SCHOOLS OF DEMOCRACY

SCHOOLS of DEMOCRACY

A POLITICAL HISTORY OF THE AMERICAN LABOR MOVEMENT

Clayton Sinyai

ILR Press *an imprint of*
Cornell University Press
Ithaca and London

First published 2006 by Cornell University Press
First printing, Cornell Paperbacks, 2006

Printed in the United States of America

Library of Congress Cataloging-in-Publication Data

Sinyai, Clayton.
    Schools of democracy : a political history of the American labor movement / Clayton Sinyai.
      p. cm.
    Includes bibliographical references and index.
    ISBN-13: 978-0-8014-4455-5 (cloth : alk. paper)
    ISBN-10: 0-8014-4455-1 (cloth : alk. paper)
    ISBN-13: 978-0-8014-7299-2 (pbk. : alk. paper)
    ISBN-10: 0-8014-7299-4 (pbk. : alk. paper)
    1. Labor movement—United States—History. 2. Labor policy—United States—History. 3. Labor unions—United States—Political activity—History. I. Title.
    HD8066.S53 2006
    322′.20973—dc22
                                                    2005032188

Cornell University Press strives to use environmentally responsible suppliers and materials to the fullest extent possible in the publishing of its books. Such materials include vegetable-based, low-VOC inks and acid-free papers that are recycled, totally chlorine-free, or partly composed of nonwood fibers. For further information, visit our website at www.cornellpress.cornell.edu.

Cloth printing   10 9 8 7 6 5 4 3 2 1
Paperback printing   10 9 8 7 6 5 4 3 2 1

To my wife Alison,
without whose love and support
I never could have completed this work

How many things that are difficult to have at the same time does the democratic form of government not presuppose? First, a very small state, where the people may be readily assembled and where each citizen may easily know all the others. Secondly, a great simplicity of manners and morals, to prevent excessive business and thorny discussions. Thirdly, a large measure of equality in social rank and fortune, without which equality in rights and authority will not last long. Finally, little or no luxury; for luxury is either the effect of riches or it makes riches necessary; it corrupts both the rich and the poor; it surrenders the country to indolence and vanity; it deprives the state of all its citizens by making some the slaves of others and all the slaves of opinion. . . . It is under this constitution, more than others, that the citizen must be armed with strength and fidelity, and repeat from the bottom of his heart every day of his life the words a virtuous Palatine once spoke in the Diet of Poland: "Better freedom with danger than peace with slavery." If there were a nation of Gods, it would govern itself democratically. A government so perfect is not suited to men.

JEAN-JACQUES ROUSSEAU, The Social Contract III:4

CONTENTS

ACKNOWLEDGMENTS

There are many people I must thank for their invaluable assistance as I pursued this project. First and foremost, I would like to honor the memory of the recently deceased Wilson Carey McWilliams. As my Rutgers University dissertation adviser, Carey served as my primary guide through the field of political philosophy and through this research. He was also a good friend and an inexhaustible source of wisdom. He is greatly missed by me and everyone he touched.

At Rutgers I would also like to thank Jeffrey Keefe at the School of Management and Labor Relations, without whose help I could never have sorted through the industrial relations scholarship that informs much of the work. Dan Tichenor spent enormous amounts of time reviewing the research and gently reminding me that just because something is progressive doesn't make it wrong. Steve Bronner, who doesn't suffer fools gladly, frequently made this point somewhat less gently. And my colleague Eric Boehme always enjoyed kicking around these ideas with me.

Beyond the halls of Rutgers I would like to recognize Fran Benson at Cornell/ILR Press, who helped me shape an unwieldy mass of research into a decently coherent manuscript. Alan Draper, Robert Zieger, and especially Michael Merrill read the manuscript and provided suggestions that greatly improved the book.

But the influences on this manuscript were by no means all academic ones; in fact, most of my education in trade unionism came from elsewhere. I thank Marcelino Cervantes, my old coworker from the W. H. Salisbury factory in Chicago; Bob Adametz, my friend and TCU (Transportation Communications International Union) brother at the Chicago and NorthWestern Railroad; and James Davenport, my NALC (National Association of Letter Carriers) shop steward at the Chicago Post Office. And I would especially like to recognize COPE (Committee on Political Education) Director John Shea at the New Jersey AFL-CIO, who taught me nearly everything I know about labor's campaign operations. As John likes to say, pretty smart for a carpenter!

I also offer appreciation to my brothers and sisters here at LIUNA: Dennis Desmond, Dennis Martire, Terry Milstead, Steve Lanning, Erin Hutson, Robert Vigil, Orlando Bonilla, Justin Meighan, Don Foor, Gene Pinder, Bobby Myers, and Hugo Carballo, among others—each of whom took special time and effort to help me understand aspects of union operations that were unfamiliar to me.

Last but not least I thank my parents James and Laureen Sinyai. They taught me a lot of this stuff from the start, although being a kid I refused to listen until I heard it from Aristotle or Alexis de Tocqueville or Samuel Gompers.

CLAYTON SINYAI

Washington, DC

INTRODUCTION

Democracy and the Worker,
Past and Present

If you ask modern observers of American trade unions to explain organized labor's political principles and practice, you are likely to hear one of two answers. Which one you hear depends largely on the politics of your respondent. Both contain valuable insights—but they also reveal as much or more about their advocates as they do about the American labor movement.

Today's free-market ideologues tend to view trade unions with suspicion. Informed by the classical liberalism of John Locke and Adam Smith, they believe that the purpose of government is to secure the liberty of every individual to work out his own destiny, free of political coercion. They further believe that an economy is most productive when every individual is free to act according to his or her own best judgment and negotiate his or her own individual transactions, whether the individual be a producer looking to sell, a consumer looking to buy, an employer looking to hire (or fire), or an employee looking to find work (or quit a job).

In this view, labor unions, first and foremost, are *economic monopolies* in which groups of workers conspire to extract an excessive price for their labor, in much the same way that business monopolies conspire to extract an unjustified price from consumers. Indeed, free marketeers argue that these labor monopolies may be *more* dangerous than the conventional variety. After all, business corporations seeking to monopolize their market still face penalty of law. In contrast, American labor law does not only *exempt* trade unions from antitrust regulations, but the 1935 National Labor Relations Act actually commits the government to *help* unions protect their monopoly once a majority of workers in a given establishment has voted to create one. Having acquired vital political interests, union leaders deploy their members' time and money in a drive for ever-increasing political power, becoming one of the most pernicious and persistent special interests of American society.[1]

The social democrats and radicals who write much of today's labor history assume a very different perspective. Implicitly (and sometimes explicitly) adopting Karl Marx's understanding of politics and society, they generally share a belief that free-market capitalism is an economic system premised on the exploitation of labor; that politics is an instrument of class warfare; and that government is often little more than a tool of the ruling classes. They further believe that some broad economic and political transformation is necessary in order to make society more democratic, equal, free, and fair, and that labor has a key role to play in this transformation.

Looked at from this perspective—and especially in comparison with the deeply socialist labor movements of Europe—American trade unions on the whole have embraced a disappointing "business unionism." Though radical rank-and-file revolt has periodically driven these unions to temporarily adopt broader goals, a "labor aristocracy," uninterested in or even hostile to a radical social transformation, has usually captured their leadership. Content to seek better wages and benefits for a narrow segment of the nation's workers without upsetting the current economic order in any fundamental way, these leaders have failed even in this mission, as evidenced by today's declining union membership numbers.[2]

Both of these perspectives reveal important truths but leave an equally important story untold. Most of America's trade union members and leaders (like most Americans) are neither socialist radicals nor supply-side Republicans, and necessarily see what they are doing quite differently than either group. Neither of the two great contemporary ideological perspectives can do justice to one of the central and enduring political concerns of the American labor movement: educating working people for democratic citizenship.

Mechanic, Slave, or Citizen? From Athens to the Enlightenment

Few today would wish for "citizenship" in Josef Stalin's USSR or Saddam Hussein's Iraq, but it was at least a rather simple proposition: obey. Authoritarian regimes, in at least this sense, do not place many demands upon their citizens. Citizens need not be especially wise, or good, or self-disciplined, or exhibit any other special virtues. The "good citizen" is one who does what he is told.

Citizenship in a democratic republic is more complicated, because the responsibilities of rule fall upon the citizens themselves. The people are called upon to make intelligent and farsighted decisions about the welfare of their nation. Precisely *what* qualities the citizen needs to participate in self-rule, *who* has them, and *how* they may be acquired or lost are among the oldest questions in political philosophy. It has been the subject of a contentious and continuous debate from the time our Greek forbears gave us the term "democracy."

While today we are tempted to evade these concerns as irrational elitism—as if *any* person could be unfit for self-government!—the workers, reformers, and activists who drove the labor movement in the United States accepted the challenge. Throughout the history of American labor, they have asked probing questions about the nature and qualifications of democratic citizenship. And they have made their various trade unions, labor parties, and worker organizations not just engines of economic betterment but of civic education: "schools of democracy" that would make America's working people *worthy* of citizenship in a democratic republic. To understand the scope of the challenge, they turned—directly or indirectly—to the political ideas of their ancient and early American forbears. Before beginning the close examination of American labor activists' words and deeds that will comprise the narrative of *Schools of Democracy*, it is fitting that we use this introduction for a brief review of the heritage that so influenced them and shaped their thought.

For the ancient Greeks, true democracy existed only when citizens *themselves* deliberated together to draw up the rules and principles by which they would live.[3] People who merely elected leaders to deliberate *for* them in representative institutions were not full citizens in the true sense of the word. "The citizen in this strict sense is best defined by the one criterion, 'a man who shares in the administration of justice and in holding of office,'" explained Aristotle. "The good citizen must possess the knowledge and capacity requisite for ruling as well as being ruled." Furthermore, the purpose of politics was certainly *not* to find out what the people wanted and give it to them. It was to secure moral excellence and the common good. According to the Philosopher, "The main concern of politics is to engender a certain character in the citizens and to make them good and disposed to perform noble actions."[4] Given such demanding political ideals, could those who spent their days in manual labor meet the demands of political participation? Not merely to vote, but to hold office and contribute to public deliberations with valuable insights into the commonweal?

Many Greek commentators found reason to doubt it. Aristotle himself divided society between a private, household sphere where bodily needs were met (the "oikos," the origin of our term "economics") and a public arena where common affairs were conducted (the "polis," from which "politics" is derived). He also imagined two corresponding polar opposites in the human race distinguished by their nature or character: the freeman or citizen, and the slave. The freeman (always, for Aristotle, a *man*) was rational and capable of education, independent judgment, and thus self-rule and citizenship. The slave was unreflective, a "living tool" or "animate instrument" lacking a capacity for reason and independent judgment and so suited only to follow directions. Their relationship was mutual and complementary, but based upon their fundamental differences. The ideal Aristotelian *polis* would have freemen participating as citizens in deliberations under the rule of law. Slaves would remain in the *oikos,* performing household labor under the command of a master, albeit command informed by a paternalistic concern.[5]

As legally free men pursuing "slavish" employment, workers seemed to occupy a shadowy zone between citizen and slave, partaking in certain characteristics of each. Aristotle sought to discern their civic potential by comparing them to his two polar classes—employing a remarkably subtle understanding of the division of labor and its consequences for these "mechanics." "Occupations are divided into those which are fit for freemen and those which are unfit for them," he explained.

> The term "mechanical" should properly be applied to any occupation, art, or instruction, which is calculated to make the body, or soul, or mind of a freeman unfit for the pursuit and practice of goodness. We may accordingly apply the word "mechanical" to any art or craft which adversely affects men's physical fitness, and to any employment which is pursued for the sake of gain and keeps men's minds too much, and too meanly, occupied. . . . A good deal depends on the purpose for which acts are done or subjects are studied. Anything done to satisfy a personal need, or to help a friend, or to attain goodness, will not be illiberal; but the very same act, when done repeatedly at the instance of other persons, may be counted menial and servile.[6]

The difference between freeman and slave was not necessarily innate—here it was viewed as an effect of the division of labor rather than its cause. Labors that were repetitive and trivial, and that were performed under the command and direction of another, were degrading to a freeman. Such labors were not just dishonorable but literally degrading, for these actually corroded physical, intellectual, and civic virtues; if one were not already unfit for citizenship, one could be made so by pernicious conditions of work. And interestingly the pursuit of "gain" was also unfitting for the freeman—seeking wealth beyond some rather modest standard of material need was seen as unnatural and even vicious. Perhaps Aristotle would have felt that today's capitalist and worker *alike* had minds "too meanly occupied" to be good citizens. In any case, Aristotle believed that populations consisting largely of "mechanics, shopkeepers and day laborers" were poorly suited to democratic government.[7]

But unlike his teacher Plato, who seemed contemptuous of democratic institutions, Aristotle not only found valid arguments in favor of democracy but also an ideal political economy for cultivating it. "When the farming class and the class of moderate means are the sovereign power in the constitution, they conduct the government under the rule of law," he said. "There is thus no difficulty in constructing a democracy where the bulk of the people live by arable or pastoral farming." A community of what Americans would later call "yeoman farmers" offered several advantages to the statesman crafting a democratic order. Small farmers worked, to be sure; they were not a leisured and educated class. But unlike the day laborers, freehold farmers directed their own labor and routinely exercised independent judgment. Also unlike the day laborers or mechanics, freehold farmers held a small property of their own, giving them an enduring stake in the welfare of their community. Finally, a city composed of independent farmers was characterized by a rough equality of economic condition, with no vast differences in wealth to inflame partisan hostility, undermine a sense of the common good, debase deliberations and incite destructive civil wars.[8]

The opposite was true of societies in which propertyless workers outnumbered their social betters, and the statesman who attempted to build democracies out of such civic material was likely to fail. A good politics was directed toward a shared pursuit of the good life, not the needs and desires of the flesh that properly belonged to the privacy of the *oikos*—but how could the laboring classes, often desperately poor, resist the temptation to use government to pursue vulgar material needs?[9]

Similarly, a politics devoted to the *common* good was concerned with the shared good of the whole community, not just a portion of it, even if that portion were a majority. And like Publius in the famous *Federalist Paper #10,* Aristotle emphatically believed that the majority faction—easily confusing its own desires for the common good—posed a special danger of tyranny. "When popular decrees are sovereign instead of the law," he argued, the majority "grows despotic; flatterers come to be held in honor; it becomes analogous to the tyrannical form of single-person government. Both show a similar temper." (If this sounds hopelessly elitist, consider the Red Scare, the McCarthy era, the Jim Crow South, or similar historical episodes.) The rule of law meant that the laws enjoined all impartially, permitting special pleading for none, neither privileged aristocrat nor majority party. But for Aristotle as for Publius, in a democratic republic the masses seemed even more disposed than the classes to abuse their political power.[10]

In short, the ancient writers did not hold workers to be promising civic material. Directed constantly by others, they lacked independent judgment; without property, they had no "stake" in the political community; their physical exigencies and their propensity to disregard the rule of law made them the weak link in any political order. They posed an especially attractive constituency for demagogues who aimed to overthrow constitutional government and establish tyrannical rule.

Time and time again, the Roman historians—whom the American founders would so closely study—seized upon this conventional wisdom to explain the decline of their own Republic.[11] With Rome's conquests abroad, the virtuous freehold farmers who comprised the backbone of the republic were eclipsed and displaced by a grasping aristocracy, on the one hand, and a multitude of slaves and urban *proletarii* (or proletarians), on the other. "To one who aspires to power the poorest man is the most helpful, since he has no regard for his own property, having none, and considers anything honorable for which he receives pay," Sallust wryly noted. Was it any surprise that the day came when popular favorites like Julius Caesar could topple Rome's free institutions with the support of their troops, to the cheers of an urban mob? Or that the Caesars could cement their tyranny by offering no more than bread and circuses to the milling *proletarii*?[12]

Seventeen hundred years later, the Enlightenment would turn many of these ancient verities on their head, with pioneering English liberal John Locke, would exercising enormous influence over the shape of American political thought. Locke tried to explain politics by imagining the human condition preceding society and government, a "state of nature" in which every person enjoyed "a State of perfect Freedom" and "a State also of Equality." By nature, every human being was free and independent of every other and had no obligations except those to which he or she consented.[13]

How did people in the state of nature spend their time? Not participating in politics, that's for sure. Nor, it seems, were they pursuing philosophical reflections. "God gave the World to Men," Locke explained, "for their benefit, and the greatest Conveniencies of Life they were capable to draw from it."[14] Men in the state of nature were busy laboring on the earth God had given them to acquire the greatest "Conveniencies of Life," or consumption goods, that they could extract from it. In so doing they were acquiring property, Locke explained with reference to his innovative Labor Theory of Value. Through a combination of this labor, and a free and uncoerced exchange of its products with others, each person in the state of nature acquired goods commensurate with the labor one exerted.[15]

From whence then did government and politics arise? However desirable man's natural freedom, one's liberty was "constantly exposed to the Invasion of others," Locke explained. Moreover, "enjoyment of the property he has in this state is very unsafe, very unsecure." Thus men gave up their natural freedom and came together in a social contract to create a government charged with protecting that liberty and property. Locke's account of the formation of government tells us a great deal about his attitude toward politics. The Greeks and Romans considered politics to be among the highest forms of human activity. Locke contended that government is merely a tool to protect individuals' freedom, in general, and their property, in particular.[16]

This attention to individual liberty would prove to be the signal contribution of English liberalism to political thought and an important heritage for its American admirers. In succeeding centuries, "liberal" thought on property would shift and change, but the primacy of individual liberty would remain axiomatic. It was a curious axiom, in an important sense an obstacle to democracy rather than a contribution to it. Liberty could be invoked by the citizen to defy a tyrant—but equally to defy democratic majorities. Furthermore, by promising citizens that they were free to live the life they chose, Locke's conception of liberty challenged the ancient concepts of civic virtue at their roots.

Locke's liberalism transformed both the idea of politics and the idea of democracy. By asking much less from politics and government than the ancient thinkers, Locke made possible a far more egalitarian, inclusive and open idea of democratic citizenship. Locke did not consider political participation a necessary component of the good life. He asked of government only that it protect the liberty and property of every citizen. Politics was a minimal affair where citizens need only appoint a government to keep the peace and thereafter keep that government under careful supervision.

With a politics so modest in its ambitions, the ancient philosophers' agonized reflections over each social class's ability to bear civic rights and responsibilities began to look absurd and elitist. The only skill the liberal citizen required was the ability to keep his word and honor the social contract; there was little justification for withholding the rights of citizenship from anyone. In fact, if all were free and equal in an original "state of nature," civic rights were probably not something one merited through intellectual or moral capacities at all, but entitlements nature awarded to all equally. Liberalism proposed a veritable revolution in the standards of republican citizenship.

Labor and Democratic Citizenship: The American Tradition

The founders and shapers of America's young republic—men like Thomas Jefferson, Alexis de Tocqueville, and Abraham Lincoln—were conversant both in the texts of Greco-Roman antiquity and the contemporary innovations of British liberals. They appropriated freely from each of these traditions to craft a uniquely American corpus of political thought, creating the conventional wisdom with which American labor would think and act.

If American political philosophy has any single father it is Thomas Jefferson; any examination of democratic citizenship in America must begin with him. Jefferson blended the premises of classical and liberal political thought into a novel—and perhaps untenable—American synthesis.[17] In the manner of the most progressive English liberals, he explained government as a sort of social contract, placed a primacy on individual liberty, called that government best which governed least, and embraced the *laissez-faire* economics of Adam Smith. Yet in language unambiguous enough to recall Aristotle or Cicero, Jefferson insisted that politics was something far nobler than a mere contract and judged the nation's new institutions according to their ability to create virtuous citizens. He married the liberal conviction in essential human equality to the ancient notion that humans achieve their highest end only in political participation. For good or ill, his principles permanently shaped the debate over American workers' fitness for democratic citizenship.

The ringing voice with which Jefferson affirmed in the *Declaration of Independence* that "all men are created equal" suggested an optimism about the average citizen's civic potential that most classical writers would have deemed excessive. Perhaps not excessive if, like his Federalist contemporaries, Jefferson had thought that elected leaders were enough to make a republic democratic, and voting the average citizen's only civic duty.[18] But like the men of ancient Athens, he considered popular participation in government to be both the essence of any democratic politics and its only sure foundation. The citizen must be "a participator in the government of affairs, not merely at an election one day in a year, but every day; when there shall not be a man in the State who will not be a member of some one of its councils, great or small, he will let his heart be torn out of his body sooner than his power be wrested from him by a Caesar or a Bonaparte."[19]

· The participatory democracy he cherished necessarily challenged his egalitarian sentiments, for Jefferson was asking much of his citizens. It was not enough that each vote "in an election one day a year," for each had to also "be a member of one of its councils." They could not be content to choose someone with enough wisdom, independence, and virtue to deliberate over the common good; they themselves needed enough wisdom, independence and virtue to engage in political deliberations. And that called for some hard thinking about who was up to the challenge. Like the ancient writers he prized, Jefferson decided that the yeoman farmer was equal to that challenge—and that the wage laborer probably was not.

"Those who labour in the earth are the chosen people of God, if ever he had a chosen people, whose breasts he has made his peculiar deposit for substantial and genuine virtue," Jefferson began in his *Notes on the State of Virginia*.

Corruption of morals in the mass of cultivators is a phenomenon of which no age nor nation has furnished an example. It is the mark set upon those, who not looking up to heaven, to their own soil and industry, as does the husbandman, for their subsistence, depend for it on the casualties and caprice of customers. Dependence begets subservience and venality, suffocates the germ of virtue, and prepares fit tools for the designs of ambition. . . . [G]enerally speaking, the proportion which the aggregate of the other classes of citizens bears in any state to that of its husbandmen, is the proportion of its unsound to its healthy parts, and is a good-enough barometer whereby to measure its degree of corruption. While we have land to labor then, let us never wish to see our citizens occupied at a work-bench, or twirling a distaff. Carpenters, masons, smiths are wanting in husbandry: but for the general operations of manufacture, let our work-shops remain in Europe. It is better to carry provisions and materials to workmen there, than bring them to the provisions and materials, and with them their manners and principles. The loss by the transportation of commodities across the Atlantic will be made up in happiness and permanence of government. The mobs of the great cities add just so much strength to the support of pure government, as sores do to the strength of the human body. It is the manners and spirit of a people which preserve a republic in vigor. A degeneracy in these is a canker which soon eats to the heart of its laws and constitution.[20]

Here Jefferson provides a rich summary of his thoughts on the worker as citizen. Labor did not *itself* prejudice the citizen's capabilities; he placed little stock in the idea shared my many ancient writers that a leisured and learned aristocracy produced the best politics. On the contrary, the self-reliant, industrious, and frugal yeomen "who labor on the earth" were the "peculiar deposit of substantial and genuine virtue" whose "manners and spirit" would "preserve a republic in vigor."

Notably, Jefferson rated only "husbandmen"—and maybe the "carpenters, masons, smiths," and other self-employed artisans who serviced them—as the "healthy parts" of the society; slaves and slavemasters, workers and capitalists apparently all numbered among the "unsound parts." Small proprietors engaged their fellow citizens on the basis of equality, and were prepared to meet and deliberate with others as equals. Not so all these others, whose daily life taught them a lot about giving orders like masters or taking orders like servants but nothing about cooperating with peers. Discussing slavery, Jefferson—a slaveholder himself—exposed how such relations of command and obedience despoil the civic virtue of both parties to the unhealthy relationship. "The whole commerce between master and slave is a perpetual exercise of the most boisterous passions, the most unremitting despotism on the one part, and degrading submissions on the other," he contended. A practice "permitting one half the citizens to trample on the rights of the other, transforms those into despots, and these into enemies, destroys the morals of the one part, and the *amor patriae* of the other."[21]

Jefferson's rhetoric regarding wage laborers themselves recalls the Roman historians' indictment of the *proletarii*. "The mobs of the great cities add just so much strength to the support of pure government, as sores do to the strength of the human body." This was because "dependence begets subservience and venality, suffocates the germ of virtue, and prepares fit tools for the designs of ambition," inviting the same kind of conspiracy between rich ambitious patrons and dependent clients that had deranged the Roman republic's politics.

In sum, Jefferson was torn between two notions of citizenship. His democratic temperament led him to embrace Locke's liberal premises. He was ready to assume that "all men are created equal" and that by nature they were entitled to equal rights—tendencies that led him toward an open and egalitarian civic standard. But he was also a careful student of his classical forbears. He understood that participatory democracy was demanding. Jeffersonian citizenship was hard work; it evoked strenuous and even exclusionary standards of civic virtue that obliged Jefferson to ask difficult questions about the workingman's fitness for political life.

Curiously, the writer who explored the American worker's qualifications for democratic citizenship most thoroughly during these years was a foreigner: Alexis de Tocqueville. Tocqueville was convinced that history had fated a general equality of condition for the world, a development about which he himself had mixed feelings. But he also believed that Americans had made the most out of the new equality, while continental Europeans had secured many of its vices without its benefits. He visited America to investigate its political culture and practices, reporting his findings in *Democracy in America.*[22]

Tocqueville was a particularly keen observer of America's robust practices of political participation. "It is hard to explain the place filled by political concerns in the life of an American. To take a hand in the government of his society and to talk about it is his most important business and, so to say, the only pleasure he knows," Tocqueville marveled. "If an American should be reduced to occupying himself with his own affairs, at that moment half his existence would be snatched from him; he would feel it as a vast void in his life and become incredibly unhappy."[23]

Against the fears of the ancients and Federalists, Tocqueville found that this enthusiastic political participation by Americans of every class did not undermine stability, good order, and the rule of law. In fact it *strengthened* them by giving all the nation's citizens a remarkable, almost proprietary interest in nation's well-being. Perhaps even more importantly, Tocqueville saw that democracy *was* a social contract, but not necessarily Locke's contract to preserve maximum individual freedom. Rather, the contract awarded each person a voice in deliberations—on condition that he freely and conscientiously respect the majority's decision when deliberations were complete. This being so, direct political participation made honoring the rule of law a debt of honor for every citizen. "This popular origin, though often damaging to the wisdom and quality of legislation, gives it peculiar strength," the Frenchman observed. Under the terms of the implicit social contract, "every American feels a sort of personal interest in obeying the laws, for a man who is not today one of the majority party may be so tomorrow, and so he may soon be demanding for laws of his choosing that respect which he now professes for the lawgiver's will."[24]

Conversely, this participatory political culture was a remarkable source of civic education. By participating in government at the local level, whether in a town meeting or a jury, the citizen learned the habits of deliberating, creating and obeying rules, and rising above private concerns to analyze the common good. Voluntary associations of all sorts nurtured these habits in every corner of American society. As in politics, so in civil, religious, social, economic, and moral fields, Tocqueville found that Americans disdained the action of a paternalistic state. Other peoples might look to the government to perform every public function, but Americans preferred to improvise voluntary associations. These associations were usually formed according to democratic political principles—via deliberation, elected officers, and majority votes. Through them Americans preserved a spirit of self-reliance and practiced the skills necessary for political participation. "They thus learn to submit their own will to that of all the rest and make their own exertions subordinate to the common action, all things which are necessary to know, whether the association be political or civil. So one may think of political associations as great free schools to which all citizens come to be taught the general theory of association."[25]

These free schools, and the robust local democracy they supported, worked so well because of peculiar American social conditions. "I think there is no other country in the world where, proportionately to population, there are so few ignorant and so few learned individuals as in America. Primary education is within reach of all; higher education is hardly available to anybody." This rough equality of mental condition conferred moral authority on democratic deliberations. With "few ignorant," deliberations produced prudent public choices; with "few learned," no social elite existed that could claim an expertise in political affairs that surpassed that of the majority. "In times of equality men . . . think it not unreasonable that, all having the same means of knowledge, truth will be found on the side of the majority."[26]

But the young industrial economy posed a danger, because it threatened the equality of mental condition that was the rational basis for democratic deliberations. Adam Smith had begun his *Inquiry into the Nature and Causes of the Wealth of Nations* by marveling how an intense division of labor had greatly multiplied the productivity of workers manufacturing "pins" (nails).[27] Tocqueville elaborated on that division of labor's pernicious effects for democracy.

> When a workman is constantly and exclusively engaged in making one object, he ends by performing this work with singular dexterity. But at the same time, he loses the general faculty of applying his mind to the way he is working. Every day he becomes more adroit and less industrious, and one may say that in his case the man is degraded as the workman improves. What is one to expect from a man who has spent twenty years of his life making heads for pins? And how can he employ that mighty human intelligence which has so often stirred the world, except in finding out the best way of making heads for pins? [. . .] Thus, at the same time that industrial science constantly lowers the standing of the working class, it raises that of the masters. While the workman confines his intelligence more and more to studying one single detail, the master daily embraces a vast field in his vision, and his mind expands as fast as the other's contracts. Soon the latter will need no more than bodily strength without intelligence, while to succeed the former needs science and almost genius. . . . What is this, if not an aristocracy?[28]

Like Plato and Aristotle, the French democratic theorist saw that hereditary class distinction was only a superficial expression of aristocracy; the essence of aristocracy was an inequality in intellect, talent or virtue that rendered democracy unreasonable. Democratic institutions had legitimate authority only insofar as majority deliberations expressed a wisdom superior to that of any elite. The more learned that elite became—and the more ignorant the majority—the less sense democratic procedures made. It seemed inevitable that the advancing industrial division of labor would make America steadily less hospitable for democracy.[29]

The vibrant local institutions that Tocqueville saw in America inspired in him another train of thought that, though not expressly related the condition of labor, prefigured many of organized labor's future challenges. The Frenchman found that Americans did for themselves through associations of equals many of those things for which his countrymen turned to the state. Voluntary associations established public libraries, fire departments, and indeed every type of civic improvement one could imagine. An astonished Tocqueville explained to his readers how Americans, upon finding an obstacle blocking the roads, preferred to improvise an assembly of their neighbors, choose an executive and fix the problem themselves rather than calling on the authorities to do so.[30]

Tocqueville thought this spirit of self-reliance essential to the preservation of American democracy—and a paternalistic state to be perhaps the greatest danger to republican institutions. For Tocqueville, democracy was virtually inseparable from local institutions of self-rule. Citizens could interact as peers with their fellows in a town meeting or a social club, but one necessarily approached an official of the state as a supplicant. It was certainly *easier* to delegate civic duties to an elected national government but this could not meaningfully be called "self-rule."

It does little good to summon those very citizens who have been made so dependent on the central power to choose the representatives of that power from time to time. However important, this brief and occasional exercise of free will will not prevent them from gradually losing the faculty of thinking, feeling, and acting for themselves, so that they will slowly fall below the level of humanity. I must add that they will soon become incapable of using the one great privilege left to them. . . . It really is difficult to imagine how people who have entirely given up managing their own affairs could make a wise choice of who are to do that for them. One should never expect a liberal, energetic, and wise government to originate in the votes of a people of servants.[31]

Though Tocqueville was not thinking here about the working classes in particular, the problem he described would consume two generations of labor activists. When industrial capitalism advanced, while labor organizations struggled to survive, Samuel Gompers and his successors in the American Federation of Labor would continue to argue that only voluntary associations could foster workers worthy of citizenship. They argued—as Tocqueville would have—that a working class that accepted the government's paternal protection hopelessly compromised its civic virtue. Against such "voluntarists" a series of progressive opponents would argue that this principle was an archaic luxury that workers could ill afford. The motions of the market, they argued, were dooming an ever-greater portion of the working class to misery and oppression. Organized labor had the right and even the duty to call upon the government to intervene in the workplace on behalf of their class.

Indeed, already by mid-century the motions of the market were eclipsing America's old majority of freehold farmers. The yeomen were being displaced by two polar classes—capitalists and workers—with a great and growing chasm between them. Thomas Jefferson and Andrew Jackson had argued that if government would but *treat* men equally, their natural and innate equality would shine forth, creating a happy republic of small proprietors.[32] White men in America indeed obtained a general equality before the law in the course of the Jackson era, given that institutions such as indentured servitude and property qualifications for the franchise melted away. But this did not create the idyll of equal yeoman farmers and small shopkeepers that the Democracy had promised. Instead, citizens were sorting themselves into unequal classes with astonishing speed. The American conventional wisdom that "all men are created equal" seemed increasingly at odds with observed facts.

For defenders of Southern slavery, these developments merely confirmed the obvious. The most trenchant of these Southern defenders was George Fitzhugh, who laid out his case in *Cannibals All! Or, Slaves without Masters*. With frequent reference to Aristotle, Fitzhugh argued that *inequality*, not equality, was the human condition. "The order and subordination observable in the physical, animal, and human world show that some are formed for higher, others for lower stations—the few to command, the many to obey." For Fitzhugh this was the nub of the matter. "Capital commands labor, as the master does the slave," he argued. Southern slaveholder or Northern capitalist, they were "cannibals all," engaged in the same enterprise of living off the labor of others. But to the capitalist, Fitzhugh said, "You, with the command over labor which your capital gives you, are a slave owner—a master, without the obligations of a master. They who work for you, who create your income, are slaves, without the rights of slaves. Slaves without a master!" Workers, whether white or black, were not entitled for the rights of citizenship—they were entitled to the paternal care of a master!

> We conclude that about nineteen out of every twenty individuals have "a natural and inalienable right" to be taken care of and protected, to have guardians, trustees, husbands, or masters; in other words, they have a natural and inalienable right to be slaves. The one in twenty are as clearly born or educated or some way fitted for command or liberty. Not to make them rulers or masters is as great a violation of natural right as not to make slaves of the mass.[33]

Fitzhugh proposed an utter rejection of American democratic principles. Pious Jeffersonian claptrap about how our special conditions could give every American the independence, predispositions, and civic skills for self-rule, enabling universal participation in politics, had been shown up by history. Human beings were fundamentally unequal; a free market had not produced equality but widening extremes of wealth and poverty; it was a license for the rich and clever to rob the poor and stupid. Ninety-five percent of human beings were congenitally incapable for self-rule. The American experiment had failed.

Interestingly, antislavery politicians like Abraham Lincoln did not so much defend the system of wage labor as they denied it. "In these Free States, a large majority are neither *hirers* nor *hired*. Men, with their families—wives, sons and daughters—work for themselves, on their farms, in their houses and in their shops, taking the whole product to themselves, and asking no favors of capital on the one hand, nor of hirelings or slaves on the other." For Lincoln even wage labor was not genuinely "Free Labor." Wherever one man labored for another, even by free contract, a separation of mental and manual labor followed that would poison the civic capacities of the working classes.

> A Yankee who could invent a strong *handed* man without a head would receive the everlasting gratitude of the [slavery] advocates. But Free Labor says "no!" Free Labor argues that, as the Author of man makes every individual with one head and one pair of hands, it was probably intended that heads and hands should cooperate as friends; and that that particular head, should direct and control that particular pair of hands . . . and that being so, every head should be cultivated, and improved, by whatever will add to its capacity for performing its charge.[34]

If Northern labor could be characterized as "free," it was not because wage labor was an honorable station but because it was a transitional one, experienced as men worked toward the true liberty of self-employment.[35] Like Aristotle and Fitzhugh, Lincoln believed that the "living instrument," the strong *handed* man directed by the head of another, bore the nature of a slave—in other words, that despite their profound differences, the wage slave and the chattel slave shared a fundamental similarity of condition. Unlike Fitzhugh and Aristotle, however, Lincoln was certain the average person was fit for much more. Still, despite his insistence that the "large majority" in the North remained self-employed, the famous words of Lincoln's Second Inaugural seem curiously confessional. "It may seem strange that any men should dare to ask a just God's assistance in wringing their bread from the sweat of other men's faces; but let us not judge that we be not judged."[36]

The labor movement received another interesting inheritance from the Civil War era: an enduring association of the term "Union" with democracy itself. This association was no linguistic accident. "The seceders insist that our Constitution admits of secession," Lincoln began, explaining their political fallacy to the Congress. "To be consistent they must secede from one another, whenever they find it the easiest way of settling their debts, or effecting any other selfish, or unjust object. The principle itself is one of disintegration, and upon which no government can possibly endure."[37]

The structure of this argument should be familiar to labor, for it is the same one used by twentieth-century labor activists to justify the union shop as a democratic institution.[38] As Tocqueville and Lincoln sensed, democracy is at root a rather simple bargain. The citizen receives a share or voice in making group decisions, and in exchange agrees to honor the group decision when the deliberations are over. Democracy is not possible when individual citizens reserve the right to withdraw and refuse obedience whenever they dissent from the collective decision—"the principle itself is one of disintegration." It is also the principle of the free market.

1

SCHOOLS OF DEMOCRACY
AND INDEPENDENCE

*The Labor Movement and
the Democratic Republic*

In the era preceding industrialization, figures like Thomas Jefferson, Alexis de Tocqueville, and Abraham Lincoln argued that only a high standard of civic virtue could sustain a democratic republic. They also tended to believe that only a community of small proprietors, sharing a rough equality of mental and material conditions, could preserve that level of civic virtue, and that vibrant local institutions of self-rule were necessary to nurture it. For Americans who treasured these precepts, Gilded Age America was filled with menacing signs. The egalitarian political economy that had made America uniquely fertile soil for democratic and republican institutions was giving way to Old World inequality. Vast class cleavages and a centralized national government much enhanced by the Civil War mobilization were daily effacing the characteristics that Tocqueville had praised in *Democracy in America* and creating those he rued in his *Ancien Regime.*

Explosive economic growth propelled this social transformation. America's rail system, already 35,000 miles strong in 1865, was increased almost fivefold in the succeeding twenty-five years. Railroad freight operations, in turn, created national markets for industrial manufactures. Between 1860 and 1900, pig iron production increased by more than 1,700 percent; soft coal by over 2,000 percent; crude oil by over 9,000 percent. By 1890, American industrial output surpassed that of Britain, France, or Germany. It was an era of technological innovation: Bell's telephone was a product of the 1870s, as was Edison's light bulb. The widespread adoption of electricity as a source of illumination and industrial power made modern manufacturing possible. The

17

Bessemer process, popularized in the 1870s and 1880s, made the mass production of steel economical for the first time.

But this was also an age of social and organizational innovation. The new industries operated on a scale that defied ownership by small proprietors. In 1870, the United States had perhaps one industrial facility employing as many as 500 workers, but thirty years later more than 1500 such plants had appeared on the landscape. The great American economic empires were being born: the 1870s saw the flowering of the transcontinental railroad systems, the construction of Andrew Carnegie's first steel plant, and the establishment of John D. Rockefeller's oil monopoly.[1] Colossal economic endeavors like these were transforming America into a society of two classes: capitalists and workers.

The new breed of capitalists barely resembled the thrifty and industrious small proprietors of yore. As employers whose income depended on the labor of others, they did not *work* in the traditional sense of the word, and many favored conspicuous consumption over deferred gratification. Nor did their economic practices always meet Adam Smith's description, producing commodities in a rational response to supply and demand. The new capitalists were sharp dealers who often preferred speculating in commodities as opposed to producing them; who created monopolies rather than competing in open markets; who sold suspect financial instruments as opposed to paying their honest debts; and who traded in adulterated goods instead of selling a quality product. They were colloquially known as "robber barons," more reminiscent of feudal lords than the frugal, hardworking and modest bourgeois of Benjamin Franklin's writings. No paragons of civic virtue, these hard men of capital had often acquired their first stakes as profiteers exploiting the Northern war effort, and made their careers on a series of swindles.[2]

These new entrepreneurs quickly racked up a record of remarkable industrial achievements—and contempt for both democratic government and the rule of law. "What do I care about the law?" crowed Cornelius Vanderbilt. "Hain't I got the power?"[3] The railroads, depending on government privileges and land grants for their growth, became synonymous with political corruption. And finding the duly elected authorities unreliable allies, a growing number of companies chose to address their labor problems with an almost studied insult to republican norms: recruiting and deploying private armies and police against their own employees, to bloody effect.

Thus they addressed the other social product of these economic developments, America's new working class. This emergence of a permanent proletariat was the event that Jefferson, Lincoln, and other students of the

Roman republic's fall had so feared. America was no longer the nation in which wage labor was a transitional stage before setting up one's own shop or farm, a point that the depression of 1873–1879 drove home. In past American economic contractions, the unfortunate had generally vacated the cities to wait out the crisis on farms owned by relatives. But now the nation's cities teemed with milling and often desperate unemployed workers seeking public relief.

If this were not bad enough, the very *foreignness* of the American working class further disturbed many native-born Americans who cherished their republican traditions.[4] Large numbers of the new proletarians were immigrant workers whose commitment to democratic and republican values seemed highly suspect. The Irish and German immigrants of mid-century had seemed dangerous enough to many American eyes. But the rising "New Immigration" drawn by industrialization from corners of southern and eastern Europe that were untouched by either the Reformation or the Enlightenment offered even greater cause for alarm. Not a few Americans shuddered at an influx of foreigners with strange beliefs that were too reactionary (Catholic and Jewish Orthodox) or too radical (socialist and anarchist) to participate productively in America's republican institutions. The political culture of these immigrants' native lands had certainly done nothing to school them in the habits of self-rule, and they were unlikely to learn those habits in America's mills and packinghouses.

Contemporary events conspired to give credence to these fears. The metastasizing urban political machines seemed to confirm Jefferson's thesis that an urban working class "prepares fit tools for the designs of ambition" rather than good politics.[5] Periodic eruptions of class warfare further heightened concerns. In a notorious 1874 incident, a crowd of unemployed workers (including none other than trade union pioneer Samuel Gompers) was demonstrating for relief in New York's Tompkins Square; the protesters were charged by police, triggering a major riot. In 1875, the violent activities of the Molly Maguires, a secret society of Irish coal miners, ended in ten hangings. Two years later, a nationwide strike rippled across the country's rail lines, bringing riots to several cities that were suppressed only with federal troops. The strikes resulted in over a hundred dead. And in the famous Chicago Haymarket Square riot of 1886, an anarchist rally in support of the eight-hour day erupted in violence (Chicago's German community nourished an active anarchist movement), taking eleven lives and injuring ten times that number.[6] Those who believed that the new political economy was undermining America's democratic republic did not suffer for lack of evidence.

Labor Reform Movements and the Knights of Labor

American workers crafted two major responses to the challenges of the Gilded Age. On the one hand, they created the national trade unions that would coalesce in the American Federation of Labor (AFL). On the other, they formed a more heterogeneous "reform" tradition that climaxed in the rise and fall of the Knights of Labor.

Scholars have proposed two distinct interpretations of the reform tradition. The older perspective, embraced by John Commons, Selig Perlman, Gerald Grob, and Richard Hofstadter, among others, understood the reform movements that culminated with the Knights mainly as futile efforts to restore the old small property economy and republican norms of America's past. These movements refused to accept the rise of industry and of classes in America. They spoke in a Jeffersonian and Jacksonian accent of uniting all productive workers, farmers, laborers, and small businessmen alike in a fight against speculators and monopolists—those ersatz aristocrats who secured wealth without labor.

The other view, popularized by many modern, left-leaning labor historians like Leon Fink, Kim Voss, and Paul Buhle held that the Knights and other reform groups constituted a progressive and forward-looking alternative challenging the "business unionism" of the national trade unions.[7] Where the AFL unions isolated skilled workers in narrow craft divisions, these authors note, reform groups sought broad alliances uniting all workers, skilled and unskilled, together with other classes oppressed by capital. And where the national trade unions generally confined themselves to bargaining with employers, the Knights sought broad social and political reforms.

Despite their opposing normative evaluations, both schools offer sound points, and the two interpretations are not entirely contradictory. But the heated dispute, then and now, has obscured how much the two great labor factions of the late nineteenth century held in common. Both the AFL and the Knights of Labor feared that the new political economy was destroying the sociopolitical conditions and the civic virtues on which American democracy rested. Both wanted, in the words of Knights of Labor activist George McNeill, to "engraft republican principles into our industrial system,"[8] but they advanced very different ways of doing so.

For the Knights and like-minded reformers, producers' cooperatives seemed an ideal way to reconcile the new large-scale means of production with a democratic and republican political economy. Cooperative ownership by producers could reconcile the material benefits of economies of scale with the civic virtues of independent proprietorship. "The aim of the Knights of Labor, properly understood, is to make each man his own employer," declared Terence V. Powderly, the Knights' most important leader. If the cooperative system worked, America could have large-scale industry without classes. Best of all, McNeill observed, "more and more labor-saving machinery will be introduced, the hours of work continually decreased, and the buildings devoted to work so improved that labor shall become a blessing instead of a curse, a pleasure instead of a pain. Instead of, as now, the poor, ignorant, physically and mentally, and sometimes morally, deformed, unskilled worker . . . *he will be a man upon whom the honors and duties of civilization can safely rest.*"[9]

McNeill's comment indicates how much he and his comrades remained concerned with civic virtue, with making workers fit for democratic citizenship. The wage-labor system, McNeill said, "engenders disease, enfeebles the mind, corrupts the morals, and thus propagates misery, vice, and crime" and "makes the employer a despot, and the employee a slave." He took all too seriously the danger that capitalism would degrade the working class intellectually and morally, stripping workers of the talents and predispositions they needed as democratic citizens. But in a remarkable turn of events, McNeill saw American wage workers taking the field to defend the democratic republic from a rebellion by the propertied classes. "These extremes of wealth and poverty are threatening the existence of the government. In the light of these facts, we declare that there is an inevitable and irresistible conflict between the wage-system of labor and the republican system of government—the wage-laborer attempting to save the government, and the capitalist class ignorantly attempting to subvert it."[10]

The organ by which McNeill hoped labor would rescue America's democratic republic from capitalist subversion was the Knights of Labor. Established by Uriah Stephens in 1869 as a secret society among tailors, it was intended to uplift and unite workers of every nationality, race, creed, and sex. The group expressly rejected class conflict and strikes, and novices were solemnly instructed that "we mean no conflict with legitimate enterprise, no antagonism to necessary capital." Consequently membership in the Knights was in time opened to all wage earners and even former wage earners, excluding only peddlers of vice, such as gamblers and liquor dealers, and "social parasites" such as lawyers and stockbrokers. Stephens hoped to create a "cooperative commonwealth" uniting all the productive classes through peaceful education and agitation for reform.[11]

McNeill's heated rhetoric suggested that American democracy confronted a social and political crisis already much advanced and beyond such mild methods of repair. His essay carefully paralleled the biblical cadences of Patrick Henry's 1775 speech rallying Americans to Revolution.[12] McNeill's reference to "wage slavery" and an "irresistible conflict between the wage-system of labor and the republican system of government" directly recalled William Seward's legendary 1858 "irrepressible conflict" speech and Lincoln's similar "House Divided" remarks the same year. A few years after the slavemasters of the South had raised their hand in rebellion to destroy the republic, and very nearly succeeded, the "capitalist class" was engaged in the same enterprise. The Knights duly made "the *abolishment* of the wage system of labor" their primary goal.

This vocabulary was not chosen lightly. For wage workers of the 1880s slavery was no abstract concept or distant memory, but a familiar evil recently defeated at a dear price in blood and treasure. Moreover, scholars like Fitzhugh had made abundantly clear how ancient Greek slavery, American chattel slavery, and "wage slavery" carried the same *political* implications: whereas one class labors, another thinks, plans, and rules. Lincoln and the Republicans in turn held that a slave aristocracy had steadily accumulated political power, trampling free labor and endangering America's republican institutions.[13] McNeill and the reformers saw their social struggle as nothing less than saving America's democratic republic from a usurpation like that attempted by the "slave power" a few decades before. And his martial slogans indicated that American democracy could not be preserved and redeemed on the cheap.

But the leadership of the Knights of Labor certainly had no stomach for the kind of industrial warfare that imminently beckoned. Succeeding Stephens in 1879 as "Grand Master Workman" of the Knights was railroad machinist Terence V. Powderly. He would direct the Knights for the next fourteen years, first through dramatic growth and then steep decline. Powderly was fully devoted to educational and cooperative activities and eschewed industrial conflict wherever possible.

Powderly greeted newcomers to the order with the words, "We welcome you to the army of peace, where we bring the producer and the consumer together, render useless the mere handler or jobber, and save the extortion of the speculator, the drone and the non-producer." In an early address to the General Assembly of the Knights, he urged his listeners to "lay siege to the bulwark of oppression" that was "the wage system." But not by industrial action, for as Powderly declaimed: "Today that system has so firm a hold upon us that every attempt at shaking off the fetters, by resorting to a strike, only

makes it easier for the master to say to his slave, *You must work for lower wages.*"
Powderly continued,

> Organization once perfected, what must we do? I answer, study the best
> means of putting your organization to some practical use by embarking on a
> system of COOPERATION which will eventually make every man his own
> master—every man his own employer; a system that will give the laborer a
> fair proportion of the products of his toil. It is to cooperation, then, as the
> lever of labor's emancipation, that the eyes of workingmen and women of the
> world should now be directed.[14]

Originally based upon trade districts in particular crafts, the Knights instead soon became dominated by "mixed assemblies" embracing all workers and former workers in a given geographic area. These heterogeneous clubs were well designed for educational and reform projects but less so for bargaining with particular employers, an area where the craft unions usually exhibited greater competence. The Knights' General Executive Board in fact saw the Knights' charge as a different and higher one than that of mere trade unions: "Our Order contemplates a radical change in the existing industrial system, and labors to bring about that change, while Trades' Unions and other orders accept the industrial system as it is, and endeavor to adapt themselves to it." But at this late date, educational and reform activity alone could hardly restore the democratic republic of virtuous small proprietors: the Knights' cooperative experiments were failures.[15] Against their will, the Knights were inexorably drawn onto the industrial battlefield.

Though psychologically and structurally unprepared for strike action, the Knights held one asset that their trade union rivals lacked: a broad-based solidarity uniting a wide array of working people. The Knights, who shared the strong suspicion of foreigners characteristic of nineteenth-century American republican thought, have an unearned reputation for internationalism. Nevertheless, where many AFL unions were narrow, homogeneous organizations of skilled tradesmen that excluded African Americans, the Knights included both unskilled laborers and black workers alongside skilled white craftsmen in their diverse assemblies.

Indeed, despite McNeill's alarm that modern industry was creating workers so "poor, ignorant and . . . morally deformed" that they were unfit for "the honors of duties of civilization," in practice the Knights adopted a generous and open ideal of citizenship. Like Jefferson, they combined their mission of civic education with liberal and egalitarian standards. They ruled all productive labor honorable and invited every worker to enlist under their banner.

They popularized a slogan derived from Athenian lawgiver Solon—"An Injury to One is the Concern of All"—which would endure in American labor long after its classical origins and meaning were forgotten.[16] This broad but shallow solidarity proved to be the source first of great strength and later of great weakness.

An engagement with the Wabash Railroad, controlled by financier Jay Gould, propelled the Knights to national prominence. Gould's men, alarmed at the growing strength of the Knights on the Wabash line, began targeting members of the Order for dismissal. The Knights' District Assembly there struck, and in solidarity Knights of Labor in every craft on every railroad line quickly brought the Wabash—as well as Gould's other railroads—to a halt. Suddenly facing staggering losses, the financier was forced to capitulate.

The Knights had been fortunate in their enemy. In contrast to industrial pioneers like Andrew Carnegie and John D. Rockefeller, Gould's forte was as a speculator, a manipulator of the stock market, a dealer in suspect financial instruments. Against such a villain straight out of republican central casting, the Knights became instant heroes, champions who could protect America's working people and the democratic republic itself from sinister operators like Gould. In the year that followed, the Knights expanded their ranks sevenfold to embrace almost three-quarters of a million workers. And they found themselves involved in an increasing number of industrial disputes.

But the Knights' leaders saw this shift toward industrial warfare and collective bargaining as a betrayal of the organization's true purpose. Edward Lee, a leader of the Knights on the New York Central Railroad, complained to Powderly, "accessions to our ranks are recruited from the ranks of dissatisfied, poorly paid men, who come into the Order for the sole purpose of bettering their condition financially, for you know that success is the god that they worship."[17] Powderly's naïve attempts to conciliate industrial conflicts by acting the honest broker between his striking members and their employers led him to be slandered as a sellout.[18] He echoed Lee's sentiments and frustrations, saying that these strikes were provoked by "raw recruits who were unacquainted with the aims and objects of the Knights of Labor." He noted how,

> as the Order grew in numbers and influence, discussion of the best means of relieving present-day pressing necessities occupied the attention of the larger part of the membership. Demands for leave to work fewer hours for others, rather than a study of how to work for themselves, occupied the time and attention of the majority of our members. Demands for higher wages from another instead of distributing the proceeds of their toil among them-

selves caused most of our members to overlook the important question of cooperation.[19]

Neither was the Knights' solidarity in diversity a blessing in the long run, for reasons that are perhaps evident in their slogan. The motto "an injury to one is an injury to all," if it is more than a charming expression, might mean one of two things. Either it can mean designing social structures under which an injury to one is shared by all of his or her comrades. (Solon spoke in this vein, for he was proposing legal reforms allowing one man to bring another's injuries before a jury to demand justice.) Or the motto can be an expression of felt identity, a sort of "mechanical solidarity" in which members are so much akin to one another that they lash out almost instinctively when group norms or values are challenged. But such solidarity is mitigated by diversity itself.[20]

The Knights' craft union rivals could command both types of solidarity. By drawing narrow craft lines—and even, sometimes, by pernicious practices of racial and ethnic discrimination—they created homogeneous organizations with strong felt identities. Moreover, union laws obliged members to support their brothers and sisters in a conflict with management, on pain of monetary fines or even loss of employment. The Knights, to the contrary, united a great diversity of members in a loosely bound organization with few or no available sanctions. They could draw on neither form of solidarity to give their slogan substantive meaning. And slogans, however progressive, cannot sustain convictions in a crisis.[21] The Knights of Labor were a house of labor built upon sand, sure to collapse when the rains came.

These rains were not long in coming. In the spring of 1886, workers on Gould's Texas and Pacific Railway walked out when a Knights of Labor foreman was fired. Gould later suggested that he had deliberately provoked the strike in order to break the union; in any case, on this occasion he was not caught unprepared. He had secured strikebreakers, hired private guards, and obtained the protection of state militias in advance to keep his railroads running. Powderly, opposed to the action from the start, failed to salvage anything for the Order from the catastrophic broken strike. As other defeats followed, the organization shrank almost as fast as it had grown, dropping 500,000 members in two years. Just as Powderly had suspected, the new Knights who had enrolled in the aftermath of the Wabash strike lacked any real commitment to the Order's purposes to sustain them in adversity. And the Knights' structural weaknesses and diversity prohibited the kinds of solidarity that would have made an injury to one truly an injury to all.

The American Federation of Labor

Vying against the Knights to represent America's workers were the great the national trade unions coalescing in the decades following the Civil War. Emerging from the combined efforts of local unions in each particular craft, these unions clashed regularly with the Knights of Labor. In 1886 they banded together in the American Federation of Labor (AFL) and with the Knights' collapse they assumed leadership in the American labor movement.

Progressive academics have come to view this AFL ascendance as a tragedy of American political and social history. The Knights of Labor—with their expansive and egalitarian membership, and proposal to end wage labor through broad social reforms—were defeated by a far more modest if not actually corrupt type of "trade unions pure and simple."[22] Cigarmaker Samuel Gompers and other AFL luminaries counseled American workers to avoid grand social projects and revolutionary challenges to capitalism. Instead, workers should parlay their control of the labor supply in narrowly defined crafts, especially skilled ones, to achieve prudent increases in wages and benefits.

Yet in the most essential ways, the Knights and their AFL rivals were motivated by a common set of civic concerns and resembled one another more than any conceivable progressive alternative. Both feared that capitalism was destroying the preconditions of republican democracy. Both, like Jefferson, worried that wage labor corroded the citizen's capacity for self-rule and the virtues on which that capacity depended; both, like Lincoln, were alarmed by the slavery-inspired notion that mental and manual labor must be separated; both, like Tocqueville, feared the centralization of political and economic power and the erosion of local self-rule as a march toward despotism. At the same time, neither group was willing to sacrifice the benefits of the new large-scale industrial technologies that were driving these changes. Rather, each tried to create a modern equivalent of the small proprietor on which Aristotle, Jefferson, and Lincoln had premised their democratic ideas.[23]

As we have seen, the Knights proposed cooperative ownership as their solution. The craft unions adopted a different but no less ambitious approach. They tried to create labor organizations that would themselves cultivate and preserve civic virtues that the political economy could no longer provide. If private ownership of the means of production was inevitable, then craft unions would make wage workers the social equivalent of yesterday's small proprietors. Like Tocqueville's voluntary associations and local democratic institutions, the trade unions would be essential organs of civic education.

They would have to be stern schools indeed if they were to educate erst-while "wage slaves" into doughty urban yeomen. Observers from Aristotle and Adam Smith to Jefferson and Tocqueville had advanced powerful arguments that laborers lacked the independence to make desirable citizens. On the most basic level, where the small proprietor relied on himself and his family to se-cure his material needs, the wage laborer was irremediably dependent on the powerful for their provision. Whether he obtained them from an employer or the government, such a relationship smacked of an unhealthy paternalism.

But these authors also argued that workplace conditions exacerbated that dependence and further degraded the citizen. When one's activity was rou-tinely directed by others, his capacity for self-direction and discipline atro-phied for lack of exercise. As Aristotle had explained, a slave was not truly defined by legal status or poor treatment, but by his role as an "animate in-strument" directed by a master. "By nature," he "was not his own man but an-other's."[24] And as the division of labor in large-scale enterprise made the worker's duties more dull and repetitive, labor seemed to lose *any* ability to stimulate the intellectual and creative faculties and served to narrow rather than expand the worker's mind. If the survival of a democratic republic de-manded a certain measure of intelligence, independence, discipline, and civic virtue, the labor process under the "wages-system" seemed designed to de-stroy these elements in the majority of the population. How could this be averted?

Like the Knights, craft union activists were unwilling to renounce the benefits of the new technologies and economies of scale made possible by the great new enterprises. Unlike the Knights, craft union activists understood that cooperative ownership was no substitute for private ownership in the fore-seeable future. But they also suspected that many of industrial capitalism's civic defects were not products of private ownership *per se* but to the alienation of labor. If workers could retain control over the labor process, *they*—rather than the venal and sybaritic robber barons—would be the true equivalent of the small proprietors who had created the American republic. *They* could retain the independent judgment and direction of the yeoman and preserve a suit-able balance of mental and manual tasks in their daily life. Not so credulous as the liberal and egalitarian Knights, they doubted that all productive labor qualified one for citizenship: serfs and slaves were surely productive. *Citizens* needed work that cultivated the habits and virtues necessary for self-rule. Craft unions could ensure that wage labor did that.

The craft unions could call upon a long and honorable heritage in this re-spect, tracing their ancestry back to the medieval guilds by which workers of an earlier era collectively governed standards and working conditions in their craft.[25] Similar, albeit weaker, institutions existed in colonial America, but political and economic tides did much to erode them in the republic's early decades. As America's working class emerged, local "journeymen's associations" frequently assembled to regulate the terms, conditions, and practices of their craft. These waxed and waned with economic cycles, political conditions, and litigation designed to prosecute them as conspiracies in restraint of trade.[26]

But by mid-century a new national economy was calling workers to organize on a national basis. Product markets were one reason: a local textile union in Massachusetts was powerless to regulate its industry when cloth could easily be imported from Rhode Island or even further away. Labor markets were even more important. Local unions alone could not effectively discipline workers for violating collective norms when these workers could move from city to city to ply their trade.[27]

The matter of discipline should command our attention. When local union delegates gathered by craft in convention to create national unions, they were doing nothing less than constructing *governments* whose jurisdictions were defined by trade rather than territory. Like the medieval guilds, they were associations by which the workers in a given craft would collectively determine its work practices. Among the earliest unions to establish an enduring structure was the Bricklayers whose constitution asserted: that "the powers of this Union shall be executive, legislative and judicial;" that it was responsible for "the government and superintendence of subordinate unions"; and that "to it shall belong the power to determine the customs and usages in regard to all matters in relation to the fellowship of the craft." The Bricklayers echoed the constitutional language of the still older Typographers' Union, which presented many of the same claims and further asserted that "general laws for the government of the craft throughout the jurisdiction of this National Union may be enacted and enforced by this body; and any Union within its jurisdiction refusing to abide by its laws and decisions shall be expelled."[28] The trade unions that would create the AFL would be far more reluctant than their European counterparts to pursue a public policy agenda or partisan affiliation. But in their essence they were *political* associations all the same and adopted a *political* rather than economic language to explain their purpose.

The concept of exclusive jurisdiction was essential. The associated producers sought *sovereignty* over their labor, and the essence of sovereignty is exclusive power and authority. If workers were to democratically control their labor, they had to build a single representative body and lodge exclusive authority in it. If individuals or rival unions remained free to bargain independently with employers, dissident workers or factions could flout majority decisions. Establishing universal trade norms and standards would be impossible. In craft union principle, a worker in a given trade had no more right to decline union membership than a resident of a city or nation could declare himself exempt from its laws; the union possessed jurisdiction over that work. As Lincoln put it when defending the "Union" from "the right of secession": "the principle itself is one of disintegration, and upon which no government can possibly endure." In Albert Hirschman's terms, members were entitled to voice but not exit.[29]

This claim to sovereignty explains the craft unions' preoccupation with the menace of "dual unionism" and "scabs."[30] A dual union that competed with the official craft union for workers' loyalties represented either a rebellion against legitimate authority or the violent encroachment of a foreign power. The scab, who rejected the authority of the union and made a private accommodation with his employer for his paycheck, did not merely violate law but actively committed treason. Jack London's characterization of the scab would achieve legendary status in American labor:

> After God had finished the rattlesnake, the toad and the vampire, he had some awful substance left with which he made the SCAB. A SCAB is a two-legged animal with a corkscrew soul, a water-logged brain, and a combination backbone made of jelly and glue. Where others have hearts he carries a tumor of rotten principles.
>
> When a SCAB comes down the street, men turn their backs and angels weep in Heaven, and the devil shuts the gates of Hell to keep him out. No man has the right to be a SCAB as long as there is a pool of water deep enough to drown his body in, or a rope long enough to hang his carcass with. Judas Iscariot was a gentleman compared with a SCAB. For betraying his master, he had the character to hang himself. A SCAB HASN'T!
>
> Esau sold his birthright for a mess of pottage. Judas Iscariot sold his savior for thirty pieces of silver, Benedict Arnold sold his country for a promise of a commission in the British Army. The modern strikebreaker sells his birthright, his country, his wife, his children, and his fellow-men for an unfilled promise from his employer, trust or corporation.
>
> Esau was a traitor to himself, Judas Iscariot was a traitor to his God. Benedict Arnold was a traitor to his country.
>
> A STRIKEBREAKER IS A TRAITOR TO HIS GOD, HIS COUNTRY, HIS FAMILY AND HIS CLASS![31]

Of course, in industry as in government, claiming sovereignty is not the same as exercising it. Defending that jurisdiction required grueling industrial warfare against always-hostile employers. An employer who hired an "unfair" worker not in good standing with his union often faced a strike by union members who refused to work alongside the scab. If the employer tried to continue production, the union might orchestrate a boycott (that most patriotic of political weapons, hallowed by its use against the British[32]) of his wares to which much of the working class would respond. Union members in other industries could and did refuse to handle the struck product as "hot cargo." The union might go so far as to direct secondary boycotts against that employer's business customers, forcing them to renounce the "unfair" employer's products.

These craft union activities were "collective bargaining" only in a loose sense. These unincorporated unions lacked the legal personality to make contracts, and in any case, they did not aspire to bargain with the employer: they aimed to unilaterally "legislate" the practices of the craft and compel employers to respect the union's work rules. The most successful craft unions achieved remarkable levels of control over their jurisdiction. The International Typographers Union (ITU) so dominated work processes in its craft that managerial employees who did not belong to the union were not permitted on the shop floor. Union rules rather than management prerogative governed hiring and firing, and if supervisors wished to discipline an employee they were obliged to plead their case before an ITU tribunal.[33]

Few unions achieved such thorough or complete control, but many went far in that direction. Building trade unions like the Carpenters and the Bricklayers controlled entry to their trades through apprenticeship systems and job allocation through their local unions or union-controlled hiring halls.[34] Skilled workers in the iron and steel industry hired and directed their own assistants and were paid by the ton like independent contractors rather than wage workers.

Such institutions of job control seemed to answer many of the charges against the worker as a citizen qualified for participation in the democratic process. These unions used their control of the labor process to thwart any division of labor that would degrade the worker. They ensured that every worker was a skilled and versatile craftsman whose labors combined conception and execution, forbidding a true separation of mental and manual tasks. Directing their own labor, these craftsmen scorned the servility of the "wage slave," adopting the "manly" independence of the republican citizen.[35] By creating and preserving wage scales in their crafts they escaped the material dependence on their employer that could make the working class suspect in a republican polity. This job control, the union's sovereignty over a craft, was supplemented by a host of other trade union practices designed to cultivate civic virtue in the new working classes.

The American trade union spokesman who best interpreted the new union philosophy was Samuel Gompers, the first president of the American Federation of Labor (AFL). Progressives routinely conjure Gompers' ghost to symbolize American labor's rejection of revolutionary or social-democratic values, or even (with some hyperbole) go so far as to castigate him as the very archfiend who made the AFL a "circle-the-wagon movement of relatively privileged workers, 'the aristocracy of labor.'"[36] We should do better to listen to the ghost than to fear the divination. Gompers' work and thought was guided by a consistent trade union philosophy, but "aristocracy" had little to do with it.

In fact, Gompers embraced much the same set of American democratic and republican precepts that his rivals in the Knights did—even if he proposed different solutions for the period's problems. His observations on American democracy, the state, and voluntary associations aligned rather comfortably with Tocqueville's. His easy facility with the themes and practices of American civic principles belied his origins as a European and Jewish immigrant to the United States who (in his own words) "secured the privilege and obligation of citizenship" only at age 22. "Gradually experience and outside contacts made me feel the freedom of opportunity and the bigness of the ideal on which American conditions and institutions were founded. Unwittingly, I was reborn to become spiritually a child and citizen of the United States."[37]

Together with a group of fellow trade union pioneers trying to solve the same problems—the self-styled "ten philosophers"—the young cigarmaker created a uniquely American vision of trade unionism and its purposes that would be known as "voluntarism." Its premises would resonate happily with all the (small-d) democratic and (small-r) republican conventional wisdom that Americans prized. Voluntarism generally opposed increased government activity in industrial relations, believing that the state would *at best* exercise a paternalistic care for workers incompatible with their claim equal and independent citizenship, and *more likely* would discriminate against workers in favor of capital. Better, they argued, that workers rely on their own fraternal associations, the trade unions, independent of both employer and state. Strong and independent unions would even benefit the republic as a whole by serving as democracy's bulwark against those latter-day aristocratic usurpers, the robber barons.

This rejection of government action to improve the lives of workers has led many to consider voluntarism an "antipolitical doctrine."[38] But their champions saw these craft unions as political organizations in at least two major and related respects. They were associations that would check the power of large firms and organized money to dominate society and polity. And they were associations that in their everyday practices equipped workers with the habits and skills that democratic citizens needed.

Trade union activists saw clearly that the great new firms were *themselves* political associations, and autocratic ones at that. American democracy had traditionally understood civil society as a community of independent and equal freemen linked only by voluntary, contractual associations. People subject to authority in private life, whether women subordinate to husbands, Catholics obedient to their clergy, or minors in the custody of parents, were dependents with dubious claims to the rights of citizens.[39] Although the massive new trusts and corporations adopted the *language* of contract to describe their organization, this language was clearly misleading; the large enterprise was a hierarchy based on relations of command and obedience, a "state within a state," as McNeill had described.[40] As McNeill had also noted, these concentrations of private economic power were a danger to the republic itself. The robber barons would persistently seek to evade the laws or even capture the power of the state for their private ends. As Gompers put it in his famous 1893 address, "What Does Labor Want?": "The laborers know that the capitalist class had its origin in force and fraud . . . always in cynical disregard of all law save its own arbitrary will."[41]

The craft unions thought they alone could protect American democracy from this threat. "Modern society is beginning to regard the Trade Unions as the only hope of civilization," Gompers continued in his address. The workers, associated in craft unions, could block the arbitrary power of capital over the workplace. They must, for "there never yet existed coincident with each other autocracy in the shop and democracy in political life."[42] Gompers and his comrades were thus challenged to create unions that endured. If labor organizations were to perform the lofty functions craft unionists sketched out for them, they had to be built to last. The trade unions that had appeared in America heretofore had been fragile institutions, almost inevitably destroyed by a failed strike or economic downturn. More than just a practical problem, this was a political scandal. The manic growth and sudden collapses of labor organizations like the Knights lent credence to the charge that workers were bad citizens who lacked the discipline, judgment, and persistence to be prudently trusted with the fate of the nation. Building sound and lasting labor organizations would meaningfully answer this charge.

In fact, Gompers and his allies called for the trade union to preserve and certify the worker's claim to equal citizenship in a host of ways. Workers who relied on their fraternal associations for pension, welfare, and social insurance benefits, instead of a paternalistic government or employer, conserved their material independence. Workers who administered their own organizations had an opportunity to practice the habits and skills of self-rule, cultivating their mental independence through regular political participation. "Unions," declaimed the AFL journal *American Federationist,* almost echoing Tocqueville, "are the schools of the workers where they learned the lessons of democracy and independence."[43] Gompers regarded the practices and structures of his own union as a model in this respect. "The Cigarmakers' International Union is now one of the most democratically conducted bodies to be found anywhere. It was developed by men who really believed in democracy," he said. "We made of the International an organization controlled and conducted by the membership with the initiative and referendum, not only in all legislation of the organization, but the nomination and election of candidates for international offices by the members."[44]

One of the most misunderstood aspects of Gompers' philosophy was the practice of exacting high union dues. Critics past and present argued that high dues reflected an exclusive concern with the most skilled and well-paid sectors of the working class, at the expense of the unskilled majority, and could even indicate a corrupt desire by union bureaucrats for a privileged lifestyle. While both problems surfaced often enough to cause craft union advocates discomfort, strong arguments commended high dues as well.

Antagonists point to statements like "the financial organization of a trade union must be based on sound business principles" as *prima facie* evidence of co-optation by capital without relating Gompers' own logic. The AFL president continued, "High dues regularly paid will inevitably lead to greater self-reliance, mutual interdependence, unity, solidarity, fraternity and federation."[45] Gompers' premise was that both the dues themselves and the benefits the dues made possible would enhance solidarity among union members.

In the first place his argument reflected a moral economy. "Men must earn things in order to appreciate their real value," Gompers contended—in labor as in other fields of human endeavor. A person who has earned something and sacrificed for its maintenance is likely to feel a stronger sense of membership and commitment (not to mention self-respect) than one who gets something for nothing. Furthermore, as Hirschman has spelled out at some length, a person who has made a substantial investment in an association has purely pragmatic reasons for not walking away over trivial or casual disagreements.[46] High dues prevented the AFL unions from enjoying the explosive growth that the Knights of Labor had experienced, but also shielded them from a similar sudden collapse. "Cheap unionism, we were convinced, did not contribute to stability or effectiveness."[47]

Furthermore, "as union dues are increased it is possible to extend the system of union benefits." A union that could provide pensions, burial insurance, or unemployment relief offered its members a salutary independence from state and employer. The craft union activists desired to prove their claim for independent, democratic citizenship by shunning paternalistic care, so an opportunity to secure assistance from their own fraternal association was to be cherished. Such benefits also gave the trade unions an enhanced organizational stability, since "participation in such beneficent undertakings would undoubtedly hold members even when payment of dues might be a hardship."[48]

Craft unionists also discovered that only well-disciplined national trade unions could act rationally and strategically to impose labor's will on industries and crafts. Gompers argued in 1887 that "we are opposed to sympathetic and foolish strikes. Ignorance is not discipline. It requires more discipline to pay an assessment of $1 a week to help those on strike than it does to strike in sympathy with them."[49] Gompers appreciated that radical demands for spectacular challenges to capital, although often crowd-pleasing, did not always advance the cause of labor. A sound, elected national leadership, wielding a significant strike fund, could more effectively campaign for control of its industry. By targeting specific employers, the union could establish a generous standard in national bargaining or to punish a recalcitrant firm resisting union demands; by withholding strike funds national leaders could discourage local unions from impetuous action.[50]

A common accusation holds that "labor aristocrat" Samuel Gompers was hostile to the cause of unskilled, and often foreign-born, industrial workers. Indeed, many craft union activists doubted these workers would ever amount to much, and Gompers resisted compromising his stringent voluntarist ideals in order to make their entry to union ranks easier. But the cigarmaker stood out among his peers as a prominent advocate of unions for this new American workforce. The early craft unions had made control of the work process their founding principle, and in economic arenas like the building trades where technological change was glacial or nonexistent this was an important, worthy, and practicable end. But Gompers perceived that the dynamism of American industrial development made such a rigid position undesirable in modern manufacturing. He observed,

We notice trade after trade being encroached upon by the daily introduction of machinery and improved tools. The skilled worker of yesterday becomes the unskilled laborer of today and tomorrow. We, therefore, view with increasing interest the growth of the organizations of the unskilled workers. . . . Organization has accomplished so much for the workers. It has not only secured higher wages, shorter hours, and better conditions of employment, but it has also instilled [such] a degree of independence and manhood and intelligence resulting from the changed conditions that none should remain outside of its ranks.[51]

Note the substance of Gompers' position: the trade union's goal is not just procuring better salaries but preparing democratic citizens. The labor movement must secure not only "higher wages" but also "a degree of independence and manhood and intelligence" for American workers. And since industrialization was producing more and more unskilled workers, America's future depended on organized labor's success in improving their living conditions *and* cultivating their civic virtue. Gompers concluded that "every advance step made by them can only tend to raise the entire economic, social, and moral position of the wage earners, and hence the entire people."

A variety of influences pressed Gompers toward this conclusion. His fellow cigarmakers had fought a losing battle against new machinery in their craft. The union survived only by choosing to organize the unskilled, mostly immigrant workforce operating the new machines. But Gompers was a bit skeptical of the distinction between skilled and unskilled labor in any event, at least as many of his contemporaries imagined it. "Every occupation calls for skill," he was wont to observe—a dubious claim often affirmed in certain quarters more for its political value than its truth content. But Gompers was making a more subtle point.

> Organized labor has often been criticized for not jeopardizing its whole organization to rescue the unorganized or the "unskilled" workers as our critical friends diplomatically term them. That which labor's adverse critics define as "unskilled labor" is really unorganized labor. There are now a large number of workers who formerly were regarded as unskilled but who have been organized. Standards of work, wages, and hours have been so far improved that these critics no longer refer to them as "unskilled." As I look back over the years I have spent in service to the labor movement and review the various groups of workers that have been designated as unorganizable because unskilled, lack of organization stands out clearly as due wholly to lack of courage, lack of persistence, lack of vision.[52]

What Gompers saw in the colloquial term "unskilled," whether by other craft unionists or his progressive critics, was actually a complex of social characteristics. Workers were labeled unskilled because they worked under degrading and oppressive conditions; they worked under oppressive and degrading conditions because they were unorganized; they were unorganized at least in part from a dearth of courage, persistence, or vision—in short, civic virtue.

Conversely, successful organization could imbue apparently *unskilled* foreign-born workers with the civic virtues characteristic of the American citizen. For this reason, Gompers labeled the massive 1902 anthracite coal strike in Pennsylvania the single most important incident in American labor history.[53] Five years prior, members of the United Mine Workers had launched a great strike that imposed uniform union standards across the Central Competitive Field, a vast range of bituminous coal deposits stretching from Illinois to Central Pennsylvania. Now the union reached out to workers in the anthracite fields of Eastern Pennsylvania. The environment Gompers described there preceding the 1902 strike was a political nightmare for anyone who valued the future of democratic and republican government in America.

The coal operators had shrewdly recruited immigrant Europeans to fill the mines with men (and often enough boys) unfamiliar with American democratic or trade union norms. Moreover, in Gompers' words, "there were so many varieties of nationalities, of politics, of religious antagonisms that concerted action was practically impossible." The coalfields became vulgar replicas of European fiefs where workers were poor and degraded serfs, living in company towns controlled by their employers, under the thumb of private police forces hired by the coal operators and dependent on company stores for their necessities. "It was a common saying the children were brought into the world by the company doctor, lived in a company house or hut, were nurtured by the company store, baptized by the company parson, buried in a company coffin, and laid away in a company graveyard."

In the course of the 1902 strike these men, who had been such refractory civic material, overturned that cheapjack aristocracy, established their own organizations, and transformed themselves into men worthy of participation in American democracy. "The strike of the miners abolished that whole system. They secured the shorter work-day with higher pay, and from then on the miners became not merely human machines to produce coal but men and citizens, taking their place among the fairly well-paid, intelligent men, husbands, fathers, abreast of all the people not only of their communities but of the republic."

Of all the voluntarist principles Gompers and the AFL preached, their rejection of a class-based party politics has confounded progressive observers the most. From the days when Werner Sombart asked why socialism failed to find an American mass following, critics have dunned the AFL unions' political posture as a reactionary narrowing of labor's vision. For almost as long, AFL admirers like John Commons, Selig Perlman, and Philip Taft have seen this policy as evidence of American labor's "democratic, tolerant, and flexible" character.[54]

The Federation eschewed a labor or socialist party politics for several related reasons. One, interestingly, was the "ten philosophers'" interpretation of Marx. Gompers grew up in a Marxist milieu in New York and had taught himself German in order to read the movement's basic texts. Marx's key insight, Gompers came to believe, was that the economy was society's base and politics its superstructure. "Whoever or whatever controls economic power directs and shapes development for the group or the nation," Gompers concluded.[55]

If Marx convinced Gompers of the primacy of the economic over the political, the history of American labor reform politics seemed to confirm that judgment. The Knights had proposed that educational and political reform could restore the democratic conditions of the young republic, but found themselves dragged into industrial action against their will. The trade union activists realized from the beginning that workers would have to rely on the strike as their key weapon. "Trade unions pure and simple are the natural organizations of the wage workers," Gompers concluded. The ten philosophers "refused to subordinate the trade union to any 'ism' or political 'reform.' We knew that the trade union was the fundamental agency through which we would achieve economic power, which would in turn give us social and political power." Wherever labor had run its own candidates in the Gilded Age they had found that "politically they were defeated and the trade union movement more or less divided and disrupted" as a result.[56]

Radical reformers seemed to spend a good deal of time reinforcing this thesis. Gompers was appalled by the scene he witnessed at Tompkins Square in January 1874, where radical agitators helped provoke a police riot at a protest by unemployed workers. "As the fundamentals came known to me, they became guide-posts for my understanding of the labor movement for years to come," Gompers recalled. "I saw that leadership in the labor movement could be safely entrusted only to those into whose hearts and minds had been woven the experiences of earning their bread by daily labor. I saw that betterment for workingmen must come primarily through workingmen. I saw the danger of entangling alliances with intellectuals who did not understand that to experiment with the labor movement was to experiment with human life."[57] The cigarmaker became increasingly skeptical of both radical political movements and the intellectuals who so often brought them to the labor movement. "We had faith in the democratic theory that wage-earners understood their problems and could deal with them better than outsiders," he insisted.[58]

Trade unions formed the foundation for labor's social action: political action was secondary and could not be allowed to interfere with or endanger these more basic class organizations. "Political movements are ephemeral. The trade union movement is not alone for today. Its continued existence is too valuable to be gambled in the political arena," Gompers' protégé, Matthew Woll of the Photoengravers, would later summarize. "The solidarity of the labor movement must not be endangered by any attempt to identify it with a partisan political movement. For the success of the trade union movement, we must have with us men of all parties as well as of all creeds. . . . Industrial, not political unity, is the prime object to be attained."[59]

Woll's last point suggests the key reason, intrinsic to the craft union structure, that the AFL's unionists were obliged to reject close partisan identifications of any kind, especially with controversial class-based political initiatives and parties. These unions were conceived and built as *democratic governments* exercising *sovereign* control over the work in a craft. To declare an official "labor" party or ideology would compromise their democracy or their sovereignty. If the union was to *govern* the trade, it had to embrace *all* workers in it. And where workers in many European nations could generally rally around social democracy, American workers had no ideological or partisan consensus. Union members had to be allowed to choose their own party identification; given the diversity of opinion within labor's ranks on the issue, the unions could not promulgate an official party or ideology without overriding the most basic tenets of democratic administration. In a society and proletariat as diverse as America's, unity required an objective basis—membership in the working class and a focus on issues directly inferred from workplace concerns—not an ideological litmus test.[60]

Was this "apolitical" stance of American labor unbearably conservative, as progressive intellectuals have often held? Perhaps, but by most *objective* indicators—as opposed to political orientation—one might conclude that the American labor movement was one of the world's *most* radical and class conscious. Our nation has historically experienced *more* strike activity than most industrialized countries, and before World War II suffered levels of industrial violence far greater than in most of Europe. Craft unions exhibited a level of solidarity, and often exercised a degree of control over the workplace, that shocked European visitors.[61]

Gompers and his peers felt that avoiding "purely political," "theoretical," and "speculative" issues which could divide workers was the only way to build solid, cohesive labor organizations. The cigarmaker was impatient with *any* attempt to introduce "speculative" ideologies to the labor movement; his AFL criticized sectarian labor organizations like the United Hebrew Trades, and thwarted attempts to establish Catholic trade unions.[62] But socialists offered the most persistent challenge to the policy. So confident were they that their views represented the "true" interests of the working classes, socialists could not or would not recognize that they were in fact calling on the trade unions to endorse a controversial ideology. In an illuminating 1914 exchange before the U.S. Commission on Industrial Relations, Gompers told socialist Morris Hillquit, "we decline to commit our labor movement to your species of speculative philosophy." "I have not introduced speculative philosophy, Mr. Gompers. If I cannot make myself clear, please tell me so," answered Hillquit. With an almost comical lack of self-awareness, he continued, "*I am speaking merely about the aim to abolish the wage system, and about the program to secure to the workers the full product of their labor.*"[63]

In truth, the craft unions were hardly "apolitical." Voluntarism was an ideological commitment of a sort, a commitment both to American democracy and civic education. A vocal socialist minority continued to agitate for *its* viewpoints in AFL conventions, and was active in securing Gompers' brief 1895 ouster from the federation presidency. But workers earned their admission to the house of labor by objective criteria—working at a trade and holding union card—and not by adhering to an official ideology.

This was the real issue behind the Federation's controversial rejection of Lucien Sanial, a Socialist Labor Party (SLP) activist, as a delegate to its 1890 convention. *Contra* AFL policy, New York City's Central Labor Federation allowed this political party to affiliate directly with the trade union body and even went so far as to send Sanial, who was not a union member, to the annual AFL convention as a delegate. Gompers objected; he said that he could not evaluate the "merits" of SLP politics but that only card-carrying union members could serve as delegates at a convention.[64] To Sanial, however, the "merits" of SLP politics were exactly the point. The SLP was a socialist labor party, and thus claimed a special right to representation at labor's convention.

A convention committee investigated the dispute and upheld Gompers. "The trade unions of America, comprising the AF of L, are committed against the introduction of matters pertaining to partisan politics, to the religion of men or to their birthplace. We cannot logically admit the Socialist Labor Party to representation, and shut the door in the face of other political organizations formed to achieve social progress." This indeed was the nub of the issue. The AFL could admit the SLP to representation at its conventions only by giving the party's particular (and highly unpopular!) speculative ideology an official stamp of approval—or by admitting every self-styled labor reformer to labor's counsels. The committee reached the only conclusion it logically could. "We are of the opinion that a political party of whatsoever nature is not entitled to representation in the American Federation of Labor."[65]

Yet if the AFL embraced no official ideology, certainly Gompers' republican and voluntarist principles exercised a special influence in the craft union movement. Unions like the Mineworkers might adopt a more flexible view of government intervention in economy and society, but Gompers nursed a rigid anti-state bias shared by many of his craft union peers. Unlike many of those peers, the cigarmaker's beliefs were part of a well-thought out political system echoing Tocqueville's concerns about centralized power.

In the first place, the old American democratic faith assumed that an expansive state was dangerous because an activist government was less likely to serve the general welfare than to be captured by social and economic elites for nefarious ends. Gompers was quite convinced of this, and the corruptions of Gilded Age politics (to put it mildly) did not overwhelm him with disconfirming evidence. Workers, like all producers, shared the public interest; wealthy employers were a special interest that sought to capture and expand the state power in order to pursue private ends. In truth it would be unjust to use the power of government to further *any* class interests, even those of the working classes. Government should serve the common good by treating all people equally. In the republican idiom, class legislation was abhorrent on its face because it subordinated the state power to a partisan interest. Labor objected to capital's special influence over the government, and consistency demanded labor renounce the government's favors with equal vehemence.

But class legislation on behalf of workers carried especially sinister implications. As Gompers argued in opposing a German-style state-sponsored medical insurance system, "that the state should provide sickness insurance for workers is fundamentally based upon the theory that these workers are not able to look after their own interests and the state must interpose its authority and wisdom and assume the relation of parent or guardian. There is something in the very suggestion of this relationship and this policy which is repugnant to a free born citizen."[66] To say that workers required special government protection would imply that they were not *fit* for the role of independent citizen, the premise that labor sought to refute. It would reflect a throwback to the world of master and servant law in employment where the government had to structure economic relations—not only to uphold the authority of the master, as is commonly understood, but also to protect the helpless servant.[67]

Gompers wished instead to limit the coercive power of government in American society, contending that any offer of vigorous state action to "help" wage earners was a devil's bargain.[68] Opposing government arbitration of labor conflicts, Gompers argued that "the industrial freedom of wage-earners depends upon their keeping control over industrial relations within their own hands. Once delegate even a particle of that authority to the government and they limit their freedom and forge a chain that retards normal free action in all times. The tendency of government is always to increase its power and scope of action."[69]

If expanding new business enterprises were rapidly undermining the foundations of America's republican democracy and conferring unprecedented social power on their owners, and if the expansion of government to check these trends was itself a powerful menace to the liberty of workers and indeed the republic, what then could be done? Gompers counted on a federation of sturdy craft unions to do what the government ought not and could not.

> For our own part, we are convinced that the state is not capable of preventing the development, or the natural concentration of industry. All the propositions to do so which have come under our observation, would, beyond doubt, react with greater force and injury upon the working people of our country than upon the trusts. . . . In the early days of our modern capitalist system, when the individual employer was the rule under which industry was conducted, the individual workmen deemed themselves sufficiently capable to cope for their rights; when industry developed and employers formed companies, the workingmen formed unions; when industry concentrated into great combinations, the workingmen formed their national and international unions; as employments became trustified, the toilers organized federations of all unions, local, national and international, such as the American Federation of Labor.[70]

Craft unions were a better mechanism than government for both checking private autocracy and protecting the interests of working people, because they were voluntary associations of equals. Compulsion, whether by employer or state, stunted the free development of individuals. It was "the duty of every wage worker to belong to the union of his trade or calling," Gompers said, "but as to coercive methods, they are not employed."[71] The American Federation of Labor "was at once a rope of sand and yet the strongest human force—

a voluntary association united by common need and held together by mutual self-interests."[72]

An initial attempt to form a national federation of trade unions, the Federation of Organized Trades and Labor Unions (FOTLU), had been launched in 1881. It quickly sputtered, but the exigencies of the day inspired renewed efforts. In December 1886, delegates from some twenty-five labor organizations met in Columbus, Ohio, to establish the American Federation of Labor. Among the most important unions participating were the Iron Molders, Miners and Mine Laborers, Typographers, Carpenters, and Cigarmakers; the assembled delegates represented perhaps 150,000 workers.[73] Samuel Gompers was named the president and only full-time officer of the new organization. His friend P. J. McGuire, head of the Brotherhood of Carpenters and Joiners, became secretary-treasurer.

The young AFL's challenge was to make the voluntarist craft union vision an organizational and social reality. Exclusive jurisdiction over each trade by an appropriate national union was the federation's founding principle, and this principle dictated much of the AFL agenda. Exclusive craft jurisdiction meant that every worker in America belonged by right to one and only one international union. An AFL charter was a symbolic grant of legitimacy to a trade union asserting sovereignty over a craft. Where no single national union existed, the AFL guided rival unions or unaffiliated local unions through mergers into newly chartered internationals. In these early years the AFL supervised or assisted the formation of the United Mine Workers of America (UMW), the Teamsters, the Laborers, and the American Federation of Musicians, to name a few.

Exclusive craft autonomy also meant that the powers of the AFL were extremely limited. It possessed no coercive power, just "moral force."[74] The affiliated craft unions retained complete sovereignty: when the AFL observed a *bona fide* trade union operating outside its ranks, the federation recognized its authority over the craft, and might spend decades wooing it to affiliate, as in the case of the railroad brotherhoods or the Bricklayers. (For the AFL leaders, a *bona fide* trade union essentially meant a national union organized on craft lines—excluding industrial unions like the American Railway Union, politicized labor organizations like the Knights, and combinations of both like the SLP's Socialist Trades and Labor Alliance and the Industrial Workers of the World.) In truth, the AFL was not a federation but a *confederation,* afflicted with the problems of any organization so governed. In conflicts over jurisdiction, for instance, important affiliated unions like the Carpenters and Plumbers could usually get favorable decisions by threatening to withdraw from the AFL.

The recession of 1893–96 offered a crucial proving ground for the AFL model of craft unionism. Conventional wisdom held that wage workers lacked the patience and discipline demanded of the citizen, and the experience of the Knights of Labor seemed to prove this. Yet while the Knights had self-destructed in prosperous times, the AFL unions withstood hardship, demonstrating a new constancy and persistence in the American proletariat. Gompers proudly announced to the 1893 AFL annual convention, "While in every previous industrial crisis the trade unions were literally mowed down and swept out of existence, the unions now in existence have manifested, not only the powers of resistance, but of stability and permanency. This fact in itself is the best answer to all trade union antagonists, carping critics, and sophists."[75]

As a political and social matter, the AFL activists had convincingly shown that wage workers, *when organized in craft unions and exercising control over their labor,* exhibited the civic virtues customarily demanded of American citizens. As a practical matter, the institutional survival of the AFL unions provided a solid base for renewed growth when economic conditions favored them. There was no longer a need to reinvent the wheel every economic cycle. The modest but enduring growth of the AFL between 1886 and the 1893 depression had seen the organization's rolls climb from 150,000 to 250,000.[76] After weathering that downturn, growth resumed, with AFL membership doubling by 1900 and climbing to 1.7 million in 1904.

Yet in an important sense Gompers' optimism was excessive. That union workers could preserve all the civic virtues attributed to yesterday's yeoman farmers was too much to ask. Powderly's doubts that private ownership of large-scale industry could be reconciled with traditional ideas of republican democracy were well-founded, and major developments during the nineteenth century's last decade would bear them out.

One of these major developments was the violent confrontation between labor and management at Andrew Carnegie's Homestead works in Pennsylvania. In the early 1870s, wrought iron was the work the Sons of Vulcan, a union of highly skilled "iron puddlers." The puddlers, not management, directed the work of their teams. They were paid not by the hour but by the ton, according to their union contract. If the craft unions seemed to imagine a society in which workers directed and managed their labor even as the means of production were privately held, the Sons of Vulcan approached this ideal as closely as did any craft. When the Bessemer process of steel production threatened labor's position in the mills, the affected crafts combined to form the Amalgamated Association of Iron, Steel and Tin Workers (AAISW). In

1892, as steel production began to surpass that of wrought iron, the 24,000-member AAISW emerged as one of the largest metal unions in the world.[77]

The steelworkers' fate would be decided at the Homestead Works. Carnegie had acquired a near-monopoly over the young industry, an empire replete with mine and railroad subsidiaries, and Homestead was his flagship. It was also the heart of the union, and a striking example of the craft union vision of worker-citizenship. Homestead's steelworkers exercised enormous control over both the works and the town. Company officials groaned against the union, "the method of apportioning work, of regulating the turns, of altering the machinery, in short, every detail of working the great plant, was subject to the interference of some busybody representing the Amalgamated Association."[78] Meanwhile the town's mayor was an AAISW member, its police force off-duty steelworkers.

The Carnegie Company set about breaking the union in ways almost calculated to offend American democratic mores. Carnegie repaired *to his castle in Scotland* for the duration, leaving the works in the hands of his partner Henry Clay Frick. Frick, a coal baron who had gained notoriety for his violent suppression of striking miners, outfitted the works like a fortress. He then locked out the union workers, promising to reopen the mill on a nonunion basis. "While the Amalgamated dealt at Homestead, they seemed to run our mill. We are going to do that ourselves hereafter," a company official announced.[79] Frick contracted with the Pinkerton Detective Agency for three hundred heavily armed agents to occupy the works, and in the predawn hours of 6 July 1892, two barge loads of Pinkerton men were towed up the Monongahela River toward Homestead.

The workers had in the meantime organized a union militia to prevent the introduction of scab labor at the works. Until the dawn of 6 July, the town remained peaceful and orderly, the workers' respect for private property and the rule of law having led them to close the taverns and even to carefully secure the company's property against vandalism. Their discovery of the arriving Pinkertons brought a more violent reaction. Concluding that *a foreign tyrant* had dispatched *a mercenary army* to trample their republican liberties—*not two days after Independence Day*—they quickly deduced their own role in the impromptu historical reenactment. The steelworkers prevented the barges from landing and instead subjected them to a daylong siege of rifle fire, flaming oil, and leftover fireworks. Seven Homesteaders and three Pinkertons were killed in the fighting before the "detectives" surrendered. The Homesteaders released them to the custody of the County Sheriff with the understanding the Pinkertons would be tried for murder.

The arrival of the militia a few days later to restore order initially delighted the Homesteaders. They believed that the lawful authorities had come to protect the community after the attempted usurpation by Carnegie's mercenaries. Their faith was misplaced: the strike leaders were arrested and charged with murder, and the scabs resumed work at the mill under militia protection. The lockout became a national *cause célèbre* for labor, with Gompers and the AFL rallying support for the union and its accused leaders.

"You refused to bow down to this wonderful autocrat, and the first answer he gave you was to send that band of hirelings into this peaceful community to force you to bow down to him, and ultimately drive you from your peaceful homes," Gompers lauded the strikers. "I am a man of peace and I love peace, but I am like that great man, Patrick Henry, I stand as an American citizen and, 'give me liberty or give me death.'"[80] But in the end there was little that Gompers and the AFL could do to relieve the Homestead workers. Labor solidarity was invaluable to the courtroom defense of the accused labor leaders, and the AFL agitated widely for anti-Pinkerton laws forbidding the use of these private armies.[81] But the Homestead lockout had been lost as soon as the state militia entered the lists, and even the battle for public opinion was irremediably handicapped after anarchist Alexander Berkman shot Frick in a failed assassination attempt.[82]

The fallout for the steelworkers was devastating. In the years following the Homestead defeat, steel producers routed the union from its remaining strongholds, and the steel industry became an open-shop bastion. Thus steel became the first of several emerging mass-production industries apparently immune to union organization. In these industries, generally characterized by unskilled labor, foreign-born workers, and mechanization, unions seldom met success in the following decades. Organized labor seemed to be barred from the most rapidly growing and modern segment of the economy.

A second event that boded poorly for Gompers' craft union republicanism was the 1890 passage of the Sherman Antitrust Act. Designed to thwart the robber barons, the legislation dictated that a combination or conspiracy in restraint of interstate commerce was illegal. Those injured by such a combination were entitled to pursue triple damages in court.

The Act deeply alarmed Gompers. The new concentration of industry, he believed, was caused by economic and technological advances that no law could stop—and any powers the government assumed to regulate economic activity could readily be turned against labor. "I did not believe that it would be effective in curbing trusts, but fearing that attempts would be made to use the law against collective action by wage-earners, I went to several members of Congress and told them my fears," Gompers recalled.[83] Though the legislators assured him that the legislation was not aimed at workers, they rebuffed his requests for a specific labor exemption from the law's scope. The cigarmaker, as it happened, had a better grasp of American politics than the legislators. Within the decade, the U.S. Supreme Court declared that manufacturing was *not* trade, excluding most trusts from Sherman Act regulation.[84] With equal speed the courts concluded that labor unions *did* belong under its purview—allowing employers to turn to the federal courts when local elected officials lacked the requisite enthusiasm to break a strike.

The famous Pullman strike drove this point home to all concerned. In 1892, future Socialist Party presidential candidate Eugene Debs resigned as an officer of the Locomotive Firemen's craft union to build a great union embracing all rail employees.[85] His American Railway Union (ARU) was an overnight sensation, enlisting 150,000 workers before its fatal confrontation with the Pullman Palace Car Company.

George Pullman manufactured luxury train cars in a "model" village he built on the outskirts of Chicago. Pullman employees were obliged to rent accommodations in company houses, purchase goods in the company store, buy company-supplied water and gas, and subscribe to the company library. Such terms and conditions surely bruised the American workers' pride even at the best of times, and with the onset of the depression the best of times vanished. The Pullman company laid off more than half its employees and substantially cut wages on the remainder—while freezing in place the high rental rates for company housing.

The confrontation between Pullman and his employees spiraled toward a strike led by the young rail union. For a time the action was remarkably successful: ARU members in every craft on every Western rail line sidelined Pullman cars. But railroad managers soon obtained the support of the federal government (over the vehement objections of Illinois Governor John Peter Altgeld, a labor ally who resented the federal intrusion). President Grover Cleveland and Attorney General Richard Olney exhibited an unseemly desire to intervene in the dispute with force, and the strike's incidental interference with the mails gave them a pretext to send federal troops to the scene.[86]

More important for the long term were judicial developments. Pullman was a rail car *manufacturer;* actions directed against the carriers who *used* his cars constituted an illegal secondary boycott. Inspired by the rulings of Judge William Howard Taft, federal courts throughout the affected states laid down broad injunctions forbidding advocacy of sympathy strikes and boycott activities. The ARU strike made Taft, then a federal appeals court judge, somewhat hysterical. In his private correspondence during the dispute he expressed "hope" that rumors that federal troops had killed thirty strikers were true; the next day he moaned that "they have only killed six of the mob as yet. This is hardly enough to make an impression." His use of sweeping injunctions was widely imitated by other judges during this and subsequent crises.[87]

The AFL did not have much sympathy for the radical new rail union. Gompers, who earnestly wished to bring the traditional, craft-based railroad brotherhoods (like the Firemen and the Brotherhood of Locomotive Engineers) into the federation, earned Debs's everlasting enmity when he declined to call a national general strike on the ARU's behalf.[88] But the posture of the federal courts alarmed all labor unions alike. Authenticated by the Supreme Court's imprimatur in *In Re Debs* (1895), the new injunctions constituted a grave threat to basic democratic principles. For one thing, they made the government an instrument of class interest. "The injunction converted the strike of the American Railway Union against the Pullman Company into a strike against the government," Gompers reflected. "When the employer tries to sidestep and induce the government to make his fight for him, the working man feels he is the victim of conspiracy." Furthermore, labor activists considered the injunction a quasi-aristocratic trampling of democratic legislative power by unelected judges. Labor injunctions were based on a "feudal legal concept" leaving unions "at the mercy of an unlimited judge-made law," the AFL contended.[89]

Members of the bench, enchanted with their shiny new juridical toys, set out to see just what they could do. The courts quickly concluded that *most* union boycott activity was illegal at common law or under the Sherman Act; that sympathetic refusal to handle struck goods was also a conspiracy in restraint of trade; that when unions urged workers to strike or join a union in violation of a contract with an employer, they engaged in illegal conspiracy; that mass picketing was illegal intimidation. And they gave a sympathetic ear to employers who demanded relief from such activities by means of a labor injunction. The injunction had heretofore been an extraordinary measure, issued only when the possibility of irreparable damage to the plaintiff rendered the glacial pace of normal court proceedings futile. Hereafter, an employer's word that an ongoing labor action was dealing his business irreparable harm was good enough for many a judge.

The Irresistible Conflict

The small proprietor's eclipse by the capitalists and workers of the great industrial concerns and trusts challenged fundamental tenets of American democratic thought. Americans had inherited the idea that a community of small property holders of modest but secure means was ideally suited to democratic government—and that a society dominated by polar classes was a poor candidate for republican self-rule.

The power wielded by the new large employers and the corruptions their money brought to American politics demonstrated the dangers large concentrations of wealth posed for a democratic politics. But Americans also feared that work practices at these vast enterprises stripped employees of the virtues and talents democratic citizens needed. They created mental and material inequalities between the classes that recreated aristocracy in fact, if not in name. In Tocqueville's words, "One is in a state of constant, narrow, and necessary dependence on the other and seems born to obey, as the other was to command. What is this, if not an aristocracy?"[90]

Both the Knights of Labor and the American Federation of Labor took it as their task to defend American democracy. They sought both to check the usurpations of the powerful new employing class and to cultivate in workers the civic virtue needed for self-rule. But they adopted very different strategies to do so.

The Knights adopted the more radical approach. It was more radical not only because the Knights reached out to all workers, crossing boundaries of race and craft that the AFL unions often did not, but because they thought wage-labor and democracy were ultimately irreconcilable. With their producers' cooperatives they hoped to restore an economy of small proprietors while conserving the new technologies and economies of scale made possible by large, advanced firms. But the cooperatives were economic failures, and the Knights found themselves drawn into industrial warfare they were poorly equipped to wage.

The AFL unions adopted a different but also extremely ambitious strategy. Accepting private ownership of the means of production, they hoped nonetheless to remove from wage labor the features that degraded the worker as citizen. Under the correct conditions, the worker could be a modern equivalent of yesterday's small proprietor. The associated workers would retain control and direction over their craft and prevent any division of labor that stunted the mind and body. They would combine to resist the arbitrary power of the boss, certifying their independence. They would mutually insure one another against extremity and want, escaping reliance on a paternal employer or state. They would direct and administer their own institutions, giving them the same habits and practice in self-rule that former generations had found in the town meeting.

But the American Federation of Labor's success at these tasks was mixed, and at the dawn of the twentieth century its status was highly ambiguous. Workers had finally succeeded in building craft unions and a labor federation that endured. Perhaps more importantly, they had constructed unions that conserved the worker's civic virtues in the face of a new political economy designed to degrade and insult them. Craft union activists *believed* old republican precepts about how the *res publica* must not enact class legislation and thus become the tool of private ends, and how a democratic republic demanded from its citizens a remarkable degree of civic virtue. Their employers, however, were not interested in building a society where virtue was rewarded and the excellence of every citizen cultivated; the employers were out to make a buck. Success was the god that *these* men worshiped, to turn Lee's phrase, and they were all too willing to appropriate government as a means to their end. Skillful use of state power by Pullman, Carnegie, and a host of clever corporate lawyers exploiting the Sherman Act steadily reduced labor's room to maneuver and increased pressure on the infant federation.

2

A WOODEN MAN?

*Industrialization, Democracy,
and Civic Virtue*

By 1900, banker J. P. Morgan had parlayed his command of financial resources into a power over the U.S. economy unparalleled before and probably since. Morgan's forte was the elimination of "wasteful cut-throat competition" by means of creating monopolies through corporate mergers. In early 1901, Morgan and his industry allies wrested Carnegie's holdings from him to create the largest corporation in the world: U.S. Steel.[1]

The age of the industrial corporation had arrived. The great firms multiplying on the national economic landscape resembled *governments* more than business enterprises in the traditional sense of the word. U.S. Steel "receives and expends more money every year than any but the very greatest of the world's national governments; its debt is larger than that of many of the lesser nations of Europe; it absolutely controls the destinies of a population nearly as large as that of Maryland or Nebraska, and indirectly influences twice that number," Ray Stannard Baker explained in *McClure's*. "The Steel Corporation is a republican form of government, not unlike that of the United States, with a president; a cabinet, or executive committee, which is like a supreme court. . . . Each man on the board was chosen, like a political committeeman, for the influence he could wield. . . . [T]he board is the law-making power, having very much the same duties and responsibilities as a parliament."[2] The reader will note that if U.S. Steel was a sort of political association, it was an inverted and rotten one. For Aristotle, Jefferson, and Tocqueville, economic activity was a means to serve nobler political goals; with the corporation, a sort of political association was established to serve economic ends.

Less and less was the American economy one of small proprietors, market competition, and *laissez-faire;* more and more it was an arena where great institutions—corporations, governments, and labor unions—cooperated or clashed. A new economics was needed to interpret the new order, and a series of innovative "institutional economists"—most notably John Commons of the University of Wisconsin—set out to create one. Commons' modest countenance concealed vast ambitions: in 1919, like a latter-day Aristotle, he sent forth his students to gather the various "constitutions" governing enterprises of the day to produce a comprehensive study titled *Industrial Government.* Traditional economics, he would come to argue, dealt merely with "bargaining" by actors on the free market. It ignored the growing sphere of social life where "managerial" and "rationing" transactions, based on principles of authority and command rather than exchange, held sway. His attempt to systematize in *Institutional Economics* was nothing less than an attempt to displace Adam Smith and Karl Marx.[3]

His early work on the staff of the National Civic Federation (NCF) gave Commons much food for thought. A brainchild of entrepreneur and Republican kingmaker Mark Hanna, the NCF solicited prominent political, business, and labor leaders to tackle the problems created by industrialization—especially labor disputes, which the Civic Federation sought to mediate. The NCF included trade union leaders like Samuel Gompers from the AFL, John Mitchell of the UMW, and James O'Connell of the Machinists; industrialists like oil heir John D. Rockefeller Jr. and Carnegie protégé Charles Schwab (now president of U.S. Steel) also participated, along with community leaders, politicians and prominent clergy.

The principal actors were attacked from all sides for their initiative. Anti-union employers attacked Hanna and his employer allies for conferring legitimacy on the labor movement by meeting as equals with trade union leaders. Meanwhile, the left lashed NCF trade union participants for class collaboration. At the 1905 AFL Convention, ITU delegate and Socialist, Victor Berger, (vainly) pressed a resolution condemning Gompers for joining with "plutocrats" to persuade workers that "the interests of labor and capital are identical."[4]

The centerpiece of NCF mediation work was the "trade agreement," under which representatives of labor and employers in a given industry could gather and hammer out a standard agreement governing work in that field. A trade agreement of this sort would assure a role for the union in the workplace, but at a price. As NCF leader Ralph Easley put it, wages would be "determined by mutual concessions in conferences with employers rather than by a demand submitted by the union as an ultimatum." Unions would "abandon arbitrary restrictions on output," and would scrupulously adhere to the contract as the very "principle of unionism" itself.[5] The union would no longer seek to *legislate* the terms of employment but rather *negotiate* them with the employer.

Commons analyzed the system of trade agreements politically in a 1901 essay, "A New Way of Settling Labor Disputes."[6] The trade agreement, he said, represented a new era in industrial government. "This higher form of industrial peace—negotiation—has now reached a formal stage in a half-dozen large industries in the United States, which, owing to its remarkable likeness to parliamentary government in the country of its origin, England, may well be called constitutional government in industry." By way of illustration, he examined how structured negotiations and the rule of law had replaced industrial conflict and violence as a means of settling disputes in soft-coal mining.

Representatives of labor and of capital met periodically "in a grand parliament of two houses—the House of Lords and the House of Commons" in order to "legislate for an industry." However, a trade agreement crafted by this bicameral legislature needed an executive to enforce it. The fractious and divided Bituminous Coal Operators Association (BCOA) was hardly up to the task; it had no machinery to discipline the recalcitrant "cutthroat operator" who would undermine the agreement for short-term profits. However, a single organization represented all the coal miners. Consequently, "enforcement falls solely upon the miners' organization." The UMW had achieved hegemony over the soft-coal industry after the grueling 1897 strike, so the union "not only can suspend their own local unions which violate the agreement, but they can absolutely shut up the mine of the rebellious operator and drive him out of business." In other words, John Mitchell was expected to serve as the president of this joint "industrial government" as well as of the UMW.

Mitchell's awkward position illuminated the system's greatest weakness. If one party was strong enough to impose its will on the other, the system obliged that party to act as judge in its own cause. Yet if neither party exercised that power, the "grand parliament" would amount to no more than a talking shop. Commons hoped and believed that the system would soon develop an independent judicial machinery to arbitrate disputes for these constitutional governments, but none were as yet in sight.

In an industry such as coal, where a strong and united union under statesmanlike leadership confronted a fragmented industry, this system of constitutional government could work remarkably well. Its value was demonstrated in the 1902 anthracite strike. The union had earned a solid public reputation for fair dealing through its activities in the soft-coal industry's Central Competitive Field (CCF), which stretched from Southern Illinois to Central Pennsylvania. By helping operators effectively regulate production, the union smoothed the wild cycles of boom and bust—and the slashed wages that attended the market's downswings—that traditionally marred the industry. Yet union organizers turning met harsh resistance when they tried to bring the UMW to Eastern Pennsylvania's hard-coal fields, and the union felt obliged to call a strike against the anthracite operators there in spring 1902.

The NCF proposed member Archbishop John Ireland as a mediator in the dispute, but the stubborn operators would have none of it. With a sentiment that George Fitzhugh would have recognized, the churlish George F. Baer responded for the coal companies that "the rights and interests of the laboring man will be protected and cared for—not by the labor agitators, but by the Christian men to whom God in His infinite wisdom has given control of the property interests of this country." Many miners urged a sympathy strike in soft coal, but Mitchell counseled otherwise: such action would have violated the CCF trade agreement without bringing any perceptible aid to the strikers. Instead he persuaded the members to accept a special dues assessment on miners working in the bituminous industry, creating a strike fund that would allow the anthracite strikers to stay out as long as necessary. By fall, President Theodore Roosevelt, enraged by the recalcitrance of the operators and fearing a winter coal shortage, threatened to intervene with federal troops on the miners' behalf. The employers agreed to arbitration and the UMW secured its beachhead in the mining towns of Eastern Pennsylvania.[7]

Strong unions pitted against fractious and competitive small producers in coal and construction had found remarkable success. Labor organizations had an important role to play, policing their industry against those who would hurt the trade's functions and reputation by fostering dangerous work conditions, cutting wages to gain a momentary edge, and marketing substandard products to the public. But what of the modern mass production industries? "The unions have practically disappeared from the trusts, and are disappearing from the large corporations as they grow large enough to specialize minutely their labor," Commons recognized.[8] Typically in these industries, a handful of large firms already enjoyed limited competition, and they confronted relatively weak trade unions. What could unions offer to U.S. Steel or Ford other than aggravation?[9]

And indeed, in the metal trades—where the metal cutters of the International Association of Machinists (IAM) often represented labor's only foothold in the mass production industries—the NCF's brief class truce unraveled into bare-knuckled class war with astonishing speed. By 1903, the National Association of Manufacturers (NAM) was directing a wide-ranging campaign against organized labor and for the "open shop." The NAM and its allied trade and industrial associations held that a natural harmony of interest governed relations between a worker and his firm, so that labor problems must be the result of interference by outside union agitators with a vested interest in stirring up trouble. And in what proved to be an enduring line of argument for union opponents, they objected to collective bargaining—however democratically conducted—by appealing to Americans' deeply held commitment to individual liberty. The closed union shop, they argued, was an intolerable infringement on the personal freedom of workers.

In the courts, the American Anti-Boycott Association protected open-shop products by savaging union boycotts as an un-American interference with the free market. Trade associations in various industries carried out veritable industrial wars against their union counterparts in which the metal trades were the critical battlefield. The National Metal Trades Association set up a blacklist of union members, established its own nonunion labor exchange (the Independent Labor League of America), and cultivated a network of paid agents within the IAM.[10] A similarly determined and thorough antiunion drive by the National Erectors' Association drove the Ironworkers to respond with violence: the union's leaders launched a campaign of bombings against open shop construction, climaxing in the deadly October 1910 demolition of the *Los Angeles Times* building, taking almost two dozen lives. Shortly thereafter a private detective on the Erectors' payroll, who was running spies on the union's executive board, seized the Ironworkers' Secretary-Treasurer John McNamara and illegally arranged his extradition to California for a sensational trial.[11]

The rapid collapse of the National Civic Federation's class war detente provided ammunition to social critics of every stripe. Old-time small-"r" republicans could view the McNamara case as a grim vindication. The America of small proprietors and local democracy had been displaced by two polar classes engaged in a violent class war and subverting the rule of law to pursue their class interests.

Socialists and other radicals drew a different conclusion. They contended that the union leader who participates in the NCF "denies, in effect, the class struggle, and vainly seeks to harmonize the economic interests of these two antagonistic classes—the exploiting masters and the exploited wage-slaves; the robbers and the robbed. It cannot be done."[12] The AFL's growing socialist opposition made the National Civic Federation a key point of its political attack against the craft union leadership. Both the UMW and IAM were centers of Socialist Party strength in the labor movement, and by 1911 both unions had renounced their involvement with the NCF.[13]

Radical critics of the NCF held that "the working class and the employing class have nothing in common," while trade agreements hamstrung the class struggle by implying, as Berger had stated, that "the interests of capital and labor are identical."[14] Both claims were exaggerations. Clearly workers and employers have *some* interests in common: neither railroad crews nor railroad stockholders wish to see the company's rolling stock involved in accidents (although the crews surely find this concern much more immediate). Nor did the trade agreement imply that *all* their interests were identical. Quite the contrary, independent unions were needed precisely *because* their interests differed in many respects. Gompers affirmed that there was "no means by which the interests of the employers and the workingmen can be made harmonious in the full and broad sense of that term."[15]

There were plenty of people who *did* contend that the true interests of employers and workers were identical: the National Association of Manufacturers, the neoclassical free-market economists (who posed an alternative to Commons and his Institutional peers), the founders of company unions, the new "scientific management" pioneers. Naturally, all of them opposed independent trade unions, whether those unions be radical or conservative. The very existence of such unions was predicated on the principle that employee and employer have at least *some* irreconcilable differences demanding independent representation for labor. Gompers, Mitchell, O'Connell, and Commons were not supporters of class harmony, but of a controlled, rather than revolutionary, class struggle. American workers were not European workers confronting autocratic regimes; they were citizens of a perhaps endangered but still functioning democratic republic. They had a good deal more to lose than their chains.

In an important sense, Gompers and Commons described a more profound class struggle than their antagonists. They were convinced that conflict between workers and management was not an artifact of one or another economic order but was *inherent in the modern division of labor.* Even as the trade agreement and the NCF faded into history, this idea became perhaps the controlling feature of U.S. industrial relations scholarship growing out of institutional economics. When Gompers insisted against the socialists that that the labor movement had no definite end, he really argued that the Socialists were naïfs who thought that collective ownership offered a simple (if not easy) solution to the problem of democracy in the workplace. Instead Gompers and Commons saw the conflict of labor and management in the large enterprise as both a permanent feature of the modern condition and a challenge to democratic principles, a problem no economic system could escape. Industrial relations luminary William Leiserson, who built on many of Commons' insights, would later conclude:

> It appears also that some form of constitutional government similar to that created by trade agreements will be necessary under any system of industry that may be substituted for private capitalism. Government ownership, cooperative industry, socialism, syndicalism, or bolshevism must all meet the same difficulties that bring trade agreements into existence. For, however the form of ownership may change, there will ever be, if not wage-earners, at least workers who must obey orders, and directors or managers with authority to issue orders. . . . Unless the two classes jointly embody their ideas of the rights and privileges of individuals in constitutions and laws, those who have the power to command will act arbitrarily or autocratically.[16]

Shibboleths about class collaboration aside, the Ironworkers' catastrophe also elicited more telling radical critiques of craft union voluntarism. "Their acts are the logical outcome of the impotency and hopelessness of the craft form of unionism, typified by Samuel Gompers and his associates," Debs said of the Ironworker leaders. "If the McNamara case teaches us anything it is that we must organize along both economic and political lines."[17] Debs admired American democracy and the virtues of its civic ideal no less than did Gompers. But his experience during the Pullman strike convinced him that American workers could conserve some of the *substance* of American democracy only by more vigorous political action. Debs had challenged workers assembled to greet his release from jail after the Pullman strike:

> What is the duty of American workingmen whose liberties have been placed in peril? They are not hereditary bondsmen. Their fathers were free born— their sovereignty none denied and their children yet have the ballot. . . . It can sweep away trusts, syndicates, monopolies and every other abnormal development of the money power designed to abridge the liberties of workmen and enslave them by the degradation incident to poverty and enforced idleness, as cyclones scatter the leaves of the forest.[18]

It was an interesting observation: *this* generation of workingmen was *not* born free, but American workers were not *yet* the *hereditary* bondsmen that workers abroad were. Now they had to take quick political action to redeem themselves before their freedom was lost forever.

Confronted with the inveterate hostility of the open shop employer, the socialists organized politically, hoping they could use the democratic process to bring the force of government to bear against the malefactor. For good civic reasons, voluntarism had renounced using the state to pursue class ends. But when bargaining failed, the Ironworkers found illegal violence their only recourse, a choice that undermined the very rule of law and respect for democratic outcomes that voluntarism was designed to protect.

The Open Shop and the Managerial Revolution

The purpose of democratic deliberations is to determine the common good. Representatives of many points of view come together to discuss and debate public policy; errors are refuted, innovations shared, and individual perspectives widened by contact with others. If the deliberations are productive, they identify public policies that serve the *general* welfare and not just the interests of a particular class, segment or faction of the community.

But if the classes indeed have nothing in common, then even representative government is merely a tool for the powerful to impose on the weak, and democratic deliberations a fraud. How can I persuade an opponent to accept my arguments if they are only a cloak to serve my interests—which differ from his? For this reason, the violent and recurrent industrial conflict that rapidly became known as "the labor problem" challenged democratic and republican principles. The open shop crusaders were obliged either to renounce those principles—alienating the American public—or to find a way to reconcile the interests of labor and management.

The new industrial order challenged democratic values in other ways as well. Democratic decisions acquire moral authority only when citizens see one another as more or less equal in wisdom and talent, so that their votes *deserved* equal weight. But the new enterprises were characterized by rank and hierarchy. The republic had been founded on a community of self-directing and roughly equal yeoman farmers. But in these new industries—as in Aristotle's *oikos* or the plantation South—some labored, and others directed their labors. As Philip Selznick observed, Henry Sumner Maine's famous "law of progress" holding that societies evolve "from status to contract" in relations among citizens now seemed to be moving in reverse.[19] Apologists for this economic "progress" needed a theory reconciling a democratic system of government assuming human equality with new economic institutions that assumed the opposite.

Most early American thinkers had married their concerns with cultivating civic virtue to a general conviction of natural equality. It was "self-evident" that "all men were created equal," but only a proper civic education could make them political equals in practice. When they enjoyed a work and social life that educated them in democratic norms, they could mature into valuable democratic citizens. But a work life spent giving or taking orders was no school of citizenship, and that is exactly the work life the new management theorists prescribed.

An escape from these rigorous civic republican values was available in the form of other, equally fundamental American principles: individual liberty and equality of opportunity. Because equality of opportunity scorns hereditary classes—and for that matter, distinctions of race, ethnicity, and gender— it is often misunderstood as a democratic principle. Thomas Jefferson, who had penned the Declaration's elegy to human equality, at the same time celebrated the existence of a "natural aristocracy among men" superior in "virtue and talents." Unlike the "artificial aristocracy, founded on wealth and birth," which Jefferson scorned, this natural aristocracy was "the most precious gift of nature, for the instruction, the trusts, and government of society."[20] Like Plato and Aristotle, Jefferson frequently speculated about the system of public education and political representation that would best identify and place these "natural aristoi." But as his language indicated, the principle was aristocratic to its core. The lauded "career open to talent" made sense only if nature awarded people *different* endowments of "virtue and talent." A meritocracy may have much to recommend it over an aristocracy of wealth, or birth, or race, or gender—but it is an aristocracy all the same.

The management theorist who wrestled most exhaustively with these issues was Frederick Winslow Taylor, the creator of "scientific management." Taylor's practical efforts to introduce his system encountered very limited success. But he *did* construct a philosophy of American industrial relations that linked management not only to scientific progress but to an equality of opportunity based on individual achievement—and a theory of class cooperation based on natural difference.

Though a scion of a prominent Philadelphia family, Taylor opted out of a traditional college education to pursue an apprenticeship as a machinist. He spent his formative period in the 1880s at the Midvale Company, which crafted machine tools and other steel products. Taylor was bright; a series of experiments he began while employed at Midvale eventually led to his invention of "high speed tool steel." Machine tools thus constructed greatly outperformed conventional ones, giving Taylor the income security to retire from industrial work at a young age and the status among engineers to pursue his avocation as a management guru.[21] After a series of industrial appointments, Taylor established himself in 1901 as an independent consultant and spent the rest of his life proselytizing for his new management philosophy. Taylor's key innovations were summarized in his 1911 essay "The Principles of Scientific Management."

"The principal object of management should be to secure the maximum prosperity for the employer, coupled with the maximum prosperity for each employee," Taylor contended. There was no inherent conflict between capital and labor, for employers could obtain greater profits and workers greater wages only when they cooperated to increase production. (It will be noted that Taylor considered "high wages" to be the key interest of the worker. Taylor's favorite salutation to workers seemed to be, "Are you a high-priced man?") "Scientific management has for its very foundation the firm conviction that the true interests of the two are one and the same."[22]

"Why is it, then, in the face of the self-evident fact that maximum prosperity can exist only as the result of the determined effort of each workman to turn out each day his largest possible day's work, that the great majority of our men are deliberately doing just the opposite?" Taylor asked. Conflict was created by defective organization, but Taylor did not attribute this entirely to malicious labor agitators; the fault lay largely with "defective systems of management which are in common use, and which make it necessary for each workman to soldier, or work slowly, in order that he may protect his own best interests."[23]

Traditional management's "old-fashioned herding of men in large gangs" did not recognize and reward workers as individuals, according to their contribution. Managers did not really manage, in the sense of directing production. The initiative lay with the workers who collectively ruled the shop floor. Their "combined knowledge and dexterity" surpassed that of their supervisors. Indeed, Taylor realized as did the craft unionists that "this mass of rule-of-thumb or traditional knowledge may be said to be the principal asset or possession of every tradesman."[24]

"Traditional knowledge" allowed the tradesman to direct his own labor, though this was hardly the most efficient and productive method of work. "The science which underlies each workman's act is so great and amounts to so much that the workman who is best suited to actually doing the work is incapable (either through lack of education or insufficient mental capacity) of fully understanding the science." The manager had to assume "the burden of gathering together all of the traditional knowledge which in the past has been possessed by the workmen and then of classifying, tabulating, and reducing this knowledge to rules, laws, and formulae."[25] Such was the basis for the famous (and famously intrusive) time and motion studies Taylor conducted on the shop floor; adequate scientific measurements of work tasks were the *sine qua non* of scientific management. Only with reference to these could management replace the traditional knowledge of the craftsman with the cumulative knowledge that scientific method makes possible.

Now the problem with the "old-fashioned method of herding men in gangs" was clearer. The gang method assumed the group members were more or less equal, when in fact humans were not equal at all. Management should be "dealing with every workman as a separate individual." Managers must subdivide tasks seeking the best method and then assign each worker "the highest grade of work for which his natural abilities fit him." For the exceptionally talented that might mean management; for the "intelligent laborer" there would be relatively complex tasks; for "the mentally sluggish" ("a man of the type of an ox," he labeled one workman he observed at length) there would be rote work.[26] Taylor could thus assail the unions as unprogressive, un-American, collectivist, leveling institutions that suppressed the individual—but only by affirming that individuals are fundamentally unequal to begin with.

Taylor presented scientific management as a foolproof solution to the "labor problem," and boasted that no firm where scientific management had been introduced properly had ever experienced a strike.[27] The system would resolve labor problems for two reasons. By establishing an objective and "scientific" standard regarding work, it would remove workplace issues from dispute and bargaining. "As reasonably might we insist on bargaining about the time and place of the rising and setting of the sun."[28] Second, it would create cooperation and harmony between worker and management. Men no longer would view their supervisors as "nigger drivers" but rather "as friends who were teaching them and helping them to earn much higher wages than they had ever earned before."[29] Taylor profoundly believed that by allowing every employee to work up to the level of his ability and reap the rewards of his own efforts, his system of management was less paternalistic and more individualistic than customary practices. Apparently insensible to irony, he never marveled how much *supervision* was necessary to avoid *paternalism* and how much *standardization* of work was necessary to preserve *individuality*.

Taylor's first premise clashed with democratic values in ways that Taylor ignored but that workers would not. Taylor was the sworn enemy of arbitrary power in the workplace, but that hardly made him a friend of democracy; in fact, the opposite was true. If work rules are in fact objective and scientific, they are not subject to deliberation nor even negotiation. "What constitutes a fair day's work will be a question for scientific investigation, instead of a subject to be bargained and haggled over," Taylor promised. Questions for scientific investigation are not subject to democratic control. Under scientific management the shop becomes an autocracy: a benevolent one perhaps, or at least well-meaning, but an autocracy nonetheless. If the workplace of the past had sometimes been a school of civic education, Taylorism promised to bring that to an end. If we accept Taylor's notion that high wages and consumption are the *summum bonum,* then this may well be a good bargain, but Taylor did not acknowledge that anything of value had been sacrificed. If he had any concerns that "a man of the type of the ox" would make a poor citizen, he kept them to himself.[30]

Taylor's second premise was equally alarming. Taylor argued that mental and manual tasks must be separated, for "the workman who is best suited to actually doing the work is incapable (either through lack of education or insufficient mental capacity) of fully understanding the science." Harmonious cooperation between those who were suited to think and direct and those who were best suited to labor under command was Taylor's wave of the future. But it was truly the ghost of the past: Taylor's offensive promise to end the manager's role as "nigger driver" notwithstanding, his vision evoked Aristotle's (and Fitzhugh's) relation of freeman and "natural slave." It was a complementary relation based on an assumption of fundamental inequality. If Taylor was wrong about that inequality, his system was unjust and corrosive to the civic virtue of employer and employee alike; if he was right, and workers were "natural slaves" properly suited to the direction of others, democracy's foundational principles would stand in doubt.

Taylor wanted to reorder the division of labor by separating mental and manual work, subdividing tasks formerly executed by skilled craftsmen until they could be performed with little or no thought. The prospect of wage laborers consigned to a life of mindless work had long alarmed observers across the political spectrum, ranging from John Ruskin and Alexis de Tocqueville to Adam Smith and Karl Marx. Taylor had an answer for his carping critics, and a wonderfully progressive one at that.

> For the workman, the first impression is that this all tends to make him a mere automaton, a wooden man. As the workmen frequently say when they first come under this system, "Why, I am not allowed to think or move without some one interfering or doing it for me!" The same criticism and objection, however, can be raised against all other modern division of labor. It does not follow, for example, that the modern surgeon is any more narrow or

wooden a man than the early settler of this country. The frontiersman, however, had to be not only a surgeon, but also an architect, house-builder, lumberman, farmer, soldier, and doctor, and he had to settle his law cases with a
gun. You would hardly say that the life of the modern surgeon is any more
narrowing, or that he is more of a wooden man than the frontiersman.[31]

Although the surgeon does not suffer the same violent wrenching of mental from manual labor that the industrial worker does, Taylor's point was fundamentally sound. Opponents of his system object to the division of labor
itself. But Taylor's argument suggests how little concern he, and other champions of specialization and efficiency, had for the problems of democracy. Aristotle labeled politics a sovereign science, for it falls to politics to judge and
rank all other social actions and goods. Politics must decide how society's
common resources are allocated between, say, education, medicine, housing,
and defense—and how could the teacher who knew nothing of health, construction or arms form a valid opinion about the relative importance of each?
As Tocqueville had sensed, the much-maligned "omnicompetent citizen" of
the frontier who was surgeon, builder, architect, lumberman, farmer and soldier was ideally suited to engage in self-rule.[32] The life of the modern surgeon
is indeed "narrowing" when it comes to exercising political judgment, the
virtue of the democratic citizen. And a "man of the type of the ox" is quite useless in this regard.

Craft unionists, especially in the metal trades, grasped the essence of Taylorism immediately and scented the foul odor of wage slavery wafting from
his work. They reprinted and circulated Taylor's writings among their members and filled union journals with sharp critiques of his philosophy. The *International Molders Journal* alluded to Aristotle's definition of the slave by
saying that under Taylorism "the worker is no longer a craftsman in any sense,
but is an animated tool of management."[33] IAM president James O'Connell
said that Taylor's method "tends to wipe out all the manhood and genius of
the American workman and make him a mere machine." He echoed Lincoln
in arguing that "the whole scheme of the system is to remove the head of the
workmen."[34]

Drawing an unhappy inference from America's still-fresh history of chattel slavery, the craft unionists (like Taylor himself, with his offensive "nigger-
driver" observation) often associated wage slavery with the entry of Blacks into
formerly white occupations and trades. This unfortunate premise led the Machinists, among others, to bar African-Americans from union membership.[35]
Yet the craft unions did not lose sight of the basic issues at stake, and union
hostility to the Taylor system soon settled on the figure of the time-study man,

the "man with the stopwatch" whose job it was to time the tasks of workers as data for a "scientific" restructuring of their work. Though Taylor thought the time-study man a small part of his operation, workers regarded him as a modern slave overseer and often refused to work in his presence. Agitation and industrial warfare over scientific management continued at a slow boil until the summer of 1911, when it exploded into view with a Molders' strike at the Watertown Arsenal.

The military officers who operated the Watertown arsenal had found its productivity unsatisfactory and resolved to give Taylor's system a try. When a time-study man suddenly appeared in the foundry, however, the molders quickly resolved not to work under the stopwatch. They drafted a letter to the commanding officer reporting that during the afternoon "a man was seen to use a stop watch on one of the molders. This we believe to be the limit of our endurance. It is humiliating to us, who have always tried to give to the Government the best that was in us. This method is un-American in principle." The following day a molder was discharged for refusing to work under such observation and a general walkout immediately ensued. As another molder explained, "I don't like a man to stand over me with a stop watch because it looks to me as if it is getting down to slavery to have a man following you when you are at your job."[36]

The strike was a brief one, but because it occurred in a government facility it became an instant public issue. A congressional committee was convened to study scientific management, taking testimony from Taylor and his supporters, the molders, Molders' Union officials, and the military officers who operated the arsenal. Taylor's hopes that the Arsenal would provide a high-profile platform for publicizing scientific management were dashed. He could no longer promise a solution to "the labor problem" and boast that scientific management had never provoked a strike.[37] Taylorism never recovered from the bad publicity that attended the Watertown Arsenal strike and for over three decades Congress prohibited the use of time studies and incentive pay in federal employment.[38]

Taylor's frontal assault on democratic norms had been too great to overlook. Democratic theory traditionally counted two features of the serf or slave that made him a bad citizen: he was accustomed to others telling them what to do, and he depended on others for what he should do for himself. Taylorism encouraged a servile character in both respects, yet was oblivious to the violence it did to civic virtue. Moreover, the relish with which Taylor recounted his Midvale and Bethlehem experiences suggested that he enjoyed breaking the organized resistance of a workforce as much as he did increasing productivity. Few of Taylor's fellow managerial revolutionaries—most of them practical men and conventional thinkers—shared either Taylor's élan for a certain variety of class warfare or his blunt skepticism about cherished chestnuts of American civics. But they did embrace his faith in individual achievement and meritocracy, and his belief that properly organized workplace relations could create harmony between the increasingly unequal citizens of the firm.

Yet even without Taylor's excessive candor, introducing meritocracy at the firm in a nation that still treasured democratic values was far from easy. Each firm was governed by a rationalized hierarchy that provided a ranked sequence of occupations and titles, allowing each person to rise to the highest level his talents could take him. But if one believed that a bureaucratic or technocratic elite was best qualified to govern these firms, didn't it follow that such an elite was best qualified to govern in politics as well? Or, to the contrary, if the citizens were wise enough to govern the nation, weren't the "industrial citizens" of these enterprises in turn wise enough to govern their firms? Finally, if one argued that governments were by right accountable to their citizens, then didn't one automatically cast aspersions on management's unaccountable power in these companies?

Business historians tell us that corporate bureaucracies developed when the demands of managing vast enterprises became too great for a single entrepreneur, however wealthy or brilliant, to finance and control—either by himself or by more *ad hoc* methods of delegation.[39] As an important side effect, bureaucratic values began to displace entrepreneurial ones. The robber barons had usually been owners or major stockholders of their companies and trusts, and even their shop floor supervisors were typically subcontractors or operated much like them; risk-taking and gain-spirit pervaded the enterprise.

But the great corporations were now evolving into a different animal. The "owners" were shareholders who bought and sold their interest in a company with little genuine influence on its direction. Actual control of the firm fell into the hands of a professional management corps whose real job was preserving and administering the institution; earning profits was a means to that end rather than their *raison d'être*. At lower levels, the frontline supervisor became less a curious type of small businessman and more a simple enforcer of company rules. Life became more predictable and, in many ways, more fair. *Fair* in the sense that arbitrary power and petty tyranny diminished as objective rules came to govern work life. Personnel departments assumed control over hiring, firing, discipline, and work assignments.

The corporations soon discovered innovative personnel management techniques that could reduce labor conflict and increase productivity. An objective and merit-based system of hiring, discipline, and promotion did not only put the best workers in the best job but removed one of the major irritants—favoritism—from industrial relations. Management itself was creating a "rule of law" at work, quite without the input of labor unions.

Together with this peculiar but potent sort of "justice as fairness,"[40] personnel managers embraced a series of innovations that came to be known as "welfare capitalism." Welfare capitalism aimed to reinforce the identity of interests that Taylor preached with a heaping helping of the paternalism he disdained. Even as the National Civic Federation's conciliation activity dwindled, open-shop employers used its auspices to share innovations in industrial safety and benefits like pensions and profit-sharing.[41] Personnel specialists argued that employees satisfied in their work were more productive; more convincingly, they demonstrated that turnover was costly. Even unskilled workers required a certain amount of training and acclimation to a new job and a firm's culture, and research indicated that productivity generally increased with seniority. Retaining employees and reducing turnover became a prime objective of personnel relations.

In his automotive empire, Henry Ford approached both the separation of mental and manual labor of which Taylor dreamed, and the identity of worker and employer interest for which personnel managers yearned. Ford's technical achievements would make his name synonymous with mass production; his employment practices would make his name synonymous with high wages and mass consumption; his business acumen would enable him to capture almost 50 percent of the American automobile market by 1914.[42] Like Taylor, Ford did not think "democracy" was about self-rule, much less civic virtue, but about equality of opportunity and the "career open to talent." "Perhaps no word is more overworked nowadays than the word 'democracy,' and those who shout loudest about it, I think, want it least. I am always suspicious of men who speak glibly of democracy," he argued. "I am for the kind of democracy that gives to each an equal chance according to his ability. . . . Democracy has nothing to do with the question 'Who ought to be boss?' That is very much like asking, 'Who ought to be the tenor in the quartet?' Obviously, the man who can sing tenor. You could not have deposed Caruso. Suppose some theory of musical democracy had consigned Caruso to the musical proletariat. Would that have reared another tenor to take his place?"[43]

Also much like Taylor, Ford believed that correctly ordering production could bring everyone who was involved a steadily increasing prosperity. Hard work, high productivity, generous wages and growing consumption were the premises of the Ford political economy. And although he condemned labor unions for restricting output, like Taylor he acknowledged that "management must share the blame with labor. Management has been lazy too—management has found it easier to hire an additional five hundred men than to improve its methods that one hundred men of the old force could be released to other work." In sum, Ford explained, "It ought to be the employer's ambition, as leader, to pay better wages than any similar line of business, and it ought to be the workman's ambition to make this possible."[44]

Ford's technical achievements took the promise of Taylor's methods and made them real. He rearranged traditional manufacturing departments to put parts in continuous flow, eliminating much of the unproductive materials handling that occupies so many of the typical factory's man-hours. By subdividing tasks into minute parts, he began to escape his industry's customary reliance on skilled craft labor and employed instead unskilled machine operators in most production work. With the perfection of the assembly line he could virtually eliminate his employees' unproductive motions.

This shift transformed the profile of the Ford worker and of the workplace. Where a skilled and native-born workforce originally dominated his lines, by 1914 three-quarters of Ford's employees were foreign-born, and semi-skilled or unskilled workers comprised about the same proportion of his employment roster. The skilled workers had been valued for their experience and judgment. Ford managers now boasted that "the Ford company has no use for experience, in the working ranks anyway. It desires and prefers machine-tool operators who have nothing to unlearn . . . , who will do what they are told, over and over again, from bell-time to bell-time." The skilled craftsmen had been valued for their initiative and intellect. Ford workers observed that "Henry has reduced the complexity of life to a definite number of jerks, twists, and turns. Once a Ford employee has learned the special spasm expected of him he can go through life without a single thought or emotion," and that "workers cease to be human beings as soon as they enter the gates of the shop. They become automatons and cease to think." Indeed the whole point of the intense division of labor and the assembly line was to ensure that the worker could "perform his operation with the least expenditure of willpower, and hence with the least brain fatigue." It also ensured that the machinery rather than the foreman set the pace of production, making the worker who objected a grumbling Luddite rather than an American citizen standing up to his boss. None of this could be possible without a vast capital investment in expensive machine tools that enabled unskilled workers to perform a particular task as well—sort of—as a skilled machinist would. "Farmers' tools," they were called, since they enabled anyone who fell off the turnip truck to imitate the work of a skilled craftsman.[45]

Securing men willing to swallow all this for unskilled labor's market price proved impossible. In the booming mass production industries it was just too easy to walk out the door to a *more* human (if still not *especially* human) working environment. Ford's most modern plant in Highland Park experienced a shocking 370 percent labor turnover in 1913, generating prohibitive costs in screening, hiring, and training replacements, no matter how simple the work operations. To solve this problem, Ford now created a modern personnel department and transformed his employment practices.

The change began with a 1913 overhaul of the pay structure into a series of grades. Workers who met production targets and mastered new skills could move up the sequence, giving ambitious employees who stayed at Ford a reasonable expectation of steady pay increases. But Ford's real breakthrough came with the institution of the famous "five dollar day," an astounding sum that approximately doubled his workers' income. Offered in conjunction with the move to twenty-four hour production at Highland Park, it was not a wage but a profit-sharing plan under which workers with satisfactory performance would receive a distribution from Ford profits to supplement their wage, bringing it up to the level of five dollars.[46]

Ford was embarking on his own weird experiment in civic education, and he made good character and a healthy family life a condition of receiving the distributions. To this end, he established the notorious Ford Sociology Department in the same year. The sociology department investigated the home lives of employees, interviewing family and neighbors to see if they merited inclusion in the profit-sharing program. Unfortunately, the self-made tycoon from the rural Midwest seemed unable to distinguish civic virtue from nativist Protestant mores. Under Ford's "Americanization" program, company social workers spent their days investigating not only the drinking habits of his employees but their cleanliness, their command of English, their adoption of American styles of dress, and their predilection for nuclear families and single-family homes.

The brilliant technical innovator and crank social theorist never seemed truly to understand how profoundly *un-American* this social engineering was.[47] "It was a sort of prosperity-sharing plan," Ford said, "but on conditions. The man and his home had to come up to certain standards of cleanliness and citizenship. Nothing paternal was intended!—a certain amount of paternalism did develop, and that is one reason why the whole plan and the social welfare department were readjusted."[48]

Although the intrusive home inspections and the profit-sharing plan were later eliminated, the fundamentals of Ford's social bargain—high wages in return for absolute obedience—implied that he still regarded his employees as children, after a fashion. Parental discipline may not be undemocratic in an actual family: a family assumes that the child will in time take his or her place among the adults. In much the same way, apprentices were indentured with the idea that one day they would become self-ruling masters or journeymen. But Ford, like other corporate employers, wanted career employees; he fancied himself the great white father of a vast tribe of hunkies, dagos, krauts, and coloreds who would remain his children all their lives. When at last in 1941 his "children" abandoned him *en masse* for the embrace of their brothers in the United Auto Workers, Ford was genuinely stunned and hurt—a lesson in true "Americanization" which even then the automaker failed to absorb.

A few employers *did* seriously attempt to reconcile their commitment to the open shop with American democratic values. Managers who truly believed that employer and employee had shared interests could readily conclude that a system of employee representation would improve communication and thus work life and productivity—so long as it was not affiliated with an "outside" entity with a vested interest in conflict.

The first serious breakthrough in company-sponsored employee representation occurred in 1915 at Colorado Fuel & Iron Co. A UMW drive to organize the Rockefeller-directed firm the previous year had culminated in the infamous Ludlow massacre: a militia assault against the strikers' encampment took the lives of eleven children and two women. John D. Rockefeller Jr. remained unwilling to bargain with the UMW, but the violence clearly indicated a need for radical changes in the company's industrial relations practices. Rockefeller employed Clarence J. Hicks, perhaps the biggest name in the personnel management revolution, to introduce a new system of industrial government at CF & I.[49]

The result was the Colorado Industrial Plan, a company-sponsored system of employee representation to present employee interests and consult with management. The Employee Representation Plan (ERP) was not precisely a company union, but a mechanism by which workers at CF & I could elect representatives of their choosing to engage in collective bargaining and adjustment of grievances. That the ERP was not a union *as such* was a point on which Rockefeller and his team maintained scruples. They were convinced that it was illegitimate to demand membership in a union—whether the UMW or a company-sponsored association—as a condition of employment. Instead they proposed an "industrial constitution" with a system of representatives elected by secret ballot and wielding enumerated powers, a constitution the miners ratified by an overwhelming margin. In Rockefeller's putative "Republic of Labor," CF & I workers were officially assured of their rights of free speech and assembly, a freedom that guaranteed their right to join "any society, fraternity, or union," but similarly their right to refrain from joining any at all. Rockefeller maintained that his system of elected representatives was actually "broader and more democratic than unionism" of the UMW sort: they could join the UMW if they wished, but all workers, union or not, secured representation through the ERP.[50]

Was Rockefeller's insistence that the ERP was not a "company union" plausible? The answer touched on a theoretical problem that would vex the next generation of labor activists. AFL unionists of Rockefeller's day portrayed the union as a *government* whose jurisdiction was work performed in a given craft. Under such reasoning, a miner could no more refuse membership in the Mineworkers' Union than South Carolina could secede from *the* Union, or than a resident of that state could declare himself outside the polity and exempt from its laws. If we take this argument at face value, Rockefeller's ERP and a company union would both be but armies of occupation usurping the powers of the union and its worker-citizens.

Two decades hence a coalition of progressive labor activists, fired by the possibilities of industrial unionism and the Wagner Act, would champion the right of workers to *choose* which union they would join. But if union membership is a *choice*, it cannot fairly be compared to residency in a state or citizenship in a nation. Rather, it is akin to membership in a political party, and Rockefeller's challenge is more serious: democracy requires that we *allow* citizens to join the political party of their choice, but forbids us to *require* membership in any political party. For those interested in the fine points of political representation, Rockefeller had drawn an important distinction.

Of course, most industrial magnates who took an interest in Rockefeller's innovations were decidedly *not* interested in the fine points of political representation. What interested *them* was finding a form of collective bargaining that would thwart independent labor organization—either by the AFL unions or one of their radical rivals. Whether the institution lodged with collective bargaining functions was a company union or company-sponsored Employee Representation Plan was a pedantic distinction for business hobbyists like the Standard Oil chief's do-gooder boy. The important thing was that it be an organ of the firm and the firm's own employees exclusively, not a branch of some alien organization with a vested interest in stirring up trouble.

Indeed, the logic of the company union was impeccable, given the stated premises of open-shop employers. They agreed with Rockefeller that "both Labor and Capital are indispensable. If these great forces cooperate, the products of industry are steadily increased; whereas, if they fight, the production of wealth is certain to be either retarded or stopped altogether, and the wellsprings of material progress choked."[51] They too sought an organizational form that would facilitate better cooperation between the two sides to the mutual advantage of both. If it was true that employees and employers had shared interests—and that industrial conflict was created primarily by *outside* unions that benefited from strife and discord—then company-sponsored unions could do no harm and perhaps much good.

Though ERPs spread throughout the Rockefeller empire, other openshop enterprises showed little early interest in pursuing their convictions this far. This changed significantly after the United States entered the First World War. Accelerated union organizing activity, together with the policies and rhetoric of a war "to make the world safe for democracy" elicited from Washington, pressured employers to provide alternative visions of "industrial democracy" if they wished to ward off the AFL.[52]

Company unions and representation programs took many forms, but seldom if ever did they respect craft lines. Corporate management, no less than Taylor, realized that craft unions were irreducibly based on worker control of the labor process. As such they would almost certainly threaten the introduction of new, more productive technology which might ultimately benefit both worker and employer. After all, it had not been early industrial unions like the Mineworkers or radical challengers like the Industrial Workers of the World (IWW) who had fought the scientific managers to a draw: it had been the most craft-conscious of unions, unions like the Molders, the IAM, and the Bricklayers.

The theme that united Taylor, Ford, and the personnel managers was the fundamental identity of interest between worker and employer. Increased production meant higher wages for workers and higher profits for employers, and what was work about other than money? Gompers and his comrades in the AFL crafts argued that this reasoning was quite wrong.

> There is so much that is interesting and profoundly significant in some of Henry Ford's methods, that it is doubly regrettable that he has not given equal consideration to human nature. Because he has taken it for granted men are satisfied if they have high wages and a short work day he has taken away their right to participate in creative work. Because he fails to appreciate the spiritual meaning of craftsmanship he finds no place for the trade union movement. The trade union is something more than an organization to regulate

hours and wages—important as those material things are—it is the reposi-
tory of trade skill and information. . . . [W]e have brains as well as brawn.[53]

Contra Adam Smith and his lesser disciples, consumption was *not* the sole
end and purpose of all production.[54] Work that improved the worker was still
important. Employees and employers shared an interest in safe and productive workplaces that enabled bargaining in the first place, but they also had
an irresolvable conflict of interests that necessitated independent unions. The
workplace was not just a place to earn a buck but a place to pursue a vocation and learn the virtues of the democratic citizen. Should the workplace lose
that character forever, craft unionists thought, the republic itself would be in
danger.

The Stirrings of Industrial Unionism

While AFL activists continued to draw upon the old premises of American civics in their dispute with corporate America, a growing number of opponents urged a general reconsideration of craft union ideology and practice.
Some wished to bring the liberal revolution in citizenship to labor; they
thought that the very *idea* that self-rule demanded some evidence of sufficient
civic virtue elitist and exclusionary. Many also suspected that government was,
and was likely to remain, the tool of class interests and nothing more; a democratic and republican vision of a politics in pursuit of the common good was
a harmful delusion. Labor, like capital, should try to influence state policy in
its favor. But what united *all* these critics was the idea of industrial unionism,
an innovation in union structure under which a single union in each industry would unite workers across all crafts.

Rapid changes in technology had blurred and scrambled craft lines, leaving a variety of squabbling unions claiming the loyalties of overlapping groups
of workers in any single factory. Furthermore, workers within the great modern plants had lost much of the craft pride and identity that formed the crucial intangible glue of solidarity for the craft union. If industrial workers found
any identity at all in their work, they thought of themselves as autoworkers,
steelworkers, or rubberworkers, not as machinists, molders, or electricians
who worked in a factory.

Craft union activists continued to demand that these worker-citizens
meet the stringent standards of civic virtue that Gompers prescribed—a test
unskilled industrial workers could not or would not meet, effectively exclud-

ing their vast and growing ranks from the AFL. In their zeal to defend the rigorous civic democracy of the past, the AFL leaders could not see that a labor movement excluding the majority of American workers also failed democratic values in a rather basic way.

The leftists and progressives who championed industrial organization imagined labor unions broad enough to embrace workers of every level of skill and civic capacity. Utilizing this more liberal and inclusive standard, they essentially argued that separation of mental and manual labor need not disqualify the worker from democratic citizenship. But excluding the rapidly growing majority of mass production workers from representation in labor institutions would surely mock democratic principles. Moreover, the industrial union advocates found ways to be optimistic about the new technological order. As the crafts were eroded, they argued, workers now forgetting craft solidarity would acquire a new *class* consciousness, uniting them broadly and making a progressive transformation of society possible.

Within the AFL, the Mineworkers sustained the industrial union idea. Strictly construed, craft union sovereignty over the labor process demanded that every worker in America fall under the jurisdiction of one and only one international union that legitimately governed that work. Consequently occupational lines were rigidly marked and industrial unions were proscribed lest, say, machinists in a Ford auto plant be saddled with conflicting loyalties to the IAM and a union of autoworkers. However, the federation had chartered the UMW to represent all workers in the mines, regardless of their craft. In the "Scranton Declaration" issued at the 1901 AFL convention, the federation concluded that in geographically isolated industries, such as mining, the "paramount organization" and its need for unity superseded claims by others to the handful of craftsmen on the scene. But the AFL had invited internal conflict by allowing the federation's largest member union to organize on an industrial basis, while prohibiting industrial workers in urban areas from following its example.[55]

In the new century's first decades, Socialists and other industrial union advocates within the AFL fought to introduce industrial organizing in manufacturing, while radical groups outside, such as Daniel DeLeon's Socialist Trades and Labor Alliance and the Industrial Workers of the World (IWW), urged tearing down the AFL and rebuilding the labor movement on an industrial basis. Later, radical intellectuals in the Workers' Education Bureau and the Brookwood Labor College would educate trade union activists in industrial union programs and philosophies while the Communist Party's Trade Union Unity League sought to replace the AFL with its own rival industrial unions. While these oppositional currents diverged on many particulars, they shared an underlying faith in industrial structure as labor's progressive future. They also came to share a common critique of the American Federation of Labor's brand of trade unionism, arguing that Gompers and his peers had utterly failed to create a labor movement that honored democratic norms and values. Their critique was the theory of "business unionism."

The IWW and "Business Unionism"

Among trade unionists, the Industrial Workers of the World (IWW) deserve principal pride of authorship for the idea of "business unionism." Some of its tenets had certainly been invoked by earlier reformers, as when the Knights of Labor had attacked the AFL for accepting the wage system rather than seeking its abolition, or when DeLeon's noisy but ephemeral labor initiative accused AFL leaders of adopting bourgeois values as their incomes rose. But it was the "wobblies" of the IWW who welded the theory together and ceaselessly propagated it through the working class and beyond. The IWW succeeded where Knights had failed: they created a critique of the American Federation of Labor that stuck.

Consequently the IWW exercised an influence on American labor and social history far out of proportion to its small size. Though it swelled and shrank wildly with its industrial actions, its core membership was counted in thousands rather than millions.[56] Yet the IWW benefited from a cast of characters far more colorful than that of the AFL and perhaps any labor movement before or since. In its ranks one would have found people like metal miner "Big Bill" Haywood, songwriter Joe Hill, "Rebel Girl" Elizabeth Gurley Flynn, "Mother" Jones, less well-known figures like fiery orator Joseph Ettor and pistol-packing priest T. J. Hagerty, and in cameo appearances, luminaries like "pope of Marxism" Daniel DeLeon, the legendary Eugene Debs and radical journalist John Reed. These and hundreds whose names are unknown to history were neither bureaucrats nor organizational geniuses. They were itinerant agitators of great skill whose theory and practice transmitted a vision of industrial syndicalism, and a sour analysis of contemporary craft unionism, throughout their class and nation.

The IWW emerged from a "continental congress of the working class" convened in Chicago with the support of the Western Federation of Miners, an industrially organized metal mining union. These Miners and their small but scrappy union were schooled in the violent industrial conflict of the American West in the era of the McNamara brothers and the Ludlow massacre. The Wobblies' base would remain in the West, where their organization of migrants who worked the mines, lumber camps, and agricultural harvests proved more resilient than their dramatic occasional forays into the urban proletariat. Indeed, their social and cultural radicalism speaks of a group of men living in mining camps and timber barracks with neither family nor home. "Hallelujah, I'm a bum," they would sing, ridiculing the civic respectability for which AFL craft unionists—and many another working man and woman—strained. Whereas a man like Gompers prided himself on his work ethic, the IWW activists celebrated a shirk ethic perhaps appropriate to a world where work had been degraded and deskilled.[57] For the craft unionist, who directed his own labor, hard work connoted independence; for the industrial worker, commanded by others, it indicated servility.

The IWW began with the premise that "the working class and the employing class have nothing in common." Thus America's so-called democratic institutions were pure fraud: with nothing in common, how could any amount of democratic deliberation find common ground? Nor could there be genuine labor negotiations. What was there to talk about? "There is but one bargain that the IWW will make with the employing class—COMPLETE SURRENDER OF ALL CONTROL OF INDUSTRY TO THE ORGANIZED WORKERS." The IWW's end and purpose was uninterrupted class struggle in the workplace until workers had seized control of the means of production. "It is the historic mission of the working class to do away with capitalism." Of the AFL unions the Wobblies said,

> The trade unions foster a state of affairs which allows one set of workers to be pitted against another set of workers in the same industry, thereby helping defeat one another in wage wars. Moreover, the trade unions aid the employing class to mislead the workers into the belief that the working-class have interests in common with their employers. . . . The craft form of union, with its principle of trade autonomy, and harmony of interest with the boss, has also been proven a failure. It has not furnished an effective weapon to the working class. True, it has been able to get for the skilled mechanics improved conditions; but due to the narrow structure of the craft organization, class interest has long since been lost sight of, and craft interest alone governs the action of its membership. In the last analysis the craft union has only been able to get advantages for its membership at the expense of the great mass of the working class. . . . They have become allies of the employers to keep in subjection the vast majority of the workers. . . . The future belongs to the IWW. The day of the skilled worker is passed.[58]

For the Wobblies, the civic virtue that craft unions cultivated actually made them political liabilities to their class. Like Marx, who valued the proletarian precisely because he had nothing to lose but his chains—and even more like Ford, who preferred the untrained worker who "had nothing to unlearn"—the Wobblies believed paradoxically that the future belonged to those workers who seemingly had the least to offer. Accordingly, when labor conflict erupted among unskilled, immigrant industrial workers, IWW organizers often quickly surfaced to offer leadership, while AFL activists confined themselves to nay-saying. In the most remarkable instance, IWW organizers led twenty thousand striking textile workers in Lawrence, Massachusetts— mostly Poles and Italians—to an astounding and unexpected victory.[59]

But the outcomes of IWW initiatives in the mass production industries comforted both industrial and craft unionist advocates in different ways. Strikes like those at Lawrence and later in Paterson, New Jersey, demonstrated a large reservoir of discontent in the industrial workforce. These workers were not so docile and feckless as craft unions had come to believe. Yet, most of the Wobbly-led industrial strikes failed terribly, and even in Lawrence, IWW membership quickly evaporated when the workers achieved their goals. It appeared indeed that without outside leadership and aid these workers *were* incapable of organization; even with it they were unwilling or unable to support enduring organizations. The Wobblies gradually withdrew to their Western stomping grounds where they flourished until suppressed by the government for their opposition to the war effort during World War I.

The theory of "business unionism" was cast in a more elegant and complete form by industrial relations scholar Robert Hoxie, a Commons protégé who apparently coined the term to explain the early 20th-century labor movement.[60] Hoxie proposed a typology of unionism in which two contrasting species were particularly important: a *business unionism* common in the AFL that sought to establish stable collective bargaining relationships versus a *revolutionary unionism* exemplified by the IWW that sought radical social transformation. Of business unionism, Hoxie determined that

> It is essentially trade-conscious rather than class conscious. That is to say, it expresses the viewpoint and interests of the workers in a craft or industry rather than those of the working class as a whole. It aims chiefly at more, here and now, for the organized workers of the craft or industry, in terms mainly of higher wages, shorter hours, and better working conditions, regardless for the most part of the welfare of the workers outside the particular organic group, and regardless in general of political and social considerations, except

in so far as these bear directly upon its own economic ends. It is conservative in the sense that it professes belief in natural rights, and accepts as inevitable, if not as just, the existing capitalistic organization and the wage system, as well as existing property rights and the binding force of contract. . . . Thus it is likely to be exclusive, that is, to limit its membership, by means of an apprenticeship system and high initiation fees and dues, to the more skilled workers in the craft or industry. . . . In harmony with its business character it tends to emphasize discipline within the organization, and is prone to develop strong leadership and to become somewhat autocratic in government. . . . In method, business unionism is prevailingly temperate and economic. It favors voluntary arbitration, deprecates strikes, and avoids political action.[61]

This analysis would become conventional wisdom in progressive circles. *Business unionism* implied a small, elite body of workers organized to pursue private monetary goals. It shunned solidarity with other workers and class consciousness. It was "conservative," accepting the inevitability or justice of capitalism. It upheld the sanctity of the contract, and its favored activity was collective bargaining. Labor was a commodity, and craft unions attempted to monopolize that commodity in order to bid up its price, as would any other business enterprise. "The truth is the outlook and ideals of this dominant type of unionism are those very largely of a business organization. Its successful leaders are essentially business men and its unions are organized primarily to do business with employers—to bargain for the sale of the product which it controls."[62]

But technology itself was eroding the business unionism of the AFL craft unions. Industrialization concentrated large numbers of workers in a single location and created vast economic empires that only a wide-ranging solidarity could challenge. Perhaps even more importantly, modern mass production deskilled labor and blurred traditional craft lines, creating a social foundation for a new, broad class solidarity. Thus the propensity for revolutionary unionism would grow and the business unionism that created the craft unions wither. As the best structure for labor's new goal, a revolutionary industrial unionism had an opening.

Revolutionary unionism, as the term implies, is extremely radical both in viewpoint and in action. It is distinctly class-conscious rather than trade conscious. That is to say, it asserts the complete harmony of interests of all wage-workers as against the representatives of the employing class, and seeks to unite the former, skilled and unskilled together, into one homogeneous fighting organization. It repudiates, or tends to repudiate, the existing institutional

order and especially individual ownership of productive means, and the wage
system. . .[63]

This revolutionary industrial unionism was more progressive, nay radical, than the old craft unionism on every count. It shunned contracts. "In method, it looks askance at collective bargaining and mutual insurance as making for conservatism and hampering the free and united action of the workers." It scorned ameliorative action, because "it is the primary aim of all revolutionary unionists to overthrow the existing institutional order" and "this cannot be accomplished by a gradual process of immediate gains in the form of better wages, shorter hours, better working conditions, etc. The end is retarded rather than advanced by such immediate concessions and advantages because these tend to make the workers conservative, satisfied with the present system, and those who gain most become detached in interest from the whole working class." And for related reasons, the revolutionary unionist suspected that the relatively well-paid workers in existing AFL craft unions were too privileged to pursue radical change. "The revolution, then, must be the work of the unskilled—the true proletariat." Craft unions were pragmatic, particularistic, material, and autocratic institutions built to administer contracts; industrial unions were engines of social change. Taken together, "Craft unions tend to be businesslike, selfish, nonidealistic, nonpolitical, nondemocratic," while "industrial unions tend to be class-conscious, socialistic, and theoretical."[64]

Hoxie's dichotomy of business/craft unionism versus revolutionary/industrial unionism (or rather his spectrum; his portrait was more nuanced than that of Debs and Haywood) explained much of what he witnessed. Clearly the Socialists, Wobblies, and other leftists of the day had adopted the cause of industrial union structure, while AFL leaders, especially in the skilled crafts, led the resistance to industrial organizing. With a little elaboration, this dichotomy would become the dominant narrative for explaining conflict in the labor movement.

On one side stood a body of craft union leaders representing at most an elite segment of the workforce and sometimes just their own union's corrupt bureaucracy. They shunned political action because they were indifferent to the plight of industrial workers who needed and desired government intervention on their behalf. They scorned industrial organizing and broad solidarity again out of a jealous desire to protect institutional prerogatives. These leaders accepted capitalism and saw unions as nothing more than instruments to make a buck for themselves and maybe their members.

On the other side stood an insurgent body of industrial union advocates who sought to unite and represent the whole working class. They were idealists who wanted workers to organize for political power and favored broad solidarity across crafts in every industry. They saw unions not as tools of personal or even group advancement but as agents of broad social transformation, even of workers' control over production and of social democracy. These insurgents lacked money, power, or influence, but they did represent a progressive option for the growing majority of unskilled industrial workers, who would not forever be denied.

Although this account has much to recommend it, the evidence supporting the "business unionism" theory is a lot less consistent upon closer examination. Were industrial unions generally more radical than craft unions? By the mid-1920s, *company-sponsored* industrial unions had enrolled half as many members as the AFL itself, dwarfing anything the IWW had achieved. Were company unions and employee representation plans the true face of industrial unionism? And did craft divisions *really* weaken workers on the shop floor? They could, although the prevalence of sympathy strikes in the building trades then and now should give us pause. And the corporations that created company unions and representation schemes certainly did not choose an industrial structure in order to empower their workers. Rather, employers continually griped that jurisdictional battles between craft organizations and their employer and/or one another inhibited both production and the introduction of new technology. In other words, they felt the *craft* unions exercised too much control over the shop floor. An industrial bargaining unit could afford to embrace productive new technologies management might wish to introduce, while a craft union would often fight such changes as a matter of survival.[65]

The preponderance of evidence in fact suggests that worker control of production was (and is—witness the building trade unions) far more central to craft union life than to that of industrial unions. It was the craft unions that led the fight against Taylorism—a fact that Hoxie, the reigning expert on scientific management, should have taken into account. And, *contra* Hoxie, negotiations and arbitration were not ideals of the craft union but reluctant concessions of unions unable to unilaterally dictate the terms of work to their employers. When the Wobblies argued that "it is essential to have the form and structure of the organization conform to the development of the machinery of production and the process of concentration going on in industry," they were making a virtue of necessity.[66] To say that trade union structure had to conform to industrial technology was to concede that workers no longer should or could govern their craft. This was capital's game and workers played the hand they were dealt.

But in a deeper sense Hoxie perceived something real when he described the "business unionism" of the AFL crafts. In industrializing America, old American notions about civic virtue and participation in self-rule were slipping into hazy memory. Gompers and a few of his confidants could nurse an abstruse social philosophy, but a growing number of craft union officials, not to say union workers, saw labor unions as nothing more than instruments for securing material gain. And this was a tragedy of the first order, for such a premise was destructive of the union itself.

When members believe that the union is only a tool to secure a bigger paycheck, then only financial calculation, not any sense of moral obligation, inhibits scabbing on one's brothers and sisters—and in a free market, financial calculation is no inhibition at all. Similarly, when the movement lost any intangible, moral dimension, the working class's leading lights would necessarily be drawn out of the ranks of labor into management in pursuit of the main chance. What the Wobblies and Socialists offered labor then (and their modern counterparts excoriating "business unionism" offer labor today) was not so much a sound analysis of the labor movement but a *vision* by which unions can serve the democratic cause. Without such a vision, labor organizations are doomed to fail. "In short," Hoxie said, "if the failure of the American Federation of Labor could be simmered down to a single phrase, it would be 'lack of practical vision.'"[67]

3

THE AFL AND
PROGRESSIVE POLITICS

Gompers and the circle of trade unionists around him never adopted the cynical view of labor action attributed them by Robert Hoxie and the Wobblies. They agreed with their IWW opponents that a widening gulf between the classes threatened to destroy the republic, but unlike their radical competitors, did not find this cause for optimism. On the contrary, they continued to see craft unions as indispensable organs of civic education without which democracy's prospects in twentieth-century America were dim.

Pinkerton men, mechanization, and industrial espionage were all dangerous, but to Gompers and his peers the judicial branch of government represented the greatest threat to labor.[1] One might have expected the courts to have been natural allies of the voluntarist AFL. The courts' well-established preference for a minimal state should have left the craft unions—voluntary associations *par excellence,* Tocqueville might have called them—a maximum field in which to operate. But in the courts' vision of liberal democracy, individual liberty, not voluntary association, was paramount.

The courts proved to be society's most aggressive defenders of the individual's right of free contract, giving open-shop advocates a remarkable opportunity to wield judicial weapons against the hated labor organizations. Today, incongruously, we have come to view trade unions as institutions of the free market. But labor unions exist for no other purpose than to take liberty of contract away from workers and employers as individuals and to replace such free market exchanges with democratic, collective decisions. Such action could readily be seen as a combination in restraint of trade in the meaning of the Sherman Act. Judges and employers of the early 1900s knew this and developed a pattern of litigation against the unions to devastating effect.

A trio of cases made the danger clear. The first was *Loewe v. Lawlor,* better known as the *Danbury Hatters'* case.[2] The United Hatters had initiated a campaign to impose union standards in the industry nationwide. Danbury hatmaker Loewe & Co. spurned the union's approaches, and the Hatters in turn launched a strike. They also threatened dealers with a secondary boycott by America's union members unless they took Dietrich Loewe's products off their shelves, drying up much of Loewe's market. The bad hatter struck back in the courts with the help of the newly-established American Anti-Boycott Association. Though the litigation would drag on for over a decade, the Supreme Court found in 1908 that the Hatters' secondary boycott amounted to an illegal conspiracy, for "Congress did not provide that one class in the community could combine to restrain interstate trade and another class could not. . . . The legislative history of the Sherman Anti-Trust law clearly shows that its applicability to combinations of labor as well as of capital was not an oversight."[3]

The next case was aimed squarely at the AFL itself. When the Molders' Union declared a boycott against Buck's Stove and Range Company, the company was placed on the *American Federationist* boycott list. In 1907, the company, which was headed by National Association of Manufacturers president James Van Cleave, sought and received a federal injunction enjoining the AFL from all written and verbal reference to the dispute. The trade unionists saw this as a flagrant violation of First Amendment rights and challenged the injunction with repeated publications of the offending material. The courts found Gompers, Mitchell, and AFL Secretary Frank Morrison in contempt, sentencing them each to jail time.[4]

The case of *Hitchman v. Mitchell* confirmed Gompers' worst fears.[5] Expanding production in unorganized West Virginia soft-coal mines was rapidly undercutting UMW standards in the Central Competitive Field. Coal operators in West Virginia had long demanded employees sign "yellow-dog" contracts—promising not to join a union—as a condition of hire. Until *Hitchman,* the effect was primarily moral; after all, an operator did not need to prove a contract violation to fire an employee. But now that UMW organizers were urging miners to join the union, Hitchman Company reasoned that the union itself was a conspiracy soliciting breach of contract.

The company sought an injunction on those grounds in 1907, which were quite serious enough. But after a few years of litigation another shoe fell. In 1912 a federal district court examined the UMW constitution and its express aim of organizing all American coal miners. Judge Dayton concluded that "this organization, known as the United Mine Workers of America, is an unlawful one" because it "require[s] its members to surrender their individual freedom of action . . . seeks to control, and restrict, if not destroy, the right of the mineowner to contract with its employes independent of the organization . . . seeks to create a monopoly of mine labor such as to enable it, as an organization, to control the coal mining business of the country; and has by express contract joined in a combination and conspiracy with a body of rival operators, resident in other states, to control, restrain, and, to an extent at least, destroy, the coal trade of the state of West Virginia. It has spent 14 years time and hundreds of thousands of dollars in effort to accomplish this unlawful purpose."[6]

This was the nightmare that Gompers had anticipated as the injunctions and case law had piled up. Much as Lincoln had, the trade unionists found the idea that labor was an alienable commodity repugnant—it seemed to imply that they were no more than "wage slaves." As the series of adverse decisions came down, Gompers repeatedly invoked the Thirteenth Amendment, accusing the courts of a "judicial reenactment of slavery," and comparing their decisions to the *Dred Scott* ruling.[7] Once the Sherman Act passed, the danger to labor was compounded. If the courts should ever reach a consensus that labor was a commodity, *all* trade unions could be deemed illegal combinations. "Under the interpretation placed upon the Sherman antitrust law by the courts," an alarmed Gompers reflected on the *Hitchman* ruling, "it is within the province and the power of any administration at any time to begin proceedings to dissolve any organization of labor in the United States."[8] This danger from the courts drew Gompers and the AFL into politics, largely against their will.

Politics was not entirely new to the trade unions. Local unions were already active players in urban politics. Although the machinations of the big-city party machines could be rough and unsavory, local political activism fostered direct political participation and did little to empower a distant state— Tocqueville probably would have approved. On a national level, the unions had taken some forceful stands on foreign policy, for instance, condemning the Spanish-American war as an undesirable imperial venture— something about which socialists and small-r republicans could readily agree.

With greater enthusiasm the AFL unions had also embraced the cause of immigration restriction, insisting that the entry of Chinese workers to West Coast labor markets and Southern or Eastern European workers to the Eastern industrial cities would depress the wages of native-born workers.[9] Although the unions dwelt on defects in civic virtue—real and imagined—that these workers imported from their ancestral cultures, there were surely more fundamental and less flattering dimensions to their stance. The craft unions' rock-ribbed solidarity was at least in part a mechanical one based on social and cultural homogeneity, which would be vitiated by diversity; resisting entry of new ethnic, racial, and gender groups was a characteristic of their nature.

Heretofore the AFL unions had generally kept their distance from domestic policy disputes, but with the courts dealing daily blows against their survival, it was a distance they could no longer afford. Yet theirs was a curiously voluntarist involvement. The craft unions did not want more government regulation of the economy; they wanted less. They did not want the government to protect labor organizations from employers. They wanted merely that the courts should back away and give them the room to defend themselves, to pursue their project of labor advancement and civic education without undue burdens on their freedom of action. Rather than asking for help from a paternalistic government, John Commons astutely noted, the unions asked "simply for immunity from interference by legislatures, courts and executives."[10]

The Federation adopted an equally interesting political strategy, for Gompers sought to make voluntarism and the craft unions' nonpartisan civic education a source of political strength rather than weakness. Trade unionists would debate and deliberate political issues within their own councils, formulating a cohesive set of policy demands. They would then present labor's agenda to each of the political parties, and educate their members on the parties' response. The AFL, as in the past, would not affiliate with a political party; in fact, the strategy would only work if they did not. Gompers intended to forge union workers into a highly knowledgeable, independent bloc of swing voters, so that all parties seriously contesting elections would have to address labor's needs. Organized labor would not be apolitical or partisan but would pursue "aggressive nonpartisan political action." As he explained it, "labor does not become partisan to a political party, but partisan to a principle."[11]

Accordingly, in 1906 the Federation drew up a "Bill of Grievances" addressed to the president and to the leaders of the two houses of Congress. The central issues were linked: the exemption of labor from the purview of antitrust legislation, and relief from proliferating injunctions. At the same time the AFL also began to take interest in select legislative elections, deploying its still rather small full-time staff to grassroots political organizing, publicizing the legislative records of notoriously anti-labor legislators, and supporting trade unionists running for office.[12]

In 1908 the AFL followed up by presenting its demands to each of the major party conventions. The Republicans rejected labor's entreaties outright, and added insult to injury by nominating William Howard Taft, "father" of the labor injunction, for the presidency. In contrast, the Democrats incorporated injunction reform into their platform. The AFL found itself steadily drawn toward an informal alliance with the Democrats, especially the radical Williams Jennings Bryan wing of the party; the Great Commoner was then engaged in his third (losing) presidential run. Though a formal AFL endorsement was still taboo, Gompers and many other trade union leaders openly campaigned for Bryan in 1908. And in an act that certainly violated the spirit if not the letter of "aggressive nonpartisan political action" the Democrats seem to have paid the salaries of many AFL organizers detailed to campaign work.[13]

The Election of 1912

The epic 1912 presidential election helped harden the AFL's political predilections. This titanic clash pitted the conservative incumbent Taft against not one, but *two* candidates angling to give voice to the burgeoning progressive movement. The Democrats nominated New Jersey governor Woodrow Wilson, while former president Theodore Roosevelt came out of retirement to attack his former protégé for betraying Progressive Republicans.

Taft and his conservative allies turned back Roosevelt's vigorous challenge for the Republican Party's presidential nomination. So long as the hated Taft and likeminded successors controlled the party of Lincoln, there would be little opportunity for a rapprochement with the AFL. Of Taft, Gompers would write,

> [As] a federal judge Mr. Taft demonstrated that he is not in harmony with the newer ideals of human freedom and human justice. He established his reputation as a leader in that legal school that holds that employers have a kind of property right in the labor power of their employees. Upon this theory was built up a use of the injunction process that denied to the wage earners their rights as free men and their legal rights under the laws of our country. This injustice to the wage-earners was augmented by unwarranted extension of the application of the writ of injunction and by the fact that in contempt cases growing out of violation of injunctions, the wage-earners were denied the right of trial by jury which was assured under our constitution and laws. Mr. Taft was known as the father of this abuse of the writ of injunction.[14]

Roosevelt—a man not easily deterred by minor setbacks, like losing his party's nomination—gathered his loyalists and pursued the presidency on a third party Progressive candidacy. Roosevelt was not so easy for the AFL to dismiss. Before and during his White House years, he had achieved considerable renown as a reformer and a trustbuster. As a young New York assemblyman, he had toured tenement factories under Gompers' guidance, and pushed regulatory legislation aggressively thereafter.[15] Presidents like Cleveland and Taft led workers to expect nothing but abuse from their chief executive, so Roosevelt's sympathetic treatment of the anthracite strikers was fondly recalled. Even when the open shop campaigns were at their peak, he publicly defended the right of workers to organize. "The wage earners must act jointly, through the process of collective bargaining, in great industrial enterprises. Only thus can they be put upon a plane of economic equality with their corporate employers. Only thus is freedom of contract made a real thing and not a mere legal fiction," he declaimed in 1910. "Wherever there is organized capital on a considerable scale I believe in the principle of organized labor and the practice of collective bargaining."[16] Not surprisingly, Gompers, and American workers generally, seemed to have a soft spot in their heart for the ex-president.

Labor historians often take a more skeptical view of Roosevelt than did contemporary trade unionists and workers, doubting the sincerity of his attacks on the "malefactors of great wealth" and noting that he too was prepared to deploy federal troops against labor violence.[17] But Roosevelt could not be expected to choose for labor against employers any more than the reverse; he was proposing a New Nationalism that rose above class. "'I am for labor', or 'I am for capital', substitutes something else for the immutable laws of righteousness," he argued in 1904. "The one or the other would let the class man in, and letting him in is the one thing that will most quickly eat out the heart of the Republic."[18]

The scholarly Roosevelt was a keen student of Roman history and the class wars that preceded that Republic's fall. He seemed to have imbibed the usual lesson from the episode: that republican government was doomed the moment that men put selfish gain for themselves or their group or class ahead of the national interest and the commonweal.[19] It could not have escaped Roosevelt's attention that America was already in a class war much advanced, one that had indirectly brought him to power: Vice President Roosevelt ascended to the White House when an anarchist assassinated President William McKinley. As unfamiliar as the sentiment is to us today, Roosevelt was a true patriot and small-r republican in the classical sense. Roosevelt despised *any* segment of the nation that put its private goals above the national interest, and though labor did this periodically, such behavior was virtually "business as usual" among the captains of industry.

Roosevelt had no objection in principle to the trusts. He was convinced that large-scale organization and the elimination of wasteful competition was part and parcel of economic progress. His famous "trust-busting" was not designed to wipe out the combinations but to prevent their exploitation of the public—and sometimes even merely to chastise those who thought their firms were bigger than the nation. Meeting with J. P. Morgan early in his presidential term, he had been mortified to discover that the banker regarded him— the PRESIDENT OF THE UNITED STATES—as nothing more than "a big rival operator."[20]

"The true friend of property, the true conservative, is he who insists that property shall be the servant and not the master of the commonwealth," Roosevelt argued. For this reason he could hold himself up as a genuine conservative and defender of property, while vigorously deploying the state to regulate it, without the caution of a Taft or even a Gompers. "I am far from underestimating the importance of dividends; but I rank dividends below human character," he declaimed. "Those who oppose *all* reform will do well to remember that ruin in its worst form is inevitable if our national life brings us nothing better than swollen fortunes for the few and the triumph in both politics and business of a sordid and selfish materialism."[21]

But enthusiasm for activist government was not the only way that Roosevelt defied both American and voluntarist tradition, or even the most important one. *Roosevelt appeared completely innocent of the customary American belief in natural human equality.* He might alternatively assail American plutocracy as too vulgar (preoccupied with money rather than virtue or honor) or not vulgar enough (insofar as monopolies and hereditary wealth blocked the social ascent of men of talent from the lower classes). He did *not* assail it with pious affirmations of equal human endowments. His concern for American workers and the injustices they faced was genuine, but was uncomfortably patrician and paternalistic in its nature and expression.

Roosevelt's overarching commitment to inculcating civic virtue did give him certain areas of agreement with trade unionists of his era. Even more than Gompers and his allies, he saw trade union activity not merely as a means of raising workers' standard of living but as improving their capacity for self-rule and thus republican citizenship. "Collective bargaining" for "wage earners . . . has been demonstrated essential in the long run for their permanent progress," he told an audience in Fargo. Trade union activity and regulation of the conditions of labor were important as a matter of fairness and decent living conditions but not *merely* that. "No man can be a good citizen unless he has a wage more than sufficient to cover the bare cost of living, and hours of labor short enough so that after his day's work is done he will have time and energy to bear his share of the management of the community, to help in carrying the general load. We keep countless men from being good citizens by the conditions of life with which we surround them."[22]

But whereas Gompers and his associates hoped that trade unions could raise *all* workers to the level of equal, participating citizens, Roosevelt championed *equal opportunity*. Roosevelt wanted society to develop the gifts of each to the fullest, but since talents were unequally distributed the results of this development would be unequal as well.

> Practical equality of opportunity for all citizens, when we achieve it, will have two great results. First, every man will have a fair chance to make of himself all that in him lies; to reach the highest point to which his capacities, unassisted by the special privilege of others, can carry him, and to get for himself and his family substantially what he has earned. Second, equality of opportunity means that the commonwealth will get from every citizen the highest service of which he is capable. No man who carries the burden of special privileges of another can give to the commonwealth that service to which it is fairly entitled.[23]

In an interesting way, Roosevelt exhibited both a lower and a higher opinion of the average, working citizen than did his liberal and socialist counterparts. He held a lower opinion insofar as he was deeply convinced of that citizen's natural inferiority. He held a higher opinion in that he believed that every citizen of the republic would welcome the chance to rise above selfish material and class interests, given "a chance to reach the place in which he will make the greatest possible contribution to the public welfare."

Gompers, arguing that independent trade unions could educate *every* worker in the virtues of the citizen, seemed to affirm the traditional American beliefs in human equality and small government. Roosevelt challenged this conventional wisdom in both respects. It fell to the other intellectual author of the New Nationalism, Herbert Croly, to elaborate the relationship between the two. In *The Promise of American Life* (1909), Croly explained how Americans' conviction of natural equality had led them to create a weak central government, while the activist state preferred by progressives of all parties necessarily implied that such equality was a childish myth best cast aside in favor of equality of opportunity.

When leaders like Thomas Jefferson and Andrew Jackson assured Americans of their essential equality, the yeoman farmers of early America readily accepted their message because it reflected their experience of the world. They lived in a community of small proprietors roughly equal in wealth and learning. But it was inevitable that in a free society like America this would not last, for humans are not endowed equally with intellect, virtue, and talent. "Whenever the exceptional individual has been given any genuine liberty, he has inevitably conquered," Croly argued. "Thus in so far as the equal rights are freely exercised, they are bound to result in inequalities."[24]

Where Jefferson and Tocqueville saw in the yeoman farmer a figure whose versatile experience made him the ideal candidate for democratic self-rule, Croly shared Frederick Winslow Taylor's darker view. "The pioneer Democracy looked with distrust and aversion the man with a special vocation and high standards of achievement." The flattened social order of the young republic, where *every* man might expect to rise from apprentice or farmhand to small proprietor, suited a nation of mediocrities. But for the man of talent, it was a blessing to see factory and corporation replace the artisan's shop. "Industrial economy demanded the expert with high and special standards of achievement."[25]

The new economic order brought its own problems. For in the world of the trust, even the most talented individuals end up distinguishing themselves by pursuit of wealth rather than true excellence. Croly lashed *homo economicus*: "A man's individuality is as much compromised by success under the conditions imposed by such a system as it is by failure. . . . The kind of individuals created by such an economic system are not distinguished from one another by any special purpose. They are distinguished by the energy and success whereby the common purpose of making money is accompanied and followed."[26] Politics offered a sort of salvation. The activist national government that Roosevelt and Croly imagined would be every bit as challenging to administer as the corporation but dedicated to a far greater cause. The Progressive government could regulate the economic activities of the trusts in the interests of social justice, human advance, and the great American founding principle: democracy.

If this was democracy, it was not that described by Aristotle or Tocqueville. And indeed Croly hoped "to venture upon a more fruitful definition of democracy" than his predecessors. "Democracy does not mean merely government by the people, or majority rule, or universal suffrage," he explained. "The salutary and formative democratic purpose consists in using the democratic organization for the joint benefit of individual distinction and social improvement."[27] Democracy was not about self-rule at all. It was a system that linked the "individual distinction" of the few great to "social improvement" for the many. A reform crusade that made public servants out of Roosevelt and other men of excellence was the best democracy the new age had to offer.

Croly had interpreted Roosevelt's political activity through a new philosophical lens. Roosevelt had been fascinated by Wisconsin's "laboratory for democracy," whereby Governor Robert LaFollette—with the advice and counsel of John Commons and his University of Wisconsin students—experimented with administrative commissions of appointed experts charged with regulating industry and commerce.[28] The characteristic Roosevelt reforms similarly called upon the state to discipline economic actors in the national interest. Roosevelt pushed strenuously for the Hepburn Act, extending the government's power to regulate the railroads. And to protect a public alarmed by Upton Sinclair's lurid meatpacking exposé, *The Jungle,* he secured passage of the Pure Food and Drug Act.[29] As suggested by his handling of the anthracite strike, he seemed prepared to use the government's power to protect labor from exploitation as well.

Gompers nursed a measured affection for the man he called a "silk stocking" reformer, but he could hardly reconcile Roosevelt's ideology of *noblesse oblige* and paternalistic care for the workingman with his own voluntarist trade union ideal. Woodrow Wilson, articulating his competing progressive vision of a New Freedom, came much closer to what the cigarmaker had in mind. In his speech, "Freemen Need No Guardians," Wilson announced:

> I believe, as I believe in nothing else, in the average integrity and the average intelligence of the American people, and I do not believe that the intelligence of the people can be put into commission anywhere. I do not believe that there is any group of men of any kind to whom we can afford to give that kind of trusteeship. I will not live under trustees if I can help it. No group of men less than the majority has the right to tell me how I have got to live in America. I will submit to the majority, because I have been trained to do it—though I may sometimes have my private opinion even of the majority.

Very much in the voluntarist spirit, he continued, "If any part of our people want to be wards, if they want to have guardians put over them, if they want to be taken care of, if they want to be children, patronized by the government, why, I am sorry, because it will sap the manhood of America."[30]

Roosevelt and Croly urged Americans to accept the trusts and corporations as a permanent fact of life, a dominant feature of our political economy now and into the future; the New Nationalists had given up on fighting monopoly and were in favor of regulating it. Wilson condemned this counsel as defeatist. "Have we come to a time when the President of the United States or any man who wishes to be president must doff his cap in the presence of high finance, and say, 'You are our inevitable master, but we will see how we can make the best of it?'"[31] Wilson, like Roosevelt, promised a large and energetic federal government, but with a different purpose. It would not regulate but resist what Wilson's intellectual ally Louis Brandeis labeled "the curse of bigness"—its aim would be to shatter the great trusts and monopolies and protect economic liberty.[32] The progressive Democrat acknowledged that modern economic conditions required his party to accept activist government, but its aim was the same as the restrained and limited government of the Jeffersonian yesteryear: to restore individual liberty, equality, voluntary association, and self-rule so far as it was possible, not to give a social blessing to their modern absence.

Wilson affirmed that Roosevelt's program was appealing, that "there is beating in it a great pulse of sympathy for the human race. But I do not want the sympathy of the trusts for the human race. I do not want their condescending assistance." It was bad enough that the trusts might capture the public agencies meant to police them. But whether the regulation succeeded or failed it was fundamentally opposed to democratic values. "I don't care how benevolent the master is going to be, I will not live under a master," Wilson insisted. "Justice is what we want, not patronage and condescension and pitiful helplessness. The trusts are our masters now, but I for one do not care to live in a country called free even under kind masters. I prefer to live under no masters at all."[33]

This was not only Wilson's feeling about the trusts, but about politics as well. The New Jersey governor believed that Roosevelt's policy on the trusts spoke to a deeper quarrel he had with democracy. "The theory that the men of biggest affairs, whose field of operation is the widest, are the proper men to advise the government is, I admit, a plausible theory." He had "entire respect" for Taft and Roosevelt, and felt that "their hearts no doubt go out to the great masses of unknown men in his country." But they saw the government as an exercise in charity under which the powerful deign to care for the weak, not under which equal citizens rule themselves. "I do not want to live under a philanthropy. I do not want to be taken care of by government," Wilson said. "Give me right and justice and I will take care of myself."[34]

Wilson had begun his career as a conservative, and though many AFL trade unionists eyed him warily, labor supported him through the difficult 1912 campaign. For a moment it seemed that Gompers had succeeded beyond his greatest aspirations. The conservative, laissez-faire advocate, Taft, trailed behind *both* progressive candidates. Roosevelt's campaign had split the Republican Party, delivering both the Congress and the White House to the Democrats. Wilson granted labor social recognition of a kind no chief executive had before, appointing UMW officer (and sometime U.S. House member) William B. Wilson as the first Secretary of Labor.

Most importantly, as part of a general reform of antitrust law, the Democrats included a series of passages granting a formal exemption for trade union activity. Their Clayton Act enumerated a catalogue of trade union activities that the courts were forbidden to enjoin by injunction, and in its famous section 6 the Act declared:

> The labor of a human being is not a commodity or article of commerce. Nothing contained in the anti-trust laws shall be construed to forbid the existence and operation of labor, agricultural, or horticultural organizations . . . or to forbid or restrain individual members of such organizations from lawfully carrying out the legitimate objects thereof, nor shall such organizations, or the members thereof, be held or construed to be illegal combinations or conspiracies in restraint of trade under the anti-trust laws.

Wilson observed, "A man's labor is not a commodity but a part of his life. The courts must not treat it as if it were a commodity, but must treat it as if it were part of his life."[35]

For years, organized labor had worked for such a declaration. Not only did craft unionists find the very idea that labor was an alienable commodity abhorrent; they also saw this as the pernicious principle that enabled antilabor judges to meddle in union activities. If labor were not a commodity, trade union activists reasoned, then a concerted activity to withhold labor—even in a sympathy strike—could not be considered a conspiracy in restraint of trade. Indeed, the whole panoply of voluntarist trade union activities were designed to bring labor under the collective control of the workers united in their craft union. If labor was, in the eyes of the law, no longer a commodity in interstate trade, perhaps the federal government's power to interfere in trade union action would vanish altogether.

Gompers was jubilant. He hailed the Clayton Act as "the Magna Carta upon which the working people will rear their structure of industrial freedom" and spent the succeeding years boasting about the AFL's remarkable achievement. He missed no opportunity to upbraid his critics on the left who had opposed his strategy of "aggressive nonpartisan political action" in favor of endorsing a labor or socialist party. "Suppose in 1912 we had had a labor party in existence; do you think for a moment we could have gone as the American labor movement to the other political parties and said: 'We want you to inaugurate in your platform this and this declaration,'" he lectured in a 1919 speech. "How long would we have had to wait for the passage of a law by Congress declaring, in practice and in principle that the labor of a human being is not a commodity or an article of commerce—the most far-reaching declaration ever made by any government in the world?"[36]

The soaring rhetoric of the Act was beautiful and surely among the "most far-reaching declarations" of any government. But winged words alone do not an industrial Magna Carta make. The Act ultimately provided trade unionists little protection from the dangers they faced.[37] The abyss into which Gompers had peered in the 1912 *Hitchman* ruling closed shortly thereafter without reference to the Clayton Act, when an appellate court ruled that the Mineworkers were no monopoly in the meaning of the Sherman Act. But the Clayton Act offered no protection against the more resilient charge of unlawfully soliciting breach of contract. In 1917 the Supreme Court upheld *Hitchman* in a far-reaching decision approving the validity of yellow-dog contracts, effectively forbidding UMW organizing activities in West Virginia.[38]

The hope that the Clayton Act would exempt other tools and techniques of trade union voluntarism from judicial interference proved similarly misplaced. The AFL believed that the Act amounted to a blanket trade union exemption from federal regulation, but the Clayton Act was carefully drawn to include only "lawful" activities of labor organizations, and secondary boycotts were apparently still unlawful. *Duplex Printing Press Co. v. Deering* (1921) confirmed that unions could expect little relief under the Clayton Act. In 1913 the Machinists had declared a boycott of Duplex Co., a defiant open-shop holdout in the nation's otherwise well-organized printing press industry. Union workers at other firms refused to ship, install, and repair presses manufactured by Duplex. The company sought an injunction against the IAM in 1917. The lower courts agreed with the union interpretation of the Clayton Act, suspecting that the Act had legalized the secondary boycott, but the Supreme Court granted the injunction in 1921. The court ruled that the Machinists were engaged in a sympathetic strike against, and a secondary boycott of, Duplex customers who were not a direct party to the dispute—and that such action was illegal and beyond the protection of the Clayton Act.[39]

Nor was this the Court's last blow against the Act. The Act had been written to protect labor organizations pursuing lawful and legitimate ends; could there be any more lawful and legitimate labor union activity than striking an employer? Yet apparently no trade union activity was entirely immune from an activist and meddling judiciary. When mass picketing in a 1913 foundry strike issued in sporadic violence, *American Steel* sought and received an injunction against the pickets. Local trade unionists denied involvement in the violence and insisted that peaceful persuasion was their aim, and for years the case wound its way through the appeals process. But by 1921, when the Supreme Court decided *American Steel Foundries v. Tri-City Trades Council*, Taft had been elevated to Chief Justice and wrote the decision.

Taft's decision was consistent with his *laissez-faire* liberal ideals. America was a nation of free and equal citizens entitled to maximum liberty in arranging their contracts, contracts enforced by a "night watchman" state. That state, though minimal, was the sole sovereign authority and thus possessed a monopoly of legitimate force. If the union's real purpose was peaceful persuasion, Taft argued, then a handful of "missionaries" to disseminate information at the works would have sufficed. Such activity would be lawful and protected under the Act. But what the unionists did here was another matter. The word picket, Taft pointedly reminded observers, is military in its origins. "The whole campaign . . . became effective because of its intimidating character." Consequently "persuasion or communication attempted in such a presence and under such conditions was anything but peaceable and lawful." The injunction was upheld; in the eyes of the law, strikes would have to be conducted without "picketing" in the ordinary sense of the word.[40]

Rather than rearing a structure of industrial freedom on the Clayton Act, labor was now convinced that the courts were erecting an edifice of wage slavery or industrial serfdom on the liberal premise of free contract. Yet their very voluntarist premises dictated that the unions could do little but ceaselessly repeat the traditional democratic values that they held so dear. "A majority of the justices of the Supreme Court have swept away this strong barrier [the Clayton Act] against a feudalistic legal concept and labor finds itself again at the mercy of an unlimited use of judge-made law. The injunction as it is now used and abused in labor disputes is without sanction either in the Constitution or in the fundamental law of the land. It is a pure usurpation of power and authority," Federation leaders fumed. "The workers maintain that in their everyday life and work rights which the Constitution declares to be inalienable should in practice, as well as in theory, be inalienable. Among these rights is the right to liberty—freedom from involuntary servitude or compulsory labor, except as punishment for crime. This guarantee of the thirteenth amendment lives, and the workers are determined that it shall not be denied them."[41]

In a sense, a final insult to the Clayton Act came two years later in an unrelated decision, *Adkins v. Children's Hospital* (1923). The court here struck down a DC minimum wage ordinance for female and child labor. The Clayton Act did not enter the court's discussion in *Adkins*.[42] That is precisely the point: when Justice George Sutherland, writing for the court, pronounced that "in principle, there can be no difference between the case of selling labor and the case of selling goods," he did not intend to make a general statement about the nature of work. But such a blunt statement that labor *was* a commodity could only be made in a world where the Clayton Act did not, for all intents and purposes, exist.

Progressivism in Power

The failure of the Clayton Act and the flailing of the voluntarists was only a symptom of a far larger problem. Wilson's New Freedom rhetoric had earned him the support of trade union voluntarists and carried the day at the polls with American voters who still treasured the old democratic verities and civic virtues. But the reasoning of Roosevelt and Croly was the more sound. The modern political economy had changed America in fundamental ways. The direct democracy of the New England town meeting and the Tocqueville text was no longer possible. Although Progressives shared with the AFL voluntarists a genuine love of democracy and political participation, they also knew that in an age of large-scale organizations these terms had to be given new definition.

The worker's civic participation could be seen as the acid test for any modern definition of democracy. Progressives identified two kinds of radical dependence that damaged the worker's civic capacities in an era when vast organizations dominated economy and polity. One kind was the sort of *mental* dependence to which Tocqueville had alluded. This was not a simplistic, slavish obedience, but an unhappy byproduct of the division of labor. As the scale of administration expanded and issues became more complex, the average worker or citizen became correspondingly *less* qualified to judge its affairs or its leaders. The other kind of dependence was one of blunt material circumstance. Trusts and corporations acquired a power to dictate economic conditions to lesser economic actors, including smaller firms but especially the workers whom the trusts employed. All told, the nation's economic and political elites had secured a monopoly of mental and material resources reminiscent more of aristocracy than the freewheeling participatory democracy of the nation's founding.

The gist of the first set of problems was quite simple. Classical democratic theory had held that only small communities could be truly democratic. The Greek city-state and New England town meeting were safe democratic venues precisely because every citizen had sufficient knowledge of their political and social problems to make sound judgments concerning them. The vast scale and complexity of modern institutions vitiated that logic. Most workers—indeed most laypersons—could no longer be expected to hold reasoned opinions on antitrust regulation, foreign affairs, or monetary policy.

The progressive reformers who confronted this problem were haunted by the very real ghost of direct democracy as experienced in the New England town meeting and Jacksonian rotation in office. Though they were prepared to admit that the era of the yeoman farmer was past, they argued over how to create a functional equivalent or worthy successor to the robust participatory democracy of old. Some, like Louis Brandeis, railed against "the curse of bigness" and yearned for the government to smash the trusts, restoring a political economy with a more human scale. "The social justice for which we are striving is an incident of our democracy, not the main end." Brandeis would scold nay-sayers before Wilson's Commission on Industrial Relations that large firms like U.S. Steel "frequently grant their employees more in wages and comforts than the union standard demands. But 'man cannot live by bread alone.' Men must have industrial liberty as well as good wages."[43]

Others described the limitations of direct democracy in the modern age as pitilessly as Croly, and demanded a more modest and realistic set of political institutions to preserve some form of democratic accountability in an era so ill-suited for the old forms. "Spontaneous self-government," Walter Lippmann argued, was possible only where "one man was as competent as the next" to manage public affairs. "The doctrine of the omnicompetent citizen is for most practical purposes true in the rural township. Everybody in a village sooner or later tries his hand at everything the village does. There is rotation in office by men who are jacks of all trades." But in the "complicated civilization" we inhabit, the only democratic accountability we could reasonably demand was one in which expert leaders present relatively simple choices to the public for their mandate. "The limit of direct action is for all practical purposes the power to say Yes or No on an issue presented to the mass."[44]

The intense division of labor characterizing large firms and the expanding state placed these invisible limits on the worker's capacity for self-rule, but the massive corporations assaulted the worker's civic independence in a more overt way as well. They accumulated a power over the worker's material well-being heretofore unknown among free laborers. Progressives made two essential observations about this.

The first was that, contrary to the traditional assumptions of market economics, sellers of labor and capital did not meet on terms of equality in the market. The most common presentation of this argument relied on the familiar premise that the worker needed to sell his labor to survive. "Political economists often regard labor as a mere commodity which should be bought and sold as other commodities are, believing that the law of supply and demand will itself regulate the prices to be paid. It is true that labor is a commodity; but it is a commodity of a peculiar kind," wrote U. M. Rose in the *American Law Review.* "Usually the laborer's case will brook no delay—he must have work or he and his family must starve. Capital, however, can wait until approaching famine compels a surrender. The sale of the laborer is a forced sale; and at forced sale commodities usually bring only ruinous prices."[45] Institutional economists like Commons elaborated this argument. Laws of supply and demand governed under conditions of perfect competition, but that these conditions did not actually describe much of the modern American economy, in which prices were formed less by free markets than by tests of power between great institutions. Progressives like Commons defended labor unions much as Theodore Roosevelt did—as worker institutions that could place labor on a more equal footing with corporate capital.

But progressives from Commons to Brandeis to Roosevelt were even more enthusiastic about using government to check industrialists' arbitrary power than they were about workers' self-help. Like the Socialists, the progressive reformers sought an activist government that would intervene in the economy in pursuit of social justice. Unlike their socialist counterparts, however, they were not radicals who sought a fundamental transformation of economy and society. As John Commons put it, they were "trying to save capitalism by making it good."[46] Progressives might propose regulating wages and working conditions, or they might urge extending social programs like public health, disability and pension insurance. In either case they aimed to release the employee from a crushing material dependence on his employer that qualified his claim to citizenship—without upending the system of free enterprise.

For trade union voluntarists, it didn't matter whether corporations and company unions, on the one hand, or progressive government, on the other, tended to the workers' welfare. Either path meant a demeaning dependence on paternalistic protectors that compromised their civic credentials. And the Progressives challenged Gompers' vision of civic education in other ways too, for most were as excited about new advances in science and the division of labor as Taylor had been, and they did not find the craft unionists' alarm about the separation of mental and manual labor very pressing.

Walter Lippmann, for one, was frustrated with people whose preoccupation with archaic ideals of self-rule prevented everyone from enjoying the superior forms of happiness that progress could offer. While these scolds persisted in a single-minded, almost maniacal search for proper institutions of political participation, "mankind was interested in all kinds of other things, in order, in its rights, in prosperity, in sights and sounds and in not being bored. . . . Because the art of successful self-government is not instinctive, men do not long desire self-government for its own sake. They desire it for the sake of the results." If we could set aside our obsessive concern with direct democracy, "the whole problem changes. The criteria which you then apply to government are whether it is producing a certain minimum of health, of decent housing, of material necessities, of education, of freedom, of pleasures, of beauty."[47]

Now here was a practical progressive program. The abundance made possible by modern industry could certainly promise everyone a certain minimum of health, material necessities, education, freedom, and pleasures, if a fair distribution of its proceeds could be secured. If the growing complexity and dynamism of the state worked to preclude the robust participatory democracy of the past, there were other important civic purposes such a state could perform far better than the literally *amateurish* political regime of Jackson's and Tocqueville's America. A rationalized state operated by progressive administrators *could* check the trusts and corporations on behalf of the worker and citizen, protecting his or her freedom from the dominion of these otherwise uninhibited private governments. If the worker could get over his sentimental hang-ups about paternalistic government and the separation of mental and manual labor, he could formulate his claims as *rights* that the government was obliged to protect.

That is to say, if the craft union activists could part with their more abstruse concerns—that a paternalistic government or a stultifying division of labor might damage the worker's potential for democratic citizenship—an obvious political strategy presented itself. And in fact the Progressive moment offered great opportunities for trade unionists who lacked such commitment to voluntarist principles and who were less inclined to fight the future. The garment workers and their unions, for example, distinguished themselves by exploring new relationships between state, employer, and trade union and achieved considerable gains. In large measure recent Jewish immigrants from Eastern Europe, the garment workers and their leaders were more often socialists than voluntarists—relatively unmoved by AFL concerns about paternalistic government or craft jurisdiction, and consequently more adventurous in their methods.

The International Ladies Garment Workers Union (ILGWU) came into its own in a dramatic sequence of walkouts in 1909–1910, in which tens of thousands of allegedly unorganizable immigrant workers effectively shut down their industry. None other than Louis Brandeis oversaw the "Protocol of Peace" that ended the strike by securing a "preferential union shop" in which union standards, if not the closed shop, prevailed.[48] The Protocol was the beginning of a system of constitutional government in the ladies' garment industry much like what the NCF had promoted. For the craft unions, "constitutional government" had been a concession of sorts, a confession that workers could not unilaterally govern work conditions in their craft. For the ladies' garment workers it was the reverse—*employers* had forfeited their unilateral control in favor of negotiation and arbitration. "It was the purpose of the protocol to introduce into the relations of employer and employee a whole new element; that is, the element of industrial democracy; that there should be a beginning, at least, of a joint control, and with joint control a joint responsibility for the conduct of the industry," Brandeis summarized. "The Union, by signing the Protocol, relinquished its right to secure by strike more than it was getting, and there was substituted for that relinquished power of strike, the powers created under this agreement, which constitutes a government to control the relation between employer and employee."[49]

Whereas the AFL union in ladies' garments embraced its immigrant roots and succeeded through innovative tactics, leaders of the AFL's men's clothing affiliate resisted the demands of its growing immigrant majority. Following on the heels of events in New York, workers in the Chicago's men's clothing industry erupted in a general strike. Support from the United Garment Workers' (UGW) leadership was grudging and counterproductive, giving a young union activist named Sidney Hillman, from the strike's epicenter at Hart, Schaffner and Marx, a chance to come into his own.[50]

The strike was not the breakthrough witnessed in New York but initiated a rolling boil among the UGW's Jewish, Italian, and Polish garment workers that culminated in their 1914 departure to form the Amalgamated Clothing Workers' Association (ACWA). The new organization prospered with Hillman at the helm despite its exile from the AFL as a "dual union." It rapidly organized men's clothing workers across the industrial North, bringing them under a system of "industrial jurisprudence" similar to that of the ILGWU. As William Leiserson—who would chair the Men's Clothing Industry Board of Arbitration and later serve prominently on the National Labor Relations Board—would write, "we have, then, in these trade agreements nothing less than constitutions for the industries they cover; constitutions which set up organs of government, define and limit them, provide agencies for making, executing and interpreting laws for the industry, and means for their enforcement."[51]

The Jewish garment unions' activity foreshadowed the industrial union-ism of the future Congress of Industrial Organizations (CIO) more than they accorded with AFL voluntarism. Their close association with the socialist party suggested their more positive attitude toward government intervention and partisan political action on behalf of labor. And these unions had sub-stantially proven that immigrant workers could be organized in solid and ef-fective unions given appropriate leadership and opportunities. The prejudices of so many craft union leaders against these workers were decisively called into question.

But the peculiar circumstances of the garment industry anticipated the future of American labor in another way, namely, in the flowering relationship between Hillman's ACWA and the Taylor Society.[52] Well before the Great War, engineers and industrial relations experts like Robert Hoxie and future Taylor Society President Morris Cooke were pressing the would-be scientific man-agers for some sort of accord with the unions. Only in this way, they said, could a progressive restructuring of the shop floor secure that worker consent without which it would certainly fail. In the wake of Taylor's own death in 1915, proponents of labor-management cooperation captured leadership in the Taylor Society. Discussions between the leadership of the AFL crafts and the engineers of scientific management became civil and even warm.[53]

These discussions ultimately bore little fruit. However conservative and re-assuring their affirmation of traditional American democratic values sounded, the AFL unions were stubbornly unwilling to cede enough control over their crafts to let management manage and allow the engineers do their work. Ef-ficiency, new technologies, and a more productive division of labor always ranked a poor second to preserving jobs, jurisdictions, and skilled craftsmen. Not so for Hillman and his garment workers, who found few if any of the in-trinsic rewards enjoyed by the carpenter or typographer in their work; they were much better prepared to accept the premise of engineers and economists that maximum production of consumer goods was the ruling principle of in-dustrial relations. Hillman and his union, assisted by Cooke and the Taylor Society, and heartily encouraged by labor relations progressives like Brandeis and Leiserson, launched an ongoing program of labor-management collabo-ration to boost wages by improving efficiency.[54]

If progressive engineers had difficulty finding common ground with the craft union stalwarts, progressive political reformers could encounter an even chillier reception. John Commons and his cohort in the American Association for Labor Legislation frequently had to pursue passage of protective labor laws without the help of or even in opposition to AFL unions. Voluntarist trade union activists objected strongly to asking government to do for workers what they should do for themselves through labor organizations. An institutional imperative may well have played a part in this: without government intervention, the trade unions held a monopoly on the power to improve workers' lives.[55] But Gompers and the voluntarists had made an important point that remained unanswered. If workers needed the protection of government for their welfare, did they have the independence they needed to be democratic citizens?

And even as they persecuted AFL trade unionists, the courts echoed this voluntarist concern while striking down one Progressive protective law after another. In the famous *Lochner v. New York* (1905) decision striking down a ten-hour law for New York bakers, Justice Rufus Peckham concluded:

> There is no reasonable ground for interfering with the liberty of person or the right of free contract, by determining the hours of labor, in the occupation of a baker. There is no contention that bakers as a class are not equal in intelligence and capacity to men in other trades or manual occupations, or that they are not able to assert their rights and care for themselves without the protecting arm of the State, interfering with their independence of judgment and of action. They are in no sense wards of the State. . . . It is a question of which of two powers or rights shall prevail—the power of the State to legislate or the right of the individual to liberty of person and freedom of contract.[56]

Gompers violently disagreed with the Court's treatment of labor as a commodity, but he agreed that extending special political protections to workers vitiated their claims to independent citizenship and endangered the liberty of all. "Many conscientious and zealous persons think that every evil, every mistake, every unwise practice, can be straightaway corrected by law," Gompers argued in 1915, contending instead that "Self-Help is the Best Help." "We must not as a nation allow ourselves to drift upon a policy of excessive regulation by legislation—a policy that eats at and will surely undermine the very foundations of personal freedom." Special class legislation on behalf of workers was, if anything, even more dangerous than that extended to others, since their civic credentials were already suspect in the eyes of so many. Of another reform project, he said, "Compulsory social insurance is in its essence undemocratic. The first step in establishing social insurance is to divide people into two groups—those eligible for benefits and those considered capable to care for themselves."[57]

By this time, few union leaders still preached the voluntarist faith with the fervor Gompers did; perhaps few even understood it. Even the most "voluntary" supported protective legislation aimed at women and children, and factory inspections for industrial safety.[58] But government interference in the core of collective bargaining still divided Gompers and his allies from the more adventurous labor organizations. And these were not only the usual suspects in the mining and garment sectors but sometimes those that might least have been expected—like the venerable and highly craft-conscious railroad brotherhoods.

Perhaps the rail unions' interest in government regulation is not so surprising, given the railroads' unique role in American political economy. The railroads were inextricably bound up with American politics from the start. As the beneficiaries of public subsidies and largesse, they owed their beginnings to government assistance. These ungrateful capitalists had repaid the citizenry for this generosity by corrupting the economy with monopoly and the polity with bribes. In turn, these institutions of interstate commerce became the favored target for populists and reformers attacking corporate vice. As early as 1887, the Interstate Commerce Act created a government commission to regulate economic activity by the railroads. Theodore Roosevelt's very public crusade for the Hepburn Act empowering the Interstate Commerce Commission to effectively discipline the carriers made them the era's most potent symbol of the struggle between private enrichment and the commonweal. During the Great War, Wilson went so far as to nationalize the railroads.

Government regulation of the railroads was thus not so much a disputed policy as an accomplished fact, and the rail unions naturally sought to make sure their needs were respected by the regulatory regime. Seeing that the government would intervene to break rail strikes in the national interest—depriving workers of the power to secure their own demands in the voluntarist fashion—the rail unions demanded that government ensure safe working conditions and arrange fair arbitration of labor disputes. Thus the brotherhoods welcomed Wilson's active interest in regulating the railroads, obtaining both a mediation mechanism and an eight-hour day rule under the 1916 Adamson Act.

The railroad brotherhoods' push eventuated in perhaps the signal progressive achievement in collective bargaining legislation, the Railway Labor Act of 1926. Brandeis had urged a jointly administered sort of "scientific management" as the solution to rail labor disputes (he, rather than Frederick Taylor, had actually coined the term); in the wake of an extensive 1922 strike in the railroad repair shops, Taylor society figures helped create a noteworthy exercise in union-management cooperation to improve productivity on the Baltimore and Ohio railroad. The carriers and unions together urged passage of the 1926 Act to ensure future cooperation. The Act restrained the rail workers' right to strike, but empowered the federal government to mediate labor disputes when collective bargaining failed; it also, in language that foreshadowed the next generation's National Labor Relations Act, guaranteed railroad employees the right to select representatives free of employers' interference or coercion.[59]

Gompers saw and understood the trend of railroad labor relations during the Great War, but strenuously objected that the game was not worth the candle. In spite of his deep desire to attract the rail brotherhoods to AFL affiliation, he opposed railroad legislation limiting the right to strike in exchange for government investigation and mediation.

> The industrial freedom of wage-earners depends upon their keeping control over industrial relations within their own hands. Once delegate even a particle of that authority to the government and they limit their freedom and forge a chain that retards normal free action in all lines. The tendency of government is always to increase its power and scope of action. An immense coercive power would thereby be created which would mark the decay of industrial freedom. Economic power is the only agency which the workers have for self-protection and self-betterment. They must retain that power and oppose every effort that would take from them their birthright as free workers—free citizens.[60]

But if the mighty railroad brotherhoods needed to enlist the government in self-defense, what hope did Ford employees have? The AFL president's hesitance to accept government regulation virtually doomed the great masses of industrial workers to disorganization, dependence, and poverty. With partial exceptions like the mineworkers and needle trades—where powerful unions confronted fractious and competitive small employers rather than titanic corporations—the industrial working class had proven incapable of organizing itself without government sponsorship and assistance. Whether he admitted it to himself or not, Gompers was making the damning and even suicidal decision that the majority of workers would *never* be citizen material according to his demanding standards.

But Gompers too had a point. He appreciated something that his progressive critics within and without the labor movement did not. When labor organizations received the favor and protection of the state, such favor and protection came with a cost. What distinguishes the powers of government from mere force, what confers legitimacy on political power, is its service of the general welfare of the whole community rather than the private interest of a segment of the population. If trade unions accepted the favor of the state, they acquired with it an obligation to serve that general interest.[61] They would no longer be true voluntary associations dedicated exclusively to workers' self-rule, but rather public agencies whose leaders had to balance the interest of their members, on the one hand, with the interest of the state and nation, on the other. Political recognition, Gompers believed, was a devil's bargain that threatened trade unions and freedom itself.

The approach of World War I proved divisive for labor and its allies.[62] The left nursed a general assumption that war would usher in a political reaction. This thesis was hardly confined to the radicals of the IWW and the Socialist Party, but touched many progressives; LaFollette's friendship with Commons was broken over their opposing stances on the war. Traditional republican ideas also linked foreign entanglements, empire, and standing armies to the decline of freedom at home and abroad: on these grounds, Gompers and the AFL had denounced the annexations of the Spanish-American War. A surprisingly resilient crackpot theory seeing America as the victim of crafty British imperialists, combined with the reluctance of many Irish-American and German-American trade unionists to support Britain in the conflict, nurtured a powerful strain of antiwar sentiment in the AFL.

In hindsight, these perspectives seem bizarre: big business and the right wing were very much thrown back on their heels during the Great War, recovering their footing only in a postwar backlash. Moreover, in America, war has usually brought rising real wages, increased union membership, and expanded social recognition for labor. Like workers everywhere, American workers in a war crisis acquired the greater leverage that came with a tighter labor market—but unlike workers elsewhere they did not court the danger that the war crisis could bring an end to electoral democracy. (There were certainly restrictions and infringements on civil liberties directed against the antiwar minority, but these too were relatively mild, compared with what their overseas compatriots confronted.)[63] Indeed, American wars almost always secure their popular mandate by invoking democratic principles rather than strategic, territorial, or ethnic ones. Whether or not political leaders are sincere in this, the logic of that mandate shapes domestic politics. Waging a war "to make the world safe for democracy" in such a way that imperiled democracy at home would be a contradiction in terms.

Gompers was eager to see the labor movement grow in size and social respect, but scrupulously avoided taking advantage of the national crisis for la-bor's own class interests in a way that would prove the old accusation that workers were indeed bad citizens. When a political dispute erupted over la-bor practices on federal construction contract jobs, Gompers sought the eight-hour day, prevailing union wages, and an end to discrimination against union members in employment. He explicitly did *not* demand the closed shop on such projects. Nor, on the other hand, did Gompers want to sacrifice the fun-damental tenets of trade union voluntarism to which he was so committed. He rejected the idea of an explicit no-strike pledge and reacted with suspicion to proposals for wider government wartime regulation of industrial relations.[64]

On the latter point Gompers was obliged to accept a good deal of com-promise—as was Wilson himself, since the regulatory measures he ultimately adopted smacked more of Roosevelt's New Nationalism than his own New Freedom. Wilson's concerns about a "Big Brother" administrative state began to subside as rising industrial unrest interfered with war production. Gom-pers had argued that good-faith bargaining with *bona fide* trade unions (i.e., *not* company unions or the IWW) was the best way to reduce production losses due to strikes, but his logic had not persuaded many employers, who continued to fight labor organization of any sort. Felix Frankfurter, a Brandeis protégé in the War Department who much preferred the politics and style of Sidney Hillman and his ACWA to that of Gompers and his voluntarist allies, proposed a more active government role conciliating industrial conflict. His advocacy led to the creation of a National War Labor Board (NWLB) to help resolve labor disputes.[65]

The NWLB was composed of five labor leaders, five employers, and two public members. The two "public" co-chairs appeared to stand in for the two sides as well—they were Frank Walsh (former chair of the US Commission on Industrial Relations) and William Howard Taft. Since the prospect seemed to be perpetual deadlock, and the NWLB's powers were merely "advisory," nei-ther labor nor management expected much to result from it. The board's ac-tivism came as a shock to labor and capital alike. Advisory or not, so long as the crisis atmosphere of the war existed, it was difficult for either side to re-ject the NWLB's moral suasion (a suasion backed up by Wilson's willingness to seize factories when they scorned an NWLB proposal and remained em-broiled in a dispute). More surprisingly, Taft—who described his labor board investigations as a sharp education in the oppressive conditions faced by many American workers—generally deferred to Walsh. Walsh soon turned the board into a crusading voice for progressive labor causes like the "living wage," the eight-hour day, the right to join unions. "Political Democracy is an illu-

sion unless builded upon and guaranteed by a free and virile Industrial Democracy," Walsh ceaselessly declaimed.[66]

The combination of wartime labor scarcity, NWLB intervention, and a patriotic commitment to democracy in industry—American workers sought to
smash the autocratic "Prussian" management that characterized the open shop
and overthrow the "American Junkers" who ruled the mass production industries—created explosive union growth. AFL membership grew by about
60 percent during the war, peaking at over four million in 1920. Union leaders less reluctant than Gompers to navigate the state machinery, and better at
it than he, made out even better: Sidney Hillman's ACWA doubled in size. In
the heavily regulated coal industry the UMW had half a million men on its
rolls by the end of the war, and had pushed well into the previously forbidden West Virginia coalfields. Nor was the growth confined to *bona fide* trade
unions, for the labor board had inadvertently created a hothouse environment
for company unions in the mass production industries. Many employers who
had disdained Rockefeller and his ERP before the war now hurried to put in
place some form of employer-sponsored collective representation and grievance machinery that might both satisfy the NWLB and forestall the entrance
of an AFL or one of its radical alternatives.[67]

Congress fell back into Republican hands in 1918, and with armistice,
the President's wartime authority lapsed. If Wilson's desire to protect labor
seemed to wane, his power to do so certainly did. Congress's sudden withdrawal of wartime economic controls set the stage for a dramatic confrontation between an enlarged and invigorated labor movement and a determined
array of employers intent on rolling back labor's progress, especially in the
manufacturing sector. The industrialists repackaged their open shop campaign as "the American Plan" for industrial relations. In what would become
an enduring line of argument for labor's opponents, they challenged the industrial democracy preached by the unions by appealing to rival values,
equally deeply rooted in American culture and fundamental to the nation's
political order: individual liberty and its corollary, the free market. Of course,
the "American Plan" was not intended to open a serious dialogue about the
tensions between individual freedom and majority rule, but to invite invidi-
ous comparison between the "Americanism" of business leaders and the foreign, collectivist values imputed to the labor movement.[68] Trade unionists
retorted that nothing could be more American than their free and democratic voluntary associations, and that the employers' aspirations to stamp out
these bodies was quite as authoritarian as a revolutionary program of state
socialism.

American labor battling for the preservation of American democracy and American institutions today stands between two converging destructive forces. Standing between two opposing forces, uncompromising toward both, the American trade union movement finds itself and every American institution of freedom assailed and attacked by the conscienceless autocrats of industry and the followers of radical European fanaticism. If either of these wins, the doors of democratic freedom and opportunity can never be reopened in our time. . . . The effort to crush the voluntary organizations of the workers may be designed by employers as an effort to secure their own immediate enrichment, but no such effort can stop at that point. Whether its sponsors will it or not, it is an effort to bring upon our whole national organization of society unprecedented disaster and retrogression. The principle of voluntary agreement is the kernel from which has grown the success of this country as a democracy. If that is destroyed in our industrial life, it can not exist in any other phase of our life, and the social organization that has made America must crumble and disappear. Neither the principle of state dictatorship nor the principle of private autocratic dictation in industry can be permitted to gain a foothold in America, for where either of these comes in freedom and democracy must cease to be. American trade unionists have long since made their choice of principles. Their movement is founded upon the principles laid down in the foundation stones of the republic. . . . The road to autocracy, unfreedom and chaos is laid down by its enemies. The choice is now before the country.[69]

Consequently the year 1919 saw more strike activity than ever before in American history. The year witnessed more than its share of remarkable brief radical manifestations, ranging from the Seattle general strike to the Boston policemen's strike, and great extensive battles that shaped the American economy, such as the massive Mineworker walkout suppressed through government intervention. More important still for the future of labor were events in the mass-production industries. Tens of thousands of workers in the meatpacking, auto, and electrical products industries had enrolled in unions during the war boom—a promising start in the direction of solving labor's most fundamental problem.

The key was U.S. Steel. In 1918 twenty-four unions with jurisdiction in the steel industry pooled their resources for a massive drive to organize the open-shop colossus. Initial results were encouraging; in a year, they signed up 100,000 steelworkers and demanded recognition from the company. The company balked and in September 1919 the unions led over 300,000 workers in nine states out on strike. But in U.S. Steel, workers faced an implacably determined foe: the firm recruited thousands of strikebreakers, an army of private guards and sympathetic law enforcement agencies to guard them (in Gary,

Indiana, the company even persuaded Wilson to send in the US Army), and a vast team of labor spies. A sophisticated propaganda operation meanwhile successfully linked the strike with the Bolshevik revolution in the public mind, dovetailing as it did with the Red Scare.[70] By January, the strike had ended in abject defeat.

The experience of wartime progressivism seemed to challenge at least one premise of craft union voluntarism. Gompers thought that government intervention in the economy was inherently anti-labor, because elites were inherently better at manipulating the government than workers. The Wilson administration's actions suggested that the government might actually act on labor's behalf, at least temporarily. (Whether Gompers was correct in the long run was another question.) However, the postwar events confirmed the belief of many craft unionists that a largely immigrant, unskilled industrial labor force lacked the civic skills and predispositions for self-rule. They *could* not organize effectively without government protection, and their unions had collapsed as soon as that paternal protection was withdrawn.

The reaction that progressives had feared *during* the war had in fact materialized only after its conclusion. Trade unionism in the mass production industries was strangled in the crib, and in just two years labor unions lost 1.5 million members.[71] In politics, similarly, labor's influence declined. In 1924, both major parties treated labor with such disdain that the AFL and railroad brotherhoods endorsed Robert LaFollette's symbolic run for the presidency. Business civilization, industrial technology, and the open shop set the tone for politics and culture, and labor was unable to offer a compelling alternative vision.

The times demanded a thorough rethinking of labor's structures, principles, and practices, but the decade's events militated against any such reexamination. Gompers died in December 1924, and no leader of his intellectual caliber or stature was prepared to take his place and propose a new direction. Structural problems conspired against a fundamental reappraisal: the unions that might have attempted innovation were devastated in these years. Not only were the nascent unions in the mass-production industry destroyed, but a series of defeats saw the UMW shrink to less than a third of its 1922 size by the end of the decade. The ILGWU was shattered by the fratricidal battles between Communists and Social-Democrats, and ACWA remained estranged from the AFL. In contrast, the building trades unions, buoyed by the general economic prosperity and its attendant construction boom, continued to grow. At a time when the expansion of the open-shop mass production industries threatened to marginalize labor as a social force, the AFL was increasingly dominated by those unions most accustomed to and successful with the craft union practices that were failing to address the new world. American labor as the twenties drew to a close seemed like a creature of the past, not the future.

What Is This, If Not an Aristocracy?

As the twentieth century dawned, Gompers and many of his fellows in the American Federation of Labor remained committed to their voluntarist vision. In their view, only a set of labor institutions that disdained paternalistic schemes of improvement and uplifted workers through their own associated, fraternal efforts could prepare them for the demanding and difficult office of democratic citizenship. Industrialization offered the most severe challenge yet to Gompers' idea.

It did so not only because the great new corporations spawned by mass production achieved power heretofore undreamed of by private associations in American society, but because industrialization fundamentally challenged the preconditions of democratic citizenship as Gompers understood them. Taylor spoke well for the new technologically advanced industries that, paradoxically, demanded a division of labor that was so intense and confining that the work was more suited to oxen then men. Figures like Taylor and Ford promised that the new advanced industries would be productive enough to generate plenty for all: higher wages for the employees along with higher profits for the employers. It was justification enough for the new work regime.

If a nation of oxen—even well-fed oxen, sleek as butter—were ill-suited for the demands of self-rule, it was small concern to Taylor. The tacit assumption of the new firms and their vast economies of scale was that most men were little better than oxen, anyway. The complex bureaucratic hierarchies and articulated division of labor were not attractive only because they were efficient. They were *just*. They allowed the talented to rise to the limit of their ability and yet found suitable work for the common laborer as well. The young American democracy of yeoman farmers offended Fitzhugh, Taylor, and Croly for much the same reasons. A society that had only one rank, the small proprietor of city or country, was dreadfully unfair to many of its citizens. It was stultifying to the man of greatness, who had the potential for so much more; it was pitiless to the common man, who lacked the virtues and talents for self-rule. A social order that recognized natural inequality of mankind was a far better thing, especially if it could utilize that essential difference in the service of prosperity. But in what sense could this social order be called a democracy?

Gompers had sought an escape from this fate—for his class and for his nation—by delving into politics in the hopes that a certain kind of political action could preserve labor organizations as "schools of democracy." It was *not* a politics seeking the favors of an activist government for labor's cause. The AFL had instead renewed Jefferson's and Jackson's political crusade to protect equal rights for all, ending what they saw as government's favor toward the powerful. Specifically, Gompers sought an end to the labor injunction and a declaration that labor was not a commodity. Gompers was jubilant when he achieved both goals in the Clayton Act, but his optimism was unfounded. Labor was a commodity in fact if not in law, and the courts were not easily persuaded to withdraw and let labor organize, strike, and boycott as it willed. The strictures of the courts denied workers the very tools of self-help on which Gompers wished to rely.

The craft unions' jealous insistence that the associated workers alone govern the conditions of work led them to resist both state regulation of employment relations and a new industrial structure that seemed to mitigate their control over their labor. Unfortunately, this entailed abandoning the legions of industrial workers to the mercies of Ford and Rockefeller. It also implied the singularly undemocratic conclusion that the majority of workers did not, and perhaps never would, meet the standards demanded for self-rule. The AFL craft union leaders who remained loyal to voluntarism even after the death of Gompers in 1924 could see how industrial unions and paternal political relief clashed with their traditional goal of turning workers into independent, equal, self-reliant citizens. Perhaps they could see equally clearly the threat a new model of union organization would pose to their claims to leadership. But in any case, they stuck to their principles through the long night of the 1920s, as history increasingly seemed to be passing labor by.

4

THE NEW DEAL AND THE BIRTH OF THE CIO

By 1930, the leaders of the American Federation of Labor had struggled for at least four decades to preserve their civic values in an increasingly hostile world. They tried simultaneously to train men (and occasionally women) for the role of citizen in a democratic republic; to defend that republic by thwarting the unlawful usurpations of the corporate giants; and—not incidentally—to bring home the bacon for their members. But AFL unions represented only a small minority of American workers and showed no prospect of organizing the burgeoning ranks of industrial labor on the cutting edge of the American economy.

For at least three decades, while craft unionism stumbled, progressive labor critics heaped scorn on two fundamental premises of AFL civic education, both of which they condemned as elitist and exclusionary. The first was exclusive craft jurisdiction. While voluntarists saw it as the workers' singular path to sovereignty over their labor, progressives contended that craft lines favored the most skilled and privileged workers at the expense of all others. Labor needed a wider and more inclusive *industrial* organization, uniting workers in every craft, in order to confront the new mass production industries and the corporations that ruled them. The second premise to which progressives objected was the proud independence that inspired the AFL trades to shun the government's paternal protection of workers' welfare, or indeed any public regulation of economic life. Opponents considered this independence a luxury only the well-organized craft union elite could afford. A civic education that reached only a thin stratum of the workforce could not truly be called democratic. Better that unorganized and unskilled manufacturing workers turn to the political process for aid and succor than that they languish in an ongoing industrial serfdom.

When the Great Depression handed progressive Democrats control of both Congress and the White House, these progressive trade unionists would get their chance to act. Manufacturing workers indeed wished to organize on an industrial basis, and Franklin Roosevelt's administration was prepared to use the powers of government to help them do so. The convergence offered an unparalleled opportunity to the American labor movement—but did the benefits outweigh the costs? The American Federation of Labor would split in two over that question.

The AFL's dominant faction hesitated, and expressed that hesitance in the vocabulary of voluntarism and civic education. The American worker and his union maintained an independence from government unlike labor in any other nation: this independence was the AFL's treasured heritage and also its most profound contribution to creating a democratic civic culture in the United States. Accepting government help in organizing industrial workers meant giving up that independence, and this, AFL leaders argued, was an unacceptable price both to the labor movement and to the nation itself. But the opposition would not be denied. After a tumultuous 1935 schism, the progressive minority would secede from the AFL and seize the initiative in the labor movement. It would be the responsibility of the new Congress of Industrial Organizations (CIO) to stake out a new path for American labor and explore new forms of civic education.

The AFL on the Eve of the New Deal

When Franklin Delano Roosevelt won election to the presidency in 1932, a rather collegial bloc of voluntarist trade union leaders dominated the AFL. Two thoughtful men among their number could offer an articulate, if derivative, presentation of the old faith. One was Matthew Woll, former president of the Photoengravers. Gompers' longtime protégé, he had been widely heralded as "the old man's" successor, but Federation politics had dictated otherwise. Voluntarism's other principal ideologue was John Frey, an officer of the Molders' Union who headed the AFL Metal Trades Department. Frey's Molders, the IAM, and the other metal trades unions had occupied ground zero during the scientific management initiatives and often violent open shop drives of the early twentieth century. He and his fellow metalworkers were proud of their history of resistance to management's worst, and skeptical when industrial union apologists claimed that special hardships in the mass production sector justified departures from craft union tradition.

Men such as Woll and Frey were supported by leaders of several larger unions, who were often as concerned with defending their craft jurisdictions from industrial union inroads as they were with defending voluntarist principles. The Electricians claimed jurisdiction over the whole of the growing consumer electronics industry. Though the union could seldom make these claims effective, IBEW Secretary G. M. Bugniazet made sure they were not overlooked. "Big" Bill Hutcheson, the Carpenters' chief, sought mastery over all things wood for his Brotherhood. Principally he sought to protect his claims on the lumber industry, but his more outlandish demands—say, that the factory workers who put radios in their wooden cabinets carry a Carpenters card—were almost a parody of building trade shenanigans.[1] Hutcheson was a poker buddy of UMW President John L. Lewis, and the two were vocal Republican partisans in a generally Democratic body. Arthur Wharton's IAM probably had the most to lose if industrial union organizing took off: the Machinists could claim members in virtually every factory in the land. Small though their membership in the mass production sector was, it was almost certainly labor's most extensive foothold there. Factory workers who had affiliated with the IAM in the face of such employer defiance displayed remarkable courage; the Machinists' president admired their character, and promised that their union would not lightly abandon them. In contrast, Dan Tobin's Teamsters had a material interest relaxing jurisdictional claims. But Tobin retained a keen commitment to voluntarist ideas, and his abiding interest in Federation and national politics made him a major presence in these debates.

If the craft union group was collegial, there was no doubt who led the rival progressive camp. Charles Howard of the ITU, a thoughtful voice for industrial organization, gracefully parried Woll and Frey in debate—but he could not deliver unanimous support from even his own modestly sized organization. The garment unions also supported the "new unionism," but their influence was somewhat constrained. David Dubinsky assumed formal leadership of the ILGWU only in 1932, and even so he led an organization that existed largely on paper and teetered on the verge of bankruptcy. Hillman's ACWA had weathered the depression *somewhat* better but did not secure affiliation with the AFL until October 1933. Its history as a schismatic "dual" union led Hillman's peers to view him with a jaundiced eye.[2]

There was one leader of greatness in the AFL councils, however, and he spoke for the industrial unions. He was John L. Lewis, president of the UMW. Born into a Midwest coal mining family in 1880, Lewis developed an active

interest in union affairs as a young man. His work in the UMW brought him
to the attention of Gompers, who in 1911 appointed him an AFL organizer—
a job that saw him participate in numerous disappointing attempts to organize in the mass production industries, especially steel and rubber. In 1917
he resigned his AFL job and took a position in the Mineworkers' national
headquarters where he not only served as the UMW statistician but also ran
the union's newspaper. The following year he secured the vice presidency and
on New Year's Day of 1920 the resignation of incumbent Frank Hayes made
John L. Lewis president of the UMW.[3]

Under Wilson's friendly regulatory regime during the Great War, the
UMW enrolled some half million miners and made substantial organizing inroads in West Virginia and the South. In the next decade the union unraveled.
Coal operators violently recovered control of the Appalachian company towns
as soon as Washington's protection was withdrawn at the war's end. A steady
growth in coal output from these nonunion West Virginia mines put increasing pressure on the Central Competitive Field, and the national agreement
eventually collapsed. By decade's end, the union existed largely as a skeleton
with islands of solid membership in downstate Illinois and the Pennsylvania
anthracite fields.[4]

In the course of his experience, Lewis developed an analysis of his union's
place in the coal industry and in American society much like that of the garment unions. Lewis's thesis was fairly simple. The bituminous coal industry
was populated by a proliferation of small operators in highly competitive conditions. It suffered extreme cycles of boom and bust that victimized responsible operators and working miners alike. The primary responsibility for this
misery belonged to a nonunion sector of marginal "cutthroat" operators: they
relied on slashing worker salaries to undercut more ethical and farsighted employers who favored an economy of high wages, high productivity, and labor
peace. The UMW could provide a stabilizing force for the industry by regulating national production levels and obliging all operators to adopt mecha-
nized, high-productivity mining techniques. But it could do so only if it could
organize freely and impose unified production standards on all mines producing soft coal for the national market.

Lewis's ideas were best laid out in a 1925 book published under his
name—though probably written largely by his economic advisor W. Jett
Lauck, onetime secretary of Wilson's National War Labor Board—*The Miners'
Fight for American Standards*.[5] The autocratic company towns of Appalachia
and elsewhere lent themselves easily to attacks in the old republican mold,
and Lewis laid into them as a threat to American democratic norms. This "in-

dustrial feudalism" was "an offense against the sovereignty of the nation," Lewis wrote. America "cannot live 'half slave and half free,'" he declaimed, appropriating Lincoln's rhetoric. "The American Constitution must mean what it says in every coal field of America."[6]

Of course it was the Constitution itself, as applied in the *Hitchman* decision, that kept the union out of the Appalachian fields in the 1920s. But then, Lewis's attraction to democratic norms was at best irregular; his ambition was constant. In a remarkably courageous—and disloyal—1921 gesture, Lewis presented himself as a militant challenger for the AFL presidency against his recent patron, Gompers. Now, when a sober assessment of the coal industry seemed to call for a unified and disciplined national leadership in the traditionally fractious and democratic UMW, Lewis had little hesitance about providing that leadership by fair means or foul.

Lewis's bid for the AFL presidency had failed, due in large part to the defection of part of the UMW delegation. The Mineworkers possessed a highly decentralized district structure that had been dictated by the varying geography of the coal mines. This structure bred a rich, democratic political life in the UMW; it also decreed internal turbulence, rapid turnover in high office, and relatively weak national leadership. Lewis's sense that soft coal was now sold on a national market and that the union needed a leadership capable of executing a national policy was probably correct, but achieving it was no easy task. His campaign to monopolize control over the UMW and use the union's leverage to stabilize the industry in partnership with the operators required a decade of war with district and local union opponents. Some were leftists who resented Lewis's "conservative" politics; others merely resented a man who had climbed to national leadership mostly through bureaucratic appointments rather than the rough-and-tumble of union elections. In a series of bitter fights, Lewis used administrative takeovers, lawsuits, and brass-knuckle tactics (usually carried out by his brother Dennie and his associates) to oust his rivals from the UMW and subordinate the union's branches.[7]

The internecine strife took a heavy toll on a union already in retreat. With its problems compounded by the Depression, by 1932 its dues-paying membership had plunged to perhaps 100,000 miners. But the organization's momentary weakness belied the potential of the union and its president. Unlike the garment unions, not to say the more radical industrial organizing experiments, the UMW had five decades of history as one of America's premier labor organizations. Over half a million miners schooled in the habits and functions of trade unionism stood in reserve, ready to act when the opportunity arose.

Furthermore, on the two principal issues that divided the progressive trade unionists from voluntarist orthodoxy, the UMW could claim a tradition of innovation. It was the only AFL union of the first rank to be organized along industrial lines, and had been associated with the cause of industrial unionism at least since the Scranton Declaration in 1901. And the Mineworkers had always left room in their ideology for government regulation of economic conditions. The UMW employed political means to limit work hours and enforce safer conditions in the industry, and Lewis called on the government to assist and sanction the union's efforts to bring order to the chaotic industry. With these assets and traditions, and now a unified leadership under a man whose ambition and rhetoric far surpassed that of his peers, Lewis and the UMW would be uniquely prepared to lead a furious challenge to the craft union cohort.

The unhappy job of trying to reconcile the two contending blocs fell to Gompers' successor in the AFL presidency, William Green. Lewis, who despised Woll, had blocked his ascent to the high office and persuaded the executive council to accept Green—a UMW brother—as a compromise candidate.[8] Interestingly, Green was not merely a Mineworker but a more consistent progressive than Lewis himself, for the UMW president's own rhetoric revealed a residual fondness for the independent and voluntarist roots of the AFL.

Green had actually been something of Lewis's senior in the UMW. He was active in the Ohio District around the turn of the century and had participated in the Mitchell era's "constitutional government" of the coal industry on which John Commons had lavished admiration. He later won election to the Ohio state Senate as a Democrat and even secured the presidency of that chamber. There he sponsored a laundry list of progressive legislation, ranging from workmen's compensation and direct election of senators to a minimum wage law and state health insurance. On his return to full-time trade union service, Green preceded Lewis as UMW statistician before rising to Secretary-Treasurer; he also served on the AFL executive board, where he was its foremost advocate of industrial unionism. In the twenties, his support for labor-management cooperation schemes brought him into dialogue with like-minded scientific management luminaries like Taylor Society President Morris L. Cooke.[9]

Lewis apparently saw the vacant AFL presidency as a chance to kill two birds with one stone. Green's punctilious ethical standards and good-government principles made the Secretary-Treasurer an obstacle to the UMW President's political maneuvers and creative financial accounting. Propelling him to the AFL presidency would put a progressive mineworker at the head of American labor and at the same time remove a stubborn do-gooder from his own union headquarters.

But how was it that the voluntarist faithful could accept this progressive figure for the AFL presidency? Green had a lot of respect for labor's civic traditions, and his democratic principles were deeply held. He well understood that democracy, especially in a labor organization, could function only if everyone agreed to obey the decision of the majority when deliberations were complete. He always vocally affirmed that "the policies of the American Federation of Labor are formulated by majority rule" and that once a vote was taken "it becomes law by which the whole of the American Federation of Labor is bound."[10] The Executive Council craft union leaders judged—correctly—that the upright Green would carry out his duty to execute the will of the body, and not substitute his own preferences.

FDR and the First New Deal

The new president, Franklin Delano Roosevelt, would couch *his* progressive agenda in the language of traditional American democratic and republican values. "There are two ways of viewing the government's duty in matters affecting economic and social life," he told the delegates to the 1932 Democratic convention. "The first sees to it that a favored few are helped and hopes that some of their prosperity will leak through, sift through, to labor, to the farmer, to the small-businessman. That theory belongs to . . ." The party of big business? The party of trickle-down economics? The party of the bosses? The party of capitalism? No, "that theory belongs to the party of Toryism, and I had hoped that most of the Tories left this country in 1776. But that is not and never will be the theory of the Democratic Party."[11]

The Democracy had always construed its political opponents as second-rate Tories who used the government's power to favor the few at the expense of the many. But the Democracy of Jefferson and Jackson had played the Liberal in response—the classical liberal of Smith and Locke. They said that a large and costly government was indelibly associated with artificial privilege and elite manipulations, and demanded a minimal state that allowed man's natural equality and its concomitants—individual liberty, local self-rule, and the free market—to flourish. Roosevelt cast aside this long-held Democratic paradigm and in the process redefined the word liberal itself.[12] The distinction between the Tory and the Democrat was not *whether* or not there would be a strong, activist government, but whether activist government would serve the few or the many.

Roosevelt contended that economic cooperation, sanctioned and enforced by government, could enable an economic recovery.

> The responsible heads of finance and industry instead of acting each for himself, must work together to achieve the common end. They must, where necessary, sacrifice this or that private advantage; and in reciprocal self-denial must seek a general advantage. It is here that formal government—political government, if you choose, comes in. Whenever in pursuit of this objective the lone wolf, the unethical competitor, the reckless promoter, the Ishmael or Insull whose hand is against every man's, declines to join in achieving an end recognized as being for the public welfare, and threatens to drag the industry back to a state of anarchy, the government may properly be asked to apply restraint.[13]

Upon election the president proposed a National Industrial Recovery Act (NIRA) to make this possible. The NIRA exempted participating businesses from antitrust laws and created a body known as the National Recovery Administration (NRA) as a forum for working out this "managed competition" in practice. "Democratic self-discipline in industry" achieved through "cooperative action" was needed, he told the nation. This democratic self-discipline would bring about "general increases in wages and shortening of hours sufficient to enable industry to pay its own workers enough to let workers buy and use the things that their labor produces." A body like the NRA would allow competitors to come together and establish basic codes of wages and work conditions in the common interest. "Without united action, a few selfish men . . . will pay starvation wages," the president warned, and all their competitors obliged to follow suit.[14]

Yet Roosevelt, interestingly, spurned heavy government regulation for a rather voluntarist plan of action. The industrial codes were not supposed to be written by government bureaucrats but drawn up by "boards representing the great leaders in labor, in industry, and in social service." If this "cooperative action" was to be in any sense "democratic"—that is, if it were to be distinguished from the "managed competition" pursued by yesterday's robber barons and trusts—the boards had to have labor representation. With the aid of New York Senator Robert Wagner, trade union leaders like Hillman, Tobin, and Wharton successfully lobbied for recognition of labor's rights in the NIRA. The UMW made an especially powerful impact. Lewis testified before Congress about the precedent of Wilson's War Labor Board during World War I, and Lauck worked with Wagner's staff to draft the Act's famous section 7(a).[15] In language recalling the 1926 Railway Labor Act, it held that every NRA code must guarantee:

> (1) That employees shall have the right to organize and bargain collectively through representatives of their own choosing, and shall be free from the interference, restraint, or coercion of employers of labor, or their agents, in the designation of such representatives or in self-organization or in other concerted activities for the purpose of collective bargaining or other mutual aid or protection; (2) that no employee and no one seeking employment shall be required as a condition of employment to join any company union or to refrain from joining, organizing, or assisting a labor organization of his own choosing.[16]

Echoing Gompers almost two decades before, Green hailed section 7(a) as "Labor's Magna Carta."

Labor under the NRA

Green's optimism would ultimately prove exaggerated, but Roosevelt's June 1933 signing of the NIRA elicited a burst of organizing activity all the same. The earth-shaking labor event of that year was the resurrection of the United Mine Workers. Roosevelt's vision of managed industry was not too different from what Lewis and Lauck had detailed in *The Miners' Fight for American Standards*. Indeed, both figuratively and literally (given the participation of Lewis, Lauck, and Green in its drafting) the NIRA had been tailor-made for the UMW. Its effect on the soft-coal industry was electric, for in a matter of weeks the Mineworkers' field of dry bones in the Central Competitive Field sprang to life. In the West, the union ousted Rockefeller's ERP from Colorado Fuel & Iron. Organizers swept into West Virginia and the South with leaflets bearing the text of section 7(a) and the admonition that "The President Wants You to Join the Union!" (President Roosevelt or President Lewis? That was left ambiguous.) Operators who just a year or two before had casually resorted to force and violence to bar the union from their towns were demoralized by the federal government's change of heart and put up only desultory resistance.[17] Almost overnight the UMW had recovered its Great War powers as the nation's largest union representing some half-million members. The union dominated negotiations creating an NRA bituminous coal code.

The garment sector unions enjoyed a similar recovery. Sidney Hillman's

ACWA consolidated its position in the New York area men's clothing business and pursued the many jobs that had escaped the union's reach in the 1920s when runaway shops had spread across the Northeast. The union enrolled an additional 50,000 members to reach a total of 125,000 in 1934. No union saw a more dramatic reversal in its fortunes than Dubinsky's ILGWU. On the verge of extinction before passage of the NIRA, the union greeted the new system with a series of lightning strikes that reorganized the women's clothing industry and pushed the union's membership over 200,000. In both cases, the sanction of the NRA allowed the respective garment unions to bring order and decent work conditions to an industry long identified with poverty and sweatshops.[18]

Other AFL unions secured more moderate returns from the NIRA. Many achieved significant growth, and established unions received a new national significance through their participation in developing the NRA codes. However, few of these unions had leadership that shared either the crusading zeal or the organizing élan that characterized the mining and needle trades unions. Perhaps more importantly, outside of the coal and garment sector only the railroad brotherhoods were familiar with the tripartite industrial government envisioned in the NIRA, the code boards composed of firms, unions, and public administrators. Most unions lacked both the desire and the experience needed to take full advantage of the new environment. A yawning gap opened between the apparent immobility of international union leaders and the raised expectations of their members.

On notable occasions that gap burst open with explosive results. The summer of 1934 saw West Coast longshoremen—led by radical young dockhand Harry Bridges—shut down Pacific ports when the International Longshoremen's Association (ILA) failed to secure a hiring hall to replace the bosses' arbitrary selection of laborers. When San Francisco employers and California National Guardsmen tried to end the stoppage by force, killing two and injuring dozens, a general strike enveloped the city. Similarly, the Trotskyist Dunne brothers of Local 574 defied Tobin and the national leadership of the Teamsters to lead a massive organizing campaign among drivers and warehousemen in Minneapolis. In the largely open-shop town, employers refused to recognize the workers' right to organize or their inclusion under the relevant NRA codes. Again, violent battles between strikers and employers—with erratic participation by the authorities—occupied city streets much of the summer and caused two deaths.[19]

In both these cases, the workers won important concessions; their brothers and sisters in the mass production industries were less successful. The AFL

attempted to capitalize on the organizing spirit of 7(a) by use of Federal Labor Unions (FLUs). These were industrial bodies, of a sort, directly affiliated
with (and generally both supervised and subsidized by) the AFL. They were
chartered to organize individual plants with the notion that as they achieved
stability, those members qualified for membership in an established craft
union would be transferred to the appropriate international. Close to two
thousand such charters were issued and tens of thousands of workers rushed
to enroll in the new organizations.[20]

But here organizing efforts in mass production stalled. Union leaders
would argue whether craft union structure or the character of industry and
industrial workers was to blame, but one thing was clear: the FLUs were ill-
designed for organizing under the National Recovery Administration. Representing individual workplaces, they were poorly suited to serve as labor
partners in drawing up NRA codes. Indeed, the large manufacturing corporations were keenly interested both in monopolizing control of the NRA code
boards and in staying union-free. The corporations sponsored an extensive array of new company unions and found the NRA administrators cooperative
partners, partners (understandably) unwilling to try to fashion a coherent independent labor voice out of the jumbled local union materials with which
they had to work.[21]

The sad situation in auto manufacture, where the AFL exerted the most
effort, indicated some of the key problems. Organization among autoworkers
was so weak that Green himself had to stand in for employees to help develop
an NRA code for the industry. An AFL organizing drive in the auto plants encountered some initial enthusiasm, but the manufacturers resisted recognizing the auto FLUs, and Washington would not force them to do so. When the
restless auto unions agitated for a strike, Roosevelt's team brokered a settlement: elections would determine proportional representation for the different
organizations claiming to represent autoworkers. Roosevelt tried to present
this as a variant on the "works councils" common in continental European
democracies, where different unions compete for workers' votes and support.
In fact, it functioned mostly as a means of protecting the legal status of company unions sponsored by the manufacturers while they harried, harassed,
disciplined, and fired bona fide union activists. Membership in the automotive FLUs spiraled downward.[22]

Thus for labor it was something of an anticlimax when the Supreme Court
struck down the NIRA in 1935. The Mineworkers and garment unions, with
their large dormant memberships and extensive experience of tripartite corporate governance, enjoyed explosive gains. Most AFL unions had recovered

a measure of vigor but had not experienced dramatic transformations. The mass production industries remained unorganized.

Trade unionists could draw three obvious lessons from the NRA experience. First, the unions that prospered under Roosevelt's "cooperative action" in industry were those who could contribute to the welfare and prosperity of their industry and of the NRA system. The UMW, ILGWU, and ACWA were all essential to generalizing high-productivity and high-wage practices in their fields, for reasons John Commons had commented upon long ago when studying the constitutional government in industry achieved by Mitchell's UMW. Roosevelt's sermons and legislation notwithstanding, soft-coal mining generated an endless supply of "cutthroat operators" all too eager to say, "Call me Ishmael." The only actor capable of disciplining such a renegade producer was a powerful Mineworkers' union. Similarly, in the garment industry (where costs of entry were even lower than in mining) every tenement could potentially produce a substandard sweatshop subcontractor if a strong garment union did not exist to force them into line or out of business.[23]

Thus these three unions played an important role in the management and organization of their industry, by regulating supply, by ensuring universal adoption of the most technologically sound methods, by enforcing uniform standards in wages and work conditions on firms in the industry, and by preventing the entry of the undercapitalized substandard competitors that damaged union and high-wage operator alike. But what could labor unions offer the mass production industries? These were generally efficient, modern oligopolies that could exploit the possibilities of the NRA antitrust exemptions quite without the help of labor organizations. Management needed nothing from their workers but obedience, and labor unions would certainly contribute little to that. The one mining sector that eluded the UMW was the series of "captive mines" owned by the steel companies in order to supply their mills with fuel. Unconcerned with the problems of cyclical overproduction and cutthroat competition that plagued most operators, and doggedly determined to keep labor organization out of the steel mills proper, the steel firms effectively resisted recognizing the UMW despite substantial pressure from Roosevelt himself.[24]

A second point exhibited by the NRA experience was that the "cooperative action" worked best for those who were already organized and powerful enough to advance their interests under its umbrella.[25] The case of the textile industry is instructive. As in the case of mining and garment work, the industry suffered greatly from boom and bust cycles in a highly competitive market; a powerful union could have been an important partner in rationalizing the industry. And in Vice President Francis Gorman, the United Textile

Workers (UTW), had a leader with the same organizing enthusiasm as did the
UMW, the ILGWU, and the ACWA. But *unlike* the garment and mining workers, the textile workers relied on an unsteady union with under 30,000 members and little presence in the Southern mill towns that now dominated its
industry. Although Gorman's massive organizing drive in the South climaxed
in September 1934 with the year's largest and most violent strike, involving
some 350,000 workers, militancy—as so often for labor—was a sign of weakness rather than strength. Unlike those who participated in the 1933 resurrection of the miners' and garment workers' unions, most of these men and
women were inexperienced in trade union action. They were both hot for an
immediate confrontation with employers and the NRA board and unlikely to
successfully resist the sort of violence Southern employers and local authorities would certainly employ.[26] The strike was a total failure.

But although labor leaders were aware of these points, their own disputes
revolved instead around a third issue: the relative merits of craft and industrial organization. Advocates of industrial unions had come to believe that
building unions with an inclusive structure was the only way to organize the
mass production industries. Critics of industrial organization believed that
even were this possible, the action would destroy the foundations of craft sovereignty and voluntarism on which the AFL had been built. There was good
evidence for both viewpoints, and discussants at the October 1934 AFL convention sought a compromise to satisfy both groups.

The AFL and Industrial Unionism

Debate over industrial unionism in AFL circles would be emotionally
charged, even vitriolic at times, but lacked the apocalyptic stakes of similar
arguments three decades before. After all, the Socialists and Wobblies of yesterday had proposed structural reform in order to transform American labor
into a radical political movement, and their opponents fought it as such. Now
the newly resurgent mining and garment unions pressed the AFL to issue industrial charters for workers in the factories and steel mills, but neither Lewis
nor Dubinsky nor even Hillman suggested a complete overhaul of the AFL
and its political aims. For their part, the craft union defenders shared the concern of their opponents about the growing open shop mass production sector.

There seemed to be some middle ground between the two positions, and
therefore a committee anchored by Lewis and Frey drew up a compromise
resolution to present to the body.

The trade unionists focused special attention on the auto industry, a convenient choice that symbolized the whole open-shop mass production sector, yet whose work lay largely outside the jurisdictional claims of established AFL trades. The resolution acknowledged that "experience has shown that craft organization is most effective in protecting the welfare and advancing the interests of workers where the nature of the industry is such that the lines of demarcation between crafts are distinguishable." However, the union leaders conceded that in modern manufacturing this was often no longer the case. "New methods" had "brought about a change in the nature of the work performed by millions of workers in the mass production industries which it has been most difficult or impossible to organize in craft unions."[27] Because their continued unfettered domination by management was unacceptable, the AFL would charter international unions in the auto, cement, aluminum, and perhaps other industries. These infant unions would remain under the AFL's provisional direction until they matured.

Lewis began the floor discussion by noting that "peculiar conditions exist . . . having to do with the psychology of workers employed in great numbers in those industries," making them resistant to organizing on a craft basis. He assured the assembled delegates that the proposed charters would not "interfere in any manner" with "the form or structure of any existing trade union of the craft form." He also made an interesting concession to inherited voluntarist craft union tradition. These national unions had to be chartered on a probationary basis because the workers in these industries, with no experience of trade union practice, would lack the civic skills necessary for self-rule.

> It is almost too much to expect, and experience in the past has demonstrated that fact, that in newly formed organizations in industries where men have just joined a trade union or labor organization, there could be immediately found in such industries and such organizations, men of sufficient experience, sufficient business ability, sufficient training, sufficient foresight and sufficient judgment to take over and conduct the executive work and the financial affairs of a great national or international union.[28]

But how could the AFL charter any industrial unions without infringing on the jurisdiction of some craft, and thus denying that craft's claim of absolute sovereignty over its trade? Frey and Woll, for their part, evaded the issue. Frey asserted that the industrial charters were being offered to "workmen who are not craftsmen in the accepted sense of the word." Woll suggested that the compromise initiative "deals more with the unorganized, and perhaps unorganizable, than it deals with questions of craft or industrial organizations, horizontal or vertical."[29]

Charles Howard of the ITU took the bull by the horns.[30] Howard spoke, he said, "as a representative of what is as strictly a craft union as is represented at this convention." This was no idle boast, for his was the *single* labor organization to live up to the voluntarist ideal of craft union as school of democracy. No union could claim a greater control over the work process than did the Typographers, whose typesetters controlled work rules and discipline in the print shops and newspapers. Nor could any union claim a superior record in civic formation and internal democracy than the ITU. The printers were distinguished from most other workers by both a remarkably intense autodidactic tradition and a lively subculture of clubs and associations outside of the union hall. Most remarkably the Typographers developed a two-party system that endured for decades, a record unparalleled in the labor movement.[31]

Nonetheless, Howard argued, however desirable craft unions were, the mass production workers wanted industrial unions. The AFL was unreasonable to demand from these workers virtues that were hard enough for existing unions to elicit from craftsmen; labor must give these workers a type of union that suited them. "We have reached the point where we realize we should mold the policies of the American Federation of Labor to meet the desires of those who are to be served, rather than to attempt to continue a policy of molding the minds of millions of human beings to suit our desires." The pressing point was to "see the unorganized workers organized and to see that they are organized under the banner and with the ethics of the American Federation of Labor." If new workers could not meet the standards craft unionism demanded, then the AFL had better create a structure under which they *could* organize. One way or another these workers would be organized in industrial units. If the AFL did not do this, the company unions or the Communists would—each of whom were enemies both of the AFL and of American democracy.

Howard had identified, better than the others, the meat of the issue. Adhering to the old standards of workers' control meant sacrificing the opportunity to organize unskilled workers in the mass production industries; organizing them would do unavoidable violence to those standards. Howard contended that both labor and American democracy would be better served by organizing these millions of workers into AFL-sponsored industrial unions than by fighting a losing battle to preserve noble but dated principles.

But the AFL leadership was unwilling or unable to make these hard choices. In February 1935, the executive council met to determine the con-

ditions under which they would issue the United Auto Workers (UAW) a charter, and the dispute between industrial and craft union organization inevitably
surfaced. The skilled tool and die makers were destined to play a leading role
in any union effort in the industry. They were the only workers in the auto
plants who had proven an ability to organize enduring institutions of their
own, and their strategic role in production gave them extraordinary power.[32]
They might be enrolled in the Machinists, affirming that craft's claim to govern its work; or they might serve as the backbone of an industrial union in automobile manufacture. They could not do both. Despite Green's pleading that
these men were "mass minded" and could be organized only along industrial
lines, the craft unions were unwilling to accept such a brazen assault on the
rights of one of their own. They upheld the IAM's claims.[33] The UAW, emerging from a national convention of auto FLUs in the summer of 1935, seemed
hobbled at birth.

Wagner and His Act

As the AFL wrestled with the issue of industrial structure, Senator Robert
Wagner of New York moved on the other major issue animating craft union
critics: government regulation of labor relations. Wagner, a true progressive,
exhibited little appreciation for American labor's historic fears concerning
government involvement in this field.[34] Rather, his perspective was that of the
piqued author of the NIRA's famous section 7(a) whose intent the great corporations had thwarted. The legislation guaranteed workers the right to organize but provided no real mechanism to guarantee that right. To fulfill the
promise of 7(a) required new legislation and more aggressive government
intervention.

Almost immediately after enactment of the NIRA, its flaws became conspicuous to Wagner. Strikes occasioned by the promise of section 7(a) had created industrial chaos without actually securing union membership for most
unorganized workers. Roosevelt created a tripartite National Labor Board of
employer, labor, and public representatives, chaired by Wagner himself, to investigate and mediate industrial disputes. The board soon struck upon a favored method of determining the legitimate representative of workers in a
given establishment: it held representation elections in the workplace, desig-
nating the winning labor organization as the exclusive representative of that
unit's workers, entitled to sit on NRA code boards.

For a voluntarist, certain drawbacks of the system were apparent. Gompers would have noted immediately that a union which secured recognition through a strike or boycott controlled its own destiny, while Wagner had made union recognition something awarded by the government. Moreover, under the AFL's principles, a craft union claimed sovereignty over *all* work performed in a given craft. Its legitimacy was quite independent of what representation workers in a *particular* firm wanted. Carpenters in a particular location could no more vote for membership in a union other than the Brotherhood than residents of South Carolina could vote for membership in the Confederacy.

Wagner's National Labor Relations Act (NLRA) would generalize this system of representation elections even as the code boards themselves passed away. By the time the NLRA became law in the summer of 1935, the Supreme Court had struck down the NIRA and eliminated NRA code boards altogether. Wagner was undeterred by this minor setback, reinterpreting NLRA itself as the great progressive attempt to secure industrial democracy. He laid out his argument in a 1937 *New York Times Magazine* essay on "The Ideal Industrial State."[35]

Like other progressive reformers, Wagner was concerned about the private power accumulated by the large industrial firms and the threat this posed to democratic life, but was contemptuous of attempts to turn back the clock to a political economy of small proprietors and their modest civic virtues. "Rhapsodizing about the virtues of the small business man" with his "independence" and "self-reliance" would mean sacrificing the "greater efficiency, larger output, and at least the opportunity for higher wages, lower prices and a wider enjoyment of goods" that new technologies and economies of scale made possible. Wagner (rather immodestly) had begun his essay by dismissing Plato's philosophizing about the ideal State as parochial: wisdom and goodness interested him even less than independence or self-reliance. "All those in modern times who have talked and written about the ideal State have regarded it as a concomitant of the plenty of the machine age. They have looked forward to the end of back-breaking toil and the emergence of standards of comfort and leisure."

Understandably, then, Wagner's primary argument for trade unions and collective bargaining was that only such institutions could face down the nation's great corporations and make sure that working people got the share of leisure and plenty that was their due in a democracy. Wagner disdained the robust and uniquely American local democracy and decentralized government celebrated by Jefferson, Tocqueville, and Gompers. Instead, he envied the "trained and expert" administrative bureaucracies of Europe, believing effective central economic planning necessary to economic growth and prosperity. "The complexities of modern life demand an increasing concentration of the power to formulate and unify decisions," Wagner contended. "People cannot all join in as they joined in the old New England town meeting."

Yet the very need for administration by expert bureaucrats led Wagner to a second defense of labor unions and collective bargaining. Trade unions were essential *because* citizens were unable to participate meaningfully in forming national policy. If not in the nation's great matters, then at least on the shop-floor, there was a venue small and modest enough that a citizen might participate intelligently in its direction. Here was the one place that workers might exercise political and social muscles grown flabby from disuse in the age of organization. But it was precisely in the most modern mass production industries that citizens were daily subjected to autocratic rule!

> That is why the struggle for a voice in industry through the process of collective bargaining is at the heart of the struggle for the preservation of political as well as economic democracy in America. Let men become servile pawns of their masters in the factories of the land and there will be destroyed the bone and sinew of resistance to political dictatorship. Fascism begins in industry, not in government. The seeds of communism are sown in industry, not in government. But let men know the dignity of freedom and self-expression in their daily lives, and they will never bow to tyranny in any quarter of their national life.

Despite his breezy dismissal of "independence" and "self-reliance," it seemed that Wagner agreed that the labor process must mold the character of the worker and not merely secure his comfort. With the grander arenas of politics and policy out of reach for the average citizen, the workplace must be his or her civic school. But it could be so only if democracy reached the workplace. If people lost the capacity for freedom and democracy on the shop floor, the republic, already only tenuously responsive and responsible to the popular will, had no chance at all. Consequently, the National Labor Relations Act guaranteed workers "full freedom of association, self-organization, and designation of representatives of their own choosing," and prohibited employers from interfering with that right or dominating labor organizations. The Act in effect ruled labor unions an important instrument of the commonweal and thus worthy of government protection.

Such protection was offered at a price. Claiming public privileges meant accepting the responsibilities that went with them. To accept the support of the government *for* labor organizations meant accepting the power of the government *over* those formerly autonomous labor organizations. The NLRA gave the National Labor Relations Board (NLRB), a public agency created the previous year, the power to define jurisdictions and to certify bargaining unit representatives through elections determining exclusive representation. If the Wagner Act was effective, these powers—which formerly belonged to labor's own body, the AFL—would be assumed by the federal government. To industrial organizing activists the NLRA represented a tremendous opportunity—to craft union voluntarists it represented a potential danger. The two sides fought it out at the historic AFL Convention of October 1935.

A Cry from Macedonia: The Split in American Labor

When the trade unions of the AFL gathered in Atlantic City for their 1935 convention, both historic issues that divided labor's voluntarists and progressives were on the agenda. The failure of millions of mass production workers to organize reignited debate over industrial unionism. New Deal industrial relations initiatives, culminating in the Wagner Act, gave renewed impetus to arguments over organized labor's relation to the government and to partisan politics.

Once again, a committee wrestled with these issues, but this time no compromise was found. The craft union majority on the committee reported a resolution calling for moderation and staying the course. But progressives believed that a friendly government in Washington, combined with an indus trial organizing program, offered an unparalleled opportunity for expanding union membership—an opportunity that the craft unionists were throwing away, out of a misplaced adherence to archaic principles or even darker motives. The minority presented a report to the floor of the convention calling for wholesale issuance of industrial union charters and a massive organizing campaign in the mass production industries.

Voluntarist stalwarts struck a consistent theme in the debate that ensued. It was no deficiency in the craft union structure, they held, but rather the inadequate virtues or capacities of the industrial workers themselves that hindered their organization. Leaders of the established craft unions had constantly stressed that the industrial workers, languishing so long in their industrial serfdom, were not yet prepared for the trade unions' institutions of self-government.[36]

Arthur Wharton of the Machinists was the most persistent inquisitor into the character of the industrial worker. Speaking before the AFL's executive council, he had reminded his peers of the rapid growth and sudden collapse of industrial organizations during World War I. "During the war my experience was that when men were organized overnight they came not as union men and they went out of it the minute they were confronted with difficulties." Wharton suspected that the Federation subsidies and low dues now offered the Federal Labor Unions had taught industrial workers to expect something for nothing. In any case, he had no use for workers unwilling to suffer the hardships that union Machinists had endured through decades of vicious open-shop drives and Taylorist tyranny. "Who are these people on the outside who want to come in?" he asked. "Don't you think we went through difficulties? Don't you think we had to risk our lives at times in organizing men and in conducting strikes? [. . .] If you ask me what I think about the situation I will say it is a lack of a will to organize, a willingness to accept the gains of the organized workers without fairly contributing their share in this struggle."[37]

These people wanted a free lunch: cheap unions with no effort. The Machinists had discovered early that low dues made for unstable organizations. Now the IAM was moving slow and steady; it was organizing members who were committed for the long haul and was making good progress. In an uncharitable remark, Wharton added that his method was better than "going out on so-called new highways and byways and picking up people that have not the will nor the desire to become affiliated with an existing institution that has proven its ability to withstand all attacks of organized employers."[38]

Lewis rose to support the minority report with a historic speech condemning craft union organizing attempts in the mass production industries as "a record of twenty-five years of constant, unbroken failure."[39] Even if one conceded that the craft union offered a civic education superior to the industrial union, if it failed to reach the vast majority of workers, then it failed in its duty to the republic. Better for both American labor and American democracy that the AFL find *some* way to organize these millions into unions, than to make the perfect the enemy of the good by insisting on noble but archaic craft union norms and organize no one.

What of the future of our country? Who among us does not know the hazards of the present moment? The teachings of the false prophets falling upon the ears of a population that is frightened and disturbed and depressed and discouraged, the nocturnal and surreptitious attempts of interests to form a philosophy, the philosophy of the Communists on the one hand and the philosophy of the Nazis on the other hand, equally repugnant and distasteful to the men of labor. And yet it is constituting a serious, deadly menace for the future. . . . How much more security would we have in this country for

the future for our form of government if we had a virile labor movement that
represented, not merely a cross-section of skilled workers, but that represented the men who work with their hands in our great industries, regardless of their trade and calling?

You may say that we are willing to give them that right, we are willing
to have them come in, if they will only accept our rules. That evades the question, because they have had that right all these years and they have not prof-
ited thereby, and they have found themselves unable to accept the invitation
on that basis. I stand here and plead for a policy that I think will do more to
perpetuate the American labor movement as an aggressive, fighting movement in our country, and a policy that will protect our form of government
against the isms and the philosophies of foreign lands that now seem to be
rampant in high and low places throughout the country.

In short, leaving these workers to the tender mercies of their employers
and the designs of radical ideologues was a greater danger to the republic than
any conceivable consequence of industrial unions and the Wagner Act. "Heed
this cry from Macedonia that comes from the hearts of men," Lewis called on
his audience. "Organize the unorganized and in so doing you make the American Federation of Labor the greatest instrumentality that has ever been forged
in the history of modern civilization to befriend the cause of humanity and
champion human rights."[40]

Frey and Woll defended the majority report. Woll articulated the voluntarist case against the Wagner Act. Howard, Lewis, and the others were excited that Roosevelt and Wagner were prepared to bring the government into
the fray on the side of the worker—but were they not at all concerned about
legislation that took from the Federation and gave to the federal authorities
power to determine "the form and character of organization that shall hereafter prevail in the labor movement"?[41]

But Frey presented the major speech directed against the minority report.[42] He began with a history lesson recalling the decades since the AFL's
foundation. Any impartial examination of these years, he suggested, would
vindicate the principles of craft union voluntarism and cast industrial organization in a poor light. The term "industrial union" was itself "an exotic im-
portation from groups who do not believe in the American Federation of
Labor." At present "the only thoroughly industrial unions I know of in this
country are company unions." What about outside this country? "Free trade
unions" once thrived in Germany, Italy, and Russia, but they were destroyed
by the totalitarian movements in those nations. When "free institutions and
free expression had been suppressed," the ruling cliques compelled their
workmen to enlist in industrial unions created and supervised by the state.

The modern record, then, suggested that industrial unions were not agencies of democratic self-rule but of social control.

In a dig at Lewis, Frey said that critics who proposed an overhaul of AFL policy must provide "something much more effective and convincing than either eloquence or sarcasm." To persuade him that their method is superior to that of his own Molders' Union they had to demonstrate success. The AFL, in short, must not give away its organizational cow for a handful of magic beans—that was a good bargain only in socialist fairy tales. This was indeed a turning point for labor, Frey acknowledged, and the AFL must "lay down a solid foundation" and not build "on shifting sands."

Like Wharton and others, Frey suspected the constancy of industrial workers and industrial unions, both of which seemed to lack commitment and endurance. The record of industrial unionism in the United States was a sorry one. Of The Knights of Labor, the American Railway Union, DeLeon's Socialist Trades and Labor Alliance, and the Wobblies, none had endured and prospered. All had ended up "in the graveyard of those labor movements launched in this country which had high ideals, which desired to serve the workers, as we know, but who lacked the capacity to build up a practical organization that would stand the test of good times and bad times alike," Frey observed. Yet, "no trade union movement in any country at any time except when it encountered the armed forces has had to contend with the problems we have had to face, and going through the battle, the so-called craft unions were at least able to hold their own." The verdict of history seemed clear. Craft unions in metal trades like the molders and the machinists took the brunt of the attack by the open shop employers and Taylorists, and survived. Industrial unions, built on shifting sands, collapsed all too readily when the rains came.

After Frey, Phil Murray, vice president of the Mineworkers, rose to support the minority cause. The Irish immigrant miner had become Lewis's most trusted UMW lieutenant.[43] Much like Green, he was well known for his gracious manner and personal rectitude. And despite an attraction to Catholic social thought that grew more pronounced as he aged, Murray, like Green, was a rather more conventional American progressive than Lewis—as his remarks made clear.[44] Murray gently chided craft union advocates for maintaining an "old-fashioned, fossilized attitude," slavishly adhering to the old craft union principles in a world that had changed. Frey's invocation of the Wobblies and the Communists was a red herring: today's industrial union movement was being led by established and respected AFL leaders. They "recognize their responsibility, not only to their membership, but to their Government as citizens of the United States of America." He noted that Frey in 1933 had still opposed unemployment insurance, citing the tradition of Gompers and the fear of government paternalism. Similarly, "with poetry on his lips and tears coursing down his cheeks," he now begged the delegates to respect "the sacred traditions of this grand old institution" and reject industrial unionism. But the AFL's official position on unemployment insurance had now changed, and the sky had not fallen; nor would it fall if the AFL embraced industrial unions.

Next, Murray turned to Woll's charge against the Wagner Act. He noted that the Act was also attacked by the Chamber of Commerce, the National Association of Manufacturers, and all manner of conservative politicians and business elites. Woll's skepticism expressed the same "reactionary" mindset that had responded to every social reform and experiment of the New Deal: "let well enough alone, let us resort to no new schemes, no new methods, no new panaceas, no new solutions. What we have done in the days gone by is good enough for us now and will be good enough for us in the future. That is a quaint, old-fashioned philosophy that does not seem to have any particular place in our modern-day civilization." This was a telling rhetorical strike. Craft union voluntarists, Murray said, were appealing to the same conservative disposition that labor's business opponents invoked to halt progress.

Lewis, Murray, and the others had not persuaded the convention delegates, and despite strong support from the miners (including AFL President Green), the needle trades, and the printing trades, the minority report was defeated by a comfortable margin. Yet the battle was not over: the issue surfaced repeatedly as delegates from nascent industrial unions dickered with the established crafts over claims to particular groups of workers. In a confrontation—perhaps planned by Lewis and his associates—that dramatized the divide, the Mineworkers' president suddenly slugged his old friend Hutcheson during a heated dispute over the rubberworkers' jurisdiction.[45] When the fractious convention concluded, supporters of the minority report gathered under the UMW chief's aegis in a Committee on Industrial Organization (CIO), ostensibly dedicated both to supporting industrial union organizing and agitating for a change in AFL policy.

It soon became obvious that the CIO initiative was leading toward a complete split in the labor movement, for the Committee almost immediately began to lay the groundwork for dual unions in the steel and electrical industries.[46] The AFL leadership determined that the CIO group had refused to honor the decisions of the convention majority and moved—with gestures of questionable legality—to suspend the dissident unions. The ILGWU and the Typographers were unwilling to join a concerted rebellion against the AFL and distanced themselves from the CIO, leaving the new organization largely a creature of Lewis and his Mineworkers, with Hillman and his ACWA in a crucial supporting role. An exchange of correspondence between Lewis and Green, written as the schism unfolded, provides an interesting window into the issues of labor and democracy at stake.[47]

Lewis offered a pragmatic assessment of labor's situation and urged Green (with questionable sincerity) to abandon his AFL post, offering him leadership of the new CIO. Old voluntarist principles should not stand in the way of labor's progress and workers' struggles; scrupulous adherence to the rules was for the weak and indecisive. Green might ultimately choose to "sit with the women, under an awning on the hilltop, while the steel workers in the valley struggle in the dust and agony of industrial warfare." But this was not for Lewis who would hardly let mere procedural norms stand in the way of his fight for working people. "Your lament is that I will not join you in a policy of anxious inertia. Candidly, I am temperamentally incapable of sitting with you in sackcloth and ashes, endlessly intoning 'O tempora! O mores!'" Lewis mocked his erstwhile associate. "I prefer to err on the side of America's underprivileged and exploited millions, if erring it be."[48]

But for Green the debate was exactly about principles and procedural norms without which democracy could not function. These rules were not silly and petty but necessary for democratic deliberation. The debate echoed the secession of the Southern States and the issues that episode had raised for democracy. "The issue involved, which has grown out of the controversy you raised, is, Shall the Federation be maintained and preserved. . . . If you persist in your determination to divide the forces of Labor I will still continue to protect and preserve our common heritage, the American Federation of Labor." The issue was not mere unity but democracy itself. Green reminded Lewis that as AFL President he had sworn to uphold laws and policies enacted by majority vote and urged upon him that "Every rule of honor and fair-play would require that the decision of the tribunal to which you submitted an issue would be respected, obeyed and observed."

Green wanted Lewis to appreciate that democracy was a bargain under which one received the right to participate in group decisions *only* in exchange for adhering to them once they were reached. Democracy could not work if members retained the right to ignore majority decisions that didn't go their way. In a few years, he would elaborate:

The Annual Convention is the supreme authority of the American Federation of Labor. Its policies are formulated, adopted or rejected after free discussion and ample debate in which delegates have full participation. The Convention of the American Federation of Labor is a democratic institution and the policies of the American Federation of Labor are formulated by majority rule. When the majority will of labor is expressed in the Convention it becomes law by which the whole American Federation of Labor is bound. For this is the democratic way and the only way in which the express will of the majority of labor can be carried into effect. This is the process which represents the essence of self-government. Destroy the majority rule and you destroy self-government and bring anarchy in its place.[49]

An important biographer of Green has accused him of a "mechanistic" or "narrow interpretation of majority rule" for his dogged defense of the convention's decision. The majority of American workers, he rightly notes, were as yet unskilled, unorganized, and unrepresented in AFL councils.[50] But unfortunately a "narrow" or "mechanistic" view of majority rule is the only verifiable one we have. Every legislative action, referendum, or contest for office is decided according to a "narrow" view of majority rule based on counting votes. Losers are not permitted to appeal that they would represent a "real majority" if only nonvoters were included—not because such claims are always false, but because they are impossible to arbitrate. Certainly labor has a long history of radical crackpots claiming to represent the "real majority" of workers; in the absence of "narrow" numerical evidence, there is no way to resolve such claims. And though the industrial unions' massive and highly successful industrial organizing campaigns would give them a legitimacy that their radical predecessors never achieved, the CIO would never surpass its senior federation in size.[51]

Yet Green's arguments had the musty feel of the past. They might well have impressed labor philosophers like Gompers, McGuire, or McNeill. But there was no point in lecturing a man such as Lewis or Hutcheson—who respected only power—about democratic procedures and the rule of law. Green might as well have been talking to a wall. In a noble but futile gesture Green took his cause to the 1936 UMW Convention and called on the delegates to reject separation and respect the decision of the AFL majority. By this time Lewis's domination of the UMW was so total that but a single delegate supported Green when the vote was taken. By 1938, Lewis had arranged Green's expulsion from the Mineworkers.[52] The AFL president later reflected on the larger tragedy of the schism. "The problem which this issue has presented to labor is whether or not workers have the intelligence, the courage and the tolerance to meet through their chosen representatives, resolve their differences and get out on the field of economic battle to fight for the policies laid down by the majority will. The foundations of unionism in America rest upon the very principles upon which we have built our nation."[53]

For five decades the AFL had demonstrated something remarkable about the American working class. These men and women had possessed the basic skills and capacities necessary for running a democratic organization and for acting as democratic citizens. They were capable of assembling as a body, deliberating, drawing up rules for themselves, and then obeying them. This is all the *more* remarkable when one notes that the labor movement had no sanctions of force to compel obedience to the majority will. A democratic government can survive the action of a few malcontents who resist the rule of law by using police and courts to bring them into compliance. Labor had no such means to coerce obedience; it relied entirely on the voluntary respect of all for the deliberations and procedures of a democratic order.

The schism seemed to demonstrate the opposite. Whether the fault lay with the petty and parochial interests of the established craft unions or the insubordination of their progressive opponents, in 1935 American labor proved incapable of assembling and acting democratically. A remarkable exercise in self-rule had come to an end.

5

THE NEW DEAL DEMOCRACY AND INDUSTRIAL UNIONISM AT FLOOD TIDE

The founders of the CIO were uniquely positioned to blaze a new path for the American labor movement. As an AFL minority, their influence had been limited, but now the tables were turned. By allying with the unorganized millions in the strategic mass-production industries and, perhaps more importantly, with the Roosevelt administration, they would consign to history a host of cherished voluntarist practices and principles. The craft unionists suspected and feared the new industrial economy because it was premised on a separation of mental and manual labor; the industrial unionists of the CIO embraced the mass-production worker and the promises of the new technologies. The craft unionists stubbornly clung to craft jurisdiction lines, because they offered a vestige of workers' sovereignty over their labor; the industrial unionists sought to unite all workers, skilled and unskilled, in a single labor organization, valuing class solidarity higher than craft control. Gompers and his AFL successors followed an older democratic tradition that instructed them that when capital or labor used government as a means to their class ends the republic was endangered; Hillman and his comrades in the CIO saw clearly that class conflict was central to the electoral politics of the era and urged workers to join the battle with enthusiasm. AFL voluntarists felt that trade union independence could not be reconciled with a friendly government's paternal protection; CIO activists believed that such scruples were too expensive in the modern economy and that if unskilled industrial workers needed the assistance of the White House to confront Republic Steel or Ford Motor, they should do so without hesitation.

The CIO unionists did not abandon the project of civic education they inherited from the AFL, but they fundamentally recast it. They sought new ways to prepare working people for political participation by training and schooling them in political action. But if they did not entirely dismiss the AFL's historic concern for civic education, they believed that upholding a stringent standard of civic virtue was far less important than finding a form of organization that could embrace the vast majority of America's working class. Democracy might *benefit* from a working class that could indulge in both mental and manual labor and that could tend to its interests without the help of government agencies; however, democracy absolutely *demanded* that workers escape the arbitrary power of their employers, becoming free to join trade unions and act in politics for their own benefit, a task that took priority. It was the CIO that would bring the liberal revolution in citizenship to the American labor movement.

The young movement was fortunate in its leadership—John Lewis and Sidney Hillman were probably the two most talented and innovative American trade union leaders of their generation—but otherwise, the CIO confronted the AFL with rather slender resources. Despite a measure of support from Hillman's Clothing Workers, the CIO was obliged to rely on the Mineworkers for most of its finances. The fragile industrial organizations with their eager but inexperienced new trade unionists rallied to the CIO, but none were self-sustaining. The UAW and the United Electrical, Radio, and Machine Workers (UE) may have been future powerhouses, but in the mid-1930s were still small, weak, and in need of much guidance.

With most experienced organizers still affiliated with the AFL, the CIO had to turn elsewhere for its staff. The Mineworkers provided personnel as well as dollars. Not only did the union loan a large number of Lewis loyalists to the CIO and its organizing campaigns, but the Mineworkers' president mended fences with a number of radical opponents that he had driven from the UMW in former years and placed them in key CIO positions. As the cornerstone of the CIO effort, he created a massive Steelworkers Organizing Committee (SWOC), headed by Phil Murray, staffed by UMW organizers and financed through loans and credits from the Mineworkers.

But Lewis and Hillman themselves could hardly provide enough manpower to do the job. Not only were there organizing committees to launch in a plethora of nonunion industries, but the central office would need to be larger than the AFL's had been, for the CIO had to provide its green affiliates services and expertise that AFL crafts already possessed. This need for experienced trade union activists led to one of the most controversial practices of the CIO, its wholesale recruitment of Communist Party cadre.

The Communists had long established themselves in the minds of many AFL activists as inveterate opponents of American, democratic trade union norms. The 1923 AFL Convention had for the first time rejected the credentials of a delegate purely on the grounds of his political attitudes and activities. William Dunne, a reporter associated with the Communist Party, was viewed differently from socialists and anarchists in the past, which is to say, he was viewed as an agent whose aim was to subject the AFL not merely to a radical cause but to a foreign power.[1] It was an important watershed, for previously the AFL had conserved its strength, unity, and democratic principles by abjuring commitments about ultimate goals. Now it had ruled that there was a necessary conflict between the principles of American democracy and Leninist Communism. The AFL had officially ruled a particular political ideology outside the bounds of legitimate discussion.

Actions by American Communists in Stalin's "third period" reaffirmed the AFL trade unionists' belief that Communists were agents of a foreign power who fundamentally misunderstood the nature of democracy. In those years, the Communist Parties notoriously labeled their social-democratic opponents "social fascists." Students of Gompers did not especially admire European social democrats, but Communists who proclaimed that social democracy was equivalent to fascism clearly placed little value on elections, civil liberties, and other democratic norms. American Communists were directed to walk out of the AFL unions and launch a leftist federation of industrial unions, the Trade Union Unity League (TUUL). As an industrial dual union secessionist movement—one that labeled the AFL a "fascist" organization, to boot—it did not cut an impressive figure in American labor circles.[2]

The TUUL folded its tents by 1934 with the moderation of Soviet international policies, but it left behind one substantial heritage: a pool of experienced and dedicated union activists suddenly available just when the CIO needed them. The new labor federation enlisted them in large numbers as organizers and central office staff.[3]

But the CIO's first order of business was not so much organizing the unorganized as cementing its alliance with Roosevelt. The business classes, divided in 1932, had turned decisively against the president in light of his New Deal programs. Industrial workers would act to keep Roosevelt in office. Lewis and Hillman led the CIO unions in a massive campaign to get out the labor vote for him in 1936. Hundreds of SWOC organizers were pulled from the nascent steel effort to electioneer for Roosevelt; the UMW emerged as the Roosevelt campaign's biggest financial contributor.[4] The CIO push in the industrial heartland deserved a good deal of the credit for Roosevelt's landslide.

The American political environment changed rapidly in the mid to late 1930s. No sooner had the Supreme Court struck down the NRA than in its place the administration and the Democratic Congress created a series of new political institutions designed to manage the economy in light of the depression experience. The landmarks of this "Second New Deal" became foundations of the modern American political economy: the Wagner Act, Social Security, unemployment insurance, the Fair Labor Standards Act (that designated, among other things, the forty hour week and a federal minimum wage). Each of these measures employed political intervention to expand the purchasing power of poor and working people.

The activists of the CIO shared this emphasis. In a 1937 *Public Opinion Quarterly* essay, Lewis (or a ghostwriter) observed, "If there is one fact which the rank-and-file of wage and salary workers, including the humblest, unskilled employees, have learned since the fateful year 1929, it is that our farms, mills, mines and factories are able to produce an abundance for all, provided our industrial facilities are managed in the public interest, and provided our industrial output is equitably distributed." The Mineworker president's account of "what labor is thinking" radically redefined the idea of "industrial democracy" in ways that might have pleased Walter Lippmann. Self-rule and civic education were nowhere to be found; the "real significance" of the CIO was expressed in the general desire for "economic well-being and freedom."[5]

In the partisan politics of 1936, rhetoric like this—and even more pointed restatements by Roosevelt himself—challenged hallowed principles of democratic philosophy. Democratic and republican government is seen as legitimate when it serves a common good transcending partial interests, whether of class, ethnicity, or of some other group. Yet in the political and social battles of these years each side perceived the other as pushing a class agenda.

Immediately after Roosevelt's landslide 1936 reelection, these issues came to a head in two events. The first was a wave of sit-down strikes launched by CIO unions confronting the great corporate behemoths. In a sit-down strike, workers refuse to work *or* to leave the premises; by occupying the plant, they prevent the employer from using strikebreakers to resume operations. In early 1936, Ohio rubberworkers extracted recognition for their union this way; in December, the technique spread to the auto plants with dramatic results. In a historic six-week action, Flint autoworkers occupied GM facilities and forcibly warded off assaults by company guards and local police. Neither Michigan Governor Frank Murphy nor The President of the United States proved willing to provide the force necessary to evict the strikers. In February 1937, General Motors contacted Lewis to sue for peace and became the first automaker to recognize and negotiate with the UAW.

The second event was the court-packing controversy. The *Schechter* decision, which struck down the NIRA, convinced Roosevelt that the conservative court was determined to hew the line carved out in the 1920s and invalidate all of his New Deal programs that violated *laissez-faire* principles. To defend them, he proposed legislation enlarging the Court, so that he might appoint additional justices and create a liberal majority. Roosevelt's initiative achieved mixed results. On the one hand, the Court rapidly changed its tune, upholding state minimum wage legislation and the Wagner Act so as to signal a new course. On the other hand, alarmed by the President's progressive ambitions, conservative Southern Democrats entered an enduring, if informal, alliance with congressional Republicans. This grand coalition not only thwarted the court-packing legislation, but weakened the proposed Fair Labor Standards Act and prevented further substantive reform legislation from reaching the president's desk at all.

The events of the late 1930s enabled *each* side to conclude that the *other* had abandoned democratic and republican norms in political pursuit of naked class interests. Roosevelt's conservative opponents considered Roosevelt a demagogue running roughshod over the rule of law. Indeed, the actions of the sit-down strikers were obviously and flagrantly unlawful, yet Roosevelt and the liberal governors—duly elected executives sworn to uphold the law—passively allowed their labor supporters to use force and violence to achieve their ends. Furthermore, Roosevelt and his partisans enacted class legislation clearly opposed to the Constitution. Roosevelt used the power of government to redistribute wealth to his supporters, and attempted to subvert the Supreme Court when it resisted.

Roosevelt and industrial workers, on the other hand, argued that it was instead their opponents who were subverting democracy. Roosevelt had won a sweeping majority and a clear mandate in 1936. The people had spoken in a thunderous endorsement of the New Deal reforms; but now wealthy business executives were turning to batteries of high-priced lawyers with their doubletalk to overturn Roosevelt's mandate in the courts (a point highlighted early in the Flint sit-down when a judge who granted GM a sweeping injunction was promptly revealed as a significant holder of GM stock.)[6] Even more provocatively they openly engaged in massive resistance to the law of the land. Roosevelt's antagonists had assembled in a "Liberty League" that counseled employers to ignore the Wagner Act, in effect suborning lawless behavior on the part of industrial management.[7] The employers in fact did not need much persuading. General Motors, for example, brazenly rejected compliance with the NLRA—allowing the UAW and its sit-down strikers to argue that they were merely trying to bring a corporate ne'er-do-well into line with the law of the land.[8]

The conflict in the steel industry moved more quietly at first. Lewis, unable to liberate the "captive mines," had fielded a small army of 350 paid organizers and a UMW-supplied budget of a half-million dollars dedicated to organizing the steel industry.[9] Under the leadership of Phil Murray, the Steel Workers Organizing Committee (SWOC) was the CIO's flagship enterprise. Rather than building for a strike, the SWOC ran candidates in U.S. Steel's highly developed company-administered Employee Representation Plan, gradually filling out the ranks of the company program with confrontational CIO unionists. Company management, eyeing events in Flint warily, chose discretion as the better part of valor and signed a contract with SWOC less than three weeks after the GM settlement.

The mid-size firms known as "Little Steel," so accustomed to following the corporate behemoth's lead in price and market decisions, rebelled against the new path in industrial relations. ("Little" though they were, these firms together employed over 185,000 workers.) SWOC called a recognition strike against Little Steel on May 26, and employers and local authorities responded violently. In the worst incident, the Memorial Day Massacre, Chicago police armed and provisioned by Republic Steel opened fire on peaceful pickets, killing ten.[10] Roosevelt's reaction was abrupt and—in CIO quarters—unexpected: "The Nation, as a whole, in regard to the recent strike episodes . . . are saying just one thing, 'A plague on both your houses.'"

Lewis was enraged, scolding the president, "it ill behooves one who has supped at labor's table and who has been sheltered in labor's house to curse with equal fervor and fine impartiality both labor and its adversaries when they become locked in deadly embrace."[11] But Roosevelt had merely been caught in the contradictions of his position. As an elected president, executing the law of the land with "fine impartiality" was his *job,* and responding to what "the Nation" was "saying" his mandate. If he was to remain true to his office, he could no more favor labor merely because he had enjoyed labor's shelter and hospitality than he could favor a wealthy private campaign donor.

In a sense, however "progressive" they fancied themselves, neither Roosevelt nor Lewis could escape the republican principles they inherited from the past. As a class war intensified in American streets, Roosevelt remained committed to an impartial administration of the law instead of a naked assertion of partisan interest. Meanwhile, the UMW president—who had always cherished the labor movement's autonomy—perceived with increasing clarity the dangers of a close alliance between labor, a political faction, and the state. There was a lot of Samuel Gompers left in John L. Lewis.

Roosevelt and the CIO, 1936–1940

Little wonder that Lewis was irked by the president's withdrawal from the class war: it was sudden and unconvincing. Just a few months before, Senator Wagner had presented Roosevelt to a cheering crowd at Madison Square Garden for his climactic final appearance of the 1936 campaign. "Powerful influences strive today to restore that kind of government with its doctrine that that Government is best which is most indifferent to mankind," Roosevelt thundered. "And we know now that Government by organized money is just as dangerous as government by organized mob. Never before in all our history have these forces been so united against one candidate as they stand today. They are unanimous in their hate for me—and I welcome their hatred. I should like to have it said of my first administration that in it the forces of selfishness and of lust for power met their match. I should like to have it said of my second administration that in it these forces met their master."[12]

The New Dealers' radical shift toward activist government and the welfare state seemed to violate the spirit of Jefferson's libertarian, small government Democracy. But Roosevelt had by now crafted a compelling narrative rendering their principles consistent, one that he had shared with delegates to the 1936 Democratic National Convention.[13] They met in Philadelphia: a fitting place to "give to 1936 what the founders gave to 1776," Roosevelt explained. Americans fought their Revolution when "we sought freedom from the tyranny of a political autocracy—from the eighteenth century royalists who held special privileges from the crown."

Our founding fathers won that battle, but the industrial revolution in turn transformed American society. "Out of this new modern civilization *economic royalists* carved new dynasties. New kingdoms were built upon concentration of control over material things." The cruel economic oppression of these economic royalists was every bit as real as political tyranny. "The political equality we once had won was *meaningless* in the face of economic inequality . . . for too many of us life *was no longer free;* liberty *no longer real.*" In effect the economic royalists had "created a *new despotism*" and undone the American Revolution. "As a result the average man once more confronts the problem that faced the Minute Man."

But this revolution would be different. It was not to be accomplished by a free people raising arms against a tyrannical government. On the contrary, "against economic tyranny such as this the American citizen could appeal *only to the organized power of government*," Roosevelt explained. "The royalists of the economic order have conceded that political freedom was the business of the government, but they have maintained that economic slavery was nobody's business. They granted that the government could protect the citizen in his right to vote, but they denied that the government could do anything to protect the citizen in his right to work and his right to live."

Roosevelt's analogy was strained at points. The actual Minute Men of 1936 who sat down at Flint and elsewhere—like those of 1776—were ambivalent about the organized power of government.[14] And government intervention into new social realms could be justified only by creating a *new right* equal to those freedoms of speech, assembly, suffrage and the like enshrined in the Constitution. This was a "right to work and live," a right to "make a living—a living decent according to the standard of the time," and it was to be the government's job to protect this right as it protected the others.

As the conservative bloc thwarted his legislative proposals, Roosevelt increasingly placed his hopes in administrative solutions. He sought, and eventually achieved, a massive expansion of the presidential staff making the White House the center of the American political universe. Through this staff the chief executive would direct the variety of regulatory and administrative agencies, making the president's policy preferences felt in national life quite apart from—or even in opposition to—stubborn legislatures, courts, or party machines.[15]

This expansion of the executive bureaucracy corresponded with a reimagining of the problem of labor and democracy. The AFL craft unions had always placed great store on the value of labor organizations as organs of self-rule within which workers learned through practice the skills they needed for democratic citizenship. Wagner had given this ideal its due when he painted the union workplace as the sphere in which people could, in some small way, experience the democracy that had eluded them since the modern bureaucratic state eclipsed the New England town meeting. A massive bureaucracy directed by a powerful executive *necessarily* interfered with these practical experiences in self-rule, which Tocqueville, Gompers, and even Wagner considered to be key building blocks of a democratic republic. But in progressive hands, such an administration could also be a powerful protector of the rights of workers from hostile employers. Rather than exercising collective self-rule, workers would be encouraged to assert their claims as *rights* that the growing executive branch was obliged to protect. In time, Roosevelt went so far as to propose, in the language of the Founders, an "economic bill of rights."

> This Republic had its beginning, and grew to its present strength, under the protection of certain inalienable political rights—among them the right of free speech, free press, free worship, trial by jury, freedom from unreasonable searches and seizures. They were our rights to life and liberty. We have come to a clear realization of the fact that true individual freedom cannot exist without economic security and independence. . . . In our day these economic truths have become accepted as self-evident. We have accepted, so to speak, a second Bill of Rights under which a new basis of security and prosperity can be established for all.[16]

These rights included "the right to a useful and remunerative job," the right "to a decent home," the right "to earn enough to provide adequate food and clothing and recreation," and the right to "protection from the economic fears of old age, sickness, accident and unemployment," among others.

If Lewis had begun to see the labor's alliance with the administration as a mixed blessing and even a potential danger, most CIO leaders embraced Roosevelt's administration and promise wholeheartedly. None did so more fervently than Sidney Hillman. Close cooperation between the CIO and Roosevelt's New Deal Democracy was the *sine qua non* of Hillman's strategy for labor. Like Roosevelt, Hillman saw a liberal or social-democratic realignment of the Democratic Party as a consummation devoutly to be wished, bringing Northern socialists *in* and pushing certain reactionary Southern elements *out*. Hillman's ACWA sponsored a Textile Workers Organizing Committee (TWOC) aimed at organizing the textile mills of the South. The initiative depended on aggressive administration pressure against the mill owners under the NLRA and the Fair Labor Standards Act; in turn, Hillman hoped that a successful CIO campaign in the South could break the political power of the region's conservative Democrats. If Hillman saw any dangers in such a close affiliation with a Democratic Party faction, he kept his own counsel. And when Roosevelt needed a labor representative to sit on his National Defense Advisory Council, he did not select Green, who still represented the larger and more powerful labor federation of the United States. Nor did he choose Lewis, president of both the CIO and the UMW, the nation's largest and most important labor union. He did not even consult with Lewis and Green about the appointment. He chose Hillman: the leader of a young, schismatic, mid-sized union whose main qualification seemed to be his rapport with progressive politicians.

The green industrial unions were even more dependent on Roosevelt's favor than was the ACWA. Though by 1938 the CIO had established a permanent structure as the *Congress* of Industrial Organizations—replacing the provisional "committee" designation to reflect their official separation from the AFL—even the largest of the new unions were fragile organizations badly in need of Labor Board support. When the Supreme court ruled in *NLRB v. Fansteel* that sit-down strikers forfeited their Wagner Act protections, these unions lost the single significant weapon they had which did not directly rely on the administration's goodwill.[17] None of the three major industrial unions had yet fully organized their basic industries: Ford remained impervious to the UAW; the Little Steel firms resisted SWOC; the UE had obtained a contract from GE but not Westinghouse. Roosevelt's Department of Labor and NLRB were prepared to protect the CIO unions from both hostile employers and more established AFL rivals—but the president expected a loyal labor constituency in return.

When pushing for his Act, Wagner had disavowed interference in jurisdictional disputes between *bona fide* unions, whose settlement was the prerogative of labor itself. But once the disaffected minority walked out in 1935, the NLRB *was* obliged to make decisions about jurisdiction and representation between competing legitimate labor organizations, for there was no longer a united body of labor's own to mediate them. The CIO unions had walked out of the AFL *into* the arms of the Roosevelt administration, and naturally they found special favor with Roosevelt's NLRB. In some notorious cases, Board bias was quite crude: when Harry Bridges led the West Coast longshoremen in secession from the ILA, the Board ruled that the entire Pacific Coast should be regarded as a single bargaining unit—ensuring that the ILA would lose certain Puget Sound locals which were firmly loyal to the New York leadership.[18]

But the AFL's quarrel with the NLRB ran far deeper than a mere prejudice in favor of the CIO, for the Wagner policy ideals it was charged to implement were fundamentally at odds with voluntarist verities. When the IBEW extracted a contract from Con Ed, their CIO rivals, also trying to organize the utility, successfully demanded dissolution of the contract and a representation election. Wagner had created the NLRA election process so workers could repudiate company unions, not legitimate labor organizations. But its mechanisms, by allowing workers in a particular location to choose if and whether to be represented by a labor organization, did not permit that distinction— or respect traditional voluntarist methods of organizing.[19] Through the NLRA and the Fair Labor Standards Act, the government had assumed responsibility for determining union jurisdictions, the shape of collective bargaining, and in many cases wages and hours of work—all functions the AFL had claimed before the New Deal.

In Green's view, a disgruntled trade union minority was collaborating with the government to advance its own interests at the cost of American labor's independence. "Shall government control unionism?" he asked readers of the *Federationist.*[20] "One of the most difficult problems a democracy has to solve is that of maintaining freedom for all against the designs or good intentions of some." He allowed that "the union schism makes the work of the Board much more difficult" but disdained its apparent choice to "determine inter-union problems and destinies" by promoting "an insurgent group." He concluded, "surely this is not freedom for workers to choose their own unions and representatives for collective bargaining, but union development under Government patronage."

But there was little the AFL could do to thwart the New Deal Democrat/ CIO axis that now determined American labor policy, and many of its affiliates adapted to the new modes of industrial organizing with considerable success. The Carpenters plunged into the lumber sector; the IBEW organized a number of workers in the electrical products and utility industries. The Teamsters enrolled warehousemen *en masse* to become the AFL's largest affiliate. The IAM thwarted an ambitious UAW effort to dominate labor in the growing aircraft industry. Thus within a few short years many of the AFL's craft unions had become at least semi-industrial organizations.

Interestingly, there was someone more alienated from Roosevelt and the New Dealers than the AFL craft union sachems: John L. Lewis. Lewis cherished labor's autonomy—and suspected a strong centralized government— as much as any AFL craft union voluntarist. Consequently, developments in the late 1930s filled him with alarm and resentment. The stuff of the New Deal was the stuff of nightmares for a Midwestern, Republican/republican isolationist like Lewis. The growth of the industrial unions had gone hand in hand with the growth of a centralized government and a powerful executive, and moreover, with a drive to intervene in the European war. To Lewis, who entertained a belief in a plot by international capital to draw the United States into the war on Britain's side, the CIO seemed a prisoner of Roosevelt and his internationalist policies.

In 1940, Lewis resolved to make a grand effort to liberate the CIO from Roosevelt. In a dramatic October surprise, he returned to the Republican fold, endorsing Wendell Willkie for president. In a remarkable apologia, Lewis noted—correctly—that "the present concentration of power in the office of the President of the United States has never before been equaled in the history of our country." It was thus "startling" to him that Roosevelt was now violating "the traditions of the republic" by seeking a third term. It could only be explained by an "overweening, abnormal, and selfish craving for power." Under Roosevelt's influence, America was casting aside its traditions of republican liberty to adopt the autocratic, imperial, and statist forms of Old World politics. But, he retorted, "America needs no superman. It denies the philosophy that runs to the deification of the state. America wants no royal family. Our forebears paid the price in blood, agony, privation and sorrow, requisite for the building of the Republic." He expressed certainty that the rank-and-file trade unionists of the CIO treasured the nation's liberty more than Roosevelt's favors, and would reject their White House benefactor at the polls. If they supported the president he would accept this as a "vote of no confidence" in his leadership and would resign the CIO presidency.[21]

The Mineworker chief's endorsement embarrassed most CIO leaders. UAW President R. J. Thomas immediately reaffirmed his support for Roosevelt; even Lewis's loyal lieutenant Phil Murray endorsed the president's reelection. The only significant support Lewis garnered came from the CIO's Communist fraction. The Communists had little enough use for the American republican political tradition Lewis treasured, but with the Nazi-Soviet Pact in effect the Party vociferously condemned Roosevelt's antifascist stance and applauded Lewis's open break.

Come election day, it was the UMW president's turn for embarrassment; rank-and-file industrial workers ignored his counsel and supported Roosevelt by overwhelming numbers. The CIO convention two weeks after the election witnessed a brief brouhaha when Lewis—whom a number of mineworker and Communist delegates wanted to draft for reelection, despite his expressed intent to resign the presidency—lashed his critics in a speech laced with anti-Semitic overtones.[22] On a report of these events from the ACWA delegation, Hillman rushed back from Washington to Atlantic City to recapture the initiative for the progressive forces, which he did with a remarkable speech of his own.

The Clothing Workers' chief mildly observed that "part of a sound labor movement is the democratic process." The democratic process allows people of different views to deliberate, adjust their differences, and reach conclusions. "Even if a group is in the minority, it must not get peeved. It must not go and say, 'well, we won't play ball.'" But there were some people who didn't believe in the democratic process. "I know that there are elements who cannot participate in the democratic process because they don't think; they take orders.

Their loyalty is to an organization outside this organization," he said. "Whether their orders come from Rome, Berlin, or Moscow, it is the same thing." Finally, he praised Lewis's rhetorical and leadership skills that had contributed so much to the CIO cause. He expressed "regret" that the CIO was about to lose that leadership but, alas, he had promised to resign if Roosevelt was reelected and Hillman well knew that, for Lewis, his word was his bond. Hillman endorsed Philip Murray to be a successor.[23]

It was a hand brilliantly played. Hillman had not only challenged Lewis to differentiate himself from the Communists by honoring the "democratic process," but proposed an ideal candidate for succession. Murray's endorsement of Roosevelt would protect CIO relations with the White House; his Mineworker roots would indicate that the CIO still valued its relationship with Lewis. Much admired by his fellows for his intelligence, affability, and character, Murray was unanimously elected president of the CIO.

Lewis, however, continued to suspect and resent his CIO comrades whom he felt remained under Roosevelt's sway. His criticism of the "miserable mediocrities of the CIO," of the "lap dogs and kept dogs and yellow dogs" who led the industrial unions, became steadily more vocal.[24] Lewis seemed to believe that something in the personal character or intellect of his associates determined their subordination to the purposes of the presidential administration. But how could they act otherwise? Lewis led an established union with a long history against a squabbling legion of small employers; naturally, he had little need for the aid and comfort of a paternalistic administration. The industrial union leaders were charged with building organizations from scratch that could confront the nation's most powerful corporations; *of course* they needed the president's support. Moreover, as Green had noted, these unions were fundamentally creatures of the labor board, not of the struggles of independently associated bodies of workers, as were the AFL unions. By leading the schism in labor, Lewis had guaranteed that the labor unions of the future would be similar creatures of the state. But Lewis—a man not seemingly given to self-examination or regret—never gave a hint that he understood his part in creating this situation.

Murray and the Industrial Council Program

The war's approach provided the CIO further opportunities to set the future course of American labor. Though still smaller than its AFL rival, the CIO was a powerhouse in the industries vital to national defense. As the administration enacted extensive wartime economic regulations, the CIO's close ties with the White House grew in value. The industrial unions in auto, steel, and electrical products would soon complete the organization of their basic industries. With government help, the fragile prewar SWOC and UAW would emerge as sturdy labor titans dominating postwar collective bargaining.

As the labor movement's new center, the CIO and its affiliated unions were obliged to develop a new *theory* relating the labor movement to democratic citizenship and values. The CIO leaders bore a heavier burden than the AFL activists had: the beauty of voluntarism was that it was, after all, voluntary. Because the craft unions did not make major public policy demands, they did not have to explain why public policy should favor labor.

Democracy required that public policy serve the general welfare, not the interest of a particular class, and there was no obvious way to reconcile class warfare and democratic politics. The AFL and the Knights of Labor had resolved this dilemma by concentrating their fire on capital's own class warfare. They did not request extensive government support for labor, merely that government stop catering to capital's special interests. Those who did pursue a class struggle politics, whether Wobblies or Socialists or Communists, were not really saying that class struggle was a legitimate form of democratic politics: they were saying that no class society was really democratic. True democracy would be achieved only when capitalism was eliminated.

The CIO unionists had to square the circle, fighting to enshrine their own class interests in public policy without convincing employers (and their fellow citizens) that the political process itself was illegitimate. Conversely, when employers used the expanded government apparatus to secure their own interests—and frankly, they were a whole lot better at it than labor leaders—the trade unionists had to find a language to fight them without impugning the legitimacy of the government. Under Lewis's erratic leadership, the CIO had made little or no progress in this direction. Could it under Murray?

In fact, Murray oversaw the boldest attempt to conceive a theory of labor and democratic citizenship conducive to the new industrial union structure. The idea, which flourished under various guises in the early 1940s, was that of industrial councils. Like the practice of "codetermination" which it prefigured, and that informs industrial relations in much of Western Europe today, the industrial council idea had multiple roots. The fingerprints of figures ranging from Taylor Society champions of labor-management cooperation like Morris Cooke to social-democratic unionists like Walter Reuther can be discerned. Another pervasive influence was that of Catholic social thought.

It was certainly a major influence on Murray, a deeply religious Roman

Catholic with a keen interest in the social vision of Pope Leo XIII. Leo's 1891 encyclical *Rerum Novarum* explicitly honored trade union organization as a solution for the social ills created by modern capitalism, and set off a flowering of Catholic social thought in both Europe and the United States. Catholics, a plurality and perhaps a majority of America's industrial working class, could find in *Rerum Novarum* and subsequent writings an alternative vision to both socialism and voluntarism. *Rerum Novarum* and Pius XI's 1931 elaboration *Quadregesimo Anno* imagined a world in which employers and employees spurned class warfare and instead, as in the medieval guilds, worked together to improve the lives of workers and the techniques of their trade. Similarly, the encyclicals decried the minimalist government described by voluntarists and *laissez-faire* economists alike, blessing instead that state which guarded the weak in society and otherwise intervened actively to promote the common good.[25]

In the United States, the figure of Monsignor John Ryan stood out. His book *A Living Wage* (1906) derived from Leo's premises and from American social science and served as an important ideological foundation for Progressive-era protective labor legislation. After World War I, the American bishops commissioned Ryan to draft a statement of Catholic social principles that proved audacious in its advocacy of trade union organization, the minimum wage, social insurance against unemployment, disability and old age, and extensive government regulation of industry in the public welfare. Ryan's career as American Catholicism's spokesman on social issues brought him into close cooperation with Roosevelt and the New Deal reformers. Other Catholic voices soon joined the New Deal labor chorus. Catholic lay activists formed ACTU, the Association of Catholic Trade Unionists. In ACTU's network of labor schools, thousands of Catholic trade unionists learned not only the Church's social teachings but also the fundamentals of organizing, grievance handling, holding union meetings, and running for trade union office.[26]

Murray struck up a close relationship with Ryan and many ACTU activists; Catholic tendencies were a marked influence on Murray's Industrial Council proposal.[27] In Murray's view, the growing national economic regulation accelerated by the defense mobilization was an opportunity, not the affliction AFL unionists and Lewis perceived. Increasing production to aid the European democracies resisting fascism called for coordinated national industrial planning. Squabbling between competing firms in the war industries was a luxury the nation could no longer afford; America's productive plant had to be mobilized for maximum output, and labor had an important part to play. What the nation needed was a series of industrial councils—not unlike those Leo and Pius had envisioned—in each vital branch of the economy, where management and labor representatives could cooperate to schedule defense production.

If Murray's enthusiasm for Catholic social thought was not universally shared, others embraced the industrial council idea for reasons of their own. Many industrial union leaders—not least those in Murray's SWOC—were profoundly influenced by Taylor Society advocates of labor-management cooperation whom Hillman had introduced to the CIO.[28] These men argued that such plans could give to the mass production industries the same radical improvements in productivity that they had brought to the garment trade. Murray and industrial engineer/Taylor-society-president-turned-labor-consultant, Morris Cooke, were credited as co-authors of a 1940 book on labor-management cooperation, *Organized Labor and Production.*[29]

More important was the landmark attempt by two leading SWOC staffers to turn the industrial council movement into an idea for a whole new democratic, American regime of industrial relations. *The Dynamics of Industrial Democracy* was the product of SWOC Research Director Harold J. Ruttenberg and Northeast Regional Director Clinton S. Golden. Ruttenberg was a labor economist by training, Golden an organizer with important formative experiences working for Hillman in the ACWA. The authors understood that, in a fundamental sense, corporations were political associations more than commercial ones. The people brought together in the corporation were not buyers and sellers interacting sporadically and spontaneously in a free market but operated in ways more familiar to students of government than of economics.

But what *form* of government would the corporation have? "In pre-union times, each department of the large industrial firms was set aside as an entity in itself, a small kingdom. Over this kingdom the foreman or superintendent ruled as prosecutor, judge, jury or executioner," the authors argued. "Collective bargaining changes all this. The foreman or superintendent's kingdom is converted into a republic. . . . Thus collective bargaining establishes an industrial citizenship for workers, enforced by the union-management contract. This parallels their political citizenship."[30]

The industrial democracy the authors discussed was not quite the craft sovereignty of old—indeed, they made a rather damning confession that the new unions were not fit to exercise that kind of authority. They demanded that the steelmasters accord SWOC the "union shop," under which every employee whom the company hired was obliged to join the union. They sharply distinguished this from the "closed shop" of craft union practice, where the union controlled admission to the trade and forbade employers hire workers unless they were already union members—in effect according the union rather than the employer personnel functions. The members of SWOC "are only too glad to leave to management the freedom to hire whomsoever it pleases," the authors state. "It is doubtful whether management could ever get industrial unions to share the responsibility of hiring. To have to tell an unemployed worker, 'sorry, no work today; not hiring just now,' is too unenviable a responsibility for industrial unions to desire or seek."[31] But this is precisely the responsibility that the craft union had taken on itself, that of determining rules for the sharing and distribution of work. Industrial unions abdicated this responsibility as "unenviable."

Theirs was indeed a Magna Carta or a Bill of Rights for the worker. The workers in the passage on "corporate dictatorship" did not seek to legislate work rules. They wanted a contract that would be the foundation for "a body of industrial common law."[32] The common law is not a means for democracy *per se*—i.e., collective deliberations to determine group rules—but a means for ensuring equitable treatment. It was true that workers wanted to know that through their organization they had a role in negotiating work rules and policies, but in practice they merely wanted to be treated fairly and impartially.

And what the union offered above all is security. The authors argued that industrial union members acquired through their contract a "qualified property interest" in their job. Did this "qualified property interest" make the industrial worker the modern equivalent of the yeoman farmer, whose independence guaranteed the Republic's liberty and democracy in Jefferson's conception? Did this "qualified property interest" enable industrial capital to become a source of unity rather than conflict in society, as the corporatism of Leo, Pius, Ryan, and Murray might have implied, by giving both employer and employed a certain proprietary relation to the means of production?

The authors had neither of these alternatives in mind. Having reflected how democracy was born when "the common man" exchanged the security of feudalism or slavery for an honorable but risky freedom, they conclude in a rather chilling passage: "Collective bargaining in England and more recently in the United States has tried, with some success, to recapture for the industrial worker that security enjoyed by the vassal and the slave—without losing the great advantages of a free society."[33] The authors had recapitulated an argument familiar from the defense of slavery penned by George Fitzhugh nearly a century before—without, of course, citing Fitzhugh or accepting his conclusions. Could the worker in fact at the same time enjoy the security of the slave and the freedom of the citizen? Gompers had spent his life arguing no; progressives like Wagner, Roosevelt, Golden, and Ruttenberg asked, why not?

The authors' main point about the union shop, however, was a broader one about the problems of democracy and collective action. Management was determined to resist the union shop on the grounds that it violated the individual freedom of those workers, perhaps a minority, who objected to union membership. The authors and the SWOC were convinced that this was a "pretense" and the company in fact wanted to bust the union. Much of their argument constituted a somewhat awkward but accurate exposition of what Mancur Olsen would famously explain in *The Logic of Collective Action*.[34] The gains that the union secured from the company were public goods, not unlike the peace and order secured by government: all members of the group enjoyed them, whether they individually paid for them or not. This created an incentive for each member of the group to evade paying their share, since they obtained the benefits of the group's action in any event. However, if each member followed through on this course of action, the organization—whether union or government—would dissolve for lack of support, an outcome most members would not have chosen. The only solution is for the group to mandate that each member pay their share— dues to the union and taxes to the government.

The authors related how company officials regularly denied the union shop in negotiations with SWOC with the argument that it would be "un-American" for the company to force any unwilling employees to join the union. The union's supporters invariably responded with a short and lucid discourse about democracy and majority rule. "The philosophy of the union shop, therefore, is rooted in the basic democratic principle that governs our political life; namely, the rule of the majority," they declaimed. "Of course it's coercion. . . . But this is not a legitimate objection to the union shop, as coercion is the fundamental basis of organized society. In fact, civilization can be said to have attained maturity when men became intelligent enough to order their affairs and compel the recalcitrant man, the ignorant man, to submit to certain compulsory rules for the common good of all men."[35]

The authors' shrewdest interlocutor responded, "my conclusion is that your contention is not valid in this case, any more than it would be for the Democrats to contend that us good Republicans should be compelled to join their political party because, for the moment, it is the majority party." The authors had compared the union to a municipal government that must provide city services and exercise police powers, untenable projects without compulsory membership. But their interlocutor improved the analogy; with the Wagner Act in place—protecting the rights of workers to choose membership in any union or even none at all—union membership had become more like membership in a political party than citizenship in a state. "A productive enterprise cannot be operated peacefully or successfully with more than one bargaining agency for the same group of workers," the authors tried to explain. "It is, therefore, a fact of industrial democracy, written into the law, that it is a one-party system of democracy." In short, CIO partisans were obliged to make the unhappy argument that one-party democracy was the best that modern America could do, at least in the workplace.

Despite such troubling issues, the CIO thinkers had registered a remarkable achievement. Their breakthrough paralleled that of Gompers and the "ten philosophers" who had created voluntarism and given the AFL its ideology. Past champions of industrial unionism had been social engineers whose ERPs were tools of social control rather than self-rule—or social revolutionaries (whether anarchist or socialist) who argued that, whatever electoral procedures it practiced or civil liberties it preserved, a "democracy" that included private ownership of the means of production was somehow illegitimate and unreal. Now, at last, the CIO activists had created an industrial union philosophy whose vocabulary was drawn from America's democratic and republican traditions.

The innovation could not have happened at a more portentous time. For as Roosevelt told delegates to the 1940 Democratic Convention,

> The fact which dominates our world is the fact of armed aggression, the fact of successful armed aggression, aimed at the form of government, the kind of society that we in the United States have chosen and established for ourselves. . . . In Europe, many nations, through dictatorships and invasions, have been compelled to abandon normal democratic processes. They have been compelled to adopt forms of government which some call "new and efficient." They are not new, my friends, they are only a relapse—a relapse into ancient history. The omnipotent rulers of the greater part of modern Europe have guaranteed efficiency, and work, and a type of security. But the slaves who built the pyramids for the glory of the dictator pharaohs of Egypt had that kind of security, that kind of efficiency, that kind of corporative state. . . . It has well been said that a selfish and greedy people cannot be free. The American people must decide whether these things are worth making sacrifices of money, of energy, of self.[36]

In late 1939, having concluded a non-aggression pact with Stalin's USSR, Nazi Germany had struck forcefully against the European democracies. Now, less than a year later, most of continental Europe was under the control of the totalitarian powers, and Britain stood alone against the fascist armies. In America, knowledgeable observers began to wonder if this war would dictate whether government of the people, by the people, for the people would perish from the earth.[37] Roosevelt reached instinctively for America's republican past to explain what was at stake.

In a return to customary themes of civic virtue, the president argued that only a people capable of subordinating their private interests to the common good could effectively preserve their freedom. Did freedom merit sacrifices of money, energy, and self? For most CIO unionists the question could only have one answer: a resounding and heartfelt yes. Whatever their preoccupation with the distribution of wealth, the industrial unions held fast to civic ideals much larger than a fatter pay envelope for their members. The notion of solidarity itself required the worker to subordinate his private interests and concerns for the welfare of the group; the trade union activist was conditioned to make sacrifices for the good of his brothers and sisters and of the cause. The trade union was a political organization whose very existence was premised on the civic virtues of its members.

And the business enterprise was a commercial organization whose very existence was premised on selfishness. The firm did not and could not accomplish civic education; it could at best teach enlightened self-interest (and too often failed even at that). The corporation's only "citizen" is *homo economicus* who coolly and rationally maximizes his utilities. This foundation made industrial capital a notoriously poor partner for the war effort. Exploiting the common extremity rather than sacrificing for the common good is the natural reaction of the firm. For a company to sacrifice its material welfare to the nation's general welfare—or to pursue any other noble purpose—would have been illogical.

Trying a more pragmatic approach, industrial council advocates tried to persuade the steel, auto, and electrical firms that labor-management cooperation could help improve productivity in *their* trades, just as unions did in the construction, coal, and garment sectors. Workers join unions as "an outlet for creative desires," Golden and Ruttenberg explained, and would as soon use them to help the firm as to fight their bosses. "Workers have a passion for efficiency, detest needless wastes, and love to work in an orderly shop, mill, or mine where production flows smoothly." Industrial autocracy encouraged managers' delusions that they must think and plan while workers labor and obey. But "management officials no longer can afford to operate on the basis that they know it all," for there is "an immense reservoir of human knowledge that remains virtually unorganized," dispersed among their workforce. A company prepared to produce "jointly with workers as intellectual equals" and deal fairly with the unions—the only institutions capable of organizing that untapped knowledge for cooperation—would acquire a dividend in exploding levels of productivity.[38]

Business leaders were not persuaded. The carpenter was in fact an "intellectual equal" of his employer—who was most likely a small contractor and a former carpenter himself. True, the industrial worker knew a thing or two about his own machine or task that the engineer did not. But whereas the craft unions in the building trades had rather successfully kept their industry's knowledge and skills in the hands of its workers, there was no convincing way to assert intellectual equality between the machine operator and the engineer. Golden and Ruttenberg conceded as much when defending the industrial worker's honor by pointing out that former General Motors president and Roosevelt defense production advisor William S. Knudsen began as "a bench mechanic." They continued, "all workers cannot rise to the corporation's presidency. But all workers, in varying degrees, possess some knowledge of producing goods." This was the nub of the matter. William Knudsen, Walter Chrysler, and Henry Ford could rise from the workbench to become captains of industry—but the average industrial worker was no William Knudsen. He or she could only "in varying degrees" offer suggestions for improving production.

SWOC called upon steel companies to give the union a share of the power to determine production on the debatable grounds that the "varying degrees" of assistance the workforce could offer would outweigh the inevitable losses incurred when a centralized plan was disrupted by democratic procedures. The UMW and the garment unions offered, if not know-how, then at least the muscle to bring rational management and planning to competitive industries prone to disruptive cycles of boom and bust. Could industrial unions do much the same through industrial councils?

Intrafirm competition did obstruct efficient industrial production for the defense effort, but the problem was hardly something workers could fix. Businesses were incapable of sacrificing profits to competitors even when the national interest demanded it, as Walter Reuther's proposal to produce "500 planes a day" in Detroit auto plants would illustrate. "Britain's battle, for all her people's bravery, could be lost, and our own country left to face a totalitarian Europe alone," the rising UAW leader warned in 1940, urging a rapid mass conversion of auto plants to military aircraft manufacture.[39]

The "Reuther Plan" indeed showcased the industrial council idea, but not the way Murray and Reuther hoped. On the one hand, the plan itself was technically impractical, for reasons Knudsen described in some detail. On the other, automakers who were profiting handsomely from even modest civilian production resisted converting their facilities to what were then uncertain materiel markets. There was money to be made, and if fascist aggression threatened to bring an end to electoral democracy in Europe, auto companies were uninterested. (With the exception of Ford, who actually seemed to be rooting for its demise: the anti-Semitic automaker rejected a rich contract for aircraft engines when he found they were to be shipped to Britain.)

The industrial council idea was never implemented in the United States. Instead, as war approached, Roosevelt created a series of *ad hoc* agencies to regulate defense production and wartime labor relations—agencies usually dominated by "dollar-a-year men" released from corporate offices for service in Washington. Their name referred to the token annual salary that they received from the federal government, a salary that implied disinterested public service but in fact indicated the opposite. In a sad commentary on the patriotic spirit of America's business class, these "production experts" were unwilling to leave their positions as presidents and CEOs of the nation's largest firms in order to serve their country in war. They retained their corporate titles, salaries, and loyalties even as they took on public responsibilities.

Labor and the War

Even so, Roosevelt's defense mobilization and wartime economic regulation proved conducive to the CIO unions' attitudes and fortunes. The defense buildup accelerated demand in industries with a significant CIO union presence; the economic recovery in these sectors aided their organizing efforts enormously. Their advantage over AFL rivals in the defense industries was further enhanced by the administration's favor, indicated by Roosevelt's selection of Sidney Hillman as labor's representative on the successive Washington agencies designed to supervise defense mobilization. In the new environment, the major industrial unions completed the organization of their respective sectors. The UE obtained recognition from Westinghouse, and the SWOC successfully extracted contracts from the resistant Little Steel firms. The marquee battle, however, pitted the UAW against Ford.

The personnel regime governing Ford operations before the First World War had long dissipated. The wage premiums that distinguished Ford from the other automakers diminished considerably and the "sociology department" had closed its doors.[40] Instead of withholding fat bonuses to discipline his workforce, Ford hired thug Harry Bennett, directing a gang of toughs known as the "service department." In the spring of 1937, when other auto companies began to cautiously negotiate with the union, Bennett's wiseguys made headlines by savagely beating Reuther and fellow UAW pioneer Richard Frankensteen as they tried to leaflet Ford's flagship River Rouge plant. By now the elderly automaker's paternal instincts were pretty much confined to the dictum "spare the rod and spoil the child."

But the enveloping war crisis left Ford increasingly isolated. Many of those who before 1940 might have cheered his contempt for the NLRA now found Ford to be bad company. His isolationism and flagrant anti-Semitism could all too easily be melded in the popular mind with his authoritarian work regime and his temerity in placing himself above the law of the land to create a monstrous image. CIO publicists were quick to seize on the possibilities. "Fordism is fascism," picket line signs proclaimed. Union leaders declared that the UAW was challenging "Hitler's Henry."[41]

An unauthorized 1941 strike at his flagship River Rouge plant finally broke Ford's resistance. Confrontations between Bennett's service department and UAW committeemen in the plant led to a sudden mass walkout by the men. Work resumed under an agreement brokered by Michigan Governor Murray D. Van Wagoner arranging NLRB elections in late May, and Ford, convinced he was still the beloved father of a contented workforce, was confident he would defeat the union. When the results arrived, he was mortified. Almost 52,000 workers, or 70 percent, voted for UAW representation. Most of the remainder chose an AFL alternative; less than 3 percent agreed with Ford that they needed "no union." Ford was first enraged by the ingratitude of his "children" and threatened to close the plant, but after anger and denial, resignation speedily followed. Ford conceded everything the union asked—not just recognition, but the union shop and "dues checkoff" (where the company itself collects union dues out of the worker's paycheck) as well. Overnight, Ford's firm had been transformed from the industrial fortress of the open shop to the CIO's most secure base.

The extraordinary industrial regulation occasioned by the defense effort further stabilized the young industrial unions. Labor relations in critical industries were governed by the National Defense Mediation Board before the war, replaced after Pearl Harbor with a National War Labor Board (NWLB) possessing still greater powers and jurisdiction. Both were tripartite bodies that consisted of an equal number of employer and labor representatives, plus public representatives, nominated by the president.

For reasons both philosophical and practical, the CIO welcomed the new NWLB. At first glance, this might seem peculiar, since industrial relations policy under the Board made so many demands on labor. The CIO unions had

greeted Pearl Harbor with a pledge that they would abjure strikes for the duration of the war. Since mobilization would surely tighten labor market demand, this was no small concession: labor would soon be in an excellent
position to win strikes. Furthermore, restraining inflation by containing wage
increases became one of the board's great preoccupations. In the landmark
July 1942 "Little Steel" decision, mediating a wage dispute between the
smaller steel firms and their employees, the NWLB limited annual wage increases to 3.5 percent, a pattern imposed on other industries thereafter.

The CIO unions nonetheless supported the NWLB. Although dissatisfied
with the Little Steel formula, they were willing to live by the decision. On one
level, this was simply another indication of labor's willingness to sacrifice in
the national interest. At President Roosevelt's request, the CIO unions also
agreed in the spring of 1942 to forfeit overtime premiums—even in the face
of rapidly increasing overtime work. The UAW presented these concessions
on strikes and overtime as a fight for "Victory through Equality of Sacrifice,"
calling upon business in turn to accept limits on profits and executive salaries.
Naturally, employers balked, reminding the public that in modern America
(unlike ancient Greece and Rome) it was the *propertied* rather than the *propertyless* who typically refused to subordinate their private interests and desires
to the general welfare. Or as UAW President R. J. Thomas expressed it, "we
may have to take it on the chin here and there for a time," but by adhering to
the no-strike pledge "we can present the nation and the returning soldier with
a clean record."[42]

The NWLB mechanism also, in a way, suggested the labor-management
cooperation expressed in the industrial council program. If it wasn't exactly
what Murray and his associates had sought, it was certainly an agency that
brought together labor and industry representatives to jointly regulate economic activity. In any case, labor's representation on the NWLB demanded
that labor abide by the decisions the board reached. To the extent that unions
accepted this role of creating public policy and coordinating the war effort, labor's obligation to act responsibly and adhere willingly to the board's rulings
increased.

Industrial unions secured certain tangible benefits from the new order.
The board's wage stabilization efforts did help establish industrial bargaining
patterns: workers performing equivalent jobs in a given industry began to secure similar salaries, regardless of which particular automaker or steel manufacturer employed them. More importantly, the National War Labor Board
offered these new unions security. Outside of the breakthrough at Ford, few
CIO unions secured the union shop from their employers by using their own

devices. They remained highly unstable institutions in need of protection. Although the Board would not go so far as to make the union shop obligatory—the government would not coerce workers to join unions, something obnoxious to American political traditions and to employers—it did grant unions "maintenance of membership" and the dues checkoff. Maintenance of membership required that workers joining the union remain members through the duration of the contract; dues checkoff meant that the company would collect dues out of employees' paychecks rather than requiring union representatives to do so.

Under NWLB supervision, the government, unions, and manufacturers erected a whole new structure of industrial relations in mass production.[43] The structure called for industrial unions and employing corporations to negotiate contracts governing work norms and create an effective grievance machinery (often culminating in arbitration) to settle periodic disputes without recourse to strikes and lockouts. This new order in labor relations placed important demands on both sides. Employers had to recognize and negotiate with unions; unions were obliged to uphold the contract they had negotiated and use a grievance procedure rather than strike action in order to solve day-to-day disputes. National union leaders found themselves in the uncomfortable but necessary position of disciplining workers and even union locals engaged in unsanctioned walkouts. Layers of bureaucracy charged with administering the contract and governing the expanding labor organizations multiplied. Fractious, democratic unions like the UAW saw their international headquarters assume steadily greater power over union locals. And the United Steelworkers of America (USWA)—which emerged when the highly disciplined and bureaucratic SWOC at last held a constitutional convention in May 1942—came to enjoy the forms of democracy without ever having experienced the substance.

The AFL unions viewed the totalitarian threat abroad with the same or greater alarm than their CIO brethren. Voluntarism taught them that a democratic republic was defined by the variety of associations that flourished free of government and party control. Consequently, for those who learned their trade unionism in the school of Gompers, fascism and communism were the stuff of darkest nightmares. But though the AFL endorsed the democratic crusade against fascism—taking a similar no-strike pledge following the Japanese attack on Pearl Harbor—they were more wary than their CIO counterparts of Roosevelt's aggressive program of wartime labor controls.

Indeed, the same premises that led voluntarists to abhor fascism, ensured their suspicion of NWLB encroachment on free collective bargaining. Voluntarists had preserved their unions' autonomy by keeping a respectful distance from government bodies and public policy. By asking less of the government than their CIO peers, AFL unions could concentrate more on the needs of their members and less on the demands of the public. Moreover, the promise of union security through maintenance of membership and dues checkoff meant little to the AFL craft unions: they were independent organizations that neither needed nor desired the government's help in conducting their affairs. If the industrial unions needed the protection of the government to collect dues and sustain bargaining patterns, this suggested to voluntarists that the CIO unions were creatures of the Roosevelt administration with dubious pretensions to *bona fide* trade union status.

The two world views collided in spectacular form in 1942 as the IAM battled the UAW to represent the workers of Curtiss-Wright Aircraft in Buffalo.[44] The Machinists assailed the Autoworkers for their stance on overtime premiums. "The CIO sacrifices worker's pay, worker's overtime as the CIO's contribution to the war effort. Big of them, huh?" IAM publications asked aircraft workers. "While the AFL has been loyal to the country it has also been loyal to its members. IT HAS NOT FELT CALLED UPON TO MAKE SACRIFICES OF WORKERS' PAY OR OF LABOR'S GAINS." The UAW lost the representation election and immediately protested to the NWLB, saying that the Machinists "sought to create the impression that employees of the company could disregard the need for unity and sacrifice requested by the President of the United States and could safely concern themselves with their own selfish interests isolated from the welfare of the country at war." A letter to Roosevelt signed by Murray, Frankensteen, and Thomas asked, "Is the CIO to be expected to make sacrifices which may result in its own destruction to the aggrandizement of those who are lending aid and comfort to the enemies of this country?" The president was readily persuaded and obviated the issue with an executive order eliminating premium pay for weekend work *throughout* the war industries.

But the strongest defender of labor's autonomy against the Roosevelt administration's waxing power, now as in 1940, was not the AFL leadership: it was John L. Lewis. The UMW president alone had the heart for a premeditated attack on the pillars of the wartime labor relations regime—the no-strike pledge and the Little Steel formula—and the direct challenge to the American government this would entail.

Lewis had been moving in this direction for some time. Having lost control over the CIO's direction to the progressives, he steadily distanced his union from that organization. On the one hand, he sent out feelers to the AFL, which shared his trepidation regarding state labor regulation—though those feelers were addressed not to the despised Green but more to his old (Republican) friend Hutcheson.[45] On the other hand, he turned savagely on Murray, whom he had come to believe had greater loyalties to Roosevelt and the Steelworkers than to Lewis and his own union. Murray was ejected from the UMW much as Green had been a few years before (with the curious result that now *both* labor federations were directed by alienated former subordinates of the Mineworker president). Lewis furthermore sent the CIO a bill for more than $1.6 million that the UMW had "loaned" to the CIO and its organizing committees in its first years. The CIO executive board rejected the payment demand outright, and soon thereafter the Mineworkers withdrew from the Congress entirely.

Lewis argued—correctly—that the NWLB's Little Steel formula did not contemplate wage increases significant enough to keep pace with rising prices. Consequently the war economy meant increased profits for employers and steadily falling living standards for workers.[46] His blunt conclusion: the Board was illegitimate and the no-strike pledge no longer binding on labor. A *non sequitur*, perhaps, but one which resonated with the rank-and-file industrial workers irked by the spectacle of corporate executives and stockholders making out like bandits while they experienced wage restraints, something that motivated a rising number of wildcat strikes.

From the spring to the fall of 1943, the Mineworkers engaged in an extended series of work stoppages for the sake of demanding substantial wage increases in direct violation of NWLB directives. Roosevelt called for maintaining the Little Steel formula while boosting workers' purchasing power through price controls on food. Murray, speaking for the industrial unions, endorsed Roosevelt's proposal; Lewis mocked his estranged CIO comrades as timid supplicants of their White House patron. Lewis would summarize his dispute with the CIO unions eloquently near the war's end in *Collier's* magazine, accusing them of acquiring "dual loyalties" through their alliance with Roosevelt and participation with his wartime regulatory agencies.

> For a full decade, and increasingly in the last few years, there has been a skillful and sustained drive to make organized labor part and parcel of a political "machine." The promises of favors and special privileges have alternated cleverly with threats of condign punishment, and as a consequence the effort has met with no small measure of success. Today we witness the ever-widening spread of what can only be called "political company unions," as much under the control of a party as the "industrial company union" is under the control of the employer.[47]

For their part, the CIO and the administration saw democracy and the war as the key issues, with Lewis on the wrong side. The CIO accused Lewis of placing himself and his union above the rule of law and of democratic deliberations. "This man has consistently schemed to undermine duly established war-time agencies," the Executive Board declaimed. "In times of emotional stress the labor movement of this country must be particularly wary of any person or element who seeks to substitute for sane and democratic processes willful and revengeful dictation." Lewis was a classic demagogue, exploiting "the legitimate grievances of labor for irresponsible personal and political aggrandizement, and with a studied indifference to our entire war effort."[48]

Both the CIO unions and their opponents had made valid points. The UAW in Buffalo, and the CIO assessing the 1943 coal strikes, saw rivals who put the private interests of their group ahead of the nation's interest in wartime. They further saw that their rival gained a certain advantage over their own more patriotic organizations by doing so. And in Lewis they saw a person who believed himself above the law and not bound by the outcomes of democratic deliberations.

By the same token, Lewis and the AFL unions saw a rival that collaborated with the government to advance its own interests at the expense of labor's independence. The CIO unionists had even supported the government's attempt to break the miners' strike and asked that Roosevelt usurp the unions' power to negotiate overtime pay through free collective bargaining. The new industrial unions *were* in an important sense creatures of the government, and they incurred an obligation to serve the government when they obtained its favor under the Wagner Act. The IAM and the UMW were responsible to their members alone, while the UAW and USWA had to serve two constituencies, the workers they represented and the public agencies that guaranteed their existence. These established unions saw the CIO as a body who relied on the Roosevelt administration to defend them from challenge even at the cost of the labor's self-determination.

6

THE AFL-CIO IN THE AGE OF ORGANIZATION

The CIO steadily developed its alliance with the nation's political leaders and the government agencies that regulated a growing portion of the nation's labor relations—an alliance that benefited and sheltered the young industrial unions but also brought with it all the challenges that Alexis de Tocqueville or Samuel Gompers would have predicted. A democratic government must in some sense represent the common good: it may not serve the exclusive interests of a single class, party, or faction. The closer government draws to a particular constituency, the less respect its decisions and laws will command from others. And however noble and progressive one's politics, this sort of partisanship carries further perils, because in an electoral democracy sometimes your side loses. The party or faction that uses the government to pursue its special and particular ends at the expense of the commonweal invites others to do the same in their turn.

How then must labor navigate this new world? The CIO's leadership had split over this question. By 1940, Lewis had decided that government sponsorship was a poor strategy for preserving labor's power and freedom. He would spend the rest of his life leading the UMW into a series of collisions with the government designed to bring down the new system of industrial relations and restore the autonomous trade union movement that preceded the New Deal. Hillman was more practical and saw only one solution to the problem: trade unionists had to make sure that labor's friends remained in power.

To bring this about, in 1943 the ACWA President directed the creation of the Political Action Committee (CIO-PAC). PACs are known today mainly as camouflage for campaign contributions, but Hillman's new creature was something very different. It was an instrument for mobilizing the labor vote by educating union members on public issues, registering them for elections, and getting them to the polls.

The CIO's political problem was complicated by the Democratic Party's internal divisions, for a number of elements within the Democratic coalition remained hostile to labor's agenda. Democratic electoral strategy still relied heavily on the patronage-driven local party institutions to deliver the vote—both the ideologically unreliable urban machines of the North and the ideologically hostile rural fiefdoms of the South. CIO-PAC was designed to replace or displace these machines. In an unprecedented labor political effort, the PAC organized union members shadowing party and electoral divisions down to the precinct level. As the CIO became the party's infantry, union leaders hoped, party leaders and officeholders would learn to fear labor's antipathy in the primaries or disaffection in the general elections. Labor's counsel would determine Democratic Party policy.

The CIO-PAC achieved significant victories in the 1944 primaries when the anti-labor Democrats' poster child, Texas Representative Martin Dies, and a rogues' gallery of the South's most notoriously racist officeholders were driven from office, while Southern New Deal Democrats like Claude Pepper were returned to Congress with the PAC's support.[1] But the general election offered a pointed reminder of the dangers a partisan labor politics invited. Even in 1936, when virtual *Ur*-American John L. Lewis held the helm, by mobilizing *as a class* for Roosevelt, labor had drawn charges of pursuing a foreign and undemocratic brand of politics. Hillman's more moderate political voice entering the 1944 presidential campaign did not silence such charges. On the contrary, the ACWA chief's unprecedented organizational efforts combined with lingering nativist prejudice to unleash a torrent of poisonous rhetoric evoking a Jewish-Bolshevik conspiracy. The issue erupted front and center with the selection of Harry Truman as vice presidential candidate at the Democratic convention. A report quickly emerged that Roosevelt had ordered party leaders to take the nomination and "Clear it with Sidney!"

If CIO sachems *had* been calling the shots, New Deal stalwart Henry Wallace would have remained on the ticket. But party leaders were determined to replace him with a more "electable" prospect to run alongside the ailing president. Truman emerged as a compromise candidate when party liberals vetoed James F. Byrnes, FDR's "assistant president" and author of the Little Steel Formula. Hillman was only one of many progressive Democrats who found

Byrnes unacceptable, but Republicans seized on the foreign-born ACWA president as a campaign issue, plastering billboards with the ugly message "It's Your Country—Why Let Sidney Hillman Run It?" Hearst papers organized a "Sidney Limerick Contest" publishing such delightful verses as

> Clear it with Sidney, you Yanks
> Then offer Joe Stalin your thanks
> You'll bow to Sid's rule
> No Matter How Cruel
> For that's a directive of Frank's.

The PAC may have been a mixed blessing for the Democrats in November 1944, but Hillman had bequeathed the American labor movement an enduring political strategy. His death in the summer of 1946 did not fundamentally change labor's political goals and methods. Phil Murray, who survived him as CIO elder statesman, was equally committed to the PAC and to an alliance with the liberal, New Deal Democracy—and though equally foreign, Murray's Scottish nativity and Irish brogue soothed much of the American public so discomfited by "Sidney."[2]

Two major obstacles remained between American labor and the progressive Democrats. One was Lewis: given his institutional base in the UMW, his relationships in the AFL, and his residual ties to the Republican Party, the mineworker's quixotic crusade against the New Deal order might yet demolish the political alliance still in formation. The other was a vocal CIO minority of Communists and their allies, estranged from the Democratic Party over the erupting Cold War.

In the course of World War II, a Communist-led "Popular Front" bloc had achieved important influence in the CIO.[3] The principal CIO Communist bastions were the vast UE and the strategically-placed ILWU. Communists or their sympathizers controlled the national leadership of both these unions, along with a host of smaller ones. In addition, the Communists and their allies held a strong position in the UAW, the largest CIO union, and were well-represented in the CIO's central offices. Factional conflict in the CIO had been submerged after Nazi Germany invaded the USSR in 1941; Communists and Democrats alike wanted to see the New Deal reforms and good relations between the United States and the USSR continue. But their alliance belied fundamental differences regarding the nature of democracy and the obligations of citizens in a democratic republic, and those differences were about to burst into public view.

The Cold War and Taft-Hartley

The powerful attraction foreign policy matters exerted on Communist trade unionists was unusual in the history of American labor, but it was not unique. David Dubinsky and Sidney Hillman had always taken a keen interest in the course of European politics. That peculiar preoccupation with matters abroad was also shared by the man who would guide the American labor movement in the postwar decades: George Meany. In late 1939, Teamster chief Dan Tobin recruited Meany to serve as Secretary-Treasurer of the AFL. The aging Green maintained a tight rein on domestic trade union matters, so Meany concentrated instead on labor's foreign policy. Combining the AFL's historic emphasis on independent trade unions with contemporary reflections on totalitarianism, the Bronx Plumber soon developed a workable theory of foreign affairs that would guide him throughout his life.

Meany, like contemporary theorists of totalitarianism, held that the totalitarian society—whether Fascist, Nazi, or Communist—was the polar opposite of a democratic and pluralist one.[4] Benito Mussolini and his court philosopher Giovanni Gentile had celebrated the *totalitarismo* they hoped would weld Italy into a seamless unconquerable monolith, a nation responding as one to *Il Duce's* command. In turn, Anglo-American democrats adopted the rightists' term for their own use, invidiously contrasting "totalitarian" regimes, in which the state reached for control of every aspect of social life, with pluralist democracies characterized by individual liberty and the proliferation of free, voluntary associations. The presence of competitive political parties, a variety of independent media, and a range of churches, all free of domination by the state (and vice versa), were seen as hallmarks of a democratic society. The pluralist critique of totalitarianism bore an unmistakable relation both to Tocqueville's ideas about civil associations and Gompers' voluntarism, and Meany endorsed it wholeheartedly. Free societies, he believed, were defined by the presence of free institutions—and especially, free trade unions.

In the tradition of Gompers, AFL leaders preferred their trade unions free of denominational or explicit partisan identities, and tried to urge such a model on European workers who were rebuilding their labor movement. Meany and many of his peers had come to respect industrial unionism, but "*bona fide* trade unions" still had to be "free from all government, employer and political domination." In contrast, a Soviet-bloc trade union dominated by the state was not a trade union at all but something more akin to a fascist "labor front" or a company union. As a fraternal delegate to the British Trade

Union Congress in September 1945, Meany broadcast the AFL's unwillingness to participate in a world trade union body in which the Soviet trade unions were represented.

> Let there be no quibbling or misunderstanding: we do not recognize or concede that Russian worker groups are trade unions. The Soviet worker groups are formally and actually instruments of the State. They are official branches of the government and of its ruling dictatorial political party. These so-called unions are designed to protect the interests of the Soviet State, even if this means that the interests of the workers themselves must be subordinated or injured. . . . How can the representatives of a government-controlled and dominated movement speak for workers?[5]

Was the American labor movement "conservative" because it rejected the socialist politics and class struggle ideology so familiar to European trade unionists within and without the Soviet sphere? The answer ultimately depends on one's own political frame of reference. Throughout his career, Meany would cogently argue that such commitments collided with basic democratic values. Lashing out later against anti-union business leaders, he would review the rise of totalitarian regimes in 1930s Europe and boast that "American labor has been the greatest force against the introduction of class-warfare concepts in American society. We have seen what the acceptance of class-struggle doctrines, in the guise of economic liberation, have done to destroy great countries."

Meany was convinced that a class struggle for control of society was fundamentally at odds with democratic ideals, for such a struggle reduced the government to the instrument of a particular interest. Communists, like America's more pernicious plutocrats, tried to turn the state into a tool of class war—but the American Federation of Labor would defend the constitutional order from such usurpations. "Let me make clear that we oppose control of government or the economy by any one group—whether it be labor, professional, financial, or business," he explained. "American labor has achieved a great deal under our system, and we would be the last to want to change it. We do not want a labor-controlled government any more than we would want a government controlled by finance or business."[6]

The American system of government derived legitimacy from its popular mandate and its service to the common good; to make it the tool of any section or interest would undermine the moral obligation of every citizen to respect the outcome of democratic deliberations and procedures. Like Publius in the famed *Federalist Paper #10*, Meany concluded that a flourishing factional life could exist in civil society but that no faction could be permitted to capture the state, lest injustice and tyranny follow in its train.

If Meany's anti-totalitarian ideals counseled him to support his country's Cold War initiatives, Communist-leaning labor leaders in the CIO not only opposed these initiatives but rejected the whole "totalitarian" paradigm as nonsense. ILWU President Harry Bridges insisted that "the lumping together of fascism and communism, of course, is another way to confuse the people." He elaborated: "What is totalitarianism? *A country that has a totalitarian government operates like our union operates.* There are no political parties."[7] Bridges' remarks showed how the Communist challenge at home and abroad would force industrial union activists to address some ambiguities in their politics. After all, the longshoreman was just connecting the dots, laid out five years earlier by SWOC's Golden and Ruttenberg, that explained how it was a simple "fact of industrial democracy" that it must be "a one-party system of democracy."[8] Soviet writers too had felled many a tree explaining how their one-party state could be considered a "democracy." If you could have a one-party democracy in the workplace, why couldn't you have one in the state?

Meany and Bridges represented two radically different perspectives on the foundational questions of politics. Democratic pluralists like Meany considered political forms and procedures essential, contrasting the totalitarian systems against competitive electoral polities rich in free civil associations. In this analysis the Nazi, fascist, and Communist regimes and parties were essentially similar—and essentially different from political regimes governed by competitive elections and the liberal, Christian-Democratic and social-democratic parties that flourished in the electoral arena. Leninist Communists, by contrast, basically affirmed that a society's essential nature was found in its economic base, not its political forms. Stalinist rhetoric or diplomacy which suggested that the German Social-Democrats were "social-fascists" no better than the Nazis was not illogical or inconsistent. The divergent political norms the two groups embraced were ephemeral; their shared acceptance of a market economy or private property essentially distinguished them from the Communists. For Communists, fascism was at worst a pernicious manifestation of capitalism.

Foreign policy was ever the place where Communists showcased such peculiar political judgments, creating a widespread public perception that the Communists were enemies of democracy. When Stalin's political shifts inspired the CP element to walk out of the AFL and launch its failing rival labor federation, AFL critics linked their dual unionism to a general Communist disregard for democratic deliberations and outcomes. Unwilling to live by the decision of the majority, they had abandoned their unions. When the Second World War erupted, Democratic partisans in the CIO leadership endorsed Roosevelt's efforts to arm Britain against Hitler and strained to avoid industrial conflicts in the war industries. But with the Nazi-Soviet Pact in effect, Communist activists led a spectacular UAW strike at North American Aviation, leading to charges that the Communists were collaborating with domestic Nazi sympathizers in the same way that they had cooperated with the Nazis in Germany to destabilize the Weimar democracy.[9] The wartime Alliance concealed the conflict after 1941, but with the arrival of the Cold War it reemerged more forcefully.

The passage of the anti-union Taft-Hartley law would bring the Cold War issue home to labor. Workers greeted the end of the world war with the greatest strike wave in American history. Though Lewis, as was his wont, managed to garner the most attention through a high-profile confrontation with the federal government, the heart of the strike wave was the CIO's big three: the UAW, the USWA, and the UE. All told, in the single year following Japan's surrender some five million workers walked, including a single massive industrial action involving 750,000 steelworkers.[10] Perhaps corporate employers expected the industrial unions to fold under pressure as their First World War predecessors had when the shelter of wartime controls was removed. Instead, they stood firm, and employers and the nation now discovered there existed a new species of giant labor organization, exercising power on a scale hitherto unknown.

Employer hysteria compounded labor's problems. Corporate management in formerly open-shop industries had witnessed spectacular industrial union growth in the CIO's first decade. Under wartime conditions of tight labor markets and stringently controlled wages, managers had seen a remarkable breakdown in shop floor discipline. Now with the war's end they encountered a massive strike wave, aggressive and peculiar bargaining demands from the UAW's Walter Reuther, repeated UMW confrontations with the lawful authorities, and multiplying reminders of the Communist presence in the trade unions. Events combined to persuade employers that their very right to direct their enterprises was disappearing.[11] The National Association of Manufacturers (NAM) and the U.S. Chamber of Commerce argued stridently that the Wagner Act and the friendly Democratic administrations charged with administering it had granted labor unions too much power over both management and their own members. In 1946, CIO-PAC suffered major reverses in an anti-labor electoral backlash. The CIO's showcase campaign pressing UAW luminary Richard Frankensteen for the Detroit mayoralty

crashed; more importantly, the Republicans recaptured Congress, ousting numerous stalwart labor allies in both houses. The stage was set for legislation
designed to cut the unions down to size.[12]

Two hostile Republicans, New Jersey Representative Fred Hartley and
Ohio Senator Robert Taft (reprising his father's role as American labor's neme-
sis), sponsored such a law. Most Taft-Hartley devices were ostensibly intended
to restore "balance" to the industrial relations system by eliminating a perceived labor tilt in the Wagner Act. Legislative supporters argued that recent
events demonstrated unions, like corporations, were now large and powerful
enough to engage in coercive behavior. An equitable labor relations policy had
to protect both workers and employers from union coercion. To begin with,
the new law exposed unions along with employers to unfair labor practice
charges. Unions that refused to bargain, engaged in secondary boycotts, or
used jurisdictional strikes to obtain contractual recognition—instead of using Board certification—could face charges before the NLRB.

Interestingly, these practices were all more characteristic of traditional
AFL voluntarism than CIO industrial unionism. Jurisdictional strikes and secondary boycotts were means that craft unions deployed to obtain recognition
in place of the NLRB's election machinery. Republican legislators who had
aimed at Lewis and Reuther instead hit Hutcheson.[13] And they had actually
increased the federal government's regulation of labor relations.

Despite this sudden and convenient embrace of interventionist government, conservative legislators and their business supporters were recalling the
enduring themes pioneered by the open shop and scientific management crusaders of the century's first decade and the "American Plan" advocates of the
interwar period. In the succeeding period, labor's enemies would devote
considerable resources and ingenuity to persuading the American public that
individual freedom, not democratic institutions—and thus "free enterprise" instead of labor unions—represented the most fundamental American values.[14]

In the event, Republican advocates of Taft-Hartley fancied themselves
protecting individual workers from coercion by collectivist trade union leaders, preparing "a bill of rights" for union members.[15] Consequently, they
made union security provisions a special target. Under the notorious section
14(b), for example, states were permitted to pass "right to work" laws under
which no worker could be obliged to join or pay dues to a union as a condition of employment. Section 14(b) proved a grievous blow for labor unionism in the South. Organizing in the region, always difficult, acquired heavy
new burdens as Southern legislatures leaped to exploit the new federal statute. As Golden and Ruttenberg had well understood, allowing individual

workers to obtain the benefits of union membership while declining to bear their share of the costs created immense collective action problems for workers trying to organize.

Similarly, the legislators outlawed the closed shop entirely. The closed shop was another notable vestige of AFL voluntarism, under which a craft union would negotiate "prehire agreements" with an employer requiring that every worker they hire have a valid union membership (thus the union "hiring hall"). Labor's critics believed that this arrangement, which effectively ceded personnel decisions to the union, gave labor organizations a power over the livelihood of their members that infringed dangerously on their individual liberties. (Curiously, few right-to-work advocates feel that *employers* exercise a dangerous power when they make the decisions to hire and fire—even though you can't vote out your boss like you can vote out your local union's president or business manager.) In other words, Republicans who had previously complained that the NLRB interfered with free contracts between workers and employers now wanted to tell employers and voluntary associations of workers what kind of contracts they could and could not make, and use government to enforce the labor relations legislators preferred. AFL leaders—most vocally John L. Lewis, who had returned to the AFL fold—saw the Taft-Hartley bill not as a step toward freeing labor relations from intrusive government control but as a political attempt to regulate and dominate the unions.

Taft-Hartley also helped enforce the separation of mental and manual labor in a way that might have pleased Frederick Winslow Taylor. Managerial and supervisory employees were expressly excluded from Wagner protections. Industrial managers who feared loss of control over their enterprises were protected from the danger that union contagion would spread to other echelons of the firm—a danger that loomed especially large at Ford where tens of thousands of foremen had enrolled in the Foremen's Association of America.[16] Equally important, though, was the above-cited prohibition on the closed shop. The prehire contract and hiring hall represented a model of unionism whereby personnel, training, and much of the industry's know-how remained in the hands of workers and their organizations. Though industrial unionists had rejected responsibility for hiring as "unenviable," professional employees might have found much to value in a system that gave them sovereign control over training, credentialing, and hiring in the professions just as the craft unions had done in their crafts. Later amendments to the law exempted the building trade unions from prohibitions on prehire agreements, but the law denied this path to future categories of employees who might wish to cross Taylor's lines.

The law tried to thwart efforts like CIO-PAC by forbidding labor organizations from financing partisan electoral activities with operating monies. In fact, Taft-Hartley intensified labor's political engagement: the unions were shocked into renewed political action by the punitive legislation and turned with great success to voluntary member contributions to finance it. More dangerous revisions of Wagner's purpose in the name of "balance" were the clauses giving employers the right to "free speech"—no longer were they forbidden to counsel their employees against union representation—and standing in NLRB certification procedures. In short, Taft-Hartley fundamentally altered the meaning of the Wagner Act. The 1935 Act had foreseen employees alone deciding whether they preferred to bargain collectively or individually. Their deliberation was their own, and every effort was made to exclude the employer from involvement. Now the employer was to be treated as a legitimate party to the decision his or her employees reached.

But none of these weighty and substantive issues proved the flashpoint as Taft-Hartley became law in 1947. That dubious honor was captured by a provision calling on union leaders to sign an affidavit swearing that they were not members of the Communist Party. Unions whose leaders refused would forfeit all rights and protections guaranteed under the National Labor Relations Act.

From Taft-Hartley to the AFL-CIO

The affidavit incited much hostility in labor's ranks, not all of it from the "popular front" group. What Communists in the labor movement felt about the affidavit would actually be something of a sideshow: the issue created the same heated debate in the AFL, which had virtually no Communist presence, that it did in the bitterly divided CIO. It was a debate about democratic citizenship in the postwar era—a debate in which the affidavit and the Party became symbols, but in which Communists themselves could participate only as outsiders.

Communist Party actions soon made clear that in 1948 Party members saw foreign policy, not domestic legislation, as the day's vital issue. While most labor leaders wrestled primarily with domestic policy questions, Communists inside and outside of the labor movement made attacking President Harry Truman's Cold War initiatives their top priority. But the questions about democratic theory that excited and moved mainstream labor leaders could not have much interested Communists in any event. Taft-Hartley was a powerful reminder of one of the strengths of the voluntarist argument: protections and privileges that the government extended, the government could take away. Public protections were contingent on the public interest. Both the Communists and their erstwhile associate John Lewis urged resistance to the demand for the affidavits, even at cost of sacrificing the government's shelter of labor organizations. But Lewis was a principled opponent of government's power to shape labor relations; the party's sudden discovery that labor organizations independent of government protection and sponsorship had their merits was merely convenient.

Phil Murray also initially resisted signing the affidavit on behalf of the USWA. Like the Communists, Murray had no consistent desire to see labor unions 'liberated' from their entanglements with the state, but he took umbrage at the suggestion that labor leaders were a suspect class. For Murray, the affidavit requirement was just an expression of a more general disrespect for workers seeking "industrial citizenship." The unions could become full and equal partners with industry and the state in shaping the American political economy only when business executives and political leaders recognized union officers as peers.

The Steelworker chief's concerns were justified, but the "new men of power" leading the labor unions found this social equality difficult to achieve. In an extensive series of interviews, sociologist C. Wright Mills found a group of men acutely self-conscious about their deficiencies in education, culture, and material well-being when confronting their opposite numbers in the business world. When policies failed to accord them equal recognition, they perceived calculated insults designed to underline their subordinate status. Union leaders had been deeply aggrieved when war planners exempted captains of industry from the draft because of their vital contribution to war production, but not labor leaders.[17] The anti-Communist affidavit was an analogous public policy that cast aspersion on the civic credentials and patriotism of trade unionists.

On a more pragmatic level, Murray hoped that by resisting the affidavit he could avoid a disastrous internal conflict that would weaken the CIO. Stalin and Truman, however, were creating a situation whereby a split would be unavoidable. Stalin's actions in Europe—campaigning against the Marshall Plan, abrogating his pledge to hold free elections in Poland, supporting the Communist coup in Czechoslovakia, and blockading Berlin—could not have been better designed to alienate Western social democrats, liberals, and certainly the blue-collar "ethnics" who made up so much of the CIO rank-and-file.[18] Truman's response turned the CIO's latent conflict into an open one, while at the same time joining labor and the Democratic Party in a more solid political alliance. When Congress passed Taft-Hartley over his veto, Truman ran for reelection on a promise to repeal the hateful anti-labor law, extend the liberal reforms of the New Deal with initiatives in civil rights and health care, and prosecute the Cold War.

Truman had basically offered to fight for the CIO's entire domestic political agenda, if only labor would endorse his challenge to the Iron Curtain. This put Communist sympathizers in the trade unions in an insoluble dilemma: American labor unions had a vital interest in Truman's domestic priorities, but for the Soviet Union and the Party the Cold War was the paramount issue. Would they support the Progressive protest candidacy of former Vice President Henry Wallace, a Cold War opponent, and possibly split the labor vote, giving the Republicans the White House? Or would they support the president for domestic policy reasons even as he escalated the confrontation with Soviet Communism? Prominent "popular front" union leaders like the ILWU President Harry Bridges and UE organizing director James Matles chose Wallace.

The most persistent charge leveled against the Communists by mainstream American union activists held that the Communists were agents of a foreign power, ultimately more concerned with Stalin's needs than those of American workers. Now the vocal denunciations of American foreign policy issuing from UE and ILWU conventions were no longer a mere embarrassment to the CIO. By acting to split the labor vote in a close election, the "popular front" trade unionists were not *just* endorsing a pernicious foreign tyranny, but asking that the trade union movement *sacrifice vital domestic interests* in order to do so.

The 1948 election issue gave an already growing anti-Communist faction in the CIO an opportunity for action. Walter Reuther, a social democrat by inclination and upbringing, took the lead. During the war, Reuther had made considerable progress in his march toward UAW leadership. Once Germany declared war against the Soviet Union, CPUSA chief Earl Browder became one of America's most vocal proponents of piecework, time-study, and productivity-based incentive pay as a means of increasing war production. Reuther skillfully exploited Browder's unseemly enthusiasm for piecework to identify himself with the rising tide of wildcat strikes in the auto industry, and emerged as a recognized spokesman for the rank-and-file autoworker. A high-profile confrontation with General Motors—a strike that began in November 1945, kicking off the postwar strike wave and capturing headlines—catapulted Reuther to the presidency the next year. Despite (or perhaps because of) his narrow margin of victory, Reuther boldly promised to "get rid of people whose party loyalty is above union loyalty." The following year, after the passage of Taft-Hartley, Reuther's slate swept his major rivals out of union office. Reuther's increasing prominence allowed him to lead the anti-Communist drive in the industrial union movement nationally.[19]

Reuther also joined likeminded associates within and without labor to re-cast the Democratic Party into an unmistakably liberal and progressive but also firmly anticommunist organization. Party liberals dueling for the New Deal franchise split into two factions. On one side was the Progressive Citizens Alliance (PCA), in which Communists and liberals opposed to the Cold War rallied around Henry Wallace to preserve the Popular Front. The PCA's rival was Americans for Democratic Action (ADA). In the ADA's early days, Reuther was joined by Dubinsky and Andrew Biemiller (a former Wisconsin congressman then beginning a long career as a union lobbyist) representing labor; Minneapolis mayor Hubert Humphrey; Protestant theologian Reinhold Niebuhr; NAACP President Walter White; economist John Kenneth Galbraith; and Eleanor Roosevelt. While Communist-oriented union activists followed the PCA out of the Democratic Party and into Wallace's quixotic venture, the CIO aligned itself with the ADA. ADA members' residual doubts about Truman's progressive *bona fides* were eased considerably at the 1948 convention, when Hubert Humphrey successfully lodged a civil rights plank in the Democratic platform. His action drove many Southern Democrats to walk out of the 1948 Convention, and left little of substance dividing Wallace from the incumbent, except for Truman's anticommunism.[20]

About a year after Truman's narrow reelection, the CIO gathered in a convention in Cleveland, where Reuther, in an epic speech, lashed the Communists as bad citizens incapable of participation in democratic procedures.[21] "Abe Lincoln said that a nation cannot exist half free and half slave. Nor can the CIO exist part trade union, dedicated to the ideals and objectives of the trade union movement, and part subservient to a foreign power," Reuther began. The Communists "are to be pitied more than despised, because they are not free men," he continued, "their very souls do not belong to them." But Reuther's pity did not extend very far. He wanted the Communists gone.

The Communists did not consider the trade unions venues for democratic participation but instruments of a political party, Reuther contended. One unfortunate consequence of this perspective was the death of independent trade unions in those states where Communism achieved power.

In the countries where the Communist Party has had their time of reign, where they seized political power, what has happened to the free trade unions? They have been destroyed, their leaders have been murdered and thrown into prison camps, and in place of free, democratic trade unions they have created the new tool of the modern police state—political company unionism. We in the CIO say we are opposed to company unionism, whether it comes out of Wall Street or somewhere else, and we are opposed to political company unionism even though it may come out of the Kremlin. We are opposed to all kinds of unionism except free, democratic trade unionism.

But the CIO faced a more immediate problem than the distant prospect of a similar Communist takeover. The Communists' ulterior loyalties rendered them incapable of participating in democratic deliberations within American labor unions either. "You cannot have a democratic right within a free voluntary association unless you are also prepared to accept the democratic obligations and responsibilities which parallel those democratic rights." For an "honest trade unionist . . . after the give and take of free democratic debate on the floor of the CIO, even though that fellow's point of view is not adopted, he will go out into the highways and byways of America and carry out the policies of the CIO, because it represents the democratic will of the majority." Not so "the Communist minority, because they have a double set of standards that govern their behavior." Thus their betrayal in the 1948 election. The Communists, Reuther argued, "have scabbed against us at the picket line and they have scabbed against us at the ballot box."

Under these circumstances, Murray at last found himself obliged to join Reuther and the anticommunists in their crusade, endorsing a constitutional amendment barring from CIO office anyone who "consistently pursues policies and activities directed toward the achievement of the program or purposes of the Communist Party, any fascist organization, or other totalitarian movement." The convention not only supported this amendment but empowered its executive board to expel or destroy the Communist-influenced unions.

The Association of Catholic Trade Unionists (ACTU) played a pivotal role in the drama that ensued. Catholic labor activists whose religious convictions had drawn them into the 1930s crusade against those who worshipped the almighty dollar had been unlikely to coexist well with godless Communists under the best of circumstances. Now they offered Reuther and other anticommunists in the labor leadership essential grassroots support.

Some commentators have argued that the Communists and the ACTU—two well-organized ideological CIO caucuses—mirrored one another in many respects.[22] The two factions featured some interesting parallels. Both groups nurtured a more expansive vision of labor's place in society than did the rising generation of union leaders. And though neither faithful Catholics nor committed Communists really made a democratic and participatory trade union politics their ultimate goal, *both* groups recruited and trained prodigious numbers of union activists and encouraged them to take an active part in their union's political life while pursuing their substantive ends. And in an increasingly pragmatic labor movement, only these groups were organized around ideological principles and possessed an ideology compelling enough to retain the loyalties of a significant constituency when their faction was out of power.

ACTU's factional union organizing had actually begun against venality in AFL unions, not against Communism in the CIO. ACTU's first internal union caucuses assembled to fight mob domination of select Teamster and International Longshoremen's Association (ILA) locals. With the fight against Communism underway, ACTU union chapters multiplied in the CIO.[23] Long convinced that superior organizational skills enabled a small Communist minority to dominate labor organizations, ACTU expanded its network of labor schools training Catholic unionists in subjects like collective bargaining and parliamentary procedure. ACTU also established caucuses wherever possible in the popular front-led unions.

The CIO's anticommunist crusade climaxed with a series of early 1950s "trials" expelling Popular Front unions on the grounds of Communist domination. Their outcome was preordained, given the dominant disposition in the industrial union movement, but their political reasoning was sound enough: the trials documented *ad nauseam* the shifts in the Communist Party line and the parallel statements and postures adopted by the unions under examination. Trade union leaders did not face censure because they had opposed U.S. intervention in the World War before 1941, or because they enthusiastically supported it afterwards. Neither Hillman's ardent support for Roosevelt's foreign policy, even when it demanded sacrifices of labor, nor Lewis's persistent skepticism of foreign intervention, even when it seemed unpatriotic, had placed them beyond the pale of democratic discourse. But the Communists who called the administration "war-mongering imperialists" just days before Germany's invasion of the Soviet Union, and urged American intervention immediately afterward, seemed to lack *any* independent judgment of their members' or their nation's interests.[24] Afterward, the 1948 election contretemps had confirmed the Communists' willingness to subordinate trade union purposes to Soviet political demands.

Of course, targets of this investigation—like the UE officers—could re-
tort with the equally unanswerable charge that the CIO had become "completely subservient to the dictates of the Administration and the Democratic
party."[25] It would be facile and silly to say that Reuther and Murray were prisoners of Truman as much as Communists were prisoners of Stalin. But precisely because Communists looked to a foreign power for direction and not a
domestic party, they retained an autonomy vis-à-vis the *American* government
that the CIO did not. This independence carried a price, because unions fil-
ing the affidavit retained NLRB protections withdrawn from their Communist
rivals. The CIO's "popular front" group was decimated. Some unions aligned
with the CIO mainstream when their leaders broke with former Communist
allies; others were virtually consumed by the autoworkers and steelworkers
in raids. Only the ILWU survived its expulsion from the CIO relatively un-
scathed: Bridges' popularity among West Coast dockworkers remained strong
and his organization sound, with no need of protection from federal agencies.

The title fight shattered the massive UE, a union representing 600,000
workers, rivaling the autoworkers and steelworkers in size. A Communist-
aligned slate had deposed founding president James Carey at the 1941 UE convention by a narrow margin. The union thereafter was led by James Matles,
Director of Organization, and Julius Emspak, Secretary-Treasurer, both close
to the Party's inner circles, along with President Albert Fitzgerald, a non-communist disposed to cooperate closely with the popular front. Carey did not fade
away in the customary fashion of defeated union officers, but retained his CIO
office as Secretary and thus his relations with fellow industrial union leaders.

Harry Block, one of Carey's former associates at Philco, survived these
years as the lone anti-communist voice on the UE executive board. Block led
the internal opposition and in 1946 helped found a caucus known as the UE
Members for Democratic Action (UEMDA). UEMDA garnered support from a
variety of anticommunist union activists, but its biggest grassroots resource was
the ACTU. Pittsburgh labor priest Charles Owen Rice, a friend of Murray's, was
instrumental in helping an anti-communist group capture the union's huge Local 601 at Westinghouse and provided extraordinary assistance in the national
fight.[26] Shortly after the incumbent leadership turned back a strong UEMDA
challenge at the 1949 UE convention, CIO convention delegates voted to expel the UE and charter a new union to occupy its jurisdiction. The board issued Carey a charter for an International Union of Electrical workers (IUE)
along with hundreds of thousands of dollars of financial support, and a second
and even more bitter duel for the loyalties of UE workers ensued.[27]

The UE joined the battle by authorizing local officers to sign the affidavits and secure a place on the NLRB ballots. ACTU agitation among the rank-and-file in favor of the new union made the UE leadership's job difficult, and the blows of government agencies made a UE victory unlikely. Continuing federal litigation disputed the UE's right to NLRB protection, straining the union's finances. Government attempts to revoke the citizenship of James Matles aggravated this problem; the prospect that he might soon be deported to Romania to acquire a more practical understanding of Stalinist political mores may have distracted the UE Organizing Director. Hearings of the House Un-American Activities Committee (HUAC) targeting the UE incumbents provided a continued stream of bad publicity, and Carey made a poor account of himself not merely in appearances before that committee but through an intense covert collaboration with FBI Director J. Edgar Hoover. (Block, in contrast, refused to testify before HUAC, which he thought had no business investigating internal union matters.)[28] The UE survived only as a shadow of its former self, displaced by its upstart CIO rival as the consumer electronics industry's leading union.

The third party current in American labor died in 1948, partly because such political action had proved a chimera: the Wallace campaign had apparently garnered little rank-and-file union support.[29] But the Progressives and Communists were not the only—or the most important—political parties to experience a catastrophic loss of standing in the house of labor in those years. At the end of World War II, the AFL still hosted some prominent Republican labor leaders, and it was still conceivable (if unlikely) that an alliance of political conservatives and old-school craft union voluntarists might resolve to fight the future of industrial relations. Taft-Hartley changed all that. The bringing together of the AFL and the CIO solidly behind the liberal Democratic vision helped enable a merger of the two organizations into a single labor federation—a new federation that would be the foundation of the postwar Democratic Party. That transformation was intimately bound up with the ascendancy of George Meany, whose relative comfort with the emerging welfare state distinguished him among his AFL peers.

As we have seen above, Taft-Hartley's overhaul of collective bargaining damaged AFL institutions more than those of the CIO unions that inspired its passage. Its provisions prohibited many of the practices, from pre-hire agreements to jurisdictional strikes to secondary boycotts, which enabled craft unions to operate effectively without the New Deal's political tools. Despite conservative Republican promises to reduce government intervention in social and economic life, Taft-Hartley actually delivered a massive escalation of government regulation in labor relations.

Lewis, who wanted to see not just Taft-Hartley but the whole Wagner framework fall, would seize this crisis as his last opportunity to seriously challenge the new industrial relations order. The Mineworkers reaffiliated with the AFL in 1946, enabling Lewis to run a spirited campaign in the federation's ranks for a program of massive resistance against the new law. Lewis's crusade peaked and crashed during floor debate at the 1947 AFL convention.[30] As in the CIO, the contretemps focused on the anti-communist affidavit which so many union leaders took as a personal insult. Lewis called Taft-Hartley "the first savage thrust of fascism in America," and taunted his peers as cowards if they offered such an oath. He urged a collective defiance that would in effect shut down the NLRB. Lewis allowed that under this strategy labor unions would lose the protections guaranteed under the Wagner Act but was unmoved.

> What built up the labor movement in this country? Was it protecting laws and statutes that protected the organizers of our movement when they went out to the meetings? Oh, no! The founders of our Federation had no such protection. They had to fight for the right to be heard. They had to fight for the right to hold a meeting, and men had to sacrifice and sometimes die for the right to join a union. . . . Are we going to abandon that policy and that course of action which created us, that made strong and courageous men out of our members and great leaders out of their representatives?

Meany spoke in response, urging compliance with the law and striking at the Mineworker chieftain's history of disdain for democratic processes. "It is a bad law, but it was placed on the statute books by our representatives under the American democratic system, and the only way it is going to be changed is by our representatives under that system." Meany resented the "inference" by Lewis "that there is a lack of courage in failing to start a revolution against this law." Labor was not above the law; Lewis's program of massive resistance was a nonstarter. He recalled the Mineworker president's cooperation with Communist trade union activists to split the AFL and build the CIO, assuring his listeners, "I am prepared to sign a non-Communist affidavit. I am prepared to go further and sign an affidavit that *I* never was a comrade to the comrades." When Lewis objected, Meany added a final fillip: "Whatever action this convention takes, *this* delegate will go along with it. He won't pick up his bat and ball and go home."

Lewis did just that; before the year was out he dispatched a janitor from the UMW offices with an index card bearing the legend "Green—AFL. We disaffiliate. Lewis." Meany's remarks recalled Hillman's speech at the 1940 CIO convention. An obsessive reader of trade union records and documents, Meany almost certainly recalled the ACWA leader's tart remark that the "democratic process" did not permit the minority to "get peeved" and "go and say, 'well, we won't play ball.'" In both cases antagonists invoked the anti-communist Mineworker president's cooperation with the Communists as a conceptual symbol. Lewis and the Communists, however different, shared a very casual attitude about democratic values. In 1940, Hillman implied that their joint resistance to Roosevelt's intervention against European fascism demonstrated this fundamental character trait. For Meany it was the erstwhile partners' disrespect for the outcomes of democratic procedures, both in the labor federation and in government, that revealed this fundamental similarity.

Meany did not entirely share Hillman or Murray's enthusiasm about government as a vehicle of social justice, but regarded Lewis's proposed defiance as unrealistic. He saw no alternative to Hillman's strategy, marshaling labor's electoral muscle to get labor's views onto the political agenda. After Taft-Hartley, an AFL majority shared this view, voting to launch its own muted version of CIO-PAC, Labor's League for Political Education (LLPE), to influence the election of 1948. This was "by no means a departure from the old political philosophy of the A. F. of L. of 'defeating your enemies and rewarding your friends,'" Meany contended. "That policy is just as valid today as when it was initiated many years ago by Samuel Gompers."[31]

But in truth, after the Federation's repudiation of Lewis, little was left of the vigorous voluntarism Gompers had articulated. The great craft unions that had objected to industrial organizing—the Carpenters, the Teamsters, the Machinists, the Electricians—all had now used the NLRB election process to organize significant numbers of industrial workers. The AFL affiliates had come to accept New Deal economic innovations like the minimum wage, unemployment insurance, and social security. And now, in a single legislative blow, Congressional Republicans pressing Taft-Hartley had driven labor's senior federation not only into active electoral politics but into the arms of the Democrats.

Consequently, by the mid-1950s little of substance separated the two federations. Both had basically similar views about collective bargaining, the Cold War, partisan politics, and the welfare state. When Green and Murray died, their places taken by Meany and Reuther respectively, the two successors relatively quickly negotiated the remaining jurisdictional issues. The two organizations merged into a single labor federation, with Meany as president and Reuther at the helm of its powerful Industrial Union Department. The AFL-CIO was born.

The "Golden Age" of American Labor

Labor economist Joseph Shister coined the term "social unionism" to describe the ideology of the AFL-CIO and its new president. Updating Robert Hoxie's old dichotomy, Schuster noted that although the last traces of "revolutionary unionism" had disappeared with the Communists, and many AFL-CIO affiliates were adopting the mores of "business unionism," the Federation's own preoccupation was progressive politics, not bread-and-butter issues.[32]

It fell to George Meany to expound American labor's new philosophy.[33] "Our goals as trade-unionists are modest, for we do not seek to recast American society in any particular doctrinaire or ideological image," Meany explained. "Sam Gompers once put the matter succinctly. When asked what the labor movement wanted, he answered 'More.' If by a better standard of living we mean not only more money but more leisure and a richer cultural life, the answer remains, 'More.'" But if labor did not have a doctrine or ideology that it sought to impose on society, its ambitious political agenda came very close. Labor was not a special interest seeking only its own advantage, but was guided by a vision of the common good. "Let me make it clear," Meany insisted, "We want more not only for ourselves, but for all Americans."

> The trade union movement dedicates itself to work for peace, with freedom and justice for mankind—to work for a steadily higher standard of living—to work for the full enjoyment of civil rights by all Americans, regardless of race, color, or religion—to work for improved relations between labor and management under a law that will be fair to both—to work for a broader measure of social security for the protection of all citizens against the hazards of poverty, old age, disability, and illness—to work, in short, for the highest ideals of the land we love.

Gompers tried to cultivate civic virtue in American workers by fostering their independence—not simply from their employers but from government as well. By 1948, America's labor leaders had rejected the cigar worker's voluntarist ideals as unrealistic aspirations for the modern world. Workers could not be expected to approximate the civic character of Jefferson's yeoman farmer when they confronted the vast political and corporate bureaucracies of postwar America.

The leaders of the AFL-CIO rejected Gompers' voluntarism, but not his mission of educating workers for democratic citizenship. Rather than distancing workers from government, Meany and his AFL-CIO colleagues sought to increase their participation in politics. Following the path Hillman had blazed with CIO-PAC, they would strive to educate workers about political issues, register them to vote, even recruit them to run for political office. In the process, they hoped to make American labor the engine driving a progressive transformation of American life.

If the AFL-CIO was achieving a new, higher profile in partisan politics, collective bargaining remained in the hands of its union affiliates. As we have seen, the craft unions had used bargaining for more than wages and benefits; they saw their fight for control of the labor process as part of their fight for citizenship itself. Since the New Deal, the industrial unions had confronted similar issues. And more than any other labor leader, Walter Reuther shaped postwar collective bargaining.

The autoworkers' engagements with General Motors under Reuther's leadership molded the future of American industrial relations. In the fight with GM, as in the parallel war he waged against UAW Communists and their fellow travelers, Reuther's unique leadership gifts were on spectacular display. If Gompers brought to the trade union movement a penetrating and systematic intellect, and Lewis a rare eloquence and indomitable spirit, Reuther had a bit of each—not to mention ambitions matching either man's and an appreciation of social and political realities superior to both. As a political educator, Reuther was without peer in the annals of American labor.[34]

Reuther set the terms of debate at the war's end in a *New York Times Magazine* bearing the unlikely title "Our Fear of Abundance."[35] The UAW leader was highly enamored of economist John Maynard Keynes, whose *General Theory of Employment, Interest and Money* (1935) was rapidly becoming the conventional wisdom explaining the depression. Reuther shared the British scholar's scorn for conservative chestnuts like *laissez-faire,* thrift, and deferred gratification, agreeing that managing demand was the fundamental problem of modern economics. But the erstwhile autoworker was especially concerned with role of technology.

"Our productive genius has always been stalemated by our failure at the distributive end. We have found it impossible to sustain a mass purchasing power capable of providing a stable market for the products of twentieth century technology," Reuther explained. For the UAW leader, America's productive genius was not—as for the craft unionists—meaningful or edifying work. America's productive genius was producing lots of stuff. To emphasize the point, he singled out the construction industry for attack. Trapped in a "vicious circle of primitive methods and restrictive practices," the construction industry was "geared to scarcity rather than to that abundance which is now both physically possible and socially imperative." "Respectable economic theory" did not condone primitive methods, restrictive practices, or scarcity. It called for highly productive firms that would "pass on to labor its just share of the benefits of technical progress in the form of higher wages, and seek its profits in capacity production for an expanded market."

Americans could escape "the fitful succession of boom and bust, feast and famine, and provid[e] stable mass distribution of the goods and services made available by mass production" but they needed "a general rise in the wage level without a concomitant rise in the price level." Industry-wide labor agreements taking wages out of competition—and offering wage increases that mirrored productivity increases—could assure both steady economic demand and steady economic growth. As an added bonus such agreements would obviate more intrusive government regulation. Society had a fundamental interest in the rising demand that generated economic growth, and would get it one way or another. "If private enterprise wants to stay private, it has to stay enterprising. If you [employers] won't accept a continuing commitment to employ, the Government will have to move in."

About two months after the publication of "Our Fear of Abundance," Reuther, heading the UAW's General Motors Division, led its employees into a grueling and attention-getting strike of 113 days.[36] Wartime price controls remained in effect, and the company insisted that it could not increase wages until the government released those controls. Reuther answered that increased productivity left plenty of room for a substantial raise without price increases. If the company said otherwise it ought to open its financial records and prove it.

The company took this as a fundamental assault on managerial prerogative and adopted a hard and unyielding line, going so far as to retain aging attorney Walter Gordon Merritt—notorious scourge of trade unionists in such cases as those of the *Danbury Hatters* and *Duplex v. Deering*—to fight the UAW's "revolutionary ideology." "A 'look at the books' is a clever catch phrase intended as an opening wedge whereby unions hope to pry their way into the whole field of management," GM moaned.[37] Management's hysterical reaction was rather misplaced. The union was not really demanding a share in directing the company; the UAW was no more equipped to co-manage the auto industry in 1945 than it had been in 1941 with its ill-starred "500 planes a day" program. Rather, like then, the union was merely exposing selfish corporate behavior that harmed the community. And though Reuther's concern for the consumer was of immense public relations value, in the final analysis the UAW was disputing not some ambitious social proposal but the most traditional collective bargaining issue of all: remuneration for workers.

Coming as it did, however—as the first in an avalanche of massive postwar labor actions and following the widespread wildcat strikes of the wartime auto industry—the company treated Reuther's demand as *casus belli*. As the strike ground on, massive walkouts by electrical workers and steelworkers were initiated and resolved. It eventually became clear that the company would never yield, and the UAW settled for an increase virtually identical to those the UE and USWA had secured. The respective employers obtained price concessions to finance these raises, and GM balances remained a closed book. All three major industrial unions, and a growing number of others, now engaged in "pattern bargaining" demanding similar terms from every employer in a given industry.

In subsequent rounds of bargaining, Reuther elaborated the system. In its 1948 contract, the UAW secured both a Cost of Living Adjustment (COLA) and an annual increase designed to reflect improvements in productivity. That year the UAW agreed to the COLA idea only with reservations, but two years later Reuther's team reached a similar agreement with an unprecedented five-year term. The 1950 contract was greeted as the "Treaty of Detroit" and regarded by company, union, and many observers as a groundbreaking expression of industrial statesmanship. The "Treaty," in the words of the *Fortune* magazine editors who so named it, was "the most resounding declaration yet made by any big union that the U.S. can grow prosperous only by producing more." By accepting "this all-important axiom of American progress" labor had at last definitively acknowledged management's right to direct industry. Management for its part had accepted the legitimate place of unions—which was collectively negotiating wages and working conditions rather than leaving these to the vagaries of the labor market.

It has been customary for the present generation of labor historians to argue that labor sacrificed more for this postwar peace than did capital. After all, capital preserved not only private property in the means of production but also obtained recognition of management's right to manage. However, one could make an equally persuasive case that *business* sacrificed more for the accord. There is scarce evidence of massive demand among American workers for participation in management, and certainly not for socialism. There is much evidence, however, that management considered both collective bargaining and the strict seniority rules that emerged from it to be grievous intrusions on individual liberty. Reuther had in fact bargained away a codetermination his constituents did not seem to want, while making General Motors concede principles dear to the company.[38]

But, in any case, the editors of *Fortune* were not entirely wrong when they said that "the most exciting thing about the contract" was that GM "was imaginative enough to see what it was buying." It was imaginative because Reuther's unease about the 1948 agreement was well-founded; he could see where such agreements might lead. With the COLA, unionized employers virtually announced plans to pass their increased labor costs on to consumers in the form of inflationary price increases. The COLA shielded autoworkers from this inflation but obstructed Reuther's ambition to build a just political economy using pattern bargaining. It made GM and its production workers partners in a system of "private planning for private profit at public expense," as the UAW scolded, promising to renew the fight. "General Motors workers cannot be bribed with the wooden nickels of inflation into withdrawing from the fight against the greedy industrialists and subservient politicians who caused and condoned the price rises which are now undermining the living standards of millions of families."[39]

GM workers' resolve to take no wooden nickels did not last, and like other large industrial unions, the UAW used collective bargaining to obtain benefits that workers abroad sought through their political parties and governments. The tactic seemed to offer a plenitude of virtues. It had emerged piecemeal during World War II, when unions found they could improve workers' rewards while honoring the letter of the Little Steel Formula by negotiating enhanced fringe benefits. Now this bargaining strategy served a similar function, allowing powerful unions to get more for their members without appearing to demand inflationary wage increases—or insisting that their members await the glacial pace of political change for improvements in their lives. Manufacturing workers and others secured employer-administered healthcare, pension, vacation and (in its most elaborate expressions, like the auto agreements) even supplemental unemployment insurance benefits that helped protect them from hardship in cyclical downturns. Later scholars would call the era a "golden age" in industrial relations.[40]

Golden though the era might have been relative to conditions before and since, it was increasingly clear that in this "age of organization" the modern corporation, with its advanced technology, division of mental and manual labor, and extensive system of employee protections and benefits, offered little of the civic education that Tocqueville and Gompers had prized.[41] This was surely cause for alarm, for as a host of commentators observed, the corporations were the new "free schools" where a growing number of American citizens were acquiring their political and social habits. What exactly were they learning in this grim academy?[42]

The industrial relations scholars who deemed this a "golden age" acknowledged these weaknesses, yet found reasons to honor the emerging economic order. If the new workplace could not educate in the civic virtues that Tocqueville and Gompers celebrated, with the help of newly powerful labor organizations it could offer the worker rights and freedoms proper to the modern era. Now that government and employer were insuring workers against unemployment, sickness, and old age, the laborer could no longer pride himself on his independence and self-reliance, as he might have in the AFL's early days when he had only himself and his union on which to rely in extremity. But employer and social-welfare benefits offered a stability and security that few workers or even labor organizations could match on their own; a larger number of workers enjoyed a greater measure of personal freedom than ever before. True, the division of labor in the great enterprise meant that working life could no longer guarantee every worker a challenging task combining mental and manual labor. But if "industrial citizenship" were defined more liberally, every productive worker could find dignity and individual satisfaction in his or her station. So long as firm, union, and government made sure that the promotion process was fair, the complex division of labor and workplace hierarchies could be a benefit rather than a curse: they offered every person a chance to rise exactly as high as his talent and hard work carried him.

The dominant figure of postwar American industrial relations who analyzed these issues was John T. Dunlop. In a career spanning the second half of the twentieth century—including both a long Harvard tenure and a brief stint as Gerald Ford's Secretary of Labor—he wrote or contributed to the era's landmark texts interpreting labor's social experience and role.[43] Dunlop's theory explained industrial relations through the complex interplay of trade unions, management, and the specialized government agencies that addressed both.

The framework mirrored the political economy in which Dunlop lived and worked. Radical socialists and craft unionists both dreamed of a world where workers unilaterally declared the rules under which they worked; many, perhaps most, employers envied the prewar open shop of U.S. Steel and Ford Motor where management unilaterally imposed order and working conditions. But both models had been pushed into the economic periphery. Finally, the use of government-imposed binding arbitration, not to say Leninist-style state diktat, had achieved little use and even less favor in the United

States. Thus neither could the third relevant actor, the state, unilaterally determine the rules under which work was performed. Perhaps in other lands
one or another of these groups dominated the others, but in America a pluralist industrial relations held sway where work rules were developed in
healthy negotiations between all three autonomous social actors.[44]

Dunlop joined other sociological luminaries to draw out some of consequences of this new order in *Industrialization and Industrial Man*. Industrialization generated polar classes, but, *contra* Marx, these were not capitalists and
workers but *managers* and workers. Noting developments in the socialist bloc,
the authors concluded that the fundamental cleavage in society between managers and managed remained the same, regardless of who owned the means
of production. Large-scale, technologically-sophisticated enterprises called
for a growing number of highly skilled managers. Fortunately for society this
group lacked the "will to power" that customarily characterized a ruling class;
they were "conformists" generally "preoccupied with the internal affairs of the
enterprise" and uninterested in larger social questions. They were disposed to
"constitutional" methods of directing the firm, valuing the consent of the employed expressed through their trade union representatives, in a sort of "pluralistic industrialism."[45]

In all societies, the authors argued, workers indulge a phase of resistance
against industrialization and its accompanying social changes, favoring one or
another utopian alternative. But "a century of experience has narrowed the
range of practical alternatives, since programs to escape, to avoid, or to overthrow the industrial order have lost any appeal. The choices for workers are
seen to be more limited: how to accommodate, to participate in the industrial
order, and to share in the gains." Class struggle between managers and workers does not exactly cease but matures into a "bureaucratic contest." "The battles will be in the corridors instead of the streets, and memos will flow instead
of blood. The conflict will be, by and large, over narrower issues than in earlier times when there was real disagreement over the nature of and the ar-
rangements within industrial society."[46]

The result, paradoxically, was an "essentially conservative" order where
"individual liberty and social mobility" flourished as never before. The tech-
nocracy *depended* on this individual liberty and mobility. The managerial hierarchy worked efficiently precisely because it recruited society's most talented
members, regardless of their social origin. And the technocrat's remarkable degree of command and coordination in the workplace had to be purchased with
a promise of freedom and plenty at home. "The productive process tends to
regiment. People must perform as expected or it breaks down. This is now

and will be increasingly accepted as an immutable fact. The state, the manager, and the occupational association are all disciplinary agents," the authors explained. But ominous as it sounded, this change was not to be feared. "Men may well settle for the benefits of a greater scope of freedom in their personal lives at the cost of considerable conformity in their working lives."[47]

What sort of civic education was this? For Alexis de Tocqueville, the American citizen's lawfulness, sobriety, and self-discipline was itself a mark of his liberty—he honored and respected the laws that he participated in drafting. The liberty of Industrial Man was just the opposite: government, manager, and trade union were all "disciplinary agents" that demanded regimentation and conformity in the workplace, but rewarded him with unprecedented license for self-expression, even self-indulgence, in his leisure time. "One is to be 'straight' by day and a 'swinger' by night!" as Daniel Bell exclaimed sarcastically. "This is self-fulfillment and self-realization!"[48] Industrial Man did what he wished on his free time and did what he was told at work. Nowhere did he have the opportunity to be a citizen, to deliberate with others and draw up rules binding equally on all.

If this marked a complete abandonment of civic education, understandably so, for the "career open to talent"—operating under the modern title of "equal opportunity"—challenged the very foundation of democratic deliberations. Aristocracy, after all, is not rule by a hereditary group *per se* but rule by the *aristoi,* the "best men." The Greek philosophers who coined the term did not feel that "best" was *defined* by wealth or birth: these were simply markers that helped us find these "best."[49] The proliferating intelligence and aptitude testing in school and workplace was not designed to promote "democracy," rule by the people, but rule by of an aristocracy of talent rather than heredity. Classical democrats had argued that all people had more or less equal capacities and talents, and this being so, it seemed appropriate that the judgment of the majority would be the best.[50] The new order assumed the opposite, that individuals varied widely in ability, and impartial scientific testing could determine the "best men" and entrust them with social authority. America was to be a "meritocracy."[51]

If wisdom and intellect *were* unequally distributed, it was no simple matter to explain exactly why the majority should rule. This did not go unnoticed by the American worker.[52] The principle of meritocracy held that objective achievement testing should replace arbitrary markers like race, ethnicity, gender, and social origin as the rule for evaluating ability and allocating jobs. To the very extent that promotion according to merit *succeeded* it constituted a more intellectually serious and troubling assault on the notion of equal citizenship than old-fashioned prejudice. If Thomas Jefferson's sometime dream of replacing the arbitrary and conventional Old World aristocracy with a "natural aristocracy" of talent could be realized, the worker would be called upon to acknowledge his or her own inadequacy. If the system guaranteed equal opportunity to rise, only a personal defect could be blamed for one's lowly position in the social hierarchy; the worker would not *deserve* to be respected as a citizen. Inequality was an omnipresent social reality that made politicians' pious ritualistic invocation of equal rights abstract and unreal.

Landrum-Griffin and Union Democracy

Trade unionists of every stripe resisted this conclusion: educating workers for democratic citizenship was inscribed too deeply in American labor history to be bartered away for *any* amount of social mobility or self-indulgence. Some looked to "union democracy" itself as a solution. If the modern workplace did not offer a satisfactory civic education, "union democracy" advocates hoped that the unions themselves still could. Craft union voluntarists had echoed Tocqueville by arguing that the trade unions, like the French commentator's venerated civil and political associations, were "schools of the workers where they learned the lessons of democracy and independence." Workers, by administering of their own organizations, would learn the skills needed by democratic citizens, ranging from mundane organizational tasks like running meetings and writing appeals to evaluating issues and running for union office.

But the declining vitality of the trade unions' internal political life was becoming depressingly clear. Only the ITU with its vigorous internal culture and entrenched two-party system had ever really earned the accolades Gompers had offered. In the AFL's early decades, major unions like the IAM, UMW, and ILGWU experienced spirited and lengthy factional battles over their leadership and direction, but these had vanished by the New Deal. For a brief period, as important affiliated unions like the UAW and UE developed exciting factional lives, it seemed that the CIO represented a rebirth of union democracy. But this proved to be a phenomenon of their youth. If anything, competition for leadership withered faster among the CIO's industrial unions than in their AFL craft predecessors. As soon as the postwar combat between Communist and anti-communist factions was settled on one side or the other, the contentious public battles ended.

Whether one believes that hot, issue-based contests were absent because members were uninterested, or that union members lost interest because divisive issues were withheld from debate, the effect was the same. Union administrations became political machines encountering no broad, cohesive opposition. Incumbents remained in danger of the kind of palace coup that felled James Carey of the IUE and David McDonald of the USWA, but they seldom had to fear a sustained grassroots insurgency.

The new environment posed clear hazards to the unions' mission of civic education, and not merely because fewer members were learning the fundamentals of electioneering and democratic procedure in the union hall. Reflecting on Golden and Ruttenberg's enthusiasm for one-party government, William Leiserson opined, "Is there any reason to believe that a one-party system of industrial government or union government is likely to be any less disastrous in its effects than such systems have been under political governments?" Even more ominously, he continued, "one may well wonder if the conviction that industrial democracy must function as a one-party system can long prevail among so large a proportion of the population as organized labor represents without sooner or later having some influence on workers' concepts of political democracy."[53]

Union democracy became a lively political issue in the wider public as critics of "golden age" trade unions contended with increasing volume that union officials routinely abused their power to suppress opposition. It was a convenient charge for those both left and right who were disappointed in the American worker's political behavior. Radicals preferred to believe the union rank-and-file a seething cauldron of potential class warfare stymied by conservative "business union" leaders, while conservatives painted these same rank-and-file members as rugged individualists and patriotic Americans groaning under the thumb of collectivist union bosses. But both groups held that a union bureaucracy's manipulation and abuse of the union machinery was thwarting the true will of the working classes.

Trade union governance is pretty dry stuff, but the U.S. Senate soon found a way to make it exciting. In 1950 and 1951, Tennessee Senator Estes Kefauver, a Democrat, led an investigative committee through spectacular televised hearings on organized crime. In the course of its work the committee documented *La Cosa Nostra's* influence in select labor organizations. The gangster was the perfect symbol for the issue of union democracy, the mobbed-up local an abuse of union power that everyone could readily grasp. Kefauver's work paved the way for Arkansas Democrat John McClellan to launch a 1957 Senate investigation focused entirely on trade union skullduggery. McClellan's rather ecumenical committee included figures ranging from stridently anti-union Arizona Senator Barry Goldwater to Massachusetts union ally John F. Kennedy, whose brother Robert served as chief counsel.[54]

Arguably no union was dominated so thoroughly by racketeers as the International Longshoremen's Association (ILA); certainly no union was as indelibly associated with gangsters in the popular consciousness. Corruption and crime were the warp and woof of the Port of New York, where dockhands routinely provided kickbacks to union officials to obtain work and many of the Mafia's marquee names appeared on ILA staff rosters. Kefauver brought his committee to New York and grilled a series of broken-nosed figures representing the ILA; soon thereafter, in 1954, Marlon Brando would deliver his unforgettable performance as Terry Malloy in *On the Waterfront*. The ILA was now virtually synonymous with the mobbed-up union.

Responding to these allegations, Meany persuaded the AFL to take an unprecedented step: the Federation not only expelled the ILA from its ranks, but chartered a new longshore union in its place. Like labor's radical and reactionary critics, Meany wished to believe that the longshoremen were prisoners of their notoriously corrupt leaders. Since the ILA scorned "recognized democratic procedures" that would enable "members who work on the waterfront . . . to select true and capable trade union leaders" the AFL would offer them a democratic alternative. "We took the position that the membership was not responsible for this, that this was the officers. We said the membership should have a right to be represented by a decent union."[55]

For the balance of the decade, the AFL and then the AFL-CIO poured financial and organizing resources into their "clean" alternative as it challenged the ILA in NLRB elections—only to lose repeatedly. Unlike his critics, Meany was willing to accept the obvious: the ILA leadership, however vicious, had secured a mandate from its constituents. "We spent more than a million dollars to give these people a new union, and it didn't work [. . .] despite all the corruption, there was a certain loyalty to the old union on the part of the workers." Meany announced that the rather superficial reforms that the ILA had adopted during its ostracism were substantial enough to merit readmission to the house of labor and accepted the Association into the AFL-CIO in 1959.

Sparring with the longshore racketeers was only a prelude. The elephant in the room was the massive International Brotherhood of Teamsters, which now vied with the UAW for the mantle of America's largest labor union. The Teamsters' astounding growth had begun before the war not because of Tobin's leadership but in spite of it. Tobin had no use for the "rubbish" in the warehouses and over-the-road trucking industry who would form the building blocks of his union's rapid expansion. Other Teamster organizers, though, dreamed of imposing regional or even national contracts on the fragmented freight industry, pattern agreements that would rival those of the big industrial unions. Among them were Farrell Dobbs—an associate of the Dunne brothers, the Minneapolis Trotskyists who had earned fame in the events of 1934—and Seattle's Dave Beck, whose pioneering Western Conference established the first area wide trucking agreement. Beck succeeded Tobin to the Teamster presidency.

The vain Beck had a weakness for money and the status it could buy—a weakness that the McClellan committee, exposing his regular abuse of union funds, aired before the world. Of more enduring consequence for the union was the career of his successor, James R. Hoffa. The young Hoffa, a onetime student of Dobbs' organizing techniques, had usurped the Minneapolis Teamsters' regional hegemony during the war and secured leadership of the Central States Drivers' Conference.

The Teamsters were a curious amalgam of old and new in the labor movement. Like the CIO unions, they reached out to organize a diverse group of skilled and unskilled workers, and Hoffa pushed tirelessly for greater central control and direction of the union. But in other ways the Teamsters remained in an AFL craft union world. Their industry was divided among small firms; employees in their core over-the-road trucking business often retained more enduring ties to their union than to their employer. Pension and benefit funds were usually union-controlled, not company-administered.[56] Neither did the massive union cede such contractual power to management as industrial unions did. Hoffa jealously protected the right to strike during the duration of contracts, rather than submitting grievances to binding arbitration.

In his rhetoric, Hoffa was the consummate "business unionist" of his day. As he explained in his bizarre memoir, he admired Dobbs—"a hell of an organizer"—but he scorned Dobbs's politics. Hoffa "always felt all communists were screwballs," but this was not his only objection. "I didn't like Dobbs' outspoken stand that unions should be a decisive political force. . . . I have always said in public as well as in private that unions should stay the hell out of politics unless a tremendous social issue is at stake."[57]

Here as always, Hoffa presented himself as the ultimate "bread and butter" unionist unconcerned with social change. But was "business unionism" really the right term for Hoffa and his union? As noted, the Teamsters rejected the industrial order of "management manages and the union grieves" to which industrial unions had reconciled themselves, retaining a sovereignty over their labor that the latter had long forfeited. Where people like Lewis, Beck, and Murray's USWA successor David McDonald relished the fine things and respectability of polite society, projecting an image of embourgeoisment, no one was less bourgeois than Jimmy Hoffa. Though no slouch in the misuse of union funds, Hoffa lived rather modestly and enjoyed a well-earned reputation as a rough-and-tumble, outlaw class warrior.[58]

Many then and now described Hoffa's union as a crude social bargain in which members (and union locals) forfeited both their share in directing the union and the pursuit of more elevated purposes in exchange for good wages and benefits. But a Teamster card carried intangible rewards, not just economic ones. In a labor movement that often seemed domesticated, Hoffa's was a rare trade union that retained the *élan* of a fighting force, the excitement and danger that had accompanied Depression labor struggles. (Indeed it could be *too* dangerous and exciting if you were unfortunate enough to hold a card in Genovese capo Anthony Provenzano's Local 560 in North Jersey or one of the many other mobbed-up locals.) To most of his union's rank-and-file Hoffa would always be a hero—and government investigations against him not welcome comeuppance for a crook but a malicious political attempt to suppress America's strongest labor organization.

Hoffa's anti-political stance, then, was not merely a matter of dollars and cents—but it was essential nonetheless to the Teamsters' strategy. By disavowing claims to social or political leadership, Hoffa and his Teamsters escaped the constraints that bound leaders like Meany and Reuther. Meany supported legislative action to alleviate poverty and regulate employer behavior in the public interest; this demanded he recognize the legitimacy of the democratic process and his obligation to obey the laws that resulted. Reuther desired to lead a social movement; this required him to reconcile his proposals with the common good, not just the interests of autoworkers. But Hoffa remained free to adopt the same pragmatic attitude toward the law that business executives did. For both Hoffa and employers, the law was no more than a context for pursuing personal ends; it carried no moral weight; the only real crime was getting caught.

Hoffa's widely publicized mob associates and his occasional recourse to violence against recalcitrant employers were hardly his best organizing tool. More important were the ways—relieved of the social obligations binding other union leaders—he could leverage the Teamsters' strategic economic position. To organize a hostile firm without invoking the cumbersome NLRB process, Teamsters at other firms could refuse to handle that company's freight and demand that their employers do likewise. True, that would be an illegal secondary boycott, but the targeted firm could well be bankrupt before obtaining relief from the courts. Moreover, Hoffa usually kept in reserve a number of unresolved grievances against every organized company, providing a legal pretext for instant strike action against an uncooperative employer who scorned such a secondary boycott. Using such mild, and mildly illegal economic coercion, Hoffa—alone among all labor leaders—registered significant organizing successes in the postwar South. Later, as IBT president, he would use these tools to crown his career with the historic 1964 National Master Freight Agreement.[59]

The members of the McClellan Committee were hardly interested in the details of collective bargaining, but they were fascinated with the Teamsters. Journalists and Senators ordinarily absorbed in mind-numbing legislative minutiae found in *this* union an apparently limitless catalogue of bribery, kickbacks, extortion, larceny, organized crime, and general vice. Now that's entertainment! The committee's more philosophically inclined took the opportunity to reflect on labor's role in politics and society. Supported by respective cheering sections in the press, they portrayed the hearings as a battle for labor's future, pitting Reuther's progressive and activist "social unionism" against Hoffa's more conservative "business unionism."[60]

Committee counsel Robert Kennedy, who wanted to see labor as a force for progressive social reform, used the hearings to initiate a long-running feud with Hoffa. For Kennedy, Hoffa represented perhaps the chief obstacle to that vision, and the committee's protracted investigation of the violence-plagued UAW strike against fiercely anti-union firm Kohler a conservative effort to stifle progressive unionism. He dramatized these themes in his 1960 book on union corruption, *The Enemy Within,* and would carry his war with Hoffa on to the Attorney General's office when his brother was elected president.[61]

Hoffa cleverly stoked Republican suspicions that Democrats were persecuting him to boost Reuther's fortunes and political views at the Teamsters' expense. "I do not believe that it is the original intention of labor organizations to try and control any . . . political powers in this country for their own determination," said Hoffa. "I think we both recognize that in the writing in the clouds today there is an individual who would like to see that happen in this country," replied Goldwater. "I do not like to even suggest to let you and him fight, but for the good of the movement I am very hopeful that your philosophy prevails." He would explain later, "I would rather have Hoffa stealing my money than Reuther stealing my freedom."[62]

Interestingly, Hoffa and Reuther remained relatively cordial throughout their careers; it was Meany who was outraged by Hoffa and the ethic he brought to the Teamsters. The chiseling repelled him, and he believed that a man who renounced the pursuit of larger social and political goals was no true trade unionist. Hoffa's posture, Meany said, "seemed to have its roots in the idea—which I categorically reject—that the American worker doesn't care what happens to the money he puts in his trade union as long as he gets a good fat pay envelope."[63]

Consequently, citing the ethical standards embedded in the AFL-CIO Constitution, Meany orchestrated an ultimatum to the Teamsters to clean up their act or face expulsion. Hoffa was defiant. The Teamsters were not the ILA; they were a colossus and certainly the Federation's most strategically placed affiliate. Controlling the transportation of freight, their respect for another union's pickets could make or break a strike. But once outside the Federation—released from the constraints and obligations of membership—their unique access to virtually every workplace would let them raid the jurisdictions of other unions at will. Hoffa was certain he could persuade Meany and the Federation to back down.[64]

He was wrong. For Meany, no one was so big they were above the rules; Hoffa's attitude was just another expression of his contempt for the rule of law. "I perhaps look at the [AFL-CIO] Constitution differently than the delegate who votes for it and walks away," he told the 1957 AFL-CIO Convention. "I feel that I have an obligation to live up to it."[65] Persuading many of the reluctant delegates, Meany skillfully built a solid majority in favor of evicting the Teamsters from the house of labor. The AFL-CIO president, who would devote considerable energy thereafter to a quarantine of the outlaw union leader, saw the episode as part an ongoing motif of his career. To his admirers, Meany was the shrewd, plainspoken plumber who humbled prima donnas like Lewis, Hoffa, and later, Reuther, men who put their own ambitions above the good of the labor movement. To his detractors, he was a small man who couldn't bear rivals of a more heroic mold, and who used organizational and bureaucratic tools to cut them down.

The McClellan hearings produced public policy as well as federation politics. The Labor-Management Reporting and Disclosure Act, or Landrum-Griffin, passed in 1959 over labor's objections. The bill aimed to root out corrupt and anti-democratic union practices revealed by the investigations. Union officials would have to meet stringent reporting requirements that documented the use of union funds. All local unions would have to elect their local officers by secret ballot. A "Bill of Rights" for union members guaranteed freedom of speech and assembly to encourage members to participate in the political life of their union without fear of retaliation.

The effects of Landrum-Griffin proved far milder than either its proponents or opponents predicted. Presumably the conservative Republicans who supported Landrum-Griffin anticipated a broad rank-and-file movement against union leaders whose embrace of liberal social causes like civil rights offended conservative workers interested only, as Meany put it, in "a fat pay envelope." On the other hand, the rhetoric of radicals who characterized the trade union leadership as a stifling conservative force holding back a potentially explosive working class portended a very different transformation of the AFL-CIO. Though many unions have seen brief "democracy" movements come and go—and the Teamsters themselves hosted one more persistent than most—nothing like the vibrant factional life that characterized decades of ITU, UMW, IAM, and ILGWU history, or the briefer but intense ferment of many young CIO unions, appeared. Turnover in union office did not increase with the passage of the Act and may actually have declined.[66]

Certain LMRDA features actually *hindered* the potential of trade unions for democratic civic education. New financial reporting requirements surely encouraged a more careful stewardship of members' dues, but they also demanded arcane skills. Whether the union did this by hiring outside experts for their staffs or by giving incumbent leaders extensive specialized training, it would constitute a formidable obstacle to shop floor amateurs seeking union office. As their officers' duties grew increasingly complex, it became correspondingly harder for rank-and-file members to deliberate on union matters or even judge the merits of their elected leaders.

Under voluntarism, the union was the workers' own body, its actions and fate theirs to decide. When the Wagner Act extended government protection to the labor organization, the government acquired an interest in the conduct of union affairs. With LMRDA, the American government in effect asserted that workers were unfit to direct their own organizations without outside supervision.

7

NOT A SLOGAN OR A FAD

Labor and the Great Society

Declining rates of voting and civic activism after World War II have been much analyzed at the millennium's end.[1] But American labor did not go gently into the night of public apathy; rather, the unions redoubled their Sisyphean efforts to stimulate the working class to continued social involvement. The same social conditions that depressed participation in the rest of society militated against any cumulative achievement in the federation's civic mission. In a society marked by a growing bureaucracy in which citizens easily learned to prefer passive representation by professional agents to an active role in either their union or their government, it was a challenge to merely resist the trend of such a *disengagement*. And yet, civic education was the very *identity* of American labor. Equipping America's workers for democracy was—and is—how American trade unionists find meaning. However discouraging the social environment, the crusade would continue.

While both American voting participation and union membership continued to decline, the AFL-CIO's electoral arm, the Committee on Political Education (COPE), compiled a remarkable record. COPE and the unions stepped into the vacuum left by the fading party machines with vigorous efforts to register union voters, educate them on the issues, and recruit volunteers for the campaigns of labor-friendly candidates. Union members became—and remain—much more likely to vote, and at that to vote Democrat, than the general population.[2]

George Meany was not one to philosophize about civic participation, but like his Federation colleagues believed that labor's new machinery of political mobilization could transform American politics. COPE's remarkable 1958

electoral showing had produced the most liberal Congress in decades and sti-
fled a burgeoning effort to pass state "right-to-work" laws allowed under Taft-
Hartley's Section 14(b).[3] But this was only the beginning. The leaders of the
AFL-CIO intended to drive the nation toward expanding the welfare state, leg-
islating civil rights, and prosecuting a cold war to propagate liberal democracy abroad. When in the 1960s the White House fell to equally ambitious
Democratic hands, Meany sensed an unparalleled opportunity.

If trade union leaders had considered the relationship of civic participation and democracy, they might have been better prepared for the paradox
that bedeviled their efforts. A vibrant local political life, Tocqueville had observed, was essential to the nature and function of American democracy. Citizens who actively deliberated and chose the rules under which they would
live adopted a keen interest in public affairs—and having directly participated
in making those rules, such citizens felt a special moral obligation to obey
them. In both respects Tocqueville invidiously compared his own people and
society to America's. The Frenchman, he argued, took little interest in the affairs of his community; the laws, crafted by distant authorities, had no claim
on his loyalty other than force.[4]

Beginning with the New Deal, labor turned increasingly to the federal
government to execute its political and social goals, and its postwar vision—
featuring a growing military force and welfare state—promised more of the
same. But the massive federal bureaucracy required by such progressive politics clashed with labor's ongoing desire to cultivate citizens capable of participation in self-rule. A powerful executive could secure for workers what
they were unable to secure for themselves, but democratic citizenship could
not be achieved by proxy. Labor could not have it both ways, and the AFL-
CIO's leaders constantly found themselves facing unpleasant choices between
conflicting priorities.

Meany mostly ignored such abstract issues, concentrating on the concrete
opportunities offered by the new political order. Hillman had been one of the
first to discover the power of the modern presidency, parlaying his relationship with Roosevelt into political appointments and public policy. If the
plumber never developed Hillman's comfort in elite intellectual circles, he
shared the CIO-PAC chairman's skills of organizational and bureaucratic maneuver. Like his forebear, Meany was remarkably adept at those battles Dunlop and his associates had described, wherein memos flowed instead of
blood.[5] And since Meany led a larger, wealthier, and more unified labor movement into these national political engagements, he had every reason to expect

that the ambitious political agenda laid out at the AFL-CIO's birth would soon be achieved.

Upon Kennedy's 1960 election, labor's political strategy began to reap rewards. With the stroke of a pen, the new president's Executive Order 10988 secured the right to union membership for a wide range of federal employees. The unions' privileged relations with the president had made possible what Meany called "a Wagner Act for public employees"—without a grueling legislative fight in the halls of Congress.[6] A series of state legislatures soon followed the federal government's lead and adopted statutes protecting state and local employees' right to organize.

The AFL-CIO president savored what he saw as an unqualified victory for his movement. Public employee unions organized rapidly at a time when many established affiliates in core industries were starting to lose members; their activity would avert a sharp and telling decline in organized labor's numbers and power.[7] Moreover, the new public employee unions would be a valuable resource in intramural federation politics, defending his vision of activist government and partisan politics against any stubborn voluntarists remaining in the ranks.

But was the *fiat* of a friendly executive the most appropriate and democratic way to secure basic rights? Obstinate antilabor *minorities* whose Senate filibusters denied workers legislative recourse compelled labor strategists to make the most of such administrative tools.[8] But this choice entailed perils not just to democratic principle but to political practice. Moving the political battlefield out of the public eye into private offices put unions at a profound disadvantage. Business, one could reasonably anticipate, would more often have the ear of the president and his cabinet than would labor. And if workers' rights could be extended by executive order, they could be revoked or repressed as well. Although federal workers would obtain a measure of statutory protection under the Civil Service Reform Act of 1978, their right to organize and bargain remained circumscribed and tenuous. The disastrous end of the Professional Air Traffic Controllers Organization (PATCO)—destroyed overnight when President Ronald Reagan abruptly dismissed striking air traffic controllers in 1981 and decertified their union—demonstrated that even the most militant and privileged federal labor organization was a hostage to the chief executive's goodwill.

But so long as Kennedy occupied the White House, this dilemma would be hypothetical, while the advantages of access were very real. Working people labored under enough unfairness in the ordinary operation of economy and society: it would almost have been irresponsible for labor *not* to get while the getting was good. And the access and substantive achievements JFK proffered paled before the possibilities Lyndon Baines Johnson would soon hold forth.

Johnson's vision of the "Great Society" mirrored that of Meany and the AFL-CIO. Organized labor, as the only major domestic constituency that both endorsed the president's ambitious domestic agenda and supported his war in Vietnam, enjoyed unprecedented access to the White House during LBJ's tenure. Despite Johnson's legendary skills as a congressional tactician, trade union support was crucial to major initiatives like the 1964 Economic Opportunity Act and other elements of the war on poverty; for the creation of Medicare in 1965; for the Civil Rights Act of 1964 prohibiting racial discrimination in employment and public accommodations; and for the Voting Rights Act of 1965, prohibiting discrimination in voter registration. "We never would have passed the Civil Rights Act without labor," congressional sponsor Richard Bolling observed. "They had the muscle; the other civil rights groups did not."[9]

High-profile legislative battles like these offered a more honorable and democratic path to reform than executive orders, but still posed challenges for labor's traditions of civic education. All too often they demanded new national bureaucracies of experts to administer them on behalf of the public. Nor could the AFL-CIO ever truly resolve the conflicting mandates that drove its political activism. Were the trade unions, as democratic institutions, obliged to faithfully represent the will of their members—a distinct minority of the public—and thus act as a "special interest"? Or were they exemplary civic actors advocating for the common good, whatever the sentiments of union members or consequences for organized labor? In the instructive case of Medicare legislation, Meany and the Federation organized a National Council of Senior Citizens to lead the fight for public support.[10] Opponents thus found it difficult to stigmatize Medicare as a "labor issue"—but the labor movement missed an opportunity to identify itself with the commonweal and the interests of society's most vulnerable.

Labor law administration proved more troubling still. Union organizing, outside of the public sector unions (and to some extent, the renegade Teamsters), had largely stalled. Existing labor law constituted a large part of the problem. Taft-Hartley had vitiated the potential of the Wagner Act. Section 14(b) obstructed organizing in many states by allowing them to enact "right-to-work" laws prohibiting the union shop, and other provisions encouraged employers to resist efforts at unionization by employees. In a larger sense, Taft-

Hartley made explicit a new policy goal in American labor law. Where Wagner had argued that his Act sought to facilitate collective bargaining as a tool of industrial democracy, Taft-Hartley stressed that government must protect the worker's *right to choose* between individual and collective bargaining.[11]

These unhappy trends in labor policy were happening precisely when the constraints of public opinion were melting away. Although the New Deal reformers and their immediate successors advanced policies that awarded distant Washington institutions the power to regulate labor relations, they could argue, without too much exaggeration, that they carried out the mandate of an informed public that understood the stakes. But the rarified atmosphere of post-Wagner labor law effectively insulated industrial relations policy from popular discussion, and thus from democratic deliberation. In 1946, as industrial conflict and proposed labor law changes filled pre-Cold War headlines, less than *half* the public could explain the likely effect of Taft-Hartley's passage. Of course, the arcane law resisted explanation even when Truman made its repeal the central issue of his successful 1948 presidential campaign; but what are we to make of the 89 percent who in 1955 did not know what right-to-work laws were?[12]

The ambiguities of the Wagner system as amended by Taft-Hartley, and the absence of an informed public, combined to disturbing effect. National Labor Relations Board members, appointed by the president, acquired enormous power to set American labor policy while virtually liberated from public accountability. NLRB appointments had always been highly politicized, but the procedure was now to achieve a new intensity.[13]

President Kennedy, on his accession to office, began to assemble the most pro-labor NLRB since the Roosevelt years. The AFL-CIO welcomed the creative "New Frontier" NLRB headed by Frank McCulloch, which expressly recognized the inequalities of power inherent in the workplace and acted in many areas to defend workers' right to organize against the sometimes subtle stratagems of employer resistance.[14] With its innovative *Fibreboard* decision, the Board moved into new territory. The Wagner framework designated certain potential bargaining subjects as mandatory: an employer who refused to bargain with a certified majority labor union over wages and working conditions, for instance, could be charged with an unfair labor practice. When the Fibreboard Company decided to subcontract its maintenance work to an outside firm—for purely economic reasons rather than to retaliate against the union—the Eisenhower-era NLRB rejected the Steelworkers' demand that the company be made to bargain over the issue. Reexamining the case, McCulloch's Board ruled that the company had to negotiate the move with the union. The implications were clear: management decisions were suddenly subject to collective bargaining. The European-style codetermination that Phil Murray and Walter Reuther had tried so hard to achieve through political or economic activism might be casually ordered by little-known presidential appointees.

Although a Supreme Court appeal limited the general applicability of the *Fibreboard* decision, employers quickly determined what was at stake and mobilized for massive retaliation. Initial reactions evidenced an interesting concern with the preservation of democratic norms. "The final result is a statute, revised administratively both in intent and in substance, which reflects the views of executive appointees instead of the elected representatives of the people," declaimed corporate lawyer Kenneth McGuiness. "It is fundamental to our system of government that our laws be enacted by the legislature, not the executive, branch."[15]

But the business community's touching concern for democratic principles was not very deeply held. The keenest managerial minds realized that controlling this new policy apparatus offered more rewards than denouncing it, and that in many ways the bureaucracy was a more friendly venue for corporations and their agents than was an unpredictable elected legislature. True, Meany and his cohort of postwar trade union leaders, who had achieved power by climbing the ranks of established labor organizations, had no small talent for institutional politics and bureaucratic intrigue. But in the black arts of conspiracy and influence-peddling that govern political appointments, business leaders—who traffic not in principles but interests—naturally held the upper hand. Labor's true strengths are political ones, based on public organizing in support of shared values; union influence diminishes rapidly behind closed doors.

In 1965, Douglas Soutar of American Smelting and Refining, a notable figure in the National Association of Manufacturers, joined Virgil Day of General Electric, who chaired the U.S. Chamber of Commerce's Labor Relations Committee to organize a coterie of corporate industrial relations chiefs. These industrial illuminati would spearhead the fight against *Fibreboard* and the apparent trend in labor relations law. Under the ominous moniker the "No-Name Committee," the shadowy group directed a lavishly financed campaign to turn national labor relations policy in directions friendlier to business. Although the group spawned organs devoted to lobbying Congress and to turning public opinion against labor, perhaps its most important move was to seek control of the NLRB. The committee's Labor Law Reform Group concluded that labor had seized the Board's appointment process and thus "gained control of the machinery of government to shape old laws to serve its interests."

The group proposed that business adopt a similar tack, seeking out labor board appointees who would fabricate even more creative interpretations of the Wagner statutes in employers' interest.[16]

Unsurprisingly, employers proved far more adept at this technique than labor, their effort culminating under Ronald Reagan in an NLRB led by Donald Dotson. Dotson chose as his chief assistant a staff lawyer from the National Right to Work Legal Defense Fund and led a board whose chief preoccupation was protecting the right of workers *not* to join unions.[17] If McCulloch and his associates stretched the intent of the National Labor Relations Act, Dotson's board flatly contradicted that intent—albeit in ways that could be justified by the letter of the law protecting the rights of workers to make free choices about representation.

The Challenge of Civil Rights

In the face of these setbacks on the shop floor, the labor movement did not retreat to a "business unionism" exclusively concerned with wage and benefit gains for its members, but persisted in its project of training workers for democratic citizenship. It no longer did so in the voluntarist, craft union mold, trying to combine mental and manual labor in the workplace for civic education, but largely by championing progressive causes in society. By offering enthusiastic labor support to the causes of civil rights, of improving the social safety net to protect society's most vulnerable, and propagating liberal democracy throughout the world, the AFL-CIO tried to discourage the selfish individualism that so tempted America after the war and tried to instill in labor union members a concern for the commonweal.

The Great Society agenda of extensive government programs administered by the federal government had little in common with the voluntary associations of Tocqueville or the voluntarism of Gompers. Perhaps more than any other issue, civil rights became a flashpoint where labor debated the merits of these treasured traditions of robust local democracy against modern ideals of equality and social justice.

At first glance, the AFL-CIO's public policy record on racial discrimination was remarkable. Though civil rights was hardly an issue moving vast majorities of rank-and-file union members to demand action, Meany and other union leaders identified it as a key labor priority. The Federation and its affiliates provided substantial legal and financial assistance to the major civil rights organizations, and by all accounts were essential players in the landmark civil rights legislation destroying Jim Crow segregation.[18] In spite of this, numerous critics accused organized labor in general—and Meany and his building trades fellows in particular—of indifference or hostility to racial equality. They considered labor leaders' civil rights advocacy a matter of rhetoric rather than commitment, pointing to expressions of racial discrimination within the trade union movement. Labor, such critics argued, could not be serious about racial equality if unions resisted putting their own house in order.

At the dawn of the civil rights era, a significant number of construction union locals—many but not all in the South—were effectively segregated by race. Even more notorious was the case of the Brotherhood of Railroad Firemen, which was admitted to the AFL-CIO in 1956 despite a history of violence aimed at preserving the color bar. For more than two decades, A. Philip Randolph, President of the Brotherhood of Sleeping Car Porters and a civil rights leader of considerable repute, hectored the AFL leadership by demanding action against such unions. Randolph's stirring floor speeches created a recurrent spectacle; his trade union peers resented not just his moral instruction but also his debating skills and superior education. But though many AFL affiliates quietly removed the color bar from their constitutions, the Sleeping Car Porters' president failed to prod William Green (who could not) or George Meany (who would not) to take punitive action against segregated affiliates.[19] The AFL-CIO constitution forbade racial discrimination, as much as racketeering, but Meany, who had initiated the expulsion of the mobbed-up Longshoremen and Teamsters, urged that unions like the Railway Firemen be admitted and only behind closed doors pressured to end such repellent practices.

Randolph had been a principal author of one of the major early achievements of the civil rights movement, Executive Order 8802. In early 1941, as Roosevelt moved to support those nations resisting the Axis, Randolph demanded that all defense contracts stipulate equal employment practices. The rail union leader and his supporters reasoned that an international crusade against fascist aggression and the Nazi ideology of racial supremacy was an opportune time to demand an end to racial segregation in the defense industries. He set about engineering a massive African-American March on Washington to press that demand. Roosevelt reckoned that if anyone could recruit "100,000 Negroes" to a demonstration in the capital, it would be the president of a black railroad union, so he gave Randolph what he wanted.

Reuther supported Meany on the admission of the Locomotive Firemen, but his general approach to civil rights contrasted with Meany's in increasingly obvious ways. Just as Meany preferred engaging discriminatory unions in cloistered negotiations, the plumber favored lobbying legislators to pass vital civil rights laws over the public demonstrations—not to say civil disobedience—then coming into vogue. Reuther, to the contrary, identified himself and the UAW with the civil rights movement in conspicuous ways. When the aging Randolph recruited an entire new generation of civil rights leaders for the momentous 1963 March on Washington, Meany kept the AFL-CIO at arm's length, while Reuther—who represented his union on the NAACP Board—publicly supported Randolph. The UAW provided financial and logistical support for the march, and Reuther shared the podium that day when Martin Luther King made history with his dream.[20]

Whatever one makes of accusations of racial discrimination in the trade unions, even a *rhetorical* support of civil rights exacted enormous costs. Efforts to organize the South had frequently stumbled in the face of Southern propaganda citing the CIO's endorsement of civil rights. And in the early-to-mid 1960s the heroic efforts of the southern state labor federations to support civil rights and register black voters—in the face of a mass exodus of white unions from the state feds, often accompanied by threats of Klan violence—is an unfortunately little-known story.[21] Also little-known is the 1965 episode in which Meany apparently spurned Minority Leader Everett Dirksen's offer to trade a repeal of Taft-Hartley's hated anti-union "right-to-work" provision for a key labor concession on voting rights.[22]

The persistent charge of progressive critics—that this public endorsement of civil rights legislation was not matched by an equal enthusiasm about addressing discriminatory practices within the trade unions themselves—indicated a real problem. But it was a problem rooted less in union leaders' insincerity than in irreconcilable conflicts between different democratic values. As Dunlop and co-author Derek Bok bluntly stated, "it is fatuous for scholars to extol the virtues of union democracy in one chapter, only to castigate local leaders in another for perpetuating discrimination. A local union can hardly practice an enlightened autocracy on racial matters while operating in a vigorous democratic environment on other issues."[23] Whereas the white working classes that dominated the trade unions of the 1950s, 1960s, and 1970s were hardly the gang of bigoted Archie Bunker mopes that some would have us believe, they certainly did not share the trade union leaders' expressed excitement about the civil rights cause.

Meany, an astute judge of trade union organizational politics, resolved this dilemma by making racial discrimination *outside* the labor movement's own institutions the Federation's policy focus. Black voting rights was an especially attractive venue for labor's civil rights initiatives. The cause was almost self-evidently just; it did not require disruptive and painful internal transformations of trade unions; it offered the added potential benefit of advancing labor's legislative fortunes. An influx of southern black voters would give the AFL-CIO a sweet revenge on the conservative Jim Crow Democrats who were labor's *bête noire* in the party. The hidebound racists whose high seniority enabled them to chair congressional committees and block progressive legislation could be swept aside. The AFL-CIO's legislative chief Biemiller even observed that he would not mind the appearance of a significant Republican party in the South if it made the southern Democracy more liberal.[24]

At the same time, Meany was exasperated with those who pointed the finger at trade union discrimination. Why, they asked, did he move against corrupt unions and not racist ones? Meany's belief that pressure and persuasion would end these practices faster than expulsion was probably sincere.[25] But he was also politician enough to know that corruption had no real constituency among American union members; racism unfortunately did.

Progressives from outside labor's ranks who cast aspersions on labor's civil rights commitments—most prominently Herbert Hill of the NAACP—quickly alienated Meany. Hill's reports on discrimination in the labor movement complicated relations with important allies, and his assistance in efforts to decertify discriminatory unions placed him beyond the pale. In any case, modern hiring decisions were overwhelmingly the province of employers, and labor strongly supported legislation penalizing *them* for occupational discrimination. Why couldn't civil rights movement leaders focus on the important issues and stop creating fights with their allies over lesser matters?

So long as Jim Crow segregation remained the movement's primary target, disputes between the unions and civil rights groups could be reasonably contained. However, as affirmative action emerged and assumed more controversial forms, the latent conflict erupted with increasing frequency. Affirmative action as initially based on the 1964 Civil Rights Act need not have been the "wedge issue" dividing the two social groups it would become in the 1970s and 1980s. Spokesmen for the AFL-CIO and major unions endorsed the Act's Title VII, forbidding discrimination in employment; Meany himself engineered large outreach programs to recruit minority apprentices into the building trades.[26]

But creative jurisprudence soon complicated matters. The minority workforce had traditionally been excluded from many jobs and educational opportunities. However aggressive and sincere outreach programs were, seniority rules and social disadvantage virtually guaranteed that minority workers would be underrepresented in the most desirable jobs for at least a generation. Only aggressive federal intervention—intervention that violated selection by seniority or by any conceivable objective job testing—could prevent this result. There was little in the legislative history of the Act to justify such programs, and in fact some legislative sponsors had stated expressly that Title VII was not to tamper with existing seniority rights. However, the Act's text was emphatic: it called for ending racial discrimination, not explaining its historical roots. There was sufficient room for a jurist so disposed to conclude that "the plain language of the act condemns as an unfair practice all racial discrimination affecting employment without excluding present discrimination that originated in seniority systems devised before the effective date of the act." The court reasoned that "Congress did not intend to freeze an entire generation of Negro employees into discriminatory patterns that existed before the Act," and ruled, "a departmental seniority system that has its genesis in racial discrimination is not a *bona fide* seniority system."[27]

For labor's most persistent and articulate critics, like Hill, no conclusion could be more transparent. If union leaders opposed rigid recruitment quotas and similar remedies to overcome past discrimination, they were defending white privilege and nothing more. Of the ILGWU, Hill argued that "a growing Black and Hispanic working class had tried to open an avenue for advancement in an institution controlled by an established stratum of Jewish leaders who were anxious to preserve the privileges of their group within the industry." Surveying the Southern organizing efforts, Hill concluded, "Unions used their power to structure racial inequality. . . . In retrospect it is evident that the Steelworkers Union and also the other labor organizations, both craft and industrial, functioned in the workplace as part of the apparatus of white supremacy."

The discriminatory patterns identified by Hill and other progressive critics were real. But their general unfamiliarity with the labor movement's history, traditions, and principles, coupled with a monomaniacal focus on race, made it difficult for them to understand that other things besides "white supremacy" were going on here.[28] Great battles of the industrial organizing era had been fought to enforce seniority rules against managerial discrimination; it was not to be casually gambled in social experiments like affirmative action. Seniority was a principle of justice for which blood had been shed, and had acquired a certain sanctity in the public and especially the trade union mind.

This sanctity also dictated that most union leaders could endorse remedial quotas only at the expense of union democracy. Naturally this pressure was most severely felt in the building trades in which the union rather than the employer was the arbiter of employment opportunities. Membership in a

building trades union was valuable precisely because it was scarce and difficult to secure. The craft union's trade, like the medieval guild's "mystery," was
the property of the membership to be jealously guarded and conserved. It was,
harking back to an older language of argument, a property that guaranteed
the independence and dignity necessary for a meaningful civic existence. It
was a legacy to be treasured, improved, and passed on to family, not to be
squandered on strangers in order to address abstract social problems created
by others. As one tradesman, Charles Kelly, explained in a 1963 letter to the
New York Times that was published under the heading "Apprenticeship as
Heritage":

> Some men leave their sons money, some large investments, some business
> connections and some a profession. I have none of these to bequeath to my
> sons. I have only one worthwhile thing to give: my trade. I hope to follow a
> centuries-old tradition and sponsor my sons for apprenticeship. For this sim-
> ple father's wish it is said that I discriminate against Negroes. Don't all of us
> discriminate? Which of us when it comes to a choice will not choose a son
> over all others? I believe that an apprenticeship in my union is no more a pub-
> lic trust, to be shared by all, than a millionaire's money is a public trust. Why
> should the government, be it local, state or Federal, have any more right to
> decide how I dispose of my heritage than it does how the corner grocer dis-
> poses of his?[29]

Allowing the government to regulate admission to the craft unions would
mean sacrificing much of labor's remaining autonomy from the government,
a substantial concern to Meany and like-minded union leaders. For tradesmen like Kelly, it meant even more—a surrender of the personal autonomy
supporting a claim to democratic citizenship already challenged in too many
ways. And although the searchlight naturally and rightly fell on segregated
white union locals, many black local unions resisted integration on the same
grounds. African-American trade unionists who had secured an economic and
social patrimony of their own were loath to part with it. A leader in a black
longshoremen's local articulated his opposition to a liberal scholar. "If you
merged the [black and white] locals together we are going to lose something,"
he explained. "These things that we are talking about, what the ILA mean to
the black community, as far as prestige and some influence and to help other
black people in that community, we are going to lose that."[30]

But Hill and black critics who attacked these practices had a valid point
to make as well. True, industrial seniority systems were designed to secure justice or efficiency in the assignment of jobs, not to discriminate against mi-

nority workers. But if African-Americans had historically been excluded from such jobs, seniority systems would certainly have prejudicial effects on the current generation's opportunities for advancement. True, also, it was not Kelly's intent to discriminate against black workers that led him to prefer his son for an open apprenticeship. But the practice, if continued, could guarantee the exclusion of blacks from many unions not just for one generation but for however long white ethnic social solidarity endured. It had been easy enough to forge an AFL-CIO consensus supporting voting rights for Southern blacks, precisely because it is easy to give away what is not your own. Now, circumstances had given Meany and his cohort of trade union leaders an insoluble dilemma. For many labor unions certain demands of racial justice and of self-rule were hopelessly at odds.

Labor and the New Politics

Affirmative action was but one of a series of issues now dividing labor from the panoply of intellectuals, students, devotees of the new social movements, and antiwar activists who conceived of themselves as a critical left alternative to Johnson and his heir apparent, Hubert Humphrey. Progressive intellectuals like economist John Kenneth Galbraith described an American working class that had largely escaped poverty, and despite much conflicting evidence, many observers were ready to equate organized workers' new prosperity with an "embourgeoisment" expressed in politics as a new conservatism.[31] Others argued, more persuasively, that as the unions were institutionalized they became a stabilizing social element with a significant interest in the status quo; even "countervailing power," to use Galbraith's phrase, was a sort of power.[32] Unions, with their political access, were seen as part of the "establishment" against which the left would have to contend.

Few *economic* issues divided the self-styled "left" from the trade union "establishment," but economic issues were not a top priority for progressives who organized around social issues and especially opposition to the Vietnam war. Outside the black community, the "New Politics" was primarily a project of well-educated middle-class activists who could *afford* to ignore the economic differences separating Democrats from Republicans, seeing George Meany, Hubert Humphrey, Richard Nixon, and George Wallace as minor variations on a theme of anti-communist reaction. The stage was set for a curious reprise of the 1948 election furor, and once again the ADA was in the thick of the fight.

Social movement activists increasingly set the tone at ADA, expressing growing disdain for labor's traditional anti-communist brand of liberalism. "The ADA in the past had its political base in a rough coalition between un-attached liberals and liberal trade unionists. So I trust it will continue to be," Galbraith declaimed, on is 1967 election as ADA chairman. "But we must also be aware that large sections of the labor movement are no pillar of liberal strength. On the contrary, the leadership is aged, contented, and deeply som-nambulant. And on important issues of foreign policy, its position is well to the rear of Gerald Ford."[33] In 1968 the ADA abandoned Johnson to endorse Senator Eugene McCarthy's primary challenge. Trade unionists were mortified by the decision to renounce the liberal author of the Great Society in order to oppose the Vietnam war; presidents I. W. Abel of the Steelworkers, Louis Stul-berg of the ILGWU, and Joseph Bierne of the Communications Workers of America (CWA) resigned from the ADA board in protest.

Reuther too objected to the endorsement, but remained with the ADA. "You are the best labor leader in the country," Galbraith assured the UAW pres-ident. "I think I probably class you as one of the better liberals."[34] The divi-sions in the Democratic Party were being played out in the labor movement; circumstances demanded trade union leaders make difficult choices. Were union officials first and foremost leaders of a labor movement or a progressive social movement? Their choice implied important consequences. If they rep-resented American workers, especially America's organized workers, union of-ficials would remain somewhat estranged from the New Politics of the social movements. Their primary responsibility would be to the union rank-and-file rather than to a progressive political program. They could secure a mandate from their members for Medicare, for a War on Poverty, and even, with some difficulty, for basic civil rights measures. But cultural cleavages and different priorities dictated that a true alliance with the new social movements could be achieved only at the expense of labor's own constituency.

If union leaders wished to lead a progressive movement in national poli-tics, they would have to reach accord with the constituency of the New Poli-tics. Doing so would mean subordinating labor's traditional concerns to a movement preoccupied with social issues and the antiwar effort. It would call for a massive campaign to persuade union members that their true interests lay in abandoning their traditional Cold War Democratic friends for an al-liance with left social groups to transform the American political order. It meant selling the American worker on a new progressive political vision, re-jecting anti-communism, and embracing environmental, feminist, and mi-nority concerns that went well beyond striking down Jim Crow. However obvious this program's merits seemed to its left advocates, it was not self-evidently linked to American workers' beliefs, interests, or traditions.

Walter Reuther was prepared to make that leap. Educated in socialism from his youth, Reuther's politics had always been *left* politics as much as *labor* politics. As Goldwater had sensed in the 1950s, Reuther's ambition was to use the trade union movement as an instrument for enacting progressive political change rather than as an end in itself. Labor *had* to be part of the emerging constellation of social movements in the Democratic Party, even if the AFL-CIO had to sacrifice its unique stature in party circles.

To this end, Reuther strove to maintain good relations between the UAW and the social movements—and promoted both himself and his efforts prominently in the public arena. Reuther's union provided essential financial backing to the Students for a Democratic Society in the young and heady days of the Port Huron Statement. The UAW president sat on the NAACP Board and participated in the March on Washington, alongside Martin Luther King, even as Meany directed the AFL-CIO to avoid such controversial public associations. Soon thereafter, he and the UAW initiated a Citizens' Crusade against Poverty to unite a broad array of civil rights, labor, and religious organizations in this new progressive cause. Through CCAP, trade unions and activist groups would cooperate with community groups and Johnson's Office of Economic Opportunity to prosecute the war on poverty.[35]

While Reuther carefully avoided an outright break with the Democrats' national leadership, he embraced much of the criticism that the New Left leveled at that national leadership and at labor itself. "The labor movement is becoming an extension of the business community," he argued, rather than "a dynamic force challenging the status quo."[36] Reuther's anti-communism forbade him from directly attacking Johnson and Humphrey on the war issue, but he did distance himself from Meany's aggressive Cold War posture. Reuther, and especially his brother Victor, adopted an innovative foreign policy of their own premised on UAW outreach to nonaligned Third World nations and European Social Democrats—at a time when Johnson and Meany were pressuring such groups to choose sides in the global contest.

Most of all, Reuther wanted to transform labor to accommodate the New Politics. Reuther and his UAW associates laid out their ideology in a sequence of Administrative Letters addressed to UAW locals and published in UAW periodicals. The letters presented a slashing critique of the AFL-CIO under Meany's leadership. "The AFL-CIO lacks the social vision, the dynamic thrust, the crusading spirit that should characterize the progressive, modern labor movement," UAW members heard. The Federation needed to pledge the will and resources for "an all out organizational crusade to extend the benefits and protection of organization to the millions of unorganized." It needed "deeper commitment . . . in the on-going struggle for equal rights and equal opportunity, not only at the community level and through legislation but within the labor movement itself." It needed to "assume full partnership with other groups in the community working to supplement government programs in an all-out crusade to abolish human poverty in this land of plenty." Labor needed "to develop stronger ties with labor's historic and essential allies in the liberal intellectual and academic community and among America's young people."[37] Reuther's public campaign enabled him in effect to seize the mantle of "social unionism"—a term Joseph Shister had coined for Meany's brand of unionism, no less than for Reuther's personal political vision of labor as an element of the New Politics.[38] "A growing labor movement that effectively mobilizes its own membership in the crusade for a better society can magnify its own influence many times by becoming the magnetic center of attraction of a broad coalition of oppressed minorities, idealistic youth and far-sighted intellectuals whose combined forces can translate the promise of America into practical performance."[39]

Reuther's activities brought him into conflict with Meany on both stylistic and substantive grounds. Reuther used high-profile campaigns and media opportunities as a means of building public support for his ideas. To Meany, who suspected the press and favored personalistic action outside the public view, Reuther seemed a show-boater who preferred grabbing headlines to constructive work. Though he respected Reuther's stewardship of the UAW, Meany saw the autoworker president's broader ambitions as visionary and ineffectual. Reuther repeatedly requested and received the endorsement of the AFL-CIO for massive multi-union organizing campaigns, with poor results. Reuther blamed a lack of commitment on the part of the leadership, especially of the AFL affiliates; Meany thought Reuther's highhanded manner and short attention span presented an insuperable obstacle.[40] Both views probably contained a measure of truth.

One of the era's rare private sector organizing success stories illuminated the conflict between the two men. In an America where (thanks largely to the successes of the labor movement a generation before) poverty seemed a challenge faced mainly by the chronically unemployed, the condition of migrant farm workers acquired a unique symbolic importance. A grievously exploited community of working poor, they became the focus of multiple organizing efforts. Heightening their importance was the figure of Cesar Chavez. His Farm Workers' Association, precursor to the United Farm Workers (UFW)—representing an ethnic minority workforce, excluded from the protections of the Wagner Act, and relying instead on boycotts supported by young activists— offered the public a more striking picture of "social movement unionism" than even Reuther's UAW.

Chavez had not learned his organizing skills within the trade union movement, but from community organizer Saul Alinsky and from activist priests who tutored him in Catholic social thought. Reuther recognized both the merit of the farm workers' struggle and its political importance; he worked hard to identify the UAW with the struggling young union, offering both financial and moral support. He also publicly upbraided the AFL-CIO for failing to aid the UFW. Meany resented Reuther's publicity campaigns: although the AFL-CIO president was indeed skeptical of Chavez and his methods, the farm workers' union would surely have withered without extensive and ongoing Federation support against the growers, and later, against aggressive raids by the renegade Teamsters offering sweetheart contracts to their employers.[41]

The episode was instructive. The AFL-CIO attacked Reuther for rapidly losing interest in the Farmworkers' struggle, demonstrating that the Federation's financial support dwarfed that of the UAW. Much of this aid, however, had gone not to Chavez and his movement but to earlier Federation organizing efforts of a less controversial nature—and with small returns. Reuther had indeed identified *la causa* early and provided the access and resources needed to propel Chavez onto the national stage. But the UAW was not the substantial or reliable backer Chavez needed; the AFL-CIO was. The Federation had national resources and connections that the UAW simply did not. Moreover, by the time the UFW was fighting for its life against the Teamsters, Reuther had locked the UAW in an unwise alliance with the Teamsters in order to challenge Meany's AFL-CIO.[42]

Through the 1960s, Reuther issued ever more vocal demands to the Federation leadership for renewed labor and community organizing efforts, alliances with the social movements, and a plethora of structural reforms. In a series of false starts, Reuther promised a climactic confrontation with Meany and his partisans, each time backing away at the last hour. Reuther resigned from the executive council, and in May 1968 the Federation's largest union began withholding its per capita dues payments. Reuther finally demanded a special convention of the AFL-CIO to debate the UAW's proffered labor program.

At the core of the increasingly personal dispute between Meany and Reuther lay a more substantial argument about democratic values. Meany said he would support Reuther's demand for a special convention if the UAW president would "commit your organization to accept the democratically arrived at decisions of such a convention." This, Meany said, was "a proposal which no honorable organization, believing in majority rule in a democratic order, could reasonably reject." But Reuther did object to these terms. At his prompting, the autoworkers resolved that "the UAW could not in good conscience continue to be confined within the constricted limits of an organization so dominated by the dead hand of the past that it refused without unacceptable restrictive conditions even to be confronted in open discussion." Reuther's UAW responded that Meany's stipulation was "unacceptable." "They want us," he told the UAW's 1968 convention, to "sign a loyalty oath." Soon thereafter the UAW disaffiliated from the AFL-CIO.[43]

The tragedy of the Reuther-Meany schism was that each of these very different men had exhibited excellence in about *half* the qualities necessary to democratic leadership. But they were contradictory halves, and they pointed to incompatible choices. Each could see the shortcomings of their rival's portion only too well, making a split perhaps inevitable.

Meany saw in Reuther a man whose ideological convictions left little room for the democratic process. Reuther's drive to disaffiliate really "stemmed from a condition for which the AFL-CIO has no remedy—your apparent unwillingness to live in constructive harmony within an organization in which the rights, the interests and the views of other unions and other personalities are given equal consideration with those of the UAW and its president." The Federation was democratically governed, and if Reuther could not or would not adhere to majority rule "neither size, financial resources, nor extravagance of language" entitled him and his union to dictate policy to the AFL-CIO.[44] Reuther was regarded by many of his peers in the labor movement as haughty and self-righteous, having little skill at the kind of politicking necessary to win votes and master the democratic process.

Indeed, Reuther's diffident attitude toward democratic procedures was often disturbing. The executive council's demand that the UAW agree to adhere to the decision of the special AFL-CIO convention that Reuther requested was an "unacceptable condition." "I'd hate to go in and bargain with management" on that basis, Reuther explained. "I say that is not the way to bargain. . . . They would know our hands were tied."[45] Quite apart from the gratuitous insult comparing his trade union rivals to company management, one should note that bargaining is not a democratic procedure at all. In bargaining, deliberation and sound arguments are peripheral, and the stronger party need never bow to a mere numerical majority. Was bargaining what Reuther thought democracy was about?

In fact, it often seemed as if Reuther was so convinced of the righteousness of his views that he was unwilling to undertake the work of building majority support in labor's ranks. He was certainly unwilling to compromise his views to build a coalition. Reuther and his UAW allies explained, "The UAW leadership is sufficiently sophisticated to know that if a political power drive is contemplated, it is essential to build a coalition of allies. Since we are not engaged in a power drive, we have taken no steps to create a caucus of allies and we have no intention of doing so in the future. We intend to take our stand, and what others do is a matter of their conscience."[46] Reuther considered the very *idea* of building a majority coalition unprincipled. There could be no genuine discussion on such terms; the UAW delegates could simply announce their "principled" position and hope that it aroused the "conscience" of others. Meany frequently compared Reuther's actions with John L. Lewis's repeated peevish disaffiliations. It was an important and compelling analogy, aptly comparing two men whose immense talent and ambition made it hard for them to accept the outcome of democratic deliberations.

Perhaps Meany saw something similar in Reuther's performances for the media spotlight. When Reuther failed to appear at a special meeting on foreign policy that the Autoworkers' president himself had requested, Meany joshed, "maybe this is because we don't have TV cameras or radio transmitters in the executive council room." The conditions laid down for a special convention were made "in view of the UAW's record of denouncing the AFL-CIO and advertising its so-called 'proposals for reform and revitalization' in the public press for the past two years—while at the same time evading, under various pretexts, every one of the many opportunities presented to it to bring its complaints and proposals to the proper forums of the AFL-CIO." Meany affirmed that the Executive Council was ready "to receive, consider, debate and act upon any complaint, charge, proposal or program—novel or ancient—that any affiliate or its officers may desire to advance and advocate," but "we are not, however, prepared to act upon the basis of a kaleidoscope of ever-changing allegations and demands expressed through press releases, public speeches or circular letters."[47] Rather than pursuing the democratic procedures of the AFL-CIO in good faith, Reuther seemed to want to bypass them, using a mass media platform to propagate his ideas. Moreover, his public displays were clearly intended as much for Democratic party and social movement audiences as for his constituents in organized labor—of whom only a minority shared his progressive views. Reuther did not seem to want to lead American workers so much as he wanted to lead a liberal political realignment. He was willing to withdraw his union from the AFL-CIO in order to pursue his political vision.

Meany's loyalty belonged to the American working class, not the "left," however defined. His unbridled contempt for the social movement activists who animated the New Politics was only part of the reason.[48] In a fundamental sense, the job of democratically elected leaders is to represent the interests and will of their constituency, not to use their entrusted position of power to pursue personal political preferences. Meany did not push for a progressive or social-democratic political realignment; then again, neither were union members demanding one.

But Meany's style of democratic leadership suffered from deficiencies in precisely the areas of Reuther's strengths. Strictly construed, this respect for democratic institutional norms in the trade union movement always threatened to fold labor in upon itself. Asked in 1972 why the proportion of American workers in unions was declining, Meany replied, "I don't know, I don't care. . . . Why should we worry about organizing groups of people who do not appear to want to be organized? If they prefer to have others speak for them and make the decisions which affect their lives, without effective participation on their part, that is their right."[49] On this reasoning, labor organizations might scrupulously adhere to the will of their members yet still lose much of their value for a democratic polity. If their political participation was merely an instrument to secure the parochial interests of a shrinking membership, rather than the common good, just this would come to pass. Reuther's messianic politics were immune to such a danger; Meany's scrupulous respect for democratic procedures made a temptation toward self-interest and solipsism a lurking presence in labor discourse.

An unfortunate neglect of political education was also inherent in Meany's approach. Meany's talent for politicking and building coalitions was so formidable that Reuther came to reject serious participation in AFL-CIO deliberations.[50] The Plumber's skillful use of access enabled him to achieve many of labor's political priorities quietly, without the fanfare and braggadocio he scorned—but a democratic politics is also about creating informed public opinion and persuading majority sentiment. A commercial enterprise is bound together by mere pecuniary interests, but a labor union must create a deposit of shared values to unite its members.

Reuther, far more than Meany, appreciated the necessity of such initiatives. In this sense, too, the analogy between Lewis and Reuther is instructive. While Meany preferred quiet action to publicity, Lewis and Reuther exerted great effort to educate all Americans about labor and social justice. It is revealing that in 1957, shortly after the merger that created the AFL-CIO, Gallup found that 93 percent of the public could still identify the Mineworkers' president, although his career was already in steep decline, and that 70 percent could identify the young UAW president. Only 50 percent could identify the president of the AFL-CIO.[51] Behind the scenes, Meany defeated both men to became the arbiter of labor's postwar policy; in public, he never equaled the ability of men like Lewis and Reuther (or for that matter even Hoffa or Chavez) to establish the terms of political debate.

Yet neither Meany nor Reuther completely lost sight of the other's portion. Reuther's estrangement from the "establishment" and hostility to Meany never pushed him so far as to join the New Left's war on Hubert Humphrey. Nor—within his UAW if not the AFL-CIO—did he neglect the exigencies of practical politics and political organization. For his part, Meany's commitment to the humane values on which the AFL-CIO was founded proved too enduring and sincere for him to see the Federation deteriorate into a mere special interest lobby. In the autumn of 1968 both of labor's national leaders were prepared to play their part in a remarkable common enterprise in democratic civic education.

The occasion was Alabama Governor George Wallace's 1968 pursuit of the presidency. In 1963, Wallace had earned sectional fame—and national notoriety—with an elaborate piece of political theater. The segregationist governor had briefly and symbolically resisted a judicial order to desegregate the University of Alabama, literally standing in the schoolhouse door as the first black students attempted to register. President Kennedy was obliged to federalize the Alabama national guard and force Wallace to stand down. For the governor it was the start of a second political career as a crusader against the federal government.

Wallace's campaign engendered considerable alarm when he proved himself more than a creature of the embittered South. To many liberals, he seemed to be profiting enormously from a racist backlash among white Northern blue-collar workers. Wallace's appeal in such districts was substantially overestimated: much of this kind of political discussion was the work of educated observers who did not actually *know* any working people, but had consumed a steady diet of pontification about "working-class authoritarianism" in the contemporary literature.[52] When Wallace challenged Johnson in the 1964 Wisconsin primary, dubious initial reports of a remarkable performance in Milwaukee's working-class South Side quickly metastasized into a pernicious urban legend among the literati. At the sight of the diehard segregationist governor crossing the industrial North, appealing to "this man in the textile mill, this man in the steel mill, this barber, the beautician, the policeman on the beat," credulous cosmopolitans too readily imagined the Dixie demagogue, exalted on army of Poles from flyover country, to present a serious danger to the Republic.[53]

But behind the smoke there was indeed some fire. Wallace's appearances in Milwaukee's dingy Serb Memorial Hall—where Kennedy had wowed similar crowds of East European "ethnics" in 1960—were political performances of no small art. They became the symbolic foundation of his national campaign. Both in style and substance, Wallace found a certain rapport with blue-collar whites. In the summer of 1968, disturbing signs of Wallace strength among *union* workers began to accumulate. In a series of embarrassing straw polls, several Autoworker and Steelworker locals—affiliates of two international unions especially vocal in their support for civil rights—endorsed Wallace for the presidency. Internal polling caused labor leaders to fear Wallace might capture one-third of the union vote.[54]

Though much estranged from one another, Meany and Reuther shared a common opinion of Wallace. The combative governor threatened to introduce a poisonous politics among American workers—what COPE Director Al Barkan deemed a "Wallace infection." When organized labor had expended so much effort to forge for the American proletariat an ideology both liberal and compatible with American democracy, Meany and Reuther were unwilling to see their working class dissolve into a malicious politics of recrimination. The unions responded with a massive and unprecedented election effort aimed *against* Wallace at least as much *for* Humphrey.

The contest offered a unique pedagogical moment. Wallace presented himself as the embodiment of plebeian resentments, the true friend of white workers. In opposition, Hubert Humphrey, whose name was synonymous with civil rights legislation and liberal anti-communism, was the paradigm of postwar labor's political ideals. Trade unions exerted much effort that fall airing Alabama's social record: right-to-work laws, low wages, high illiteracy, a regressive tax structure. COPE orchestrated the publication of well over a hundred million pieces of literature for the 1968 election, much of it targeted against Wallace. The UAW established a "Wallace desk" and fielded over six hundred full-time staffers to challenge the Southern governor's claim to speak for workers.[55] "He hopes to bring about nationally the kind of brutal and unjust society he promoted when he was governor of Alabama," UAW's *Solidarity* said, reporting the racial segregation and economic underdevelopment of that state. His brand of "law and order" was frankly un-American, UAW reporters argued. "Order prevailed in Stalin's Russia and Hitler's Germany—but at the price of justice."[56]

Meany's attacks on Wallace were uncharacteristically public and voluble, and he did not confine himself to bread-and-butter issues. Wallace, Meany told union members, was "waging a campaign of hate and fear," he "promised the American people a police state," and represented "fascism in America." On "Meet the Press" Meany stated flatly, "we do have some evidence that our people are being deceived by Wallace. Wallace pretends to be one thing, but we know Wallace's record. We know the standard of life in Birmingham, Alabama. We know how the Negro and minority groups live in Alabama. We identify Wallace for what he is. And he is a racist, there is no question about that."[57]

Ultimately, the labor campaign significantly blunted the Wallace vote among union members and reinforced labor's commitment to civil rights. Nowhere outside the South, and certainly not among union members, did a large working-class Wallace vote develop. Outside the South, Wallace garnered the support of less than 10 percent of manual workers, a showing similar to his share of the whole population. In the three-way race Humphrey secured a solid majority of the union vote above the Mason-Dixon line.[58]

Still, organized labor's achievement was in some respects unsatisfying. Richard Nixon, despised by labor, won the presidency—and the questions raised by the Wallace challenge were even more profound and disconcerting than this electoral setback. Despite the conventional wisdom, Wallace was not speaking simply about race. Indeed, he discerned in his first Wisconsin forays that explicit racist and segregationist appeals were not what his chosen Northern audience wanted to hear. "If Wisconsin believes in integration that is Wisconsin's business, not mine. . . . A vote for me in Wisconsin is not a vote for segregation. *It is a vote for the right to run your schools, your business, your lives as you and you alone see fit.*"[59]

Wallace's attack on the federal government was simple and devastating. Tocqueville had argued that the strength of American democracy, the loyalty it commanded of its citizens, proceeded from their sense of ownership or partnership in the polity. Because citizens *directly participated* in the *making* of the laws and rules under which they lived, they felt *obliged* to *honor* them; they loved the government because it was *theirs* in very tangible ways. But such easy identification with their government was no longer tenable; however well-intended, federal programs directed by experts and technocrats were simply not plausible institutions of self-rule. The government, Wallace told America's workers, may have been *progressive,* but it is no longer *yours.* It had been seized by "pointy-headed liberals" and "ivory tower intellectuals" to be employed against you in contemptuous programs of social engineering. Democracy had been leached of the substance of self-rule as federal bureaucrats usurped the powers of communities and even our elected representatives. "The people of this country are simply fed up with the antics of strutting bureaucrats lording it over them . . . telling them that they haven't got sense enough to run their own schools and hospitals and local governments," Wallace told cheering crowds.[60]

Meany and Reuther could not and did not engage Wallace on this territory. They could scare workers with the economic and social consequences of a retreat of the federal government. The dangers were real; few outside the South (and probably few there) wanted an America that looked like Alabama. But they could hardly portray Washington's invasive and multiplying bureaucracies as devices of self-rule. Wallace had gone a long way toward discrediting the idea of government itself in the eyes of working people. He could not take all the credit: the New Left's concern with participatory democracy sprung from much the same analysis, that power concentrated in national institutions tended to squeeze out opportunities for democratic activity. A broad social suspicion of the federal government was being born, one that would be central to the conservative resurgence of the late twentieth century.

But there was a brighter lesson from labor's 1968 crusade, and it was much larger than American workers' rejection of Wallace's racist appeals. On Labor Day 1969, Lane Kirkland—then Secretary-Treasurer of the AFL-CIO—reflected on labor and democracy in light of the recent election.[61]

> During the last election campaign, the double-jointed slogan "participatory democracy" was played up by newcomers to the game as though they had invented the wheel. The wheel, of course, has been around for some time now, and so have all the elements of "participatory democracy." That concept has been brought to its fullest development, over the years, by the trade union movement. . . . Many Americans are not familiar with the involvement of their unions and their members in political education and political action. In the minds of many citizens, unions are associated exclusively with the workplace—factory, store, construction site—where they bargain collectively for their members. This economic role is, of course, the main function of labor unions in representing their members, and through it unions have helped achieve greater security, progress and opportunity for members and their families. That function has served to build a stronger economy and a better country. But to think of unions only in this role is a one-sided view of their place in the American framework. . . . The labor movement takes citizenship most seriously. We believe that the rights and the responsibilities of citizenship are indivisible.

"No single group dedicates more time and effort to engage citizens in the democratic process than the trade union movement," Kirkland continued, reviewing the massive voter registration and get-out-the-vote drives with which labor greeted each election. He noted the year-round activities of trade unions to educate their members about contentious current issues and about the records of their elected officials. He made specific reference to the record-breaking labor efforts during the 1968 election on all these fronts. "The AFL-CIO is proud that its political programs strengthen democracy and its institutions," Kirkland concluded. "To us, this is what 'participatory democracy' means—not just a slogan or a fad, but a way of living and working in a free country where all are equal."

AFTERMATH

Labor and Civic Education
in Lean Times

Our government is not copied from those of our neighbors:
we are an example to them rather than they to us. Our constitution is named a democracy, because it is in the hands
not of the few but of the many. But our laws secure equal
justice for all in their private disputes, and our public opinion welcomes and honors talent in every branch of achievement, not for any sectional reason but on the ground of
excellence alone. . . . In our public acts we keep strictly
within the control of law. We acknowledge the restraint of
reverence; we are obedient to whomever is set in authority,
and to the laws, more especially to those which offer protection to the oppressed. . . . We are alone among mankind in
doing men benefits, not on calculations of self-interest, but
in fearless confidence in freedom. In a word I claim that our
city as a whole is an education to Greece, and that her members yield to none, man by man, for independence of spirit,
many-sidedness of attainment, and complete self-reliance in
limbs and brain.

Funeral Oration of Pericles
Thucydides, *The History of the Peloponnesian War*

With the 1968 election, "history" draws perilously
near "current events." Here my study ends, and America's labor movement entered a new period of lean times whose ultimate end cannot yet be seen. But
it is suitable that I end with a few words bringing the story up to the present.

In 1969, business leaders, politicians, and journalists still saw labor as a
social behemoth whose power shaped the American economy and government more than ever before. Labor leaders themselves understood that union
organizing in private industry had stalled, but felt confident that vast, well-

established trade unions like the Autoworkers, the Steelworkers, the Team-sters—not to say the century-old building trades unions dominating the con-struction industry—had become a permanent feature of the social order. Consequently, the precipitous 1980s decline in union density was greeted with various degrees of shock.

The numbers were indeed disconcerting. In the first decade after World War II, union members made up approximately one-third of the American workforce, almost entirely concentrated in the private sector. About the time the AFL-CIO was born, a steady decline in the share of private-sector work-ers belonging to unions began, but accelerated organizing of public employ-ees masked the magnitude of the problem. Union membership remained at or near a quarter of the American workforce until George Meany's retirement in 1979.

But by then the pace of public sector organizing had slowed, and Meany's much-maligned successor Lane Kirkland inherited a catastrophe. At first, Meany's urbane, cosmopolitan protégé seemed positioned to give the AFL-CIO a fresh political start. If Kirkland honored his mentor's anti-communist principles, he shared neither the plumber's immersion in the culture and val-ues of the American working classes nor his stubborn commitment to ancient feuds. Kirkland not only successfully reunited the house of labor—bringing the Autoworkers, Mineworkers, and Teamsters back into the AFL-CIO—but developed a rapport with the social movement activists powering the New Politics that would have been inconceivable for his bitter predecessor.

On the grander canvas of American political and economic life, these ini-tiatives proved of small account. The 1980s were a disaster for organized la-bor, the worst decade trade unions had experienced since the 1920s. Newly elected President Ronald Reagan, a former president of the Screen Actors Guild, may have been the first union leader to reach the White House, but he set the tone for the decade by firing the striking air traffic controllers and de-certifying their union. Corporations already exporting Rust Belt manufactur-ing jobs overseas, outsourcing them to right-to-work states, or automating them out of existence were inspired to adopt a harder line against union bar-gaining demands and organizing efforts.

The magnitude of damage suffered during labor's lost decade soon be-came depressingly clear. In the course of the 1980s, union membership in the private economy plummeted from 20 percent to a dismal 12 percent. Where in 1980 over fifteen million private sector workers belonged to labor unions, by 1990 barely ten million did. The totemic "golden age" industrial unions were especially badly hit. The sprawling Teamsters, briefly two million strong during their exile from the AFL-CIO, lost nearly one third of their membership between 1979 and 1993; the Steelworkers and Autoworkers, each reporting well over one million members in the 1970s, lost fully half their members over the same period. The venerable building trades unions fared only moderately better, enduring stagnant or declining membership rolls in a growing construction market.[1]

These steep losses naturally took their toll on labor's political and economic influence. As work was outsourced or captured by open-shop competitors, pattern bargaining eroded. Employers showed a new willingness to break strikes by hiring replacements; using unsavory tactics to defeat union organizing efforts ceased to be the mark of the industrial outlaw and became almost customary personnel practice. Politicians were emboldened to confront the AFL-CIO on even vital organizational interests, culminating in the 1993 approval of the North American Free Trade Agreement (NAFTA), the first in a series of American initiatives to liberalize global trade. Whatever the economic merits of these global free trade pacts, they necessarily infringed on the practice of self-rule, lifting important economic decisions beyond the reach of democratic institutions and bestowing them on unelected transnational bodies for arbitration. They also—lacking any serious labor standards—promised to speed the export of relatively high-paying American jobs. By 1995, only one in ten American workers outside of government still enjoyed the benefits of union membership. In that year Kirkland resigned under pressure, and an energetic new leadership under John Sweeney stepped up to take his place.

Social commentators who took the industrial relations exemplified by labor's "golden age" as their point of reference have been quick to interpret these troubles as a sign that the labor movement is on its deathbed. Those with a longer historical view will be less inclined to make rash predictions. The combination of circumstances which forged that "golden age"—remarkable economic growth and a prosperous working class; a relatively solicitous government, protective of workers' rights; an employing class largely respectful of the rule of law; high union membership and prestige in the society at large—may have been unique in American history. True, today our nation's trade unions find themselves representing only a modest segment of the American workforce, facing hostile employers willing to use illegal means to thwart organizing efforts, receiving little or no help from a cold and indifferent government. But this is not to say the American labor movement is spent—only that today's labor movement finds itself in the world before the New Deal.

Sweeney emerged from the Service Employees International Union (SEIU), one of a handful of labor unions that has successfully adapted to the new environment. Once a venerable but not especially influential AFL building janitors' union, under Sweeney's leadership the SEIU nearly doubled in size to represent over one million workers. The growth was a product of carefully structured and highly visible organizing initiatives combined with strategic mergers, a formula continued with great success by Sweeney's successor Andrew Stern. No longer merely a janitors' union, the SEIU has successfully positioned itself as the leading union of healthcare workers. With over 1.5 million members in 2004, the Service Employees have become the largest and most influential labor union in the United States: an influence born of patient planning, organizing achievements, and not least to a skillful use of the mass media to educate the public about trade unionism and the issues of low-income workers.

Such issues have acquired an unhappy new salience, for now—as before the New Deal—our nation is home to a burgeoning class of working poor. By 1945, trade unions had done their job so well it seemed that America's working families could take a middle-class lifestyle for granted. The anti-poverty crusaders of the 1960s targeted their good deeds and government programs not at working people but at the chronically unemployed of Appalachia and the inner city. But the thinning ranks of well-paying industrial manufacturing jobs and the policy choices of welfare reform have conspired to restore the proletarian face of American poverty. At the beginning of the new millennium, perhaps one in four U.S. workers earned a wage inadequate to lift a family above the poverty line, a moral scandal that mocks the work ethic and dishonors the laborer. Writer Barbara Ehrenreich's modern Nellie Bly turn, working as a maid, waitress and Wal-mart "associate," and trying to live on the resultant salaries, has created a minor sensation and helped make this social catastrophe front-page news.[2]

These unfortunate social and economic shifts have increasingly strained America's working families, but they have also restored a certain moral authority that the labor movement has not enjoyed since the 1940s. For a half century after World War II, critics successfully dominated public discourse about trade unions with peripheral (although significant) phenomena portraying a labor movement in decadence. Teamster corruption, construction union featherbedding, autoworker absenteeism, and overpaid Air Traffic Controllers filled conversations and newspapers.

But with the elimination of welfare, poverty has become the lot of a significant slice of our nation's workforce, and this discourse has changed. If there is one economic principle on which Americans can agree, it is that the laborer is worth his wages; no man or woman working full-time should live in poverty. This is no novel discovery: the mineworker, garment worker, and cigar worker unions at the turn of the last century sought no elaborate fringe benefits but simple justice. Workers deserved better than a grinding want dictated by an uncaring market—they deserved a wage allowing them to live in dignity. Today, unions like the Laborers (LIUNA), Hotel Workers (HERE, which recently merged with the garment workers), and Service Employees have recaptured that commanding moral position held by their forebears. For the building construction laborers, hotel housekeepers, and nursing home workers whom they organize and represent, a union contract is typically the difference between a poverty wage and a living wage.

These unions struggle against tough odds. After a few decades of uncharacteristic compliance with the letter (if not necessarily the spirit) of the Wagner Act, large numbers of American employers have reverted to a more historically familiar attitude toward organized labor. The campaign of massive resistance against the NLRB and the whole Wagner system that John Lewis had advocated has at last materialized—initiated by management, not unions. Belatedly appreciating that NLRB justice is excruciatingly slow and the penalty for unfair labor practices negligible, employers have indulged a campaign of lawlessness in dimensions not seen since the Liberty League incited such rebellion in the 1930s. If management no longer has easy recourse to the gun and the truncheon, the culture of impunity that characterizes today's workplace gives them weapons enough to suppress many a budding organizing campaign. Every year tens of thousands of workers face illegal reprisals for attempting to exercise their right to organize. Cynical employers reason that an unlawful firing or two can often cow the remainder of their workforce, and that by the time the victim secures redress the organizing campaign will have been broken.[3]

The most ecstatic Wobbly, the most committed Stalinist, the most cartoonish Teamster Business Agent would have been hard-pressed to imitate such contempt for the rule of law. It is certainly beyond the ken of the ordinary trade union activists, who find themselves bound by the obligations of the National Labor Relations Act while receiving few of its protections. They are denied the secondary boycott, the jurisdictional strike, and the sit-down, but left without a functional alternative.

The manifest disappointments of the National Labor Relations Act have led our nation's unions toward a modest rediscovery of voluntarist organizing traditions—traditions that relied more on labor's own resources and less on the unreliable favors of the government. They have increasingly turned away from a cumbersome NLRB election process that employers have learned to delay and manipulate against their workers. Instead, they often use innovative community organizing techniques and "corporate campaigns" targeting employers' multifarious business interests, using these levers to pressure management to sign neutrality agreements with "card check" provisions. Employers signing neutrality agreements pledge to allow their workers to exercise their right to organize without coercion or interference; "card check" is an alternative certification process by which unions secure recognition when a majority of workers sign authorization cards. In a rich irony, while the business community has done its level best to undermine and subvert the NLRB election process, its public policy flacks scold unions that pursue corporate campaigns and card check for disrespecting the secret ballot and coercively "organizing the employer" instead of organizing the workers.[4]

These techniques have proved necessary for unions merely to hold their own. John Sweeney inspired the AFL-CIO and many of its trade union affiliates to pour unprecedented quantities of money, time, and effort into organizing the unorganized, and the cascading membership losses of the 1980s slowed to a trickle. But in the face of hostile employers and an indifferent government, it has been all labor can do to organize enough new members to replace those who continue to be automated or outsourced out of their jobs in traditionally organized sectors like manufacturing, transportation, and telecommunications. Yet if the AFL-CIO under John Sweeney's leadership has struggled to maintain its numbers, this has made labor's electoral achievements even more remarkable. For over the past decade American trade unions—even in their diminished form—have transformed American electoral politics in a healthier and more democratic direction.

Back in the late 1960s and the early 1970s the progressive activists behind the New Politics had advanced a series of political "reforms"—especially the replacement of party caucuses with primary elections for candidate nominations—designed to reduce the power of "party bosses" and open the political process to new currents. While the UAW, American Federation of State, County, and Municipal Employees (AFSCME), and likeminded progressive unions endorsed the changes, George Meany and his peers, with sound reason, suspected these innovations.[5] The old system favored those who could mobilize thousands of activists to walk precincts and millions of voters to turn out at the polls. It worked to the benefit of blue-collar organizations like the labor unions and urban party machines that were rich in "people power" but relatively cash-poor.

The new system, which required candidates to appeal directly to primary voters through expensive mass media campaigns, placed a premium on campaign contributions. It boosted the prospects of everyone who commanded more money than grassroots support, to the benefit of the middle-class activists who powered the New Politics, and even more, to the business classes and multiplying corporate PACs. As an unhappy byproduct, the evolving political ecology also helped depress voter participation. The ad consultants now directing campaigns discovered that the electronic media were not very helpful for recruiting new supporters but good attack ads were a very effective tool for discrediting opponents and discouraging their admirers from coming to the polls. By 1996 electoral participation in the presidential election slumped below 50 percent, a level of civic disengagement not seen since before the New Deal.

The AFL-CIO and its affiliated unions have struggled to keep pace with the escalating arms race of financial contributions and big media buys, and one of the Sweeney administration's first major initiatives was a multi-million dollar advertising campaign meant to shape priorities in the 1996 election campaign. But trade union activists understood that a competition for campaign cash was one they could not win. AFL-CIO Political Director Steve Rosenthal began retooling the Federation's political operations in order to maximize labor's traditional strengths in the new environment.[6]

Dismissing the "checkbook politics" of campaign contributions and the media "air war" they made possible, trade unionists concentrated on rebuilding the labor's "ground war" machinery. A painstaking effort followed to recruit tens of thousands of trade union activists who would walk precincts and man telephones to talk to fellow union members about the election. Curiously, so dismal by then were rates of electoral participation—only 36 percent of American adults went to the polls in the off-year elections of 1998—anyone who could actually do effective GOTV (or "get out the vote") work among their constituents was rewarded with a disproportionate political impact. The labor-to-labor outreach directed by national, state, and local labor federations was widely credited with increasing union household voters as a share of the electorate even as total union membership continued to stagnate or ebb. In 1998, the Democrats, largely on the strength of the labor effort, enjoyed unexpected success in the House elections. In 2000, labor GOTV helped Vice President Al Gore—though down in the polls on election eve—picked up a popular vote victory over Texas Governor George W. Bush and very nearly captured the White House.

The outcome sent a shudder through the Republican Party, which realized that this was a different political world than the one they knew, and that they could no longer neglect their own "ground game." The 2000 cliffhanger persuaded both parties and their adherents to redouble efforts to recruit and mobilize new voters. The labor unions were now joined both by political parties and the new "527" organizations—named after the provision of the tax code under which they formed—in a massive effort to draw the apathetic and the alienated back into civic engagement on election day. (Rosenthal had by this time left the AFL-CIO to direct the most prominent of the liberal 527s, ACT or America Coming Together.)[7]

The result was a historic leap in civic participation. With nearly 60 percent of voting-age Americans casting a ballot—an almost unprecedented net gain of fifteen million voters over the Bush-Gore race—the nation witnessed rates of electoral participation unseen since the dramatic 1968 contest.[8] If the defeat was crushing for the unions and their Democratic allies, they may be permitted to take small comfort in this remarkably effective extension of the franchise. Even in defeat, our labor movement continues to transform American politics in more democratic directions. If we may credit the boast of Pericles that his city of Athens was an education in self-rule and civic virtue for all of Greece, we must acknowledge the House of Labor as a "school of democracy" from which our nation is still learning.

NOTES

Introduction

1. See Milton Friedman's classic *Capitalism and Freedom* (Chicago: University of Chicago Press, 1962). Partisan explications of these ideas focused explicitly on labor include Morgan O. Reynolds, *Power and Privilege: Labor Unions in America* (New York: Universe, 1984), and Howard Dickman, *Industrial Democracy in America* (LaSalle: Open Court, 1987). A lively if hysterical account of the right's political case against trade unions can be found in Linda Chavez and Daniel Gray, *Betrayal: How Union Bosses Shake Down Their Members and Corrupt American Politics* (New York: Crown Forum, 2004).

2. Although the disappointment with "business unionism" permeates modern American labor history, James R. Green's *The World of the Worker: Labor in Twentieth-Century America* (New York: Hill and Wang, 1980) stands out as an exciting and comprehensive labor history survey from this point of view. Other sharp polemical expressions include Kim Moody, *An Injury to All: The Decline of American Unionism* (New York: Verso, 1988), and Paul Buhle, *Taking Care of Business: Samuel Gompers, George Meany, Lane Kirkland, and the Tragedy of American Labor* (New York: Monthly Review, 1999).

3. For a good discussion of Athenian democracy, see M. I. Finley, *Democracy Ancient and Modern* (New Brunswick, NJ: Rutgers University Press, 1985).

4. Aristotle, *The Politics of Aristotle* (London: Oxford, 1973), 1275a, 1277b; Aristotle, *Nicomachean Ethics* (New York: Bobbs-Merrill, 1962), 1099b.

5. Aristotle, *Politics,* 1252–1255.

6. Aristotle, *Politics,* 1337b. See also 1277.

7. Aristotle, *Politics,* 1257–1258, 1319a, 1337b.

8. Aristotle, *Politics,* 1292b, 1318b–1320a.

9. Hannah Arendt, a close scholar of the classical writers, made this a major theme of her study *On Revolution* (New York: Viking, 1963).

10. Aristotle, *Politics,* 1292a, 1279b–1280a; see also Plato, *The Republic,* 565–566.

11. American political leaders of the founding generation drew their arguments from a variety of ancient sources, of which the Roman historians were perhaps the most prominent. See Charles F. Mullett, "Classical Influences on the American Revolution," *Classical Journal* 35 (1939–40): 92–104; Richard M. Gummere, *The American Colonial Mind and the Classical Tradition* (Cambridge: Harvard University Press, 1963), esp. 173–90; and Meyer Reinhold, *Classica Americana: The Greek and Roman Heritage in the United States* (Detroit: Wayne State University Press, 1984), 94–115.

12. P. A. Brunt, *Social Conflicts in the Roman Republic* (New York: W. W. Norton, 1971), 13–19, 74–100, 139–42; R. H. Barrow, *The Romans* (London: Penguin, 1949), 40, 54–55;

234
Notes to Pages 6–16

Sallust, *The War with Jurgutha,* trans. J. C. Rolfe (Cambridge: Harvard University Press, 1921), 86: 2–4; Juvenal, *Satire X:* 80.

13. John Locke, *Second Treatise of Government,* para. 4, in *Two Treatises of Government,* by John Locke (Cambridge: Cambridge University Press, 1988).

14. Ibid., 34.

15. Ibid., 27, 34.

16. Ibid., 22, 87, 95, 123–24.

17. For a similar view of Jefferson's project, see Garrett Ward Sheldon, *The Political Philosophy of Thomas Jefferson* (Baltimore: Johns Hopkins University Press, 1991).

18. Alexander Hamilton, John Jay, and James Madison, *The Federalist* (New York: Modern Library, 1937). See especially Federalist Paper # 63, pp. 407–16.

19. Jefferson, "To Joseph Cabell," 2 Feb. 1816, in Thomas Jefferson, *Writings* (New York: Library of America, 1984), 1380.

20. Thomas Jefferson, *Notes on the State of Virginia* (New York: Penguin, 1999), 170–71.

21. Ibid., 168–79.

22. Alexis de Tocqueville, *Democracy in America* (New York: Harper Collins, 1969), 705. Conversely his unfinished *The Old Regime and the French Revolution* (New York: Doubleday, 1955) examined why the French revolution failed to produce healthy democratic institutions. For an excellent brief study see Richard Herr, *Tocqueville and the Old Regime* (Princeton: Princeton University Press, 1962).

23. Tocqueville, *Democracy in America,* 243.

24. Ibid., 93–95, 240–41.

25. Ibid., 70, 189, 274, 515, 521, 522.

26. Ibid., 55–56, 435.

27. Adam Smith, *An Inquiry into the Nature and Causes of the Wealth of Nations* (Indianapolis: Liberty Fund, 1981), 13–15.

28. Tocqueville, *Democracy in America,* 555–56.

29. This understanding that the emerging modern division of labor degraded the worker's physical and intellectual virtues has largely disappeared from our discourse—more, I suspect, because it is too depressing to think about than because of any great disconfirming evidence. But it was widely acknowledged by observers of the industrial revolution across the political spectrum. See Smith, *Wealth of Nations,* 781–82; Karl Marx, *Capital* (New York: Kerr, 1906), 1:708–9; John Ruskin, *The Stones of Venice,* in *Selected Writings* (London: Penguin, 1991), 283.

30. Tocqueville, *Democracy in America,* 72, 96, 189; see also Tocqueville, *Old Regime and the French Revolution,* 69–70.

31. Tocqueville, *Democracy in America,* 694.

32. See Drew R. McCoy, *The Elusive Republic: Political Economy in Jeffersonian America* (Chapel Hill: University of North Carolina Press, 1980); and Marvin Meyers, *The Jacksonian Persuasion: Politics and Belief* (Stanford: Stanford University Press, 1957).

33. George Fitzhugh, *Cannibals All! Or, Slaves without Masters* (1856; Cambridge: Harvard University Press, 1960), 16–17, 69.

34. Abraham Lincoln, "Address to the Wisconsin State Agricultural Society," in *Selected Speeches and Writings* (New York: Vintage, 1992), 234–35.

35. "The prudent, penniless beginner in the world, labors for wages awhile, saves a surplus with which to buy tools or land, for himself; then labors on his own account another while, and at length hires another new beginner to help him. This, say its advocates, is *free*

labor—the just and generous, and prosperous system, which opens the way for all." Lincoln, *Selected Speeches and Writings*, 234.

36. Matthew 7:1–5: "Stop judging, that you may not be judged. For as you judge, so will you be judged, and the measure with which you measure will be measured out to you. Why do you notice the splinter in your brother's eye, but do not perceive the wooden beam in your own eye? How can you say to your brother, 'Let me remove that splinter from your eye,' while the wooden beam is in your eye? You hypocrite, remove the wooden beam from your own eye first; then you will see clearly to remove the splinter from your brother's eye." See also Romans 2:1: "Therefore, you are without excuse, every one of you who passes judgment. For by the standard by which you judge another you condemn yourself, since you, the judge, do the very same things."

37. Lincoln, "Message to Congress in Special Session," 4 July 1861, in *Selected Speeches and Writings*, 311–12.

38. Clinton S. Golden and Harold J. Ruttenberg, *The Dynamics of Industrial Democracy* (New York: Harper and Brothers, 1942); Mancur Olson, *The Logic of Collective Action* (Cambridge: Harvard University Press, 1965); Albert O. Hirschman, *Exit, Voice, and Loyalty* (Cambridge: Harvard University Press, 1970).

1. Schools of Democracy and Independence

1. Daniel Nelson, *Managers and Workers: Origins of the New Factory System in the United States, 1880–1920* (Madison: University of Wisconsin Press, 1975), 4; Thomas C. Cochran and William Miller, *The Age of Enterprise: A Social History of Industrial America* (New York: Harper and Row, 1942), 130–37.

2. Sean Dennis Cashman, *America in the Gilded Age* (New York: New York University Press, 1984), 34–45.

3. Cited in Eric F. Goldman, *Rendezvous with Destiny: A History of American Reform* (New York: Vintage, 1955), 3.

4. For general discussions of these themes, see John Higham's study of American nativism, *Strangers in the Land: Patterns of American Nativism, 1860–1925* (New Brunswick, NJ: Rutgers University Press, 1988), esp. 52–63, 77–96; and Maldwyn Allen Jones's examination of the demand for immigration restriction in *American Immigration* (Chicago: University of Chicago Press, 1992), 212–31.

5. But John Buenker provides convincing evidence that—against the assumptions of both progressive reformers and old-fashioned republicans—the urban political machines, rooted as they were in the working class immigrants and ethnics, were the seedbed of many critical industrial era reforms. John Buenker, *Urban Liberalism and Progressive Reform* (New York Charles Scribner, 1973).

6. Melvyn Dubofsky and Foster Rhea Dulles. *Labor in America: A History* (Arlington Heights, IL: Harlan Davidson, 1984), 108–19; Philip S. Foner, *The Great Labor Uprising of 1877* (New York: Monad, 1977); Harold Livesay, *Samuel Gompers and Organized Labor in America* (Boston: Little, Brown, 1978), 24–27.

7. Leon Fink, *Workingmen's Democracy: The Knights of Labor and American Politics* (Urbana: University of Illinois Press, 1983); Kim Voss, *The Making of American Exceptionalism: The Knights of Labor and Class Formation in the Nineteenth Century* (Ithaca, NY: Cornell University Press, 1993); Paul Buhle, *Marxism in the United States* (New York: Verso, 1987), 71–79.

8. George McNeill, "The Problem of To-Day," in *The Labor Movement: The Problem of To-Day*, ed. McNeill (Boston: Bridgman, 1887), 456.

9. Ibid., 466. My italics.

10. Ibid., 455, 459.

11. Texts are from the Knights' initiation ceremony as recorded by Terence V. Powderly, national leader of the Knights during the height of their influence. Powderly, *The Path I Trod* (New York: Columbia University Press, 1940), 47–51. See also Gerald N. Grob, *Workers and Utopia: A Study of Ideological Conflict in the Labor Movement, 1865–1900* (Chicago: Quadrangle, 1961), 38–40, 52; Fink, *Workingmen's Democracy*, 9.

12. For example, McNeill, "The Problem To-Day," 461: "It is war, and cries of 'peace, peace' when there is no peace, will only lull the thoughtless into treacherous sleep," following Patrick Henry's stirring statement, "It is in vain, sir, to extenuate the matter. Gentlemen may cry, Peace, Peace—but there is no peace. The war is actually begun!" For original see Jer 6:14, 8:11.

13. Eric Foner, *Free Soil, Free Labor, Free Men: The Ideology of the Republican Party before the Civil War* (Oxford: Oxford University Press, 1970), 69–72, 87–101.

14. Powderly, *The Path I Trod*, 64, 268–69.

15. Grob, *Workers and Utopia*, 43–48, 99–100.

16. Powderly, *The Path I Trod*, 61–62.

17. Cited in Grob, *Workers and Utopia*, 72.

18. Powderly inexplicably concluded that Gould was "pleasant, outspoken and exceedingly candid" and that he "was in earnest when he said that it was his ambition to found a great system of railroads and leave it as a heritage to the American people." He was uncertain whether to credit reports of Gould's dishonest business dealings because, after all, "the testimony on which he has been judged came largely from the lips of men who engaged in playing the game with him and lost." Powderly, *The Path I Trod*, 104–39.

19. Ibid., 120, 270.

20. See Emile Durkheim, *The Division of Labor in Society* (New York: Free Press, 1984), 84, 149–50.

21. Samuel Gompers, more sensitive to this than the socialist intellectuals with which he later sparred, considered that felt identity or mechanical solidarity far more central to the labor movement than class consciousness. "For class consciousness was a mental process shared by all who had imagination, but that primitive force that had its origin in experience only was *Klassengefuhl* (class feeling). This group feeling is one of the strongest cohesive forces in the labor movement." Samuel Gompers, *Seventy Years of Life and Labor: An Autobiography*, ed. Nick Salvatore (Ithaca, NY: Cornell University Press, 1984), 114.

22. Ibid., 115.

23. For a similar view of wage labor and citizenship—though not the AFL—see Christopher Lasch, *The True and Only Heaven: Progress and Its Critics* (New York: W. W. Norton, 1991).

24. Aristotle, *Politics*, 1253–1254.

25. Each guild, composed of those who had mastered that craft or "mystery," held its skills as collective property, controlling both standards and initiation of new members through a system of apprenticeship. Perhaps not coincidentally, the guilds sustained a set of democratic institutions in otherwise feudal societies, in which the assembled masters comprised a legislature governing the craft. For more information, see the famous treatment by social-democratic historian Georges Renard popularized by GDH Cole and the "guild socialists." Renard, *Guilds in the Middle Ages* (London: Bell and Sons, 1918).

26. John R. Commons, "American Shoemakers, 1648 to 1895," in *Labor and Administration* (New York: Sentry, 1913), 219–66; Melvyn Dubofsky, *The State and Labor in Modern America* (Chapel Hill: University of North Carolina Press, 1994), 21–29; Edward Pessen, "Builders of the Young Republic," 46–54, in *A History of the American Worker*, ed. Richard B. Morris (Princeton, NJ: Princeton University Press, 1983). The conspiracy cases—both their extent and their effect on labor—are among the most controversial subjects in labor history. Some prominent treatments include Karen Orren, *Belated Feudalism* (Cambridge: Cambridge University Press, 1991); Victoria Hattam, *Labor Visions and State Power* (Princeton, NJ: Princeton University Press, 1993); William E. Forbath, *Law and the Shaping of the American Labor Movement* (Cambridge: Harvard University Press, 1989); and Anthony Woodiwiss, *Rights v. Conspiracy* (New York: St. Martin's Press, 1970).

27. See Lloyd Ulman, *The Rise of the National Trade Union* (Cambridge: Harvard University Press, 1966), esp. 64–67, 303–18.

28. *Constitution and Rules of Order of the International Union of Bricklayers* (New York: William F. Jones, 1867); *Proceedings of the 12th Annual Session of the National Typographical Union* (Detroit, 1864).

29. Albert O. Hirschman, *Exit, Voice, and Loyalty: Responses to Decline in Firms, Organizations, and States* (Cambridge: Harvard University Press, 1970); Lincoln, "Message to Congress," in *Selected Speeches and Writings*, 311–12.

30. For example, Selig Perlman, *A Theory of the Labor Movement* (New York: Kelley, 1928), 162–65.

31. Jack London, in *Jack London: American Rebel* (New York: Citadel, 1947), 57–58. Pioneer industrial relations scholar Robert Hoxie, while deploring violence against strikebreakers, similarly explained union reactions to them in terms of trade union sovereignty and legitimate authority. After a union of workers have through combined effort established "definite rules of the industrial game," Hoxie explained, "Now comes the 'scab.' He has not sacrificed to establish the rules and now he violates them for his own selfish advantage and undoes the painfully established results for which the unionists have sacrificed in the interest of the common good. He is necessarily, from their point of view—the group viewpoint—antisocial, and must be restrained just as the thief is restrained by society." Robert F. Hoxie, *Trade Unionism in the United States* (1923; New York: Russell & Russell, 1966), 16.

32. Boycotts were indeed seen as a means of "redeeming the republic" from the "money-power." See Forbath, *Law and the Shaping of the American Labor Movement*, 84.

33. See Seymour Martin Lipset, Martin A. Trow, and James S. Coleman, *Union Democracy: The Internal Politics of the International Typographical Union* (Glencoe, IL: Free Press, 1956). It is often noted that labor faces a distinct disadvantage in negotiations with capital on the grounds that its commodity is perishable while capital's is not. The ITU, with much of its strength in the newspaper industry, dealt with employers who were under the same constraints to sell their product on a daily basis as workers were to sell their labor.

34. Building trades unions in many major cities essentially dictated work rules rather than bargaining them as late as the 1930s. William Haber, *Industrial Relations in the Building Industry* (Cambridge: Harvard University Press, 1930), 512–13.

35. David Montgomery, *Workers' Control in America: Studies in the History of Work, Technology, and Labor Struggles* (Cambridge: Cambridge University Press, 1979), 11–15.

36. Paul Buhle, *Taking Care of Business: Samuel Gompers, George Meany, Lane Kirkland, and the Tragedy of American Labor* (New York: Monthly Review Press, 1999), 45.

37. Gompers, *Seventy Years of Life and Labor*, 12.

38. Michael Rogin, "Voluntarism: The Political Functions of an Antipolitical Doctrine," *Industrial and Labor Relations Review* 15 (1962): 521–35. Curiously, although the IWW also shunned the state as an engine for labor emancipation, no one suggests that the IWW was anti-political.

39. While his trade union colleagues often adopted a paternalistic attitude toward women workers, Gompers, a feminist, supported women's suffrage and opposed state regulation of women's wages and working conditions. Livesay, *Samuel Gompers and Organized Labor,* 134; Gompers, *Seventy Years of Life and Labor,* 126–29.

40. For the best discussion of the firm as political association rather than contractual association, see Philip Selznick, *Law, Society, and Industrial Justice* (Berkeley: Russell Sage, 1969), esp. 52–72.

41. Samuel Gompers, "What Does Labor Want?" in *The Samuel Gompers Papers,* ed. Stuart B. Kaufman and Peter J. Albert (Urbana: University of Illinois Press, 1986), 3:390–92.

42. Gompers, in *Report of Proceedings of the Annual Convention of the American Federation of Labor 1894,* 14.

43. *American Federationist* (1917): 46. Tocqueville had observed that civil and political associations were "free schools" in which citizens learned the habits and practices of self-rule (Tocqueville, *Democracy in America,* 520–22). Though the similarity between Gompers' remarks on the trade unions and Tocqueville's remarks on civil associations is eerie, his use of this idea was not unique in early American trade union circles—as well we might expect, both because Americans persisted in the high value they assigned to civic education and because socialists often regarded trade unions as "schools" in which workers received a political education. Peter J. McGuire—the socialist leader of the Brotherhood of Carpenters and Joiners and a close Gompers comrade who helped launch the AFL—called the trade union movement a "great democratic training school." See Robert A. Christie, *Empire in Wood: A History of the Carpenters' Union* (Ithaca, NY: Cornell University Press, 1956), 36.

44. Gompers, *Seventy Years of Life and Labor,* 53. Gompers' basic point that trade unions were schools in which workers acquired the civic skills and opportunities they needed to be participating citizens is today fairly well established by empirical research. See Sidney Verba, Kay Lehman Schlozman, and Henry E. Brady, *Voice and Equality: Civic Voluntarism in American Politics* (Cambridge: Harvard University Press, 1995), esp. 384–88, 520–21.

45. Samuel Gompers, "The Advantages of High Dues," *American Federationist* (February 1915): , 112–13.

46. Hirschman, *Exit, Voice, and Loyalty,* 92–97.

47. Gompers, *Seventy Years of Life and Labor,* 40, 54.

48. Gompers, "Advantages of High Dues," 112; *Seventy Years of Life and Labor,* 54.

49. Gompers, *Seventy Years of Life and Labor,* 86.

50. The practical ability of the international to implement these goals can easily be exaggerated, however; see for instance Ulman, *Rise of the National Trade Union,* 169–73.

51. Samuel Gompers, "To Organize Unskilled Labor," *American Federationist* (February 1897): 257.

52. Gompers, *Seventy Years of Life and Labor,* 48.

53. Ibid., 153–54.

54. Werner Sombart, *Why Is There No Socialism in the United States?* (1906; White Plains, NY: International Arts and Sciences, 1976); David Montgomery, *The Fall of the House of Labor* (Cambridge: Cambridge University Press, 1987), 6; Victoria C. Hattam, *Labor Visions and State Power: The Origins of Business Unionism in the United States* (Princeton, NJ: Princeton Univer-

sity Press, 1993); Aristide R. Zolberg, "How Many Exceptionalisms?" in *Working-Class Formation: Nineteenth-Century Patterns in Western Europe and the United States,* ed. Ira Katznelson and Aristide R. Zolberg (Princeton, NJ: Princeton University Press, 1986), 397–455; Philip Taft, "Theories of the Labor Movement," in *Interpreting the Labor Movement,* ed. George W. Brooks, Milton Derber, David A. McCabe, and Philip Taft (Champaign: IRRA, 1952), 38.

55. Gompers, *Seventy Years of Life and Labor,* 27, 94. The most thorough account of Gompers' encounter with Marxism and socialism generally is that of Stuart Bruce Kaufman, *Samuel Gompers and the Origins of the American Federation of Labor, 1848–1896* (Westport, CT: Greenwood, 1973). Marx's influence on the AFL president's thought is generally underappreciated, and his interesting and original attempts to interpret Marxist ideas in an American setting have been neglected by almost all other authors. For these reasons Kaufman's theses are particularly interesting and provocative. That said, any presentation of Gompers as scientific socialist must ultimately rely—as does Kaufman's—mainly on his early experiences in the small, parochial political culture of American trade union disciples of Marx and LaSalle. By the time socialism acquired an American character and significant domestic following, and Gompers became a figure of national significance, the two were thoroughly estranged. Kaufman, *Samuel Gompers and the Origins of the American Federation of Labor, 1848–1896* (Westport, CT: Greenwood, 1973).

56. Gompers, *Seventy Years of Life and Labor,* 66, 115; AFL, *Report of Proceedings of the Annual Convention of the American Federation of Labor,* 1894, 14.

57. Gompers, *Seventy Years of Life and Labor,* 34–35. Gompers, probably intentionally, had invoked George Washington's Farewell Address—in which he warned that "entangling alliances" with foreign powers would endanger America's democratic republic.

58. Or as Selig Perlman pointedly remarked, "The American movement, led by leaders risen from the ranks, could withstand the political temptation with so much greater ease than the European movements, because it saw little to choose between an autocratic capitalist management of industry and a bureaucratic one by 'experts' appointed by the state." Gompers, *Seventy Years of Life and Labor,* 43; Perlman, *Theory of the Labor Movement,* 202.

59. Matthew Woll, "Stand By Your Principles," *American Federationist* (February 1919):, 150.

60. "American labor remains the most heterogeneous laboring class in existence—ethnically, linguistically, religiously, and culturally," Selig Perlman observed. "With a working class of such composition, to make socialism or communism the official 'ism' of the movement, would mean, even if other conditions permitted it, deliberately driving the Catholics, who are perhaps in the majority in the American Federation of Labor, out of the labor movement, since with them an irreconcilable opposition to socialism is a matter of religious principle. Consequently the only acceptable 'consciousness' for American labor as a whole is a 'job consciousness' with a 'limited' objective of 'wage and job control.'" Philip Taft later struck a similar note observing that "such a philosophy is not as ostentatious and lacks the architectonic grandeur of a philosophical system such as Marxism. This perhaps makes American trade unionism less attractive to those who enjoy the aesthetic experience of beholding a beautiful intellectual system. However, the absence of these qualities helps to make the American movement more democratic, tolerant, and flexible." Perlman, *Theory of the Labor Movement,* 168–69; Philip Taft, "Theories of the Labor Movement," 38.

61. In their admirably thorough catalogue of American labor violence, Philip Taft and Philip Ross conclude that "the United States has experienced more frequent and bloody labor violence than any other industrial nation." Taft and Ross, "American Labor Violence: Its

Causes, Character, and Outcome," in *The History of Violence in America,* ed. Hugh Davis Graham and Ted Robert Gurr (New York: Bantam, 1969), 380. See also Montgomery, *Workers' Control in America,* 15–26; and Perlman, *Theory of the Labor Movement,* 274.

62. Gompers, *Seventy Years of Life and Labor,* 102, 106, 138, 162, and Philip Taft, *The AFL in the Time of Gompers* (New York: Octagon, 1970), 72, 335–40.

63. Morris Hillquit, Samuel Gompers, and Max Hayes, *The Double Edge of Labor's Sword* (Chicago: Socialist Party, 1914), 126–27. My italics.

64. Taft, *AFL in the Time of Gompers,* 68–69

65. *AFL Convention Proceedings,* 1890, 22; see also Gompers, *Seventy Years of Life and Labor,* 114–15.

66. Cited in Taft, *AFL in the Time of Gompers,* 364.

67. Selznick, *Law, Society, and Industrial Justice,* 122–37.

68. Some, like Gwendolyn Mink in *Old Labor and New Immigrants in American Political Development: Union, Party, and State, 1875–1920* (Ithaca, NY: Cornell University Press, 1986), argue that the AFL endorsement of immigration restrictions give the lie to this. But as a tenet of democratic theory, the scope of government is a matter concerning the relationship between citizens and their government, not their government's relationship with foreigners.

69. Gompers, "Freedom Must Not Be Surrendered," *American Federationist* (January 1917): , 46.

70. Gompers, *Report of Proceedings of the Annual Convention of the American Federation of Labor,* 1899, 15.

71. Hillquit, Gompers, and Hayes, *The Double Edge of Labor's Sword,* 89–90. Recall that the craft unions tried to enforce closed shop conditions; by *coercion* Gompers means merely the violent power that is the legitimate monopoly of the state.

72. Gompers, *Seventy Years of Life and Labor,* 104.

73. Dubofsky and Dulles, *Labor in America,* 152–53.

74. Hillquit, Gompers, and Hayes, *The Double Edge of Labor's Sword,* 89–91.

75. *AFL Proceedings,* 1893, 12.

76. Livesay, *Samuel Gompers and Organized Labor,* 114; Dubofsky and Dulles, *Labor in America,* 154.

77. Gompers, *Seventy Years of Life and Labor,* 154; Montgomery, *Workers' Control in America,* 11–13, and *Fall of the House of Labor,* 35.

78. Cited in Paul Krause, *The Battle for Homestead, 1880–1892: Politics, Culture, and Steel* (Pittsburgh: University of Pittsburgh Press, 1992), 294.

79. Krause, *Battle for Homestead,* 294.

80. Gompers cited in Dubofsky and Dulles, *Labor in America,* 161.

81. The laws passed, however, were quite limited in their effects. Dubofsky and Dulles, *Labor in America,* 161–62; Krause, *Battle for Homestead,* 348; Taft, *AFL in the Time of Gompers,* 136–37; Arthur Burgoyne, *Homestead* (Pittsburgh: Rawsthorne, 1893), 235–40.

82. By all accounts Frick demonstrated great courage in fighting off the assault. Burgoyne, *Homestead,* 146–51.

83. Gompers, *Seventy Years of Life and Labor,* 133.

84. "Doubtless the power to control the manufacture of a given thing involves in a certain sense the control of its disposition, but this is a secondary and not the primary sense; and although the exercise of that power may result in bringing the operation of commerce into play, it does not control it, and affects it only incidentally and indirectly. Commerce succeeds to manufacture, and is not a part of it." *U.S. v. E.C. Knight,* 156 U.S. 1, 12 (1895).

85. Debs later would assert that the events of the Pullman strike and his subsequent jail term converted him to socialism. Nick Salvatore, *Eugene V. Debs: Citizen and Socialist* (Urbana: University of Illinois Press, 1982), 125–34, 149–51.

86. By pardoning the surviving Haymarket anarchists Altgeld had already forfeited whatever affection the conservative Cleveland administration had for him. Stanley Buder, *Pullman: An Experiment in Industrial Order and Community Planning, 1880–1930* (London: Oxford University Press, 1967), 182–66. Gerald G. Eggert, *Railroad Labor Disputes: The Beginnings of Federal Strike Policy* (Ann Arbor: University of Michigan Press, 1967), 152.

87. Eggert, 110–14, 152–91; Henry F. Pringle, *The Life and Times of William Howard Taft* (Hamden: Archon, 1964), 126–38.

88. Ironically, Debs himself had tried to prevent his young and untested organization from rushing headlong into the strike, realizing it might well be destroyed by such precipitate action. Nonetheless, he deeply resented Gompers for offering essentially the same counsel to his AFL peers. Salvatore, *Eugene V. Debs*, 126–27, 134–37.

89. Gompers, *Seventy Years of Life and Labor,* 167; AFL, *Report of Proceedings of the Annual Convention of the American Federation of Labor,* 1921, 59.

90. Tocqueville, *Democracy in America,* 556.

2. A Wooden Man?

1. The classic account of Morgan and his "money trust" is that of Louis Brandeis, *Other People's Money and How the Bankers Use It* (New York: Kelly, 1914). The title alludes to Adam Smith's argument that corporate management tended to be less responsible and efficient than owner-operators, because "the directors of such companies, being the managers rather of *other people's money* than their own, it cannot be well expected, that they should watch over it with the same anxious vigilance with which the partners in a private copartnery frequently watch over their own." Adam Smith, *An Inquiry into the Nature and Causes of the Wealth of Nations* (Indianapolis: Liberty Fund, 1981), 741.

2. Ray Stannard Baker, "What the United States Steel Corporation Is and How It Works," *McClure's,* 18 (November 1901), 3–13.

3. Joseph Dorfman, *The Economic Mind in American Civilization,* 3:276–94, and 4:352–53, 377–98.

4. American Federation of Labor, Report of Proceedings of the Annual Convention of the American Federation of Labor (1905), 159, 181–82.

5. Ralph M. Easley, "What Organized Labor Has Learned," *McClure's,* 19 (October 1902), 492.

6. John R. Commons, "A New Way of Settling Labor Disputes," in *Selected Essays* (London: Routledge, 1996), 1:162–71.

7. Melvyn Dubofsky and Foster Rhea Dulles, *Labor in America: A History* (Arlington Heights, IL: Harlan Davidson, 1984), 180–84; Melvyn Dubofsky, *The State and Labor in Modern America* (Chapel Hill: University of North Carolina Press, 1994), 40–42.

8. John R. Commons, "Is Class Conflict Growing, and Is It Inevitable? [1908]," in *Selected Essays,* 1:197.

9. But as Jeffrey Haydu has argued, in modern industries where management confronted *well-established* labor organizations, they might yet choose trade agreements as a

method of managing technological change. Haydu, "Trade Agreements and Open Shops before World War I," *Industrial Relations* 28 (Spring 1989): 159–13.

10. David Montgomery, *The Fall of the House of Labor* (Cambridge: Cambridge University Press, 1987), 58–61.

11. Philip Taft, *AFL in the Time of Gompers* (New York: Octagon, 1970), 275–87; see
also Louis Adamic, *Dynamite: The Story of Class Violence in America* (New York: Harper & Row,
1931), 187–242.

12. Eugene V. Debs, "Craft Unionism (1905)," in *Writings and Speeches of Eugene V. Debs*
(New York: Hermitage Press, 1948), 174–75.

13. John Laslett, *Labor and the Left: A Study of the Socialist and Radical Influences in the
American Labor Movement, 1881–1924* (New York: Basic Books, 1970), chaps. 5, 6.

14. Preamble to the IWW Constitution, 1905; *AFL Proceedings* (1905), 159, 181–
82.

15. Morris Hillquit, Samuel Gompers, and Max J. Hayes, *The Double Edge of Labor's
Sword* (Chicago: Socialist Party National Office, 1914), 132, 138.

16. William M. Leiserson, "Constitutional Government in American Industries," *American Economic Review* 12:1 (March 1922): 76.

17. Eugene V. Debs, "The McNamara Case and the Labor Movement," in *Writings and
Speeches of Eugene V. Debs* (New York: Hermitage, 1948), 344, 349.

18. Debs, "Liberty," in *Debs: His Life, Speeches, and Writings* (Chicago: Charles H. Kerr,
1908), 327, 332–33.

19. Philip Selznick, *Law, Society, and Industrial Justice* (Berkeley: Russell Sage, 1969),
61–62.

20. Thomas Jefferson, "To John Adams," 28 Oct. 1813, *The Portable Thomas Jefferson,*
ed. by Merrill D. Peterson (New York: Viking, 1975), 534–35.

21. Daniel Nelson, *Frederick Winslow Taylor and the Rise of Scientific Management* (Madison: University of Wisconsin Press, 1980), 31–38, 86–88.

22. Frederick Winslow Taylor, *The Principles of Scientific Management* (Mineola: Dover,
1998) 1, 20.

23. Ibid., 4.

24. Ibid., 6, 13, 34, 63.

25. Ibid., 15, 18.

26. Ibid., 1, 19–21, 28–31, 34.

27. Ibid., 71.

28. Taylor, cited in Robert Franklin Hoxie, *Scientific Management and Labor* (New York:
Kelley, 1966), 40. Or as Commons observed of corporate industrialization, apropos of Taylor's scheme: "Under their exact system of costs they measure a man as they do coal, iron, and
kilowatts, and labor becomes literally, what it has been by analogy, a commodity." Commons,
"Is Class Conflict Growing, and Is It Inevitable?" 1:196.

29. Taylor, *Principles of Scientific Management,* 35.

30. Ibid., 30, 75.

31. Ibid., 65–66.

32. "Omnicompetent citizen" was a rather sarcastic neologism of Walter Lippmann's—
like Taylor, Lippmann was prepared to live without such citizens as the price of progress.
Lippmann, *Public Opinion* (1922; New York: Free Press, 1965), 173.

33. Cited in James R. Green, *The World of the Worker: Labor in Twentieth-Century America* (New York: Hill and Wang, 1980), 71; for reference see Aristotle, *Politics,* 1253b–1255.

34. "This system is wrong, because we want our heads left on us." O'Connell, cited in Robert Kanigel, *The One Best Way: Frederick Winslow Taylor and the Enigma of Efficiency* (New York: Penguin, 1997), 448–49; Hugh G. J. Aitken, *Scientific Management in Action: Taylorism at Watertown Arsenal, 1908–1915* (Princeton, NJ: Princeton University Press, 1985), 173. Recall that Lincoln had said that "A Yankee who could invent a strong handed man without a head would receive the everlasting gratitude of the mud-sill advocates." Abraham Lincoln, *Selected Speeches and Writings* (New York: Vintage, 1992), 235.

35. The Machinists' story is rather complex, since Gompers and O'Connell both campaigned against the racist policy, but this unhappy prejudice was widely shared among the union rank-and-file. On the Machinists, see Taft, *AFL in the Time of Gompers,* 308–13, and Montgomery, *Fall of the House of Labor,* 198–201. The most widely read general treatment of the theme is that of David R. Roediger, *The Wages of Whiteness* (New York: Verso, 1991).

36. Cited in Aitken, *Scientific Management in Action,* 150, 216.

37. Of course Taylor had only argued that a *correct* application of his principles had not provoked a strike, and acknowledged that there were plenty of ways to misapply time study that would aggravate industrial conflict. In Watertown he pointed to the failure of management to habituate the workers to obedience before introducing time study. "It is only after a year or two of continually harassing men and making them change their ways on minor matters that it is safe to begin on time study and those steps which lead to task work." Taylor, *Principles of Scientific Management,* 70–71; Aitken, *Scientific Management in Action,* 162.

38. The restriction was eventually removed in 1949 on the initiative of "Mr. Republican," Senator Robert Taft, son of the former president and sponsor of the infamous Taft-Hartley Act. Aitken, *Scientific Management in Action,* 234–35.

39. The classic source is, of course, Alfred Chandler, *The Visible Hand: The Managerial Revolution in American Business* (Cambridge: Harvard University Press, 1977); but see also Richard Edwards, *Contested Terrain: The Transformation of the American Workplace in the Twentieth Century* (New York: Basic Books, 1979).

40. The term "justice as fairness" is that of political philosopher John Rawls, expounded in *A Theory of Justice* (Cambridge: Harvard University Press, 1971).

41. Daniel Nelson, *Managers and Workers: Origins of the New Factory System in the United States, 1880–1920* (Madison: University of Wisconsin Press, 1975), 101–21.

42. Stephen Meyer, *The Five-Dollar Day: Labor Management and Social Control in the Ford Motor Company* (Albany: State University of New York Press, 1981), 2.

43. Henry Ford, *My Life and Work* (Garden City: Doubleday, Page, 1922), 253, 266.

44. Ibid., 117, 186, 257, 259.

45. "Cheap men need expensive jigs, highly skilled men need little outside of their tool chests," one critic observed. Meyer, *Five-Dollar Day,* 10, 22, 26, 40, 52.

46. Ibid., 80, 100–110.

47. It seems that the term social engineering was coined around this time, with interesting origins of its own. Former minister William Tolman, sponsored by Andrew Carnegie and other contemporary steel masters, was a leading period advocate of improved health and safety measures in the workplace. As director of the American Museum of Safety, he tried to persuade employers that adopting the best available practices ultimately improved productivity and reduced costs. Because workers took umbrage at the "paternalistic" associations of the terms "industrial betterment" and "welfare work," he adopted the term "social engineer-

ing" for such projects. William Tolman, *Social Engineering: A Record of Things Done by American Industrialists Employing Upwards of One and One-Half Million of People* (New York: McGraw-Hill, 1909).

48. Ford, *My Life and Work*, 128.

49. Bruce E. Kaufman, *The Origins and Evolution of the Field of Industrial Relations in the United States* (Ithaca, NY: ILR Press, 1993), 46; H. M. Gitelman, *Legacy of the Ludlow Massacre: A Chapter in American Industrial Relations* (Philadelphia: University of Pennsylvania Press, 1988), 155–57, 219, 332–34.

50. John D. Rockefeller, Jr., "Labor and Capital—Partners," *Atlantic Monthly*, 117 (June 1916), 12–21; Gitelman, *Legacy of the Ludlow Massacre*, esp. 181–96, 212.

51. Rockefeller, "Labor and Capital—Partners," 13.

52. Joseph A. McCartin, "'An American Feeling': Workers, Managers, and the Struggle over Industrial Democracy in the World War I Era," 83–85, in *Industrial Democracy in America: The Ambiguous Promise*, ed. Nelson Lichtenstein and Howell John Harris (Cambridge: Cambridge University Press, 1993); Daniel T. Rodgers, *The Work Ethic in Industrial America, 1850–1920* (Chicago: University of Chicago Press, 1974), 59–61; Daniel Nelson, *American Rubber Workers and Organized Labor, 1900–1941* (Princeton, NJ: Princeton University Press, 1988), 57–60.

53. "A Challenge to Henry Ford," *American Federationist* (November 1926):, 1304.

54. Smith, *Wealth of Nations*, 660.

55. James O. Morris, *Conflict within the AFL: A Study of Craft versus Industrial Unionism, 1901–1938* (Westport, CT: Greenwood, 1958), 13–25. The other significant industrial union, the Brewery Workers, was embroiled in constant jurisdictional disputes until destroyed by prohibition.

56. Robert F. Hoxie, *Trade Unionism in the United States* (1923; New York: Russell & Russell, 1966), 139–42.

57. As "Big Bill" Haywood said, "one of the worst features about the working class is that they do not think themselves happy unless they are hard at work." Cited in Rodgers, *Work Ethic in Industrial America*, 177.

58. Vincent St. John, *The IWW* (IWW pamphlet), 9, 12–13, 36.

59. Melvyn Dubofsky, *We Shall Be All: A History of the IWW* (Chicago: Quadrangle, 1969), 227–62.

60. Hoxie's book, *Trade Unionism in the United States*, where he laid out his idea of business unionism was comprised actually of papers posthumously arranged by his wife, with the help of Commons and others, following Hoxie's suicide. Lafayette G. Harter, *John R. Commons: His Assault on Laissez-Faire* (Corvallis: Oregon State University Press, 1962), 158–59.

61. Hoxie, *Trade Unionism in the United States*, 45–46.

62. Ibid., 336.

63. Ibid., 48.

64. Ibid., 48, 88, 16–19.

65. Dubofsky and Dulles, *Labor in America*, 242; David Montgomery, *Workers' Control in America: Studies in the History of Work, Technology, and Labor Struggles* (Cambridge: Cambridge University Press, 1979), 20–25; Sumner H. Slichter, *The Impact of Collective Bargaining on Management* (Washington, DC: Brookings Institution Press, 1941), e.g., 213–14.

66. St. John, *IWW*, 11.

67. Hoxie, *Trade Unionism in the United States*, 135.

3. The AFL and Progressive Politics

1. "Abuse of the injunctive writ had grown in frequency until it had become the paramount issue in labor problems." Gompers, *Seventy Years of Life and Labor,* 169.

2. Much of the information here comes from Daniel Ernst, "The Danbury Hatters' Case," in *Labor Law in America: Historical and Critical Essays,* ed. Christopher L. Tomlins and Andrew J. King (Baltimore: Johns Hopkins University Press, 1992), 180–200; see also William Forbath, *Law and the Shaping of the American Labor Movement* (Cambridge: Harvard University Press), 90–94.

3. *Loewe v. Lawlor,* 204 U.S. 274, 9–10 (1908).

4. On appeal, the case became bogged down in technical issues for years (during the course of which the jail sentences were suspended); Van Cleave died; and the company resolved its differences with the Molders, causing the case to be declared moot. *American Federation of Labor v. Buck's Stove and Range,* 33 App. D.C. 33 (1909); *Gompers v. Buck's Stove and Range,* 33 App. D.C. 513 (1909).

5. David Brody, "Free Labor, Law, and American Trade Unionism," in *Terms of Labor: Slavery, Serfdom, and Free Labor,* ed. Stanley L. Engerman (Stanford: Stanford University Press, 1999), 235–36; Dallas L. Jones, "The Enigma of the Clayton Act," *Industrial and Labor Relations Review* 10 (January 1957): 201–21.

6. *Hitchman Coal and Coke v. Mitchell,* 236 US 1, 127–9 (1912).

7. Forbath, *Law and the Shaping of the American Labor Movement,* 136–38.

8. Jones, "Enigma of the Clayton Act," 204.

9. The most widely read contemporary study of this phenomenon—albeit with a very different political viewpoint—is Gwendolyn Mink's *Old Labor and New Immigrants in American Political Development* (Ithaca, NY: Cornell University Press, 1986).

10. John R. Commons, "The Passing of Samuel Gompers (1925)," in *Selected Essays,* 2:343–49.

11. Samuel Gompers, *Seventy Years of Life and Labor: An Autobiography,* ed. Nick Salvatore (1925; Ithaca, NY: ILR Press, 1984), 178–79; *American Federationist* 15 (1908): 1039.

12. Julie Greene, *Pure and Simple Politics: The American Federation of Labor and Political Activism, 1881–1917* (Cambridge: Cambridge University Press, 1998), 107–31, 140–41.

13. Ibid., 157–70, 181–86, 210–14; see also Melvyn Dubofsky, *The State and Labor in Modern America* (Chapel Hill: University of North Carolina Press, 1994), 51–52. Greene notes importantly that the AFL's engagement with the Democrats and Bryan was an important factor in transforming the Democratic party, taking the national leadership away from conservatives backed by the Southern Democrats and handing it to economic reformers such as Bryan, Wilson, and finally Franklin D. Roosevelt. Greene also believes that trade unionists "repudiated" Gompers' choice for the presidency at the ballot box and "renounced his political strategy," although the anecdotal nature of most available evidence would seem to call for a little caution. There is no scientific polling data to determine worker voting behavior in early twentieth century elections; our understanding is based on guesses inferred from changes in county vote totals.

14. Gompers to President Wilson, 1916, cited in Philip Taft, *The AFL in the Time of Gompers* (New York: Octagon, 1970), 404.

15. Gompers, *Seventy Years of Life and Labor,* 60.

16. "Labor and Capital," 5 Sept. 1910, in Theodore Roosevelt, *The New Nationalism* (1910; Englewood Cliffs, NJ: Prentice-Hall, 1961), 99.

17. James R. Green, *The World of the Worker: Labor in Twentieth-Century America* (New York: Hill and Wang, 1980), 54–56, 64; Dubofsky, *State and Labor in Modern America,* 42–43.

18. Roosevelt, cited in Jacob A. Riis, *Theodore Roosevelt: The Citizen* (New York: Outlook, 1904), 373.

19. The conviction that class war had destroyed the Roman republic and could destroy America's as well was very present in Roosevelt's thought. See John Milton Cooper, *The Warrior and the Priest: Woodrow Wilson and Theodore Roosevelt* (Cambridge: Harvard University Press, 1983), 112–13; Cicero, *On the Commonwealth,* 1.4.

20. In early 1902, Roosevelt had initiated his antitrust campaign with an enforcement action against the Northern Securities Company, a railroad combination Morgan had orchestrated. The banker obtained a private meeting and proposed that the president "send your man [the Attorney General!] to my man and they can fix it up." Roosevelt rebuffed him, reflecting afterward that it had been "a most illuminating illustration of the Wall Street point of view," finding that Morgan regarded him as "a big rival operator" with whom he could negotiate rather than the elected chief executive charged with impartial enforcement of the law. See Nathan Miller, *Theodore Roosevelt: A Life* (New York: William Morrow, 1992), 366–70; Edmund Morris, *Theodore Rex* (New York: Random House, 2001), 87–93.

21. Roosevelt, "The New Nationalism," in *The Essential Theodore Roosevelt,* 269, 278–79.

22. Roosevelt, "Labor," in *The New Nationalism* (Englewood Cliffs, NJ: Prentice Hall, 1961), 99.

23. Roosevelt, "New Nationalism," 268–69, 276.

24. Herbert Croly, *The Promise of American Life* (1909; Boston: Northeastern University Press, 1989), 189.

25. Ibid., 64, 102, 189.

26. Ibid., 410.

27. Ibid., 207.

28. Lafayette G. Harter, *John R. Commons: His Assault on Laissez-Faire* (Corvallis: Oregon State University Press, 1962), 91–114.

29. Though intended as a socialist propaganda tract, the eccentric Sinclair's melodramatic serial grabbed the public mainly with his portrayal of unsanitary meatpacking practices. The curious story of Sinclair, Roosevelt, and the Pure Food and Drug Act is found in Robert Crunden, *Ministers of Reform: The Progressives' Achievement in American Civilization, 1889–1920* (Urbana: University of Illinois Press, 1984), 166–99.

30. Woodrow Wilson, *The New Freedom: A Call for the Emancipation of the Generous Energies of a People* (New York: Doubleday, 1918), 64–65.

31. Ibid., 201.

32. Louis D. Brandeis, *The Curse of Bigness: Miscellaneous Papers of Louis D. Brandeis* (Port Washington, NY: Kennikat Press, 1965).

33. Wilson, *New Freedom,* 204, 207, 216.

34. Ibid., 66, 68, 198.

35. Wilson cited in 1921 *AFL Proceedings,* 59.

36. Samuel Gompers, "The Charter of Industrial Freedom," *American Federationist* (1914): 971, and "Political Labor Party—Reconstruction—Social Insurance," *American Federationist* (January 1919): 43.

37. This was apparent to many contemporaries well before the definitive Supreme Court decisions of 1921. See "Labor Is Not a Commodity," *New Republic,* December 2, 1916.

38. The Supreme Court upheld the injunction barring UMW organizers from enticing miners to violate their "yellow-dog" contracts (a term the court delicately avoided) by joining the union. The practice of demanding yellow-dog contracts was so universal in West Virginia that the court had essentially made West Virginia a no-go zone for UMW organizers. See Brody, "Free Labor, Law, and American Trade Unionism," 235–36; Irving Bernstein, *The Lean Years: A History of the American Worker, 1920–1933* (Baltimore: Penguin, 1966), 196–200.

39. *Duplex Printing Press Company v. Deering et al.,* 254 U.S. 443 (1921).

40. 257 U.S. 184. See also Stanley I. Kutler, "Labor, the Clayton Act, and the Supreme Court," *Labor History* 3 (Winter 1962): 33–36, and Henry R. Pringle, *The Life and Times of William Howard Taft* (Hamden: Archon, 1964), 1030–35.

41. Political conference report recorded in 1921 *AFL Proceedings,* 59.

42. The court did invoke the precedents of *Adair v. U.S.* (1908) and *Coppage v. Kansas* (1915) which respectively struck down federal and state laws attacking the yellow-dog contract on the grounds that such laws violated the "constitutional freedom of contract. . . . Chief among such contracts is that of personal employment." In *Adkins* the Court elaborated, "the ethical right of every worker, man or woman, to a living wage may be conceded . . . [but] [i]n principle, there can be no difference between the case of selling labor and the case of selling goods. If one goes to the butcher, the baker or grocer to buy food, he is morally entitled to obtain the worth of his money but he is not entitled to more. If what he gets is worth what he pays he is not justified in demanding more simply because he needs more." Interestingly, Taft dissented; ever the conservative, he preferred to allow elected legislatures to decide when such intervention was necessary so long as the lawmakers invoked the police power in the public interest. *Adair v. United States,* 208 U.S. 161 (1908); *Coppage v. Kansas,* 236 U.S. 1, 22–3 (1915); *Adkins v. Children's Hospital* (1923), 261 U.S. 525. See also Howard Gillman, *The Constitution Besieged: The Rise and Demise of Lochner Era Police Powers Jurisprudence* (Durham, NC: Duke University Press, 1993), 167–75; and Pringle, *Life and Times of William Howard Taft,* 1049–52.

43. "Size," Brandeis continued, "underlies all of the difficulties of the concentration of power." Food, housing, and recreation are indeed all essential, "but we may have all those things and have a nation of slaves." Brandeis became an ardent admirer of Athens' direct democracy; he spent his life trying to enact policies that would breathe life back into the democratic ideal of engaged, virtuous citizens. Citations from Louis D. Brandeis, *The Curse of Bigness: Miscellaneous Papers* (Port Washington, NY: Kennikat, 1965), 79–81; on Brandeis and the *polis* see Philippa Strum, *Louis D. Brandeis: Justice for the People* (New York: Schocken Books, 1984), 236–40.

44. Walter Lippmann, *Public Opinion* (1922; New York: Free Press, 1965), 147, 172–73.

45. U. M. Rose, "Strikes and Trusts," *American Law Review* 27 (September–October 1893): 717; see also Bruce E. Kaufman, *The Origins and Evolution of the Field of Industrial Relations in the United States* (Ithaca, NY: ILR Press, 1993), 32–35.

46. John R. Commons, *Myself: The Autobiography of John R. Commons* (1934; Madison: University of Wisconsin Press, 1963), 143.

47. Lippmann, *Public Opinion,* 196–97.

48. Irving Howe, *World of Our Fathers* (New York: Harcourt, Brace, Jovanovich, 1976), 295–303.

49. Louis D. Brandeis, "Purpose of the Protocol," in *Out of the Sweatshop: The Struggle for Industrial Democracy,* ed. Leon Stein (New York: Quadrangle/New York Times Book, 1977), 122–23.

50. Steven Fraser, *Labor Will Rule: Sidney Hillman and the Rise of American Labor* (Ithaca, NY: Cornell University Press, 1991), 46–67.

51. William M. Leiserson, "Constitutional Government in American Industries." *American Economic Review* 12:1 (March 1922): 61.

52. Milton J. Nadworny, *Scientific Management and the Unions, 1900–1932* (Cambridge: Harvard University Press, 1955), 35–47.

53. Jean Trepp McKelvey, *AFL Attitudes toward Production: 1900–1932* (Ithaca, NY: Cornell University Press, 1952), 24–26, 64–78; Nadworny, *Scientific Management and the Unions,* 74–82, 96–121.

54. Fraser, *Labor Will Rule,* 130–40, 160–77.

55. Michael Rogin, "Voluntarism: The Political Functions of an Apolitical Doctrine," *Industrial and Labor Relations Review* 15 (1962): 521–35; see also Greene, *Pure and Simple Politics,* 255–57.

56. *Lochner v. New York,* 198 U.S. 45, 20–1(1905).

57. Gompers, "Self-Help is the Best Help," *American Federationist* (February 1915): 114, and "Not Even Compulsory Benevolence Will Do," *American Federationist* (January 1917): 48.

58. Gompers himself was an avowed feminist who disdained paternalism toward women in the same way he did for men. He supported women's suffrage and opposed laws that regulated wages and hours of work for adult women. Gompers, *Seventy Years of Life and Labor,* 126–29.

59. Nadworny, *Scientific Management and the Unions,* 122–26; David Montgomery, *The Fall of the House of Labor* (Cambridge: Cambridge University Press, 1987), 421–24; Jacob J. Kaufman, *Collective Bargaining in the Railroad Industry* (New York: Columbia University Press, 1954), 57–73.

60. Samuel Gompers, "Freedom Must Not Be Surrendered," *American Federationist* (January 1917): 46.

61. Of course capital often failed to adhere to this principle and viewed, for instance, the privilege of incorporation as an entitlement that conferred no public obligations. But this only proved that the worker *could* be a good citizen while the large employer seldom was— a statement Gompers surely would have affirmed.

62. Montgomery, *Fall of the House of Labor,* 356–65; Harter, *John R. Commons,* 65; Taft, *AFL in the Time of Gompers,* 342.

63. The virtual extermination of the IWW during the war was the primary example of wartime labor suppression, but it is the exception that proves the rule. What is remarkable is not that an organization whose professed goal was the revolutionary overthrow of the state and social order was suppressed in wartime, but that it was permitted to exist at any time. More troubling was the imprisonment of war critics like Debs whose Socialist Party opposed the war only by legal and democratic means.

64. Simeon Larson, *Labor and Foreign Policy: Gompers, the AFL, and the First World War, 1914–1918.* (Rutherford, NJ: Fairleigh Dickinson University Press, 1975), 83–85, 95–98; State and Labor in Modern America, 65–9; Montgomery, *Fall of the House of Labor,* 375; Taft, AFL in the *Time of Gompers,* 347–51.

65. Dubofsky, *State and Labor in Modern America,* 69–71.

66. Montgomery, *Fall of the House of Labor,* 374; Dubofsky, *State and Labor in Modern*

America, 73; Pringle, *Life and Times of William Howard Taft,* 915–25; Joseph A. McCartin, "'An American Feeling': Workers, Managers, and the Struggle over Industrial Democracy in the World War I Era," in *Industrial Democracy in America: The Ambiguous Promise,* ed. Nelson Lichtenstein and Howell John Harris (Cambridge: Cambridge University Press, 1993), 71.

67. McCartin, "An American Feeling," 72–74; Taft, AFL in the *Time of Gompers,* 362; Dubofsky, *State and Labor in Modern America,* 74–76; Montgomery, *Fall of the House of Labor,* 413–24.

68. Taft, AFL in the *Time of Gompers,* 401–3.

69. "The Challenge Accepted," report in 1921 *AFL Proceedings,* 56, 61.

70. The strike was led by syndicalist and future CPUSA chief William Z. Foster.

71. Dubofsky, *State and Labor in Modern America,* 79.

4. The New Deal and the Birth of the CIO

1. Philip Taft, *The AFL from the Death of Gompers to the Merger* (New York: Octagon, 1970), 92.

2. Irving Bernstein, *The Lean Years: A History of the American Worker, 1920–33* (Baltimore: Penguin, 1966), 335; Robert H. Zieger, *The CIO, 1935–1955* (Chapel Hill: University of North Carolina Press, 1995), 22–29.

3. Robert H. Zieger, *John L. Lewis: Labor Leader* (Urbana: University of Illinois Press, 1986), chap. 1, 1–21; Melvyn Dubofsky and Warren Van Tine, *John L. Lewis: A Biography* (Urbana: University of Illinois Press, 1986), 18–34.

4. Dubofsky and Van Tine, *John L. Lewis,* 100–102; Zieger, *John L. Lewis,* 49–52.

5. Lewis's biographers generally name Lauck as the book's primary author; the two together developed its analysis over the years. Dubofsky and Van Tine, *John L. Lewis,* 80–82, 103–5; Zieger, *John L. Lewis,* 29–31, 53; David Brody, *In Labor's Cause* (New York: Oxford University Press, 1993). 148–53.

6. John L. Lewis, *The Miner's Fight for American Standards* (Indianapolis: Bell, 1925), 182, 189.

7. Zieger, *John L. Lewis,* 20, 37–52; Dubofsky and Van Tine, *John L. Lewis,* 56–69, 86–99, 114–23.

8. Bernstein, *Lean Years,* 94–97; Craig Phelan, *William Green: Biography of a Labor Leader* (Albany: State University of New York Press, 1989), 26.

9. Phelan, *William Green,* 20–21; Milton J. Nadworny, *Scientific Management and the Unions, 1930–1932* (Cambridge: Harvard University Press, 1955), 129–34.

10. William Green, *Labor and Democracy* (Princeton, NJ: Princeton University Press, 1939), 175; see also Phelan, *William Green,* 26–28.

11. Franklin Delano Roosevelt, "Speech Before the 1932 Democratic Convention," 2 July 32, in *The Essential Franklin Delano Roosevelt* (New York: Gramercy, 1995), 19.

12. Herbert Hoover, the true classical liberal, fought to retain the term for himself throughout the 1932 campaign but his fight proved an exercise in futility. The story is recounted in David Green, *Shaping Political Consciousness: The Language of Politics in America from McKinley to Reagan* (Ithaca, NY: Cornell University Press, 1987), 109–34.

13. Samuel Insull was the notorious 1920s impresario of interlocking directorates. Roosevelt, "Every Man Has a Right to Life," in *New Deal Thought,* ed. Howard Zinn (Indianapo-

lis: Bobbs-Merrill, 1966), 51–52; Thomas C. Cochran and William Miller. *The Age of Enterprise: A Social History of Industrial America* (New York: Harper and Row, 1965), 315–21; Genesis 16:11–12.

14. Roosevelt, "Fireside Chat on the National Recovery Administration," 24 July 1933, in *The Essential Franklin Delano Roosevelt,* 64.

15. Zieger, *John L. Lewis,* 60–64; Dubofsky and Van Tine, *John L. Lewis,* 131–33; Steven Fraser, *Labor Will Rule: Sidney Hillman and the Rise of American Labor* (Ithaca, NY: Cornell University Press, 1991), 282–88; Taft, *AFL from the Death of Gompers to the Merger,* 41–47; Christopher Tomlins, *The State and the Unions: Labor Relations, Law, and the Organized Labor Movement in America, 1880–1960* (New York: Cambridge University Press, 1985) 103–8.

16. Cited from the text of the National Industrial Recovery Act as published in Leverett S. Lyon, Paul T. Homan, Lewis L. Lorwin, George Terborgh, Charles L. Dearing, and Leon C. Marshall, *The National Recovery Administration: An Analysis and Appraisal* (Washington, DC: Brookings Institution Press, 1935), 895–96.

17. Irving Bernstein, *The Turbulent Years: A History of the American Worker, 1933–41* (Boston: Houghton Mifflin, 1970), 39–46, 61–62; Zieger, *John L. Lewis,* 62–66; Melvyn Dubofsky, *The State and Labor in Modern America* (Chapel Hill: University of North Carolina Press, 1994), 112–14; Dubofsky and Van Tine, *John L. Lewis,* 133–38.

18. Fraser, *Labor Will Rule,* 290–302; Bernstein, *Turbulent Years,* 75–77, 84–89.

19. For the full story of the two dramatic strikes, see Bernstein, *Turbulent Years,* 229–98.

20. Phelan, *William Green,* 101; James O. Morris, *Conflict within the AFL: A Study of Craft versus Industrial Unionism, 1901–1938* (Westport, CT: Greenwood Press, 1958), 158–70.

21. Dubofsky, *State and Labor in Modern America,* 111–19; Milton Derber and Edward Young, eds., *Labor and the New Deal* (Madison: University of Wisconsin Press, 1961), 288–93.

22. Phelan, *William Green,* 68–88; Taft, *AFL from the Death of Gompers to the Merger,* 98–103; Brody, *In Labor's Cause,* 232–35, and in *Restoring the Promise of American Labor Law,* ed. Sheldon Friedman, Richard W. Hurd, Rudolph A. Oswald, and Ronald L. Seeber (Ithaca, NY: ILR Press, 1994), 37–39.

23. Dubinsky gives a good account of how this worked in his memoir. See David Dubinsky and A. H. Raskin, *David Dubinsky: A Life with Labor* (New York: Simon and Schuster, 1977), 118–44.

24. In the auto field, meanwhile, Ford characteristically shunned the NRA as a plot by a "bankers' international." Leuchtenburg, *Roosevelt,* 66.

25. See Murray Edelman, "New Deal Sensitivity to Labor Interests," in *Labor and the New Deal,* ed. Derber and Young, 159–91.

26. "A few hundred funerals will have a quieting influence," a textile trade journal observed. William E. Leuchtenburg, William E., *Franklin D. Roosevelt and the New Deal, 1932–40* (New York: Harper, 1963), 112–13. See also Bernstein, *Turbulent Years,* 298–314.

27. *AFL Proceedings,* 1934, 586, 587.

28. Ibid., 588.

29. Ibid., 590, 593.

30. Ibid., 591–93.

31. For the singular story of the ITU see Seymour Martin Lipset, Martin A. Trow, and James S. Coleman, *Union Democracy: The Internal Politics of the International Typographical Union* (Glencoe, IL: Free Press, 1956).

32. Not only had significant numbers of tool and die makers enrolled in both the IAM and the FLUs, but they had also formed an independent organization, the Mechanics' Educational Society of America (MESA), that carried out a successful strike against the automakers in 1933. Bernstein, *Turbulent Years,* 94–98, 372–79; 502–9; Nelson Lichtenstein, *Walter Reuther: The Most Dangerous Man in Detroit* (Urbana: University of Illinois Press, 1997), 135–36.

33. "The workers are brought into this industry in large numbers en masse, they are employed en masse, they work together as cogs in a great machine. . . . Is it not reasonable to conclude and [sic] as a matter of fact that men who are not regarded as skilled workers, men who are not required to exercise skill, but required to perform a repetitive operation day in and day out would begin to think in mass terms? They become mass minded." Green, Minutes, AFL Executive Council, 207.

34. Of course, these concerns were hardly the exclusive property of the AFL; neither the nineteenth century anarchists nor the Wobblies trusted the government to regulate labor relations.

35. Robert Wagner, "The Ideal Industrial State—As Wagner Sees It," *New York Times Magazine,* 9 May 1937, 8.

36. "Workers governed for years by the propaganda of big corporations are not ready for participation in the democracy of labor," the *IBEW Journal* had counseled in 1934. AFL President Green had hoped that the Federal Labor Unions could serve as institutions of civic education for industrial workers, remedial schools to "educate the new members to union methods and techniques. First and most important they had to learn self-government to be able to put the democratic process to a practical test in their own organizations." William Green, *Labor and Democracy,* 172; Morris, *Conflict within the AFL,* 163.

37. *AFL Proceedings,* 1935, 569–73. AFL Executive Council Minutes, 12 February 1935, 216.

38. A strange and uncharitable allusion indeed: see Luke 14:15–24 and Matt 22:1–10.

39. Speech in *AFL Proceedings,* 1935, 534–42.

40. The greatest instrumentality in history, yet! Tobin, perhaps excited by Lewis's sometimes wonderful but always weird rhetoric, would later adapt the only piece of scripture a Catholic could reasonably be expected to know (Matt 16:18) in his response. He attributed to Gompers (!) and his peers the injunction, "Upon the rock of trade autonomy, craft trades, you shall build the church of the labor movement, and the gates of hell nor trade industrialism shall not prevail against it." *AFL Proceedings,* 1935, 659.

41. *AFL Proceedings,* 1935, 529.

42. Ibid., 552–59.

43. Murray was born in Scotland to Irish parents; his family moved to the United States when he was sixteen. Schatz, "Philip Murray," in *Labor Leaders in America,* ed. Melvyn Dubofsky and Warren Van Tine (Urbana: University of Illinois Press, 1987), 234–57.

44. *AFL Proceedings,* 1935, 559–64.

45. By most accounts Lewis sucker-punched his friend; with great success CIO publicist Len DeCaux used the fight to celebrate "the battling Lewis as a John L. Sullivan of industrial organization." Zieger, *The CIO, 1935–1955,* 22–29.

46. In the event, only the UE came into existence as a dual union; with some heavy-handed persuasion, the AAISW remnant was induced to participate in the CIO-sponsored Steelworkers' Organizing Committee (SWOC). Morris, *Conflict within the AFL,* 222–28; Zieger, The *CIO, 1935–1955,* 34–39.

47. The letters are Lewis to Green, 6 June 1936; Lewis to Green, 7 June 1936; and Green to Lewis, 6 June 1936. All are available on microfilm at the Meany Center Archives in Washington, DC.

48. Lewis to Green, 7 June 1936.

49. Green, *Labor and Democracy,* 175–76.

50. Phelan, *William Green,* 138–39, and "William Green and the Ideal of Christian Cooperation," in *Labor Leaders in America,* ed. Dubofsky and Van Tine, 153–57.

51. For a full discussion see Christopher Tomlins, "AFL Unions in the 1930s: Their Performance in Historical Perspective," in *The New Deal: Conflicting Interpretations and Shifting Perspectives,* ed. Melvyn Dubofsky (New York: Garland, 1992), 147–71.

52. This might easily have created a problem for the punctilious Green, since the AFL Constitution reserved the presidential office for union members in good standing. However, Green—who apparently played a mean fiddle—had in the meantime obtained a card from the American Federation of Musicians. This amused Lewis who said it was "appropriate" since "Like Nero, he fiddles while Rome burns." Phelan, *William Green,* 133–34, 149–51; Morris, *Conflict within the AFL,* 219–20.

53. Green, *Labor and Democracy,* 183.

5. The New Deal Democracy and Industrial Unionism at Flood Tide

1. "Anyone coming into this convention seeking to represent a State or central body who edits such a paper and who has direct connection with the Communist Party and is playing for the Soviet and Moscow government has no right in this convention as a trade unionist," said Matthew Woll. Phil Murray moved to have Dunne's credentials revoked and his motion was overwhelmingly accepted. *AFL Proceedings,* 1923, 256; see also Philip Taft, *The AFL in the Time of Gompers* (New York: Octagon, 1970), 457–59.

2. Harvey Klehr and John Earl Haynes. *The American Communist Movement: Storming Heaven Itself* (New York: Twayne, 1992), 64–73; Irving Bernstein, *The Lean Years: A History of the American Worker, 1920–33* (Baltimore: Penguin, 1966), 139–41.

3. Robert H. Zieger, *John L. Lewis: Labor Leader* (Boston: Twayne, 1988), 101.

4. William E. Leuchtenburg, *Franklin D. Roosevelt and the New Deal, 1932–40* (New York: Harper, 1963), 188–92; Robert H. Zieger, *The CIO, 1935–1955* (Chapel Hill: University of North Carolina Press, 1995), 39–41; Melvyn Dubofsky and Warren Van Tine, *John L. Lewis: A Biography* (Urbana: University of Illinois Press, 1986), 181–85.

5. John L. Lewis, "What Labor Is Thinking," *Public Opinion Quarterly* 1 (October 1937): 26.

6. Sidney Fine, *Sit-Down: The General Motors Strike of 1936–1937* (Ann Arbor: University of Michigan Press, 1969), 192–95.

7. Milton Derber and Edward Young, eds., *Labor and the New Deal* (Madison: University of Wisconsin Press, 1961), 291; Frank W. McCulloch and Tim Bornstein, *The National Labor Relations Board* (New York: Praeger, 1974), 23–27, 106–7.

8. A dubious argument. The sit-down was attractive to trade union activists because it allowed a militant minority to wage an effective strike even when the majority was indifferent, weak, or vacillating, as was apparently the case at GM. See Fine, *Sit-Down,* 51–53, 173–83, 332–36; Dubofsky, "Not So 'Turbulent Years': A New Look at the 1930s," in *Life and La-*

bor: Dimensions of American Working-Class History, ed. Charles Stephenson and Robert Asher (Albany: State University of New York Press, 1986), 205–23.

9. Nelson Lichtenstein, *Labor's War at Home: The CIO in World War II* (Cambridge: Cambridge University Press, 1982), 11.

10. Zieger, *The CIO, 1935–1955,* 60–64.

11. Frank Freidel, *Franklin D. Roosevelt: A Rendezvous with Destiny* (Boston: Little, Brown, 1990), 244.

12. Text of Roosevelt's campaign speech is reproduced in the *New York Times,* 1 November 1936, 36.

13. Roosevelt, "Speech before the 1936 Democratic National Convention," 27 June 1936, in *The Essential Franklin Delano Roosevelt* (New York: Gramercy, 1995), 113–19. My italics.

14. CIO publicists made out the Flint sit-downers as modern Minute Men taking up arms to fight for freedom—perhaps not realizing what they were saying about their own government. Zieger, *The CIO, 1935–1955,* 43.

15. The full story can be found in Sidney M. Milkis, *The President and the Parties: The Transformation of the American Party System since the New Deal* (Oxford: Oxford University Press, 1993), 98–146, and Peri E. Arnold, *Making the Managerial Presidency: Comprehensive Reorganization Planning, 1905–1996* (Lawrence: University of Kansas Press, 1998), 95–117.

16. Roosevelt, "Eleventh Annual Message to Congress," 11 January 1944, in The Essential Franklin Delano Roosevelt, 294.

17. NLRB v. Fansteel Metallurgical Corp., 306 U.S. 240 (1939).

18. James A. Gross, *The Reshaping of the National Labor Relations Board: National Labor Policy in Transition, 1937–1947* (Albany: State University of New York Press, 1981), 56–60. See also Derber and Young, eds., *Labor and the New Deal,* 110, 329–30; Christopher Tomlins, *The State and the Unions: Labor Relations, Law, and the Organized Labor Movement in America, 1880–1960* (New York: Cambridge University Press, 1985), 176–78.

19. Tomlins, *The State and the Unions,* 174.

20. Green, "Shall Government Control Unionism?" *American Federationist* 45 (August 1938): 801–2.

21. "Text of John L. Lewis' Appeal for the Support of Wendell Willkie," *New York Times,* 26 October 1940.

22. In his remarks Lewis enumerated the needle trade union leaders and charged them with disloyalty in the conflict with the AFL. "He [Dubinsky] has crept back into the American Federation of Labor. He abandoned his fellows and he abandoned what he claimed was his principle. And he has gone into that organization on the adversary's terms. He is crying out now, and his voice laments like that of Rachel in the wilderness, against the racketeers and the panderers and the crooks in that organization. And Zaritsky, he was the man representing the Millinery and Cap Workers. He said, 'Me too.' And now above all the clamor comes the piercing wail and the laments of the Amalgamated Clothing Workers. And they say, 'Peace, it is wonderful.' And there is no peace. . . . Dubinsky took the easy way. Zaritsky took the easy way. If there is anybody else in CIO who wants to take the easy way, let them go on." It is the subject of much dispute among Lewis's historians whether or not Lewis was making a calculated appeal to anti-Semitism among the delegates, but that is certainly how the ACWA delegates interpreted it. (And I find it hard to imagine Lewis intoning "peace, it is wonderful" without affecting a Yiddish accent.) For the transcript of Lewis's remarks see Congress of Industrial Organizations, *Daily Proceedings of the Third Constitutional Convention* (Atlantic City,

1940), 159, 162. For accounts of the CIO convention see Dubofsky and Van Tine, *John L. Lewis*, 261–67; Steven Fraser, *Labor Will Rule: Sidney Hillman and the Rise of American Labor* (Ithaca, NY: Cornell University Press, 1993), 447–52; Zieger, *The CIO, 1935–1955*, 108–10; for Woll's remarks see Philip Taft, *The AFL from the Death of Gompers to the Merger* (New York: Octagon, 1970), 184.

23. *CIO Convention Proceedings, 1940*, 182–92.

24. Zieger, *John L. Lewis*, 123.

25. Both Encyclicals can be found reprinted in David J. O'Brien and Thomas A. Shannon, *Catholic Social Thought: The Documentary Heritage* (Maryknoll, NY: Orbis, 1992).

26. John A Ryan, *Economic Justice: Selections from Distributive Justice and A Living Wage* (Louisville: Westminster, 1996); Jay P. Dolan, *The American Catholic Experience* (Garden City: Doubleday, 1985), 342–44, 405–7; David J. O'Brien, *American Catholics and Social Reform: The New Deal Years* (New York: Oxford University Press, 1968), 51–57, 68–69, 109–10, 134–43; Francis L. Broderick, *Right Reverend New Dealer John A. Ryan* (New York: Macmillan, 1963), 212–39; Douglas P. Seaton, *Catholics and Radicals: The Association of Catholic Trade Unionists and the American Labor Movement, from Depression to Cold War* (Lewisburg: Bucknell University Press, 1981), 53–64; Neil Betten, *Catholic Activism and the Industrial Worker* (Gainesville: University of Florida Press, 1976), 71–76.

27. The text of the Industrial Council Plan as presented before the CIO convention in November 1941 can be found as an appendix in Clinton S. Golden and Harold J. Ruttenberg, *The Dynamics of Industrial Democracy* (New York: Harper & Brothers, 1942), 343–47. See also Ronald W. Schatz, "Philip Murray and the Subordination of the Industrial Unions to the United States Government," in Melvyn Dubofsky and Warren Van Tine, eds. *Labor Leaders in America* (Urbana: University of Illinois Press, 1987), 249; Lichtenstein, *Labor's War at Home*, 40–2, 83–89; Zieger, *The CIO, 1935–1955*, 142–46.

28. Fraser, *Labor Will Rule*, 173, 429–30.

29. There is some debate over whether Murray actually contributed to or even *read* the book. See for instance the remarks of John Hoerr in Paul F. Clark, Peter Gottlieb, and Donald Kennedy, eds., *Forging a Union of Steel: Philip Murray, SWOC, and the United Steelworkers* (Ithaca, NY: Cornell University Press, 1987), 122.

30. Golden and Ruttenberg, *The Dynamics of Industrial Democracy*, 17, 40–42.

31. Ibid., 215.

32. Ibid., 49. A 1940 UAW publication makes the analogy explicit. "The contract is your constitution, and the settlement of grievances under it are the decisions of an industrial supreme court." Cited in Lichtenstein, "Great Expectations: the Promise of Industrial Jurisprudence and Its Demise, 1930–1960," in *Industrial Democracy in America: The Ambiguous Promise*, ed. Nelson Lichtenstein and Howell John Harris (Cambridge: Cambridge University Press, 1993), 130.

33. Golden and Ruttenberg, *The Dynamics of Industrial Democracy*, 119.

34. Indeed, Golden and Ruttenberg seem to award coinage of the term "free rider" to crusty SWOC local president and pipefitter Tommy Morgan. Golden and Ruttenberg, *The Dynamics of Industrial Democracy*, 25.

35. Ibid., 192, 205, 210–12, 217.

36. Roosevelt, "Radio Address to the 1940 Democratic National Convention," 19 July 1940, in *The Essential Franklin Delano Roosevelt*, 181–89.

37. Robert C. Brooks, "Reflections on the 'World Revolution' of 1940," *American Political Science Review* 35 (February 1941): 1–28.

38. Golden and Ruttenberg, *The Dynamics of Industrial Democracy,* 229, 233, 236, 238, 243.

39. Nelson Lichtenstein, *Walter Reuther: The Most Dangerous Man in Detroit* (Urbana: University of Illinois Press, 1997), 159–71.

40. Stephen Meyer, *The Five-Dollar Day: Labor Management and Social Control in the Ford Motor Company, 1908–21* (Albany: State University of New York Press, 1981), 195–200.

41. See James Brough, *The Ford Dynasty: An American Story* (Garden City: Doubleday, 1977), 99, 115–20, 144–45, 212–16; Upton Sinclair, *The Flivver King: A Story of Ford-America* (New York: Dodd, 1937), 110; James Brough, *Ford, Life and Work,* 250–52; Lichtenstein, *Walter Reuther,* 81–87, 178–79; Zieger, The *CIO, 1935–1955,* 122–25; Irving Bernstein, *The Turbulent Years: A History of the American Worker, 1933–41* (Boston: Houghton Mifflin, 1970), 735–51; Barnard, *Reuther,* 66–69.

42. Lichtenstein, *Walter Reuther,* 194–98, and *Labor's War at Home,* 98–101, 185.

43. James N. Baron, Frank R. Dobbin, and P. Devereaux Jennings, "War and Peace: The Evolution of Modern Personnel Administration in U.S. Industry," *American Journal of Sociology* 92 (September 1986): 350–83.

44. The account is drawn from Lichtenstein, *Labor's War at Home,* 98–108.

45. Hutcheson seems to have imagined a Carpenter-Mineworker axis that would obstruct the AFL's own increasing association with Roosevelt's New Deal Democracy. Taft, *AFL from the Death of Gompers to the Merger,* 476–77.

46. Though this was expressed not in falling real wages but in extended working hours without corresponding increases in take-home income. Lichtenstein, *Labor's War at Home,* 110–17, 166; Dubofsky and Van Tine, *John L. Lewis,* 304–6; Zieger, *John L. Lewis,* 136–37.

47. The article exhibits the combination of keen insight, slashing rhetoric and paranoid conspiracy notions that made Lewis the remarkable labor figure of his age. The thesis of his remarks was that "there is no labor movement" but rather "a Tower of Babel" created by contending voices. Lewis identified the *absence* of a "government labor policy" as the root of labor's problems and divisions. This initially seems at odds with his concern about growing government power at the expense of labor union autonomy and popular liberty, but his point actually foreshadows the one made by Ted Lowi a generation later in *The End of Liberalism.* Roosevelt, he argued, had created corporate bodies empowered to govern labor relations *without* defining a policy; the War Labor Board acted arbitrarily, played favorites, and bargained with the forces it was supposed to regulate. He also believed that this arbitrary regulatory power was responsible for creating divisions within and weakening the labor movement. But Lewis was also convinced that Roosevelt was *deliberately* acting to divide and subordinate the American labor movement. Though the New Deal labor regime in fact depended on a divided labor movement, Roosevelt certainly did not see this and encouraged every effort toward AFL-CIO unity as a potential boon to the Democrats' political fortunes. Lewis, "There Is No Labor Movement," *Collier's,* 5 May 1945.

48. Cited in *CIO News,* 24 May 1943.

6. The AFL-CIO in the Age of Organization

1. On the CIO-PAC in the 1944 election cycle, see James Caldwell Foster, *The Union Politic: The CIO Political Action Committee* (Columbia: University of Missouri Press, 1975), 16–48; Steve Fraser, *Labor Will Rule: Sidney Hillman and the Rise of American Labor* (Ithaca, NY:

Cornell University Press, 1993),503–38; Nelson Lichtenstein, *Labor's War at Home: The CIO in World War II* (Cambridge: Cambridge University Press, 1982), 171–77; Robert H. Zieger, *The CIO, 1935–1955* (Chapel Hill: University of North Carolina Press, 1995), 181–88.

2. Regarding the "Clear it with Sidney" brouhaha see Foster, *Union Politic,* 39–48; Fraser, *Labor Will Rule,* 526–36; and James F. Byrnes, *All in One Lifetime* (New York: Harper, 1958), 216–30. Arthur Krock, "In the Nation," *New York Times,* 25 July 1944, 18.

3. Scholars usually estimate that at the war's end between one-fifth and one-third of the CIO unions were "Communist-dominated" or "Left." The name given this group varies with the author's political sympathies, but it signifies that party members and sympathetic political allies opposed to the Cold War held leadership in a union. See Zieger, *The CIO, 1935–1955,* 253–61; Harvey A. Levenstein, *Communism, Anticommunism, and the CIO* (Westport, CT: Greenwood, 1981), 213, 230; Max Kampelman, *The Communist Party versus the CIO: A Study in Power Politics* (New York: Praeger, 1957), 37, 45–47; and Judith Stepan-Norris and Maurice Zeitlin, "'Who Gets the Bird?' or, How the Communists Won Power and Trust in America's Unions: The Relative Autonomy of Intraclass Political Struggles," *American Sociological Review* 54 (August 1989): 503–23.

4. See Carlton J. H. Hayes, "The Challenge of Totalitarianism," *Public Opinion Quarterly* 2 (January 1938): 21–22; Robert Nisbet, "Rousseau and Totalitarianism," *Journal of Politics* 5 (May 1943): 93–114, and "The Politics of Social Pluralism: Some Reflections on Lamennais," *Journal of Politics* 10 (November 1948): 764–86; and Emil Lederer, *State of the Masses: The Threat of the Classless Society* (New York: Norton, 1940).

5. George Meany, "Trade Unions Must Be Free," in *Vital Speeches of the Day,* 1 October 1945, 760–61; Philip Taft, *AFL from the Death of Gompers to the Merger* (New York: Octagon, 1970), 238, 372–73, 386–97; Joseph C. Goulden, *Meany* (New York: Atheneum, 1972), 125–26; Federico Romero, *The United States and the European Trade Union Movement, 1944–1951* (Chapel Hill: University of North Carolina Press, 1992), 131–37.

6. Meany's remarks cited here came from his heated response to the First National Bank's campaign in support of "right-to-work" laws. Meany, "What American Labor Seeks for America," *U.S. News and World Report,* 27 April 1959, 115–16.

7. *ILWU Convention Proceedings,* 1947, 178. My italics.

8. Clinton S. Golden and Harold J. Ruttenberg, *The Dynamics of Industrial Democracy* (New York: Harper and Brothers, 1942), 211.

9. For the collaboration of Nazis and Communists to topple Social Democrat governments in Germany, see Julius Braunthal, *The History of the International* (London: Nelson, 1967), 2:354–90; to see how Reuther and other Americans interpreted same, see Lichtenstein, *Labor's War at Home,* 59–60, and *Walter Reuther: The Most Dangerous Man in Detroit* (Urbana: University of Illinois Press, 1997), 269.

10. See Melvyn Dubofsky, *The State and Labor in Modern America* (Chapel Hill: University of North Carolina Press, 1994), 192–95; Zieger, *The CIO, 1935–1955,* 212–14.

11. For the most thorough explanation of this theme, see H. J. Harris, *The Right to Manage* (Madison: University of Wisconsin Press, 1982).

12. On the 1946 election cycle, see Foster, *Union Politic,* 49–69. A thorough discussion of the politics of Taft-Hartley is to be found in R. Alton Lee, *Truman and Taft-Hartley: A Question of Mandate* (Westport, CT: Greenwood, 1966). Two contemporary treatments that assess the environment of the Taft-Hartley legislation and its merits are Philip Taft, "Democracy in Trade Unions," *American Economic Review* 36 (May 1946): 359–69; and Sumner H. Slichter, "The Taft-Hartley Act," *Quarterly Journal of Economics* 63 (Feb. 1949): 1–31.

13. Robert A. Christie, *Empire in Wood: A History of the Carpenters' Union* (Ithaca, NY: Cornell University Press, 1956), 282–83, 301–16.

14. A story ably told by Elizabeth A. Fones-Wolf in *Selling Free Enterprise: The Business Assault on Labor and Liberalism, 1945–1960* (Urbana: University of Illinois Press, 1994).

15. Lee, *Truman and Taft-Hartley,* 66–68.

16. Harris, *Right to Manage,* 79–89.

17. See C. Wright Mills, *The New Men of Power: America's Labor Leaders* (New York: Harcourt, Brace, 1948), 148; Nelson Lichtenstein, *Walter Reuther: The Most Dangerous Man in Detroit* (Urbana: University of Illinois Press), 19970, 168–69.

18. Romero, *The United States and the European Trade Union Movement,* 96–113.

19. Lichtenstein, *Walter Reuther,* 203–6, 232–42, 248–53, 266–70; and *Labor's War at Home,* 140–56; Irving Howe and B. J. Widick, *The UAW and Walter Reuther* (New York: Random House, 1949), 114–17.

20. Indeed, Wallace—now editor of *The New Republic*—had long before acknowledged that "the liberals in the so-called warring groups are about 90 percent in agreement." Wallace, "The Enemy Is Not Each Other," *New Republic,* 27 January 1947, 22–23. For the background of the PCA and the ADA, see Steven M. Gillon, *Politics and Vision: The ADA and American Liberalism, 1947–1985* (New York: Oxford University Press, 1987), 16–32; Foster, *Union Politic,* 89–93,101–5, 115–17; and David Brody, "The Uses of Power II: Political Action," in *Workers in Industrial America* (New York: Oxford University Press, 1980), 215–37.

21. The floor debate is found in the CIO *1949 Convention Proceedings,* 239–281, Reuther's speech is on 266–72.

22. See Levenstein, *Communism, Anticommunism, and the CIO,* 113–16, and Steve Rosswurm, "Catholic Church and Left Unions," in *The CIO's Left-Led Unions* (New Brunswick, NJ: Rutgers University Press, 1992), 125–28.

23. And in the ILA, where ACTU had initially fought gangster control, the organization changed sides and aligned with corrupt ILA President Joe Ryan when the Communists seemed on the verge of capturing leadership of the opposition. Douglas P. Seaton, *Catholics and Radicals: The Association of Catholic Trade Unionists and the American Labor Movement, from Depression to Cold War* (Lewisburg: Bucknell University Press, 1981), 23, 106–8, 143–45, 154.

24. Joel Seidman, *American Labor from Defense to Reconversion* (Chicago: University of Chicago Press, 1953), 49–50. Zieger, *The CIO, 1935–1955,* 287–90.

25. Zieger, *The CIO, 1935–1955,* 287; see also Ronald Filippelli and Mark D. McColloch, *Cold War in the Working Class: The Rise and Decline of the United Electrical Workers* (Albany: State University of New York Press, 1995), 116.

26. The local featured a remarkable internal political life and its leadership changed hands repeatedly in the 1940s. Ronald W. Schatz, *The Electrical Workers: A History of Labor at General Electric and Westinghouse* (Urbana: University of Illinois Press, 1983), 188–204; and Filippelli and McCulloch, *Cold War in the Working Class,* 68, 97.

27. Filippelli and McColloch, *Cold War in the Working Class,* 121–40.

28. See ibid., 103–4, 122–24, 141–54; Zieger, *The CIO, 1935–1955,* 292.

29. Although our information is limited, Wallace's 2.38 percent of the popular vote seems to have come primarily from middle-class activists moved by his championship of the peace issue.

30. *AFL Convention Proceedings,* 1947, 490–97; see also Melvyn Dubofsky and Warren Van Tine, *John L. Lewis: A Biography* (Urbana: University of Illinois Press, 1986), 338–40; Robert H. Zieger, *John L. Lewis: Labor Leader* (Boston: Twayne, 1988), 163–67; Goulden, *Meany,*

146–54; Archie Robinson, *George Meany and His Times* (New York: Simon & Schuster, 1981), 147–53; "Weak Must Fall," *Time,* 22 September 1947, 25–26.

31. Cited in Taft, *The AFL from the Death of Gompers to the Merger,* 312–13.

32. Joseph Shister, "Unresolved Problems and New Paths for American Labor," *Industrial and Labor Relations Review* 9 (April 1956): 447–57.

33. Meany laid out his mid-50s priorities in two reflections on Gompers and postwar American labor, "What Labor Means by 'More,'" a *Fortune* magazine essay published shortly before the merger (clearly with the merger in mind), and a 1956 Labor Day speech, "What Does Labor Want?" *Vital Speeches of the Day,* 15 September 1956, 722–24.

34. For a good discussion of Reuther as political educator, especially in the context of the 1945 strike against General Motors and his contemporary factional battles in the UAW, see Irving Howe and B. J. Widick, *The UAW and Walter Reuther* (1949; New York: Da Capo, 1973), 126–71.

35. Reuther, "Our Fear of Abundance," *New York Times Magazine,* 16 September 1945, 5.

36. Lichtenstein, *Walter Reuther,* 232–47; Zieger, *The CIO, 1935–1955,* 218–27; Harris, *Right to Manage,* 139–43; Howe and Widick, *The UAW and Walter Reuther,* 130–46; William Serrin, *The Company and the Union: The 'Civilized Relationship' of the General Motors Corporation and the United Automobile Workers* (New York: Vintage, 1974), 157–69.

37. GM pamphlet, cited in Howe and Widick, 137.

38. To see the case made by contemporary labor historians, see for instance Ronald W. Schatz, "From Commons to Dunlop: Rethinking the Field and Theory of Industrial Relations," in *Industrial Democracy in America: The Ambiguous Promise,* ed. Nelson Lichtenstein and Howell John Harris (Cambridge: Cambridge University Press, 1993), 87–112, and Harris, *Right to Manage.* To get the business-eye view, see *Fortune,* 1 July 1950, 53–55.

39. 1948 comments from UAW press release, cited in Lichtenstein, *Walter Reuther,* 179; see 276–98 for an excellent discussion of the "Treaty of Detroit" and UAW pattern bargaining realities.

40. Bruce E. Kaufman, *The Origins and Evolution of the Field of Industrial Relations in the United States* (Ithaca: ILR Press, 1993), 75.

41. The term "age of organization" was coined by political philosopher Sheldon Wolin, who—much like this author—feared that democracy was being squeezed out of modernity by bureaucracy at the top and individualism at the bottom. Sheldon Wolin, *Politics and Vision: Continuity and Innovation in Western Political Thought* (Boston: Little, Brown, 1960).

42. Peter Drucker, *The Concept of the Corporation* (1946; New Brunswick: Transaction, 1993); David Riesman, *The Lonely Crowd: A Study of the Changing American Character* (New Haven: Yale University Press, 1950); Daniel Bell, *Work and Its Discontents* (Boston: Beacon, 1956); and William H. Whyte, *The Organization Man* (New York: Simon and Schuster, 1956).

43. The most important being John T. Dunlop, *Industrial Relations Systems* (New York: Holt, 1958); Clark Kerr, John T. Dunlop, Frederick Harbison, and Charles A. Myers, *Industrialism and Industrial Man* (1960; New York: Oxford University Press, 1964); Dunlop and Derek C. Bok, *Labor and the American Community* (New York: Simon and Schuster, 1970).

44. *Industrial Relations Systems,* intended as a value-neutral social scientific framework, indulges in relatively little such "express advocacy." But see for instance Dunlop's spirited debate with A. H. Raskin of the *New York Times.* "Two Views of Collective Bargaining," in *Challenges to Collective Bargaining,* ed. Lloyd T. Ulman (Englewood Cliffs: Prentice-Hall, 1967), 155–80.

45. Kerr, Dunlop, et al., *Industrialism and Industrial Man,* 132, 135, 228, 232.

46. Ibid., 185, 235.

47. Ibid., 228, 237–8.

48. Daniel Bell, *The Cultural Contradictions of Capitalism* (New York: Basic Books, 1978), 72.

49. Plato, *Republic,* 415a; Aristotle, *Politics,* 1293b–1294a.

50. Alexis de Tocqueville, *Democracy in America* (New York: Harper Collins, 1969), 435.

51. When a ruling class is not hereditary Americans have a hard time seeing it at all. For the meritocracy revealed, see Nicholas Lemann, *The Big Test: The Secret History of the American Aristocracy* (New York: Farrar, Straus and Giroux, 1999), and Michael Young, *The Rise of the Meritocracy, 1870–2033: An Essay on Education and Inequality* (Baltimore: Penguin, 1970 [1958]).

52. The most important American social-scientific examination of this problem is Richard Sennett and Jonathan Cobb's *The Hidden Injuries of Class* (New York: Norton, 1972).

53. William M. Leiserson, *American Trade Union Democracy* (New York: Columbia University Press, 1959), 75.

54. R. Alton Lee, *Eisenhower and Landrum-Griffin* (Lexington: University Press of Kentucky, 1990), 45–54.

55. *AFL Convention Proceedings,* 1953, 55; Robinson, *George Meany and His Times,* 190; Vernon H. Jensen, *Strife on the Waterfront: The Port of New York since 1945* (Ithaca, NY: Cornell University Press, 1974), 105–11, 121–35,179–81, 239–43.

56. As in the case of the UMW and the building trades, after Taft-Hartley these were, strictly speaking, jointly administered funds financed by employer contributions and reserving half the trustee positions for employer representatives. However, the union tends to dominate funds in such industries—thus we refer to the "Teamsters' pension" or the "Carpenters' fund," rather than the joint fund.

57. James R. Hoffa, *Hoffa: The Real Story* (New York: Stein and Day, 1975), 60.

58. An excellent work on Hoffa and his union informing much of this discussion is Ralph and Estelle James's *Hoffa and the Teamsters: A Study of Union Power* (Princeton, NJ: Van Nostrand, 1965). Hoffa, at the height of his career, granted extraordinary and unique access to the two academic researchers. They provide the best account of the mechanics of Hoffa's operations, and provide an especially interesting character study of America's most notorious "union boss." Arthur Sloane's biography, *Hoffa* (Cambridge: MIT Press, 1993), offers another well-documented and thorough treatment. Thaddeus Russell's *Out of the Jungle: Jimmy Hoffa and the Remaking of the American Working Class* (New York: Knopf, 2001) posits the Teamsters as the business union *par excellence*—but his narrative, intentionally or not, is drenched in the romance of Hoffa's brand of class war.

59. Hoffa's lawlessness, of course, caught up with him. In 1964 he was convicted of jury tampering, and later, additional charges; in 1967 he began serving a sentence in Lewisburg prison; after his release, he was banned from union activity for a decade, and finally in 1975 he disappeared under mysterious circumstances.

60. Two notable such accounts were those of A. H. Raskin, "Reuther vs. Hoffa: A Key Struggle," *New York Times Magazine* (22 September 1957), and Sidney Lens, "Hoffa and Reuther," in *The Crisis of American Labor* (New York: A. S. Barnes, 1959), 133–171.

61. Robert F. Kennedy, *The Enemy Within* (New York: Harper and Brothers, 1960); see also Russell, *Out of the Jungle,* 181–212.

62. Quoted in Rick Perlstein, *Before the Storm: Barry Goldwater and the Unmaking of the*

American Consensus (New York: Hill and Wang, 2001), 36–37. See also Lee, *Eisenhower and Landrum-Griffin*, 65–73.

63. See Sloane, *Hoffa*, 99–103, 134–5, 182, 256; Goulden, *Meany*, 235, 243–56; Robinson, *George Meany and His Times*, 196; "Hoffa on the AFL-CIO," *Newsweek* (25 November 1963), 87; *AFL-CIO Executive Council Minutes*, October 1961, 4.

64. Sloane, *Hoffa*, 95–103; Goulden, *Meany*, 243–54.

65. 1957 *AFL-CIO Convention Proceedings*, 93.

66. For discussions see Philip Taft, "The Impact of Landrum-Griffin on Union Government," *Annals of the American Academy of Political and Social Science* 333 (January 1961): 130–40; Marvin Snowbarger and Sam Pintz, "Landrum-Griffin and Union President Turnover," *Industrial Relations* 9 (October 1970): 475–76. For a more optimistic assessment, see Doris B. McLaughlin and Anita L. W. Schoomaker, *The Landrum-Griffin Act and Union Democracy* (Ann Arbor: University of Michigan Press, 1979).

7. Not a Slogan or a Fad

1. Important treatments of this theme include Sidney Verba, Kay Lehman Schlozman, and Henry E. Brady, *Voice and Equality: Civic Voluntarism and American Politics* (Cambridge: Harvard University Press, 1995); Ruy A. Teixeira, *The Disappearing American Voter*; and Robert D. Putnam, *Bowling Alone: The Collapse and Revival of American Community* (New York: Simon and Schuster, 2000).

2. Though the differential between voting participation by union and nonunion workers has not been as satisfactorily examined as one might like, most researchers have agreed that union members participate in politics, including voting, at significantly higher rates than nonunion voters who otherwise fit their demographic profile. Better established is the Democratic partisan "union effect" on vote choice. A persistent "union effect" of ten points or more in the Democrats' favor during national elections has been observed; its decline has often been predicted but never seems to materialize. See Arthur Kornhauser, Albert J. Mayer, and Harold L. Sheppard, *When Labor Votes: A Study of Auto Workers* (New York: University Books, 1956), 29–31, 72–73; Ruy A. Teixeira and Joel Rogers, *America's Forgotten Majority: Why the White Working Class Still Matters* (New York: Basic Books, 2000), 131–33; and Steven J. Rosenstone and John Mark Hansen, *Mobilization, Participation, and Democracy in America* (New York: Macmillan, 1993). See Warren E. Miller and J. Merrill Shanks, *The New American Voter* (Cambridge: Harvard University Press, 1996), 275–76; and David J. Sousa, "Organized Labor in the Electorate, 1960–1988," *Presidential Research Quarterly* 46 (December 1993): 741–59.

3. Alan Draper, *A Rope of Sand: The AFL-CIO Committee on Political Education, 1955–1967* (New York: Praeger, 1989), 60–76, and Gilbert J. Gall, *The Politics of Right to Work: The Labor Federations as Special Interests, 1943–1979* (New York: Greenwood, 1988), 93–128.

4. Alexis de Tocqueville, *Democracy in America* (New York: Harper Collins, 1969), 72, 93; *Old Regime and the French Revolution* (New York: Doubleday, 1955), 69.

5. Clark Kerr, John T. Dunlop, Frederick Harbison, and Charles A. Myers. *Industrialism and Industrial Man* (1960; New York: Oxford University Press, 1964), 235.

6. Joseph C. Goulden, *Meany* (New York: Atheneum, 1972), 327.

7. In 1960, nearly 30 percent of American workers belonged to labor unions; two decades later, as the 1970s drew to a close, that proportion had slipped slightly to 25 per-

cent. While the downturn among private-sector employees was considerably greater than that, the net effect was blunted as the share of public employees belonging to unions more than tripled.

8. Filibusters blocked labor law reform legislation in 1965 under Lyndon Johnson and again in 1978 under Jimmy Carter. Taylor Dark, *The Unions and the Democrats: An Enduring Alliance* (Ithaca, NY: Cornell University Press, 1999), 59–63, 107–14.

9. Goulden, *Meany,* 322. For the whole story, see Dark, *Unions and the Democrats,* 47–59; J. David Greenstone, *Labor in American Politics* (New York: Knopf, 1969), 336–43; Vaughn Davis Bornet, *The Presidency of Lyndon B. Johnson* (Lawrence: University of Kansas Press, 1983), 236–38; Eric Goldman, *The Tragedy of Lyndon Johnson* (New York: Knopf, 1969), 284–96.

10. Goulden, *Meany,* 341–42; Greenstone, *Labor in American Politics,* (337–39; Dark, *Unions and the Democrats,* 57–58

11. For discussion see James A. Gross, *Broken Promise: The Subversion of U.S. Labor Relations Policy, 1947–1994* (Philadelphia: Temple University Press, 1995).

12. Most of the public opinion information here was gathered from Roper polls and can be found in Michael X. Delli Carpini and Scott Keeter, *What Americans Know About Politics and Why It Matters* (New Haven: Yale University Press, 1996), 73–82.

13. The account below comes largely from Gross, *Broken Promise,* esp. 146–52, 172–74, 189–241.

14. See Frank McCulloch and Tim Bornstein, *The National Labor Relations Board* (New York: Praeger, 1974), 71, 163–65.

15. Kenneth C. McGuiness, *The New Frontier NLRB* (Washington, DC: Labor Policy Association, 1963), 245.

16. Gross, *Broken Promise,* 198–223.

17. Ibid., 246–66.

18. Even labor's most forceful critics acknowledge this point. See Herbert Hill, "Black Workers, Organized Labor and Title VII of the 1964 Civil Rights Act: Legislative History and Litigation Record," in *Race in America: The Struggle for Equality,* ed. Herbert Hill and James E. Jones (Madison: University of Wisconsin Press, 1993).

19. Jervis Anderson, *A. Philip Randolph: A Biographical Portrait* (New York: Harvest, 1972), 247–61, 285–307.

20. Other major unions that supported the march included the IUE, ILGWU, and AFSCME. "Meany vs. Reuther: Clash on Rights March," *US News and World Report,* 26 August 1963, 22; Nelson Lichtenstein, *Walter Reuther: The Most Dangerous Man in Detroit* (Urbana: University of Illinois Press, 1997), 370–95; Kevin Boyle, *The UAW and the Heyday of American Liberalism, 1945–1968* (Ithaca, NY: Cornell University Press, 1995), 161–71; Anderson, *A. Philip Randolph,* 320–30.

21. To see some of it, read Alan Draper, *A Rope of Sand: The AFL-CIO Committee on Political Education, 1955–1967* (Westport, CT: Praeger, 1989), 105–17.

22. Dirksen promised to drop his filibuster against repeal of the despised section 14(b) if labor would withdraw its opposition to his constitutional amendment overturning a key Supreme Court decision. *Baker v. Carr* held that the principle of "one man, one vote" forbade state legislative apportionment schemes that favored rural areas—a subterfuge used widely in the South to enable conservative white rural districts to dominate state politics and reduce the clout of urban black ones. See Goulden, *Meany,* 347–48; Dark, *Unions and the Democrats,* 61–62; Gall, *Politics of Right to Work,* 170–9; Greenstone, *Labor in American Politics,* 344–55;

Neil MacNeil, *Dirksen: Portrait of a Public Man* (New York: World Publishing, 1970), 244–49, 260–67.

23. Derek C. Bok and John T. Dunlop, *Labor and the American Community* (New York: Simon and Schuster, 1970), 135.

24. Be careful what you ask for, as they say, you just might get it. Dark, *Unions and the Democrats,* 57; see also Greenstone, *Labor in American Politics,* 340–42.

25. Meany was not always so restrained, however, especially in dealing with the state federations over which he exercised more authority than over international union affiliates. When the Massachusetts State Federation of Labor defied the national AFL-CIO by opposing busing to integrate south Boston schools, Meany informed this particular federation that it faced expulsion if it did not rescind its stance. The Massachusetts Federation quickly fell into line. See Marc K. Landy, "The Political Imperative: George Meany's Strategy of Leadership," in Peter Dennis Bathory, *Leadership in America: Consensus, Corruption, and Charisma* (New York: Longman, 1978), 79–96.

26. See Goulden, *Meany,* 407–11, and Jill Quadagno, "Social Movements and State Transformation: Labor Unions and Racial Conflict in the War on Poverty," *American Sociological Review* 57 (October 1992): 626–28.

27. Quarles et al. v. Philip Morris, Inc., 279 F. Supp. 505 (1967). See also 1960s EEOC consultant and future Clinton NLRB Chairman William B. Gould's *Black Workers in White Unions: Job Discrimination in the United States* (Ithaca, NY: Cornell University Press, 1977), 67–80.

28. Hill, "Black Workers, Organized Labor and Title VII," 274, 287, 302–3, 311, 312. Hill's tendentious account indulges in a good deal of unsubstantiated speculation about the motives of his opponents. "*It may be assumed* that many proponents of the bill, including the leaders of organized labor, hardly envisioned Title VII as an instrument for major social change." "*The pretext* for the UAW's complaint was that the NAACP had not informed the union of its activity in a proper, formal manner, *but the real problem* for the UAW, *as everyone understood,* lay in the contrast between the direct action of the NAACP in mobilizing an effective campaign and the failure of the union to challenge the auto industry's racial practices," and, "*To divert attention from the central issue* of racial discrimination in the Holmes case, union officials mounted an intensive public relations campaign, trying to make anti-Semitism the issue instead." Hill was so shockingly blind to trade unions needs and norms that he dismissed union leaders' angry reactions to *decertification efforts* he led against an ILGWU local accused of discrimination as nothing more than a knee-jerk defense of white supremacy.

29. Charles Kelly's eloquent (rather *too* eloquent, to my lights) letter to the *Times* appeared 8 August 1963 and was cited by Jill Quadagno in "Social Movements and State Transformation: Labor Unions and Racial Conflict in the War on Poverty," *American Sociological Review* 57 (October 1992): 616–34.

30. See Benjamin W. Wolkinson, *Blacks, Unions, and the EEOC: A Study in Administrative Futility* (Lexington, MA: Lexington Books, 1973), 28, and Gould, *Meany,* 126–35.

31. The definitive voter study of the era, *The American Voter,* concluded that the general prosperity of the postwar era was making social class less salient among American workers both as an identity and as a predictor of voting behavior. Moreover, to this day it is hard to speak with union political activists without hearing them morosely observe that labor, having made its members prosperous, has turned them into Republicans. Ironically, the authors

of *The American Voter* also observed that "*union members* receiving wages normally associated with higher occupation strata *maintain their identification with the working class.*" Being part of the union "establishment" had not made these workers more conservative but rather more class-conscious. Angus Campbell, Philip Converse, Warren E. Miller, and Donald E. Stokes, *The American Voter* (New York: Wiley, 1960), 357, 379. Authors' italics. From Galbraith see John Kenneth Galbraith, *American Capitalism: The Concept of Countervailing Power* (Boston: Houghton-Mifflin, 1952), and *The Affluent Society* (Boston: Houghton-Mifflin, 1958).

32. See Richard A. Lester, *As Unions Mature: An Analysis of the Evolution of American Unionism* (Princeton: Princeton University Press, 1978), esp. 21.

33. "The Galbraith Acceptance," *ADA World Magazine,* May 1967.

34. Steven M. Gillon, *Politics and Vision: The ADA and American Liberalism, 1947–1985* (New York: Oxford University Press, 1987),, 123, 210–14.

35. Dark, *Unions and the Democrats,* 58, 70; Lichtenstein, *Walter Reuther,* 389–95; Boyle, *UAW and the Heyday of American Liberalism,* 158–60, 189–93.

36. Reuther, cited in Boyle, *UAW and the Heyday of American Liberalism,* 237.

37. "To Clarify UAW's Position with the AFL-CIO," *UAW Solidarity* (February 1967): 10–11, and "A Matter of Principle," *UAW Solidarity* (March 1967): 7–10.

38. To this day a notion of "social unionism" is central to the self-identity of the United Autoworkers. In the December issue of the union's magazine *Solidarity,* for instance, we find that "The social union philosophy of Walter Reuther, the UAW's third and longest serving international president, lives on today. . . . In contrast to the business unionism of many labor leaders, Reuther was concerned about more than grievances, contracts, and other traditional union business. As a social unionist [he was] concerned about changing society as well as the workplace." Sam Stark, "Social Unionism: Reuther's Legacy to the UAW," *UAW Solidarity* (December 2000): 11.

39. From a UAW leadership resolution on "Relations with AFL-CIO" presented to the delegates of the 1968 UAW convention, the resolution was approved overwhelmingly. *Proceedings of the 21st Constitutional Convention of the UAW* (May 1968), 341.

40. Goulden, *Meany,* 324–27; Lichtenstein, *Walter Reuther,* 351–52, 368.

41. See Richard Griswold del Castillo and Richard A. Garcia, *Cesar Chavez: A Triumph of Spirit* (Norman: University of Oklahoma Press, 1995), 22–38, 49–55, 122–26; J. Craig Jenkins, *The Politics of Insurgency: The Farm Worker Movement in the 1960s* (New York: Columbia University Press, 1985), 59–62, 131–37, 172–79, 186–90; *Proceedings of the AFL-CIO Convention, 1969,* 465; Goulden, *Meany,* 398; Lichtenstein, *Walter Reuther,* 410–11.

42. Reuther was by this time dead, but his ill-conceived Alliance for Labor Action survived him. Jenkins, *Politics of Insurgency,* 178–79; Lichtenstein, *Walter Reuther,* 432–33.

43. *AFL-CIO Convention Proceedings* (1969), 430; *Proceedings of the 21st Constitutional Convention of the UAW* (May 1968), 345; Lichtenstein, *Walter Reuther,* 408–10.

44. Meany, cited in *AFL-CIO Convention Proceedings,* 1969, 408, 434.

45. Reuther, cited in *Proceedings of the 21st Constitutional Convention of the UAW* (May 1968), 345.

46. "A Matter of Principle," *UAW Solidarity* (March 1967): 10.

47. Goulden, *Meany,* 387; *AFL-CIO Proceedings* (1969), 408–9, 430.

48. Dark, *Unions and the Democrats,* 83–101; William J. Crotty, *Decision for the Democrats: Reforming the Party Structure* (Baltimore: Johns Hopkins University Press, 1978), 110–12, 222–23, 244–57.

49. "Interview with George Meany," *US News and World Report* (21 February 1972): 27–28.

50. Dark, *Unions and the Democrats,* 72–73; Lichtenstein, *Walter Reuther,* 366–68.

51. *The Gallup Poll: Public Opinion, 1935–1971* (New York: Random House, 1972), 1483–84.

52. The theme of most of this literature was that the common run of citizens had only a causal commitment to democratic norms, with widespread authoritarian predilections concealed just below the surface. Theodor Adorno and his collaborators inked the genre landmark *The Authoritarian Personality* (1950), although Seymour Martin Lipset earned dubious honor of coining the term "working-class authoritarianism" to characterize the worker's alleged civic deficiencies. Studies documenting the lower classes' putatively inadequate adherence to democratic values continue to this day, as can be seen in Verba, Schlozman, and Brady, among others. T. W. Adorno, Else Frenkel-Brunswik, Daniel J. Levinson, and R. Nevitt Sanford. *The Authoritarian Personality* (New York: Harper and Brothers, 1950), 267, 269; Samuel Stouffer, *Communism, Conformity, and Civil Liberties: A Cross-Section of the Nation Speaks Its Mind* (Garden City: Doubleday, 1955); William Kornhauser, *The Politics of Mass Society* (New York: Free Press, 1959); Seymour Martin Lipset, *Political Man: The Social Bases of Politics* (Garden City: Doubleday, 1960), 97–130; see also Philip Converse, "The Nature of Belief Systems in Mass Publics," in *Ideology and Discontent,* ed. David E. Apter (New York: Free Press, 1964), 206–61; Verba, Lehman Schlozman, and Brady, *Voice and Equality,* 500–506, 555. A good critical discussion of this body of research can be found in Christopher Lasch, *The True and Only Heaven: Progress and Its Critics* (New York: W. W. Norton, 1991),, under the heading "The Politics of the Civilized Minority."

53. Wallace, cited in Stephen Lesher, *George Wallace: American Populist* (Reading, PA: Addison-Wesley, 1994), 390. Some actual analysis of the 1964 Wisconsin primary can be found in Richard F. Hamilton, *Class and Politics in the United States* (New York: John Wiley, 1972), 460–67.

54. Lichtenstein, *Walter Reuther,* 427–29; Goulden, *Meany,* 367–69; Lesher, *George Wallace,* 412–13; Dan T. Carter, *The Politics of Rage: George Wallace, the Origins of the New Conservatism, and the Transformation of American Politics* (New York: Simon and Schuster, 1995), 351–52; "How Wallace Campaign Is Splitting the Labor Vote," *US News and World Report,* 23 September 1968, 98–99.

55. See Lichtenstein, *Walter Reuther,* 427–29; and Goulden, *Meany,* 367–69; "Labor's Battle Cry Now: Stop Wallace," *US News and World Report,* 14 October 1968, 108–9.

56. *UAW Solidarity* (October 1968): 9.

57. Meany, cited in Archie Robinson, *George Meany and His Times* (New York: Simon & Schuster, 1981), 277–78.

58. Theodore White, in his classic account of the 1968 presidential race, describes labor's electoral assault on Wallace as "unprecedented" and credits the unions with transforming a working class largely sympathetic to Wallace in the summer of 1968 into a hostile force in November. Theodore H. White, *The Making of the President, 1968* (New York: Atheneum, 1969), 362–70; see also Hamilton, *Class and Politics,* 460–63; see also Sousa, "Organized Labor in the Electorate."

59. Harold H. Martin, "George Wallace Shakes Up the Political Scene," *Saturday Evening Post,* 9 May 1964, 85–88.

60. Cited in Lesher, *George Wallace,* 369.

61. Lane Kirkland, "Making Democracy Work," *American Federationist* (September 1969): 16–19.

Aftermath

1. Marick F. Masters, *Unions at the Crossroads:* (Westport, CT: Quorum, 1997), 66–70; Jeff Grabelsky and Mark Ehrlich, "Recent Innovations in the Building Trades," in *Which Direction for Organized Labor?* ed. Bruce Nissen (Detroit: Wayne State University Press, 1999).

2. See Barbara Ehrenreich, *Nickel and Dimed: On (Not) Getting By in America* (New York: Metropolitan Books, 2001); Beth Shulman, *The Betrayal of Work: How Low-Wage Jobs Fail 30 Million Americans and Their Families* (New York: New Press, 2003); David K. Shipler, *The Working Poor: Invisible in America* (New York: Knopf, 2004).

3. By the late 1990s the NLRB was reporting more than 20,000 back pay awards to workers for such illegal reprisals; Cornell University researcher Kate Bronfrenbrenner estimated that workers unlawfully fire union advocates or sympathizers in some 25 percent of organizing campaigns. See *Unfair Advantage: Workers' Freedom of Association in the United States under International Human Rights* (Human Rights Watch, 2000). Those who doubt that such defiance is willful should consult Martin Jay Levitt and Terry Conrow, *Confessions of a Union Buster* (New York: Crown, 1993).

4. Daniel V. Yager and Joseph J. LoBue, "Corporate Campaigns and Card Checks: Creating the Company Unions of the Twenty-First Century," *Employee Relations Law Journal* 24 (Spring 1999): 21–50.

5. Taylor E. Dark, *The Unions and the Democrats* (Ithaca, NY: Cornell University Press, 1999), 76–92.

6. *Ibid.*, 208–16, and Taylor E. Dark, "Labor and the Democratic Party: A Report on the 1998 Elections," *Journal of Labor Research* 21 (2000): 627–40; Glenn Burkins, "Labor Plans to Shift to Its Foot Soldiers in 1998's Congressional Campaigns," *Wall Street Journal,* 20 January 1998, 1; Aaron Bernstein, "Labor Helps Turn the Tide—the Old-Fashioned Way," *Business Week,* 16 November 1998, 45.

7. Kathy Kiely, "In the End, 'Ground Game' May Decide Closest Races," *USA Today,* 4 November 2002, A1; Ann Gerhart, "Ground War: Steve Rosenthal Wages a $100 Million Battle to Line Up Democratic Votes," *Washington Post,* 6 July 2004, C1; John Harris, "Boasts and Bluster in the Ground War," *Washington Post,* 4 October 2004, A1; Howard Fineman, "The Ground Game," *Newsweek,* 4 October 2004, 32–35.

8. "President Bush, Mobilization Drives Propel Turnout to Post-1968 High; Kerry, Democratic Weakness Shown," Press Release, Center for the Study of the American Electorate, 4 November 2004.

SELECTED BIBLIOGRAPHY

Adamic, Louis. *Dynamite: The Story of Class Violence in America.* New York: Harper & Row, 1931.

Adorno, T. W., Else Frenkel-Brunswik, Daniel J. Levinson, and R. Nevitt Sanford. *The Authoritarian Personality.* New York: Harper and Brothers, 1950.

Aitken, Hugh G. J. *Scientific Management in Action: Taylorism at Watertown Arsenal, 1908–1915.* Princeton, NJ: Princeton University Press, 1985.

American Federation of Labor. *American Federationist.* Washington, DC: 1894–1976.

——. *Report of Proceedings of the Annual Convention of the American Federation of Labor.* 1888–1955.

American Federation of Labor–Congress of Industrial Organizations. Report of Convention Proceedings. Washington, DC: 1955–present.

Anderson, Jervis. *A. Philip Randolph: A Biographical Portrait.* New York: Harvest, 1973.

Arendt, Hannah. *On Revolution.* New York: Viking Press, 1963.

Aristotle. *Nicomachean Ethics.* Translated by Martin Ostwald. New York: Bobbs-Merrill, 1962.

——. *The Politics of Aristotle.* Translated by Ernest Barker. London: Oxford University Press, 1973.

Baker, Ray Stannard. "What the U.S. Steel Corporation Really Is, and How It Works." *McClure's* 18 (November 1901): 3–13.

Barber, Benjamin R. *Strong Democracy: Participatory Politics for a New Age.* Berkeley: University of California Press, 1984.

Baron, James N., Frank R. Dobbin, and P. Devereaux Jennings. "War and Peace: The Evolution of Modern Personnel Administration in U.S. Industry." *American Journal of Sociology* 92 (1986): 350–83.

Bell, Daniel. *The Cultural Contradictions of Capitalism.* New York: Basic Books, 1976.

Berle, Adolph, "American Capitalism." *Review of Economics and Statistics* 35 (February 1953): 81–84.

Berle, Adolph, and Gardiner Means. *The Modern Corporation and Private Property.* New York: Macmillan, 1933.

Bernstein, Irving. *The Lean Years: A History of the American Worker, 1920–33.* Baltimore: Penguin, 1966.

——. *The Turbulent Years: A History of the American Worker, 1933–41.* Boston: Houghton Mifflin, 1970.

Betten, Neil. *Catholic Activism and the Industrial Worker.* Gainesville: University of Florida Press, 1976.

Blanshard, Paul. *American Freedom and Catholic Power.* Boston: Beacon Press, 1949.

Blauner, Robert. *Alienation and Freedom: The Factory Worker and His Industry.* Chicago: University of Chicago Press, 1964.

Boesche, Roger. *The Strange Liberalism of Alexis de Tocqueville.* Ithaca, NY: Cornell University Press, 1987.

Bok, Derek C., and John T. Dunlop. *Labor and the American Community.* New York: Simon and Schuster, 1970.

Bokenkotter, Thomas. *A Concise History of the Catholic Church.* New York: Doubleday, 1990.

Boyle, Kevin. *The UAW and the Heyday of American Liberalism, 1945–1968.* Ithaca, NY: Cornell University Press, 1995.

Brandeis, Louis D. *The Curse of Bigness: Miscellaneous Papers of Louis D. Brandeis.* Port Washington: Kennikat, 1965.

———. *Other People's Money and How the Bankers Use It.* 1914. New York: Kelley, 1971.

Braverman, Harry. *Labor and Monopoly Capital: The Degradation of Work in the Twentieth Century.* New York: Monthly Review, 1974.

Brecher, Jeremy. *Strike!* Boston: South End, 1972.

Brody, David. *In Labor's Cause.* New York: Oxford University Press, 1993.

———. *Workers in Industrial America.* New York: Oxford University Press, 1980.

Bronfrenbrenner, Kate, Sheldon Friedman, Richard W. Hurd, Rudolph A. Oswald, and Ronald L. Seeber, eds. *Organizing to Win: New Research on Union Strategies.* Ithaca, NY: Cornell University Press, 1998.

Brooks, George W., Milton Derber, David A. McCabe, and Philip Taft, eds. *Interpreting the Labor Movement.* Champaign, IL.: IRRA, 1952.

Brooks, Robert C. "Reflections on the 'World Revolution' of 1940." *American Political Science Review* 35 (February 1941): 1–28.

Buenker, John D. *Urban Liberalism and Progressive Reform.* New York: Charles Scribner, 1973.

Buhle, Paul. *Taking Care of Business: Samuel Gompers, George Meany, Lane Kirkland, and the Tragedy of American Labor.* New York: Monthly Review, 1999.

Burgoyne, Arthur. *Homestead.* Pittsburgh: Rawsthorne, 1893.

Burnham, James. *The Managerial Revolution: What Is Happening in the World.* New York: John Day, 1941.

Burhnam, Walter Dean, "The Changing Shape of the American Political Universe." *American Political Science Review* 59 (March 1965): 7–28.

Burns, James MacGregor. *The Lion and the Fox: The First Political Biography of Franklin Delano Roosevelt.* New York: Harcourt, Brace & World, 1956.

Campbell, Angus, Philip Converse, Warren E. Miller, and Donald E. Stokes. *The American Voter.* New York: Wiley, 1960.

Carnegie, Andrew. *Triumphant Democracy, or, Fifty Years' March of the Republic.* New York: Scribner's, 1886.

Carter, Dan T. *The Politics of Rage: George Wallace, the Origins of the New Conservatism, and the Transformation of American Politics.* New York: Simon and Schuster, 1995.

Cashman, Sean Dennis. *America in the Gilded Age.* New York: New York University Press, 1984.

Chamberlain, Neil, and James Kuhn. *Collective Bargaining.* New York: McGraw-Hill, 1986.

Chandler, Alfred. *The Visible Hand: The Managerial Revolution in American Business.* Cambridge: Harvard University Press, 1977.

Chavez, Linda, and Daniel Gray. *Betrayal: How Union Bosses Shake Down their Members and Corrupt American Politics.* New York: Crown Forum, 2004.

Chenery, William. *Industry and Human Welfare*. New York: Macmillan, 1922.

Christie, Robert A. *Empire in Wood: A History of the Carpenters' Union*. Ithaca, NY: Cornell University Press, 1956.

Clark, Paul F., Peter Gottlieb, and Donald Kennedy, eds. *Forging a Union of Steel: Philip Murray, SWOC and the United Steelworkers*. Ithaca, NY: Cornell University Press, 1987.

Coase, R. H. "The Nature of the Firm." In *The Nature of the Firm: Origins, Evolution, and Development,* edited by Oliver E. Williamson and Sidney G. Winter. Oxford: Oxford University Press, 1991.

Cochran, Thomas C., and William Miller. *The Age of Enterprise: A Social History of Industrial America*. New York: Harper and Row, 1965.

Commons, John R. *Myself: The Autobiography of John R. Commons*. 1934. Madison: University of Wisconsin Press, 1963.

——. *Selected Essays*. 2 vols. London: Routledge, 1996.

Commons, John R., Ulrich B. Phillips, Eugene A. Gilmore, Helen L. Sumner, and John B. Andrews, eds. *A Documentary History of American Industrial Society*. Cleveland: Arthur H. Clark, 1910.

Congress of Industrial Organizations. *Daily Proceedings of the Constitutional Convention*. Washington, DC: 1938–1955.

Converse, Philip. "The Nature of Belief Systems in Mass Publics." In *Ideology and Discontent,* edited by David E. Apter. New York: Free Press, 1964.

Cooke, Morris Llewellyn, and Philip Murray. *Organized Labor and Production*. 1940. New York: Arno, 1971.

Cowie, Jefferson. "Nixon's Class Struggle: Romancing the New Right Worker, 1969–1973." *Labor History* (August 2002): 257–86.

Croly, Herbert. *The Promise of American Life*. 1909. Boston: Northeastern, 1989.

Crotty, William J. *Decision for the Democrats: Reforming the Party Structure*. Baltimore: Johns Hopkins University Press, 1978.

Crunden, Robert. *Ministers of Reform: The Progressives' Achievement in American Civilization, 1889–1920*. Urbana: University of Illinois Press, 1984.

Dahl, Robert. *A Preface to Economic Democracy*. Berkeley: University of California Press, 1985.

Dahl, Robert A. *Who Governs? Democracy and Power in an American City*. New Haven, CT: Yale University Press, 1961.

Dark, Taylor E. *The Unions and the Democrats: An Enduring Alliance*. Ithaca, NY: Cornell University Press, 1999.

Davis, Mike. *Prisoners of the American Dream: Politics and Economy in the History of the U.S. Working Class*. London: Verso, 1986.

Debs, Eugene V. *Debs: His Life, Speeches, and Writings*. Chicago: Charles H. Kerr, 1908.

——. *Writings and Speeches of Eugene V. Debs*. New York: Hermitage Press, 1948.

Derber, Milton, and Edward Young, eds. *Labor and the New Deal*. Madison: University of Wisconsin Press, 1961.

Dickman, Howard. *Industrial Democracy in America: Ideological Origins of National Labor Relations Policy*. LaSalle: Open Court, 1987.

Dorfman, Joseph. *The Economic Mind in American Civilization*, 5 vols. New York: Kelley, 1969.

Dorfman, Joseph, C. E. Ayres, Neil W. Chamberlain, Simon Kuznets, and R. A. Gordon.

Institutional Economics: Veblen, Commons, and Mitchell Reconsidered. Berkeley: University of California Press, 1963.

Douglas, William A., and Roy S. Godson, "Labor and Hegemony: A Critique." *International Organization* 34 (Winter 1980): 149–58.

Draper, Alan. *A Rope of Sand: The AFL-CIO Committee on Political Education, 1955–1967.* Westport, CT: Praeger, 1989.

Drucker, Peter F. *The Concept of the Corporation.* 1946. New Brunswick: Transaction, 1993.

——. *The End of Economic Man: A Study of the New Totalitarianism.* New York: John Day, 1939.

Dubinsky, David, and A. H. Raskin. *David Dubinsky: A Life with Labor.* New York: Simon and Schuster, 1977.

Dubofsky, Melvyn. *The State and Labor in Modern America.* Chapel Hill: University of North Carolina Press, 1994.

——. *We Shall Be All: A History of the IWW.* New York: Quadrangle/New York Times Book, 1969.

Dubofsky, Melvyn, and Foster Rhea Dulles. *Labor in America: A History.* Arlington Heights, Ill.: Harlan Davidson, 1984.

Dubofsky, Melvyn, and Warren Van Tine. *John L. Lewis: A Biography.* Urbana: University of Illinois Press, 1986.

——, eds. *Labor Leaders in America.* Urbana: University of Illinois Press, 1987.

Dunlop, John T. *Industrial Relations Systems.* New York: Holt, 1958.

Dunlop, John T., and Neil W. Chamberlain, eds. *Frontiers of Collective Bargaining.* New York: Harper and Row, 1967.

Durkheim, Emile. *The Division of Labor in Society.* 1893. New York: Free Press, 1984.

Easley, Ralph M. "What Organized Labor Has Learned." *McClure's,* 19, October 1902, 483–92.

Edwards, Richard. *Contested Terrain.* New York: Basic Books, 1979.

Engerman, Stanley L., ed. *Terms of Labor: Slavery, Serfdom, and Free Labor.* Stanford: Stanford University Press, 1999.

Feller, David E. "A General Theory of the Collective Bargaining Agreement." *California Law Review* 61 (May 1973): 663–856.

Filippelli, Ronald L., and Mark D. McColloch. *Cold War in the Working Class: The Rise and Decline of the United Electrical Workers.* Albany: State University of New York Press, 1995.

Fine, Sidney. *Sit-Down: The General Motors Strike of 1936–1937.* Ann Arbor: University of Michigan Press, 1969.

Fink, Leon. *Workingmen's Democracy: The Knights of Labor and American Politics.* Urbana: University of Illinois Press, 1983.

Finley, M. I. *Democracy: Ancient and Modern.* New Brunswick, NJ: Rutgers University Press, 1985.

Fitzhugh, George. *Cannibals All! Or, Slaves without Masters.* 1856. Cambridge: Harvard University Press, 1960.

Foner, Eric. *Free Soil, Free Labor, Free Men: The Ideology of the Republican Party before the Civil War.* Oxford: Oxford University Press, 1970.

Foner, Philip, and David R. Roediger. *Our Own Time: A History of American Labor and the Working Day.* New York: Verso, 1989.

Fones-Wolf, Elizabeth. *Selling Free Enterprise: The Business Assault on Labor and Liberalism, 1945–1960*. Urbana: University of Illinois Press, 1994.

Forbath, William. *Law and the Shaping of the American Labor Movement*. Cambridge: Harvard University Press, 1989.

Ford, Henry. *My Life and Work*. Garden City: Doubleday, Page, 1922.

Form, William. *Segmented Labor, Fractured Politics: Labor Politics in American Life*. New York: Plenum, 1995.

Foster, James Caldwell. *The Union Politic: The CIO Political Action Committee*. Columbia: University of Missouri Press, 1975.

Franklin, Benjamin. *The Autobiography and Selected Writings*. New York: Modern Library, 1944.

Fraser, Steven. *Labor Will Rule: Sidney Hillman and the Rise of American Labor*. Ithaca, NY: Cornell University Press, 1993.

Freeman, Richard B., and James L. Medoff. *What Do Unions Do?* New York: Basic Books, 1984.

Friedman, Milton. *Capitalism and Freedom*. Chicago: University of Chicago Press, 1962.

Friedman, Sheldon, Richard W. Hurd, Rudolph A. Oswald, and Ronald L. Seeber, eds. *Restoring the Promise of American Labor Law*. Ithaca, NY: ILR, 1994.

Galbraith, John Kenneth. *The Affluent Society*. Boston: Houghton-Mifflin, 1958.

——. *American Capitalism: The Concept of Countervailing Power*. Boston: Houghton-Mifflin, 1952.

——. "The Galbraith Acceptance." *ADA World Magazine*. May 1967.

Gall, Gilbert J. *The Politics of Right to Work: The Labor Federations as Special Interests, 1943–1979*. New York: Greenwood, 1988.

Gallup, George H. *The Gallup Poll: Public Opinion, 1935–1971*. New York: Random House, 1972.

Garson, Barbara, "Luddites in Lordstown." *Harper's Magazine*, June 1972, 68–73.

Geoghegan, Thomas. *Which Side Are You On? Trying to Be for Labor When It's Flat on Its Back*. New York: Penguin, 1992.

Gies, Joseph, and Melvin Kranzburg. *By the Sweat of Thy Brow: Work in the Western World*. New York: G. P. Putnam's Sons, 1975.

Gillman, Howard. *The Constitution Besieged: The Rise and Demise of Lochner Era Police Powers Jurisprudence*. Durham, NC: Duke University Press, 1993.

Gillon, Steven M. *Politics and Vision: The ADA and American Liberalism, 1947–1985*. New York: Oxford University Press, 1987.

Gitelman, H. M. *Legacy of the Ludlow Massacre: A Chapter in American Industrial Relations*. Philadelphia: University of Pennsylvania Press, 1988.

Godson, Roy S., "Labor's Role in Building Democracy." In *Promoting Democracy: Opportunities and Issues,* edited by Ralph Goldman and William Douglas. New York: Praeger, 1988.

Golden, Clinton S., and Harold J. Ruttenberg. *The Dynamics of Industrial Democracy*. New York: Harper and Brothers, 1942.

Goldfield, Michael. *The Decline of Organized Labor in the United States*. Chicago: University of Chicago Press, 1987.

Goldman, Eric F. *Rendezvous with Destiny: A History of Modern American Reform*. New York: Vintage, 1955.

Gompers, Samuel. *The Samuel Gompers Papers*. Urbana: University of Illinois Press, 1986.

——. *Seventy Years of Life and Labor: An Autobiography.* Edited by Nick Salvatore. Ithaca, NY: ILR Press, 1984 (1925).

Goodwyn, Lawrence. *The Populist Moment: A Short History of the Agrarian Revolt in America.* Oxford: Oxford University Press, 1978.

Gould, William B. *Black Workers in White Unions: Job Discrimination in the United States.* Ithaca, NY: Cornell University Press, 1977. Goulden, Joseph. *Meany.* New York: Atheneum, 1972.

Green, James R. *The World of the Worker: Labor in Twentieth-Century America.* New York: Hill and Wang, 1980.

Green, William. *Labor and Democracy.* Princeton, NJ: Princeton University Press, 1939.

Greene, Julie. *Pure and Simple Politics: The American Federation of Labor and Political Activism, 1881–1917.* Cambridge: Cambridge University Press, 1998.

Greenstone, J. David. *Labor in American Politics.* New York: Knopf, 1969.

Grint, Keith. *The Sociology of Work.* Cambridge: Polity Press, 1991.

Griswold del Castillo, Richard, and Richard A. Garcia. *Cesar Chavez: A Triumph of Spirit.* Norman: University of Oklahoma Press, 1995.

Grob, Gerald N. *Workers and Utopia: A Study of Ideological Conflict in the American Labor Movement, 1865–1900.* Chicago: Quadrangle, 1961.

Gross, James A. *Broken Promise: The Subversion of U.S. Labor Relations Policy, 1947–1994.* Philadelphia: Temple, 1995.

——. *The Making of the National Labor Relations Board: A Study in Economics, Politics and the Law, 1933–1937.* Albany: State University of New York Press, 1974.

——. *The Reshaping of the National Labor Relations Board: National Labor Policy in Transition, 1937–1947.* Albany: State University of New York Press, 1981.

Gutman, Herbert G. *Work, Culture, and Society in Industrializing America.* New York: Vintage, 1976.

Hamilton, Alexander, John Jay, and James Madison. *The Federalist.* New York: Modern Library, 1937.

Hamilton, Dona Cooper, and Charles V. Hamilton. *The Dual Agenda: Race and Social Welfare Policies of Civil Rights Organizations.* New York: Columbia University Press, 1997.

Hamilton, Richard F. *Class and Politics in the United States.* New York: John Wiley, 1972.

Harris, Howell John. *The Right to Manage: Industrial Relations Policies of American Business in the 1940s.* Madison: University of Wisconsin Press, 1982.

Harrington, Michael. *The Other America: Poverty in the United States.* New York: Macmillan, 1962.

Harter, Lafayette G. *John R. Commons: His Assault on Laissez-Faire.* Corvallis: Oregon State University Press, 1962.

Hartz, Louis. *The Liberal Tradition in America.* New York: Harcourt and Brace, 1955.

Hattam, Victoria C. *Labor Visions and State Power: The Origins of Business Unionism in the United States.* Princeton, NJ: Princeton University Press, 1993.

Hayek, Friedrich A. *The Road to Serfdom.* Chicago: University of Chicago Press, 1944.

Haydu, Jeffrey, "Trade Agreements and Open Shops Before World War I." *Industrial Relations* 28 (Spring 1989): 159–73.

Hayes, Carlton J. H. "The Challenge of Totalitarianism." *Public Opinion Quarterly* 2 (January 1938): 21–26.

Heilbroner, Robert L. *The Worldly Philosophers: The Lives, Times, and Ideas of the Great Economic Thinkers.* New York: Touchstone, 1980.

Herr, Richard. *Tocqueville and the Old Regime.* Princeton, NJ: Princeton University Press, 1962.

Higham, John. *Strangers in the Land: Patterns of American Nativism, 1860–1925.* New Brunswick, NJ: Rutgers University Press, 1988.

Hill, Herbert. "Black Workers, Organized Labor, and Title VII of the 1964 Civil Rights Act: Legislative History and Litigation Record." In *Race in America: The Struggle for Equality,* edited by Herbert Hill and James E. Jones. Madison: University of Wisconsin Press, 1993.

Hillquit, Morris, Samuel Gompers, and Max J. Hayes. *The Double Edge of Labor's Sword.* Chicago: Socialist Party National Office, 1914.

Hirschman, Albert O. *Exit, Voice, and Loyalty: Responses to Decline in Firms, Organizations, and States.* Cambridge: Harvard University Press, 1970.

——. *The Passions and the Interests: Political Arguments for Capitalism before Its Triumph.* Princeton, NJ: Princeton University Press, 1977.

Hofstadter, Richard. *The Age of Reform: From Bryan to FDR.* New York: Vintage, 1955.

Holloway, Harry. "Interest Groups in the Postpartisan Era: The Political Machine of the AFL-CIO." *Political Science Quarterly* 94 (Spring 1979): 117–33.

Howe, Irving. *World of Our Fathers.* New York: Harcourt, Brace & Jovanovich, 1976.

Howe, Irving, and B. J. Widick. *The UAW and Walter Reuther.* New York: Random House, 1949.

Hoxie, Robert F. *Scientific Management and Labor.* 1915. New York: Kelley, 1966.

——. *Trade Unionism in the United States.* 1923. New York: Russell & Russell, 1966.

Huxley, Aldous Leonard. *Brave New World: A Novel.* London: Harper, 1932.

Jefferson, Thomas. *Notes on the State of Virginia.* New York: Penguin, 1999.

——. *The Portable Thomas Jefferson.* Edited by Merrill D. Peterson. New York: Viking, 1975.

Jenkins, J. Craig. *The Politics of Insurgency: The Farm Worker Movement of the 1960s.* New York: Columbia University Press, 1985.

Jevons, W. Stanley. *The Theory of Political Economy.* 1871. New York: Kelley, 1965.

Jones, Dallas L. "The Enigma of the Clayton Act." *Industrial and Labor Relations Review* 10 (January 1957): 201–21.

Jones, Maldwyn Allen. *American Immigration.* Chicago: University of Chicago Press, 1992.

Josephson, Matthew. *The Robber Barons: The Great American Capitalists, 1861–1901.* New York: Harcourt, Brace and World, 1934.

Kakar, Sudhir. *Frederick Taylor: A Study in Personality and Innovation.* Cambridge: MIT Press, 1970.

Kampelman, Max M. *The Communist Party Versus the CIO: A Study in Power Politics.* New York: Praeger, 1957.

Kanigel, Robert. *The One Best Way: Frederick Winslow Taylor and the Enigma of Efficiency.* New York: Penguin, 1997.

Karson, Marc. *American Labor Unions and Politics, 1900–1918.* Boston: Beacon, 1958.

Katznelson, Ira. *City Trenches: Urban Politics and the Patterning of Class in the United States.* New York: Pantheon, 1981.

Kaufman, Bruce E. *The Origins and Evolution of the Field of Industrial Relations in the United States.* Ithaca, NY: ILR Press, 1993.

Kaufman, Stuart Bruce. *Samuel Gompers and the Origins of the American Federation of Labor, 1848–1896.* Westport, CT: Greenwood, 1973.

Kazin, Michael. *Barons of Labor: The San Francisco Building Trades and Union Power in the Progressive Era.* Urbana: University of Illinois Press, 1987.

———. *The Populist Persuasion: An American History.* New York: Basic Books, 1995.

Kennedy, Robert F. *The Enemy Within.* New York: Harper and Brothers, 1960.

Kerr, Clark, John T. Dunlop, Frederick Harbison, and Charles A. Myers. *Industrialism and Industrial Man.* 1960. New York: Oxford University Press, 1964.

Keynes, John Maynard. *The General Theory of Employment, Interest, and Money.* New York: Harbinger, 1935 [1936].

Kirkland, Edward Chase. *Industry Comes of Age: Business, Labor and Public Policy, 1860–1897.* Chicago: Quadrangle, 1961.

Kirkland, Lane. "Making Democracy Work." *American Federationist* (September 1969): 16–19.

Klehr, Harvey. "American Communism and the United Auto Workers: New Evidence on an Old Controversy." *Labor History* 34 (Summer 1983): 449–62.

Klehr, Harvey, and John Earl Haynes. *The American Communist Movement: Storming Heaven Itself.* New York: Twayne, 1992.

Kochan, Thomas A., Harry C. Katz, and Robert B. McKersie. *The Transformation of American Industrial Relations.* New York: Basic Books, 1986.

Kornhauser, Arthur, Albert J. Mayer, and Harold L. Sheppard. *When Labor Votes: A Study of Auto Workers.* New York: University Books, 1956.

Kornhauser, William. *The Politics of Mass Society.* New York: Free Press, 1959.

Krause, Paul. *The Battle for Homestead, 1880–1892: Politics, Culture, and Steel.* Pittsburgh: University of Pittsburgh Press, 1992.

Kurzman, Dan. "Lovestone's Cold War: The AFL-CIO Has Its Own CIA." *New Republic,* 25 June 1966, 17–22.

Kutler, Stanley I. "Labor, the Clayton Act, and the Supreme Court." *Labor History* 3 (Winter 1962): 19–38.

Landy, Marc K., "The Political Imperative: George Meany's Strategy of Leadership." In *Leadership in America: Consensus, Corruption, Charisma,* edited by Peter Dennis Bathory. New York: Longman, 1978.

Larson, Simeon. *Labor and Foreign Policy: Gompers, the AFL, and the First World War, 1914–1918.* Rutherford, NJ: Fairleigh Dickinson University Press, 1975.

Lasch, Christopher. *The True and Only Heaven: Progress and Its Critics.* New York: W. W. Norton, 1991.

Laslett, John H. M. *Labor and the Left: A Study of Socialist and Radical Influences in the American Labor Movement, 1881–1924.* New York: Basic Books, 1970.

Lauck, W. Jett. "The Vanishing American Wage-Earner." *Atlantic Monthly* 110, November 1912, 691–96.

Lazarsfeld, Paul F., Bernard Berelson, and Hazel Gaudet. *The People's Choice: How the Voter Makes Up His Mind in a Presidential Campaign.* New York: Duell, Sloan and Pearce, 1944.

Lee, R. Alton. *Eisenhower and Landrum-Griffin.* Lexington: University Press of Kentucky, 1990.

———. *Truman and Taft-Hartley: A Question of Mandate*. Westport, CT: Greenwood, 1980.

Leiserson, William M. *American Trade Union Democracy*. New York: Columbia University Press, 1959.

———. "Constitutional Government in American Industries." *American Economic Review* 12:1 (March 1922): 56–79.

Lekachman, Robert. *The Age of Keynes*. New York: Random House, 1966.

———. *A History of Economic Ideas*. New York: McGraw-Hill, 1959.

Lemann, Nicholas. *The Big Test: The Secret History of the American Meritocracy*. New York: Farrar, Straus and Giroux, 1999.

Lens, Sidney. *The Crisis of American Labor*. New York: A. S. Barnes, 1959.

Lesher, Stephen. *George Wallace: American Populist*. Reading, PA: Addison-Wesley, 1994.

Lester, Richard A. *As Unions Mature: An Analysis of the Evolution of American Unionism*. Princeton, NJ: Princeton University Press, 1958.

Leuchtenburg, William E. *Franklin D. Roosevelt and the New Deal, 1932–40*. New York: Harper, 1963.

Levenstein, Harvey A. *Communism, Anticommunism, and the CIO*. Westport, CT: Greenwood, 1981.

Levinson, Harold M. "Pattern Bargaining: A Case Study of the Automobile Workers." *Quarterly Journal of Economics* 74 (May 1960): 296–317.

Levitt, Martin Jay, and Terry Conrow. *Confessions of a Union Buster*. New York: Crown Publishers, 1993.

Lewis, John L. *The Miners' Fight for American Standards*. Indianapolis: Bell, 1925.

———. "There Is No Labor Movement." *Collier's*, 5 May 1945.

———. "What Labor Is Thinking." *Public Opinion Quarterly* 1 (October 1937): 23–28.

Lichtenstein, Nelson. *Labor's War at Home: The CIO in World War II*. Cambridge: Cambridge University Press, 1982.

———. *State of the Union: A Century of American Labor*. Princeton, NJ: Princeton University Press, 2002.

———. *Walter Reuther: The Most Dangerous Man in Detroit*. Urbana: University of Illinois Press, 1997.

Lichtenstein, Nelson, and Howell John Harris, eds. *Industrial Democracy in America: The Ambiguous Promise*. Cambridge: Cambridge University Press, 1993.

Lincoln, Abraham. *Selected Speeches and Writings*. New York: Vintage, 1992.

Link, Arthur S. *Woodrow Wilson and the Progressive Era: 1910–1917*. New York: Harper & Row, 1954.

Lippmann, Walter. *Public Opinion*. New York: Free Press, 1965 (1922).

Lipset, Seymour Martin. *Political Man: The Social Bases of Politics*. Garden City: Doubleday, 1960.

Lipset, Seymour Martin, Martin A. Trow, and James S. Coleman. *Union Democracy: The Internal Politics of the International Typographical Union*. Glencoe, IL: Free Press, 1956.

Lipsitz, George. *Class and Culture in Cold War America: "A Rainbow at Midnight."* South Hadlin: Bergin & Garvey, 1982.

Livesay, Harold C. *Andrew Carnegie and the Rise of Big Business*. New York: Longman, 2000.

———. *Samuel Gompers and Organized Labor in America*. Boston: Little, Brown, 1978.

Locke, John. *Two Treatises of Government*. Cambridge: Cambridge University Press, 1988.

London, Jack. *Jack London: American Rebel*. Edited by Philip Foner. New York: Citadel, 1947.

Lowi, Theodore J. *The End of Liberalism: The Second Republic of the United States*. New York: Norton, 1979.

Machiavelli, Niccolò. *Discourses on Livy*. New York: Oxford University Press, 1997.

Marks, Gary. *Unions in Politics*. Princeton, NJ: Princeton University Press, 1989.

Marx, Karl. *Capital*. Vol. 1. New York: Kerr, 1906.

Marx, Karl, and Frederick Engels. *Selected Works*, Vols. 1–3. Moscow: Progress, 1970.

Masters, Marick F. *Unions at the Crossroads*. Westport, CT: Quorum, 1997.

Mayo, Elton. *The Human Problems of an Industrial Civilization*. New York: Viking, 1933.

McCoy, Drew R. *The Elusive Republic: Political Economy in Jeffersonian America*. Chapel Hill: University of North Carolina Press, 1980.

McCulloch, Frank W., and Tim Bornstein. *The National Labor Relations Board*. New York: Praeger, 1974.

McGuiness, Kenneth C. *The New Frontier NLRB*. Washington, DC: Labor Policy Association, 1963.

McKelvey, Jean Trepp. *AFL Attitudes toward Production, 1900–1932*. Ithaca, NY: Cornell University Press, 1952.

McLaughlin, Doris B., Frederick H. Nesbitt, and Charles M. Rehmus, eds. *Labor and American Politics*. Ann Arbor: University of Michigan Press, 1978.

McLaughlin, Doris B., and Anita L. Schoomaker. *The Landrum-Griffin Act and Union Democracy*. Ann Arbor: University of Michigan Press, 1979.

McNeill, George, ed. *The Labor Movement: The Problem of To-Day*. Boston: Bridgman, 1887.

McWilliams, Wilson Carey. *The Idea of Fraternity in America*. Berkeley: University of California Press, 1973.

Meany, George. "Trade Unions Must Be Free." *Vital Speeches of the Day*, 1 October 1945, 757–62.

——. "What Does Labor Want? More for All Americans." *Vital Speeches of the Day*, 15 September 1956, 722–24.

——. "What Labor Means by 'More.'" *Fortune* (March 1955).

Merrill, Michael. "Labor Shall Not Be Property: The Horizon of Workers' Control in the United States." *Labor Studies Journal* (Summer 1996): 27–50.

Meyer, Stephen. *The Five-Dollar Day: Labor Management and Social Control in the Ford Motor Company, 1908–21*. Albany: State University of New York Press, 1981.

Meyers, Marvin. *The Jacksonian Persuasion: Politics and Belief*. Stanford: Stanford University Press, 1957.

Michels, Robert. *Political Parties: A Sociological Study of the Oligarchical Tendencies of Modern Democracy*. 1915. New York: Dover, 1959.

Milkis, Sidney M. *The President and the Parties: The Transformation of the American Political System since the New Deal*. Oxford: Oxford University Press, 1993.

Miller, Warren E., and J. Merrill Shanks. *The New American Voter*. Cambridge: Harvard University Press, 1996.

Mills, C. Wright. *The New Men of Power: America's Labor Leaders*. New York: Harcourt Brace, 1948.

Milton, David. *The Politics of U.S. Labor: From the Great Depression to the New Deal*. New York: Monthly Review Press, 1982.

Mink, Gwendolyn. *Old Labor and New Immigrants in American Political Development*. Ithaca, NY: Cornell University Press, 1986.

Mishel, Lawrence, and Paula C. Voos. *Unions and Economic Competitiveness*. Armonk: M. E. Sharpe, 1992.

Mitchell, Wesley C., "Bentham's Felicific Calculus." *Political Science Quarterly* 33 (June 1918): 161–83.

Montgomery, David. *Beyond Equality: Labor and the Radical Republicans, 1862–1872*. New York: Knopf, 1967.

——. *Citizen Worker: The Experience of Workers in the United States with Democracy and the Free Market during the Nineteenth Century*. Cambridge: Cambridge University Press, 1993.

——. *The Fall of the House of Labor*. Cambridge: Cambridge University Press, 1987.

——. *Workers' Control in America: Studies in the History of Work, Technology, and Labor Struggles*. Cambridge: Cambridge University Press, 1979.

Moody, Kim. *An Injury to All: The Decline of American Unionism*. London: Verso, 1988.

Morris, James O. *Conflict within the AFL: A Study of Craft versus Industrial Unionism, 1901–1938*. Westport, CT: Greenwood Press, 1958.

Mowry, George E. *The Era of Theodore Roosevelt and the Birth of Modern America, 1900–1912*. New York: Harper and Row, 1958.

Mueller, Franz H. *The Church and the Social Question*. Washington, DC: AEI, 1984.

Mullett, Charles F. "Classical Influences on the American Revolution." *Classical Journal* 35 (1939–1940): 92–104.

Nadworny, Milton J. *Scientific Management and the Unions, 1930–1932*. Cambridge: Harvard University Press, 1955.

Nelson, Daniel. *Frederick W. Taylor and the Rise of Scientific Management*. Madison: University of Wisconsin Press, 1980.

——. *Managers and Workers: Origins of the New Factory System in the United States, 1880–1920*. Madison: University of Wisconsin Press, 1975.

Nelson, Donald M. *Arsenal of Democracy: The Story of American War Production*. New York: Harcourt, Brace, 1946.

Nisbet, Robert A. "The Politics of Social Pluralism: Some Reflections on Lamennais." *Journal of Politics* 10 (November 1948): 764–86.

——. "Rousseau and Totalitarianism." *Journal of Politics* 5 (May 1943): 93–114.

O'Brien, David J. *American Catholics and Social Reform: The New Deal Years*. New York: Oxford University Press, 1968.

O'Brien, David J., and Thomas A. Shannon. *Catholic Social Thought: The Documentary Heritage*. Maryknoll, NY: Orbis, 1992.

Okin, Susan Moller. *Women in Western Political Thought*. Princeton, NJ: Princeton University Press, 1979.

Orren, Karen. *Belated Feudalism: Labor, the Law, and Liberal Development in the United States*. Cambridge: Cambridge University Press, 1991.

Olson, Mancur. *The Logic of Collective Action: Public Goods and the Theory of Groups*. Cambridge: Harvard University Press, 1965.

Patterson, James T. *Mr. Republican: A Biography of Robert A. Taft*. Boston: Houghton Mifflin, 1972.

Perlman, Selig. *A Theory of the Labor Movement*. New York: Kelley, 1928.

Perrow, Charles. *Complex Organizations: A Critical Essay.* Glenview, IL: Scott, Foresman, 1979.

Phelan, Craig. *William Green: Biography of a Labor Leader.* Albany: State University of New York Press, 1989.

Piven, Frances Fox, and Richard A. Cloward. *Poor People's Movements: Why They Succeed, How They Fail.* New York: Vintage, 1977.

Plato. *The Dialogues of Plato.* Vols. 1–2. Translated by M. A. Jowett. 1892. New York: Random House, 1937.

———. *The Republic of Plato.* Translated by Allan Bloom. New York: Basic Books, 1968.

Plutarch. *The Lives of the Noble Grecians and Romans.* New York: Modern Library, 1932.

Polanyi, Karl. *The Great Transformation: The Political and Economic Origins of Our Time.* 1944. Boston: Beacon, 1957.

Popper, Karl. *The Open Society and its Enemies.* London: Routledge, 1945.

Powderly, Terence V. *The Path I Trod.* New York: Columbia, 1940.

Preston, William. *Aliens and Dissenters: Federal Suppression of Radicals, 1903–1933.* New York: Harper, 1963.

Pringle, Henry F. *The Life and Times of William Howard Taft.* Hamden: Archon, 1964.

Putnam, Robert. *Bowling Alone: The Collapse and Revival of American Community.* New York: Simon and Schuster, 2000.

Quadagno, Jill. "Social Movements and State Transformation: Labor Unions and Racial Conflict in the War on Poverty." *American Sociological Review* 57 (October 1992): 616–34.

Radosh, Ronald. *American Labor and United States Foreign Policy.* New York: Random House, 1969.

Raskin, A. H. "Reuther versus Hoffa: A Key Struggle." *New York Times Magazine,* 22 September 1957.

———. "Why They Cheer for Hoffa." *New York Times Magazine,* 9 November 1958.

Rawls, John. *A Theory of Justice.* Cambridge: Harvard University Press, 1971.

Reinhold, Mayer. *Classica Americana: The Greek and Roman Heritage in the United States.* Detroit: Wayne State University Press, 1984.

Renard, Georges. *Guilds in the Middle Ages.* London: G. Bell and Sons, 1918.

Reuther, Victor. *The Brothers Reuther and the Story of the UAW.* Boston: Houghton Mifflin, 1976.

Reynolds, Morgan O. *Power and Privilege: Labor Unions in America.* New York: Universe, 1984.

Rice, Charles Owen. "Confessions of an Anti-Communist." *Labor History* 30 (Summer 1989): 449–62.

Riesman, David. *The Lonely Crowd: A Study of the Changing American Character.* New Haven, CT: Yale University Press, 1950.

Riis, Jacob. *How the Other Half Lives: Studies among the Tenements of New York.* 1890. New York: Dover, 1971.

———. *Theodore Roosevelt, the Citizen.* New York: Outlook, 1904.

Robinson, Archie. *George Meany and His Times.* New York: Simon & Schuster, 1981.

Robinson, Joan. *Economic Philosophy: An Essay on the Progress of Economic Thought.* Garden City: Doubleday, 1962.

Rockefeller, John D., Jr. "Labor and Capital—Partners." *Atlantic Monthly,* 117, June 1916, 12–21.

Rodgers, Daniel T. *The Work Ethic in Industrial America, 1850–1920.* Chicago: University of Chicago Press, 1974.

Roediger, David R. *The Wages of Whiteness: Race and the Making of the American Working Class.* London: Verso, 1991.

Rogin, Michael. "Voluntarism: The Political Functions of an Antipolitical Doctrine." *Industrial and Labor Relations Review* 15 (1962): 521–35.

Roosevelt, Franklin D. *The Essential Franklin Delano Roosevelt.* New York: Gramercy, 1995.

Roosevelt, Theodore. *The New Nationalism.* Englewood Cliffs, NJ: Prentice-Hall, 1961 [1910].

Rose, U. M. "Strikes and Trusts." *American Law Review* 27 (September–October 1893): 708–40.

Rosenstone, Steven J., and John Mark Hansen. *Mobilization, Participation, and Democracy in America.* New York: Macmillan, 1993.

Rosswurm, Steve, ed. *The CIO's Left-Led Unions.* New Brunswick, NJ: Rutgers University Press, 1992.

Rousseau, Jean-Jacques. *The Social Contract.* London: Penguin, 1968.

Roy, William G. *Socializing Capital: The Rise of the Large Industrial Corporation in America.* Princeton, NJ: Princeton University Press, 1997.

Ruskin, John. *Selected Writings.* London: Penguin, 1991.

Russell, Thaddeus. *Out of the Jungle: Jimmy Hoffa and the Remaking of the American Working Class.* New York: Knopf, 2001.

Ryan, John A. *Economic Justice: Selections from Distributive Justice and A Living Wage.* Louisville: Westminster, 1996.

Sallust. *The War with Jurgutha.* Translated by J. C. Rolfe. Cambridge: Harvard University Press, 1921.

Salvatore, Nick. *Eugene V. Debs: Citizen and Socialist.* Urbana: University of Illinois Press, 1982.

Sandel, Michael J. *Democracy's Discontent: America in Search of a Public Philosophy.* Cambridge: Harvard University Press, 1996.

Saxton, Alexander. *The Indispensable Enemy: Labor and the Anti-Chinese Movement in California.* Berkeley: University of California Press, 1971.

Schattschneider, E. E. *Party Government.* New York: Rinehart, 1942.

——. *The Semi-Sovereign People: A Realist's View of Democracy in America.* New York: Holt, Rinehart and Winston, 1960.

Schatz, Ronald W. *The Electrical Workers: A History of Labor at General Electric and Westinghouse, 1923–1960.* Urbana: University of Illinois Press, 1983.

Schumpeter, Joseph A. *Capitalism, Socialism and Democracy.* 1942. New York: Harper, 1950.

Seaton, Douglas P. *Catholics and Radicals: The Association of Catholic Trade Unionists and the American Labor Movement, from Depression to Cold War.* Lewisburg: Bucknell University Press, 1981.

Seidman, Joel. *American Labor from Defense to Reconversion.* Chicago: University of Chicago Press, 1953.

Selznick, Philip. *Law, Society, and Industrial Justice.* Berkeley: Russell Sage, 1969.

Sennett, Richard, and Jonathan Cobb. *The Hidden Injuries of Class.* New York: Norton, 1972.

Serrin, William. *The Company and the Union: The "Civilized Relationship" of the General Motors Corporation and the United Automobile Workers*. New York: Vintage, 1974.

Sheldon, Garrett Ward. *The Political Philosophy of Thomas Jefferson*. Baltimore: Johns Hopkins University Press, 1991.

Shister, Joseph, "Unresolved Problems and New Paths for American Labor." *Industrial and Labor Relations Review* 9 (April 1956): 447–57.

Shklar, Judith. *American Citizenship: The Quest for Inclusion*. Cambridge: Harvard University Press, 1991.

Sims, Beth. *Workers of the World Undermined: American Labor's Role in U.S. Foreign Policy*. Boston: South End Press, 1992.

Sinclair, Upton. *The Flivver King: A Story of Ford-America*. Detroit: UAW, 1937.

Slichter, Sumner H. "The Taft-Hartley Act." *Quarterly Journal of Economics* 63 (Feb. 1949): 1–31.

———. *Union Policies and Industrial Management*. Washington, DC: Brookings Institution Press, 1941.

Slichter, Sumner H., James J. Healy, and E. Robert Livernash. *The Impact of Collective Bargaining on Management*. Washington, DC: Brookings Institution Press, 1960.

Sloane, Arthur A. *Hoffa*. Cambridge: MIT Press, 1993.

Smith, Adam. *An Inquiry into the Nature and Causes of the Wealth of Nations*. Indianapolis: Liberty Fund, 1981.

Smith, Rogers M. *Civic Ideals: Conflicting Visions of Citizenship in U.S. History*. New Haven, CT: Yale University Press, 1997.

Snowbarger, Marvin, and Sam Pintz, "Landrum-Griffin and Union President Turnover," *Industrial Relations* 9 (October 1970): 475–76.

Sombart, Werner. *Why Is There No Socialism in the United States?* 1906. White Plains: International Arts and Sciences, 1976.

Somers, Gerald G. "Collective Bargaining and the Social-Economic Contract." *IRRA Proceedings,* December 1975.

Sorel, Georges. *Reflections on Violence*. 1906. London: Collier, 1950.

Sousa, David J. "Organized Labor in the Electorate, 1960–1988." *Presidential Research Quarterly* 46 (December 1993): 741–58.

Stanley, John. *The Sociology of Virtue: The Political and Social Theories of Georges Sorel*. Berkeley, University of California Press, 1981.

Stein, Leon, ed. *Out of the Sweatshop: The Struggle for Industrial Democracy*. New York: Quadrangle, 1977.

Steinfeld, Robert J. *The Invention of Free Labor: The Employment Relation in English and American Law and Culture, 1350–1870*. Chapel Hill: University of North Carolina Press, 1991.

Stepan-Norris, Judith, and Maurice Zeitlin. "'Red' Unions and 'Bourgeois' Contracts?" *American Journal of Sociology* 96 (March 1991): 1151–1200.

———. "'Who Gets the Bird?' or, How the Communists Won Power and Trust in America's Unions: The Relative Autonomy of Intraclass Political Struggles." *American Sociological Review* 54 (August 1989): 503–23.

Strauss, George, Daniel G. Gallagher, and Jack Fiorito, eds. *The State of the Unions*. Madison: IRRA, 1991.

Strauss, Leo. *Natural Right and History*. Chicago: University of Chicago Press, 1953.

Taft, Philip. *The AFL from the Death of Gompers to the Merger*. New York: Octagon, 1970.

——. *The AFL in the Time of Gompers.* New York: Octagon, 1970.

——. *Defending Freedom: American Labor and Foreign Affairs.* Los Angeles: Nash Publishing, 1973.

——. "Democracy in Trade Unions." *American Economic Review* 36 (May 1946): 359–69.

——. "The Impact of Landrum-Griffin on Union Government." *Annals of the American Academy of Political and Social Science* 333 (January 1961): 130–40.

Taft, Philip, and Philip Ross. "American Labor Violence: Its Causes, Character, and Outcomes." In *The History of Violence in America,* edited by Hugh Davis Graham and Ted Robert Gurr. New York: Bantam, 1969.

Taylor, Frederick Winslow. *The Principles of Scientific Management.* 1911. Dover: Mineola, 1998.

Teixeira, Ruy A. *The Disappearing American Voter.* Washington, DC: Brookings Institution Press, 1992.

Teixeira, Ruy, and Joel Rogers. *America's Forgotten Majority: Why the White Working Class Still Matters.* New York: Basic Books, 2000.

Tilgher, Adriano. *Work: What It Has Meant to Men through the Ages.* New York: Harcourt, Brace, 1930.

Tocqueville, Alexis de. *Democracy in America.* New York: Harper Collins, 1969.

——. *The Old Regime and the French Revolution.* New York: Doubleday, 1955.

Tolman, William. *Social Engineering: A Record of Things Done by American Industrialists Employing Upwards of One and One-Half Million of People.* New York: McGraw-Hill, 1909.

Tomlins, Christopher. *The State and the Unions: Labor Relations, Law, and the Organized Labor Movement in America, 1880–1960.* New York: Cambridge University Press, 1985.

Tugwell, R. G. "The Principle of Planning and the Institution of Laissez Faire." *American Economic Review* 22 (March 1932): 75–92.

Ulman, Lloyd, ed. *Challenges to Collective Bargaining.* Englewood Cliffs, NJ: Prentice-Hall, 1967.

Ulman, Lloyd. *The Rise of the National Trade Union.* Cambridge: Harvard University Press, 1966.

Useem, Michael. *The Inner Circle: Large Corporations and the Rise of Business Political Activity in the U.S. and U.K.* Oxford: Oxford University Press, 1984.

Van der Wee, Herman. *Prosperity and Upheaval: The World Economy, 1945–1980.* Berkeley: University of California Press, 1983.

Veblen, Thorstein. *The Theory of Business Enterprise.* 1904. New York: Scribner, 1921.

——. *The Theory of the Leisure Class.* 1899. New York: Mentor, 1953.

Verba, Sidney, Kay Lehman Schlozman, and Henry E. Brady. *Voice and Equality: Civic Voluntarism in American Politics.* Cambridge: Harvard University Press, 1995.

Voss, Kim. *The Making of American Exceptionalism: The Knights of Labor and Class Formation in the Nineteenth Century.* Ithaca, NY: Cornell University Press, 1993.

Wallace, Henry. "The Enemy Is Not Each Other." *New Republic* (27 January 1947): 22–23.

Waters, Robert C. "Leadership and Its Consequences: Technical Change in the Longshore Industry." *Industrial Relations* 32 (Spring 1993): 262–71.

Webb, Sidney, and Beatrice Webb. *The History of Trade Unionism.* 1894. London: Longmans Green, 1920.

——. *Industrial Democracy.* 1897. New York: Augustus Kelley, 1965.

Weber, Max. *The Theory of Social and Economic Organization.* New York: Free Press, 1947.

Weinstein, James. *The Corporate Ideal in the Liberal State, 1900–1918.* Boston: Beacon, 1968.

Western, Bruce. "A Comparative Study of Working-Class Disorganization: Union Decline in Eighteen Advanced Capitalist Countries." *American Sociological Review* 60 (April 1995): 179–201.

Weyl, Walter E. *The New Democracy: An Essay on Certain Political and Economic Tendencies in the United States.* 1912. New York: Harper, 1964.

White, Theodore H. *The Making of the President 1968.* New York: Atheneum, 1969.

Whyte, William H. *The Organization Man.* New York: Doubleday, 1956.

Widick, B. J. "Why They Like Wallace." *Nation,* 14 October 1968, 358–59.

Wilentz, Sean. *Chants Democratic: New York City and the Rise of the American Working Class, 1788–1850.* Oxford: Oxford University Press, 1984.

Wilson, Graham. *Unions in American National Politics.* New York: St. Martin's, 1979.

Wilson, Woodrow. *The New Freedom: A Call for the Emancipation of the Generous Energies of a People.* New York: Doubleday, 1918.

Wolfe, Arthur C. "Trends in Labor Union Voting Behavior, 1948–1968." *Industrial Relations* 9 (October 1969): 1–10.

Wolin, Sheldon S. *Politics and Vision: Continuity and Innovation in Western Political Thought.* Boston: Little, Brown, 1960.

Wolkinson, Benjamin W. *Blacks, Unions, and the EEOC: A Study of Administrative Futility.* Lexington, MA: Lexington Books, 1973.

Wood, Gordon S. *The Radicalism of the American Revolution.* New York: Knopf, 1992.

Wright, Erik Olin. *Classes.* London: Verso, 1985.

Yager, Daniel V., and Joseph J. LoBue. "Corporate Campaigns and Card Checks: Creating the Company Unions of the Twenty-First Century." *Employee Relations Law Journal* 24 (Spring 1999): 21–50.

Young, James P. *Reconsidering American Liberalism.* Boulder, CO: Westview, 1996.

Zieger, Robert H. *American Workers, American Unions.* Baltimore: Johns Hopkins University Press, 1994.

——. *The CIO, 1935–1955.* Chapel Hill: University of North Carolina Press, 1995.

——. *John L. Lewis: Labor Leader.* Boston: Twayne, 1988.

Zinn, Howard, ed. *New Deal Thought.* Indianapolis: Bobbs-Merrill, 1966.

INDEX

Commodity, 76, 82, 91–94, 96, 100, 109, 242n28
Common good: business cannot serve, 155–57; labor movement and, 40, 57, 71, 103, 153, 155, 168, 183, 195, 202, 218, 237n31; only basis for democratic government, 3, 5, 9, 11, 57, 139, 150, 164, 168–69. *See also* Public interest
Common law, 47, 152
Commons, John, 20, 37, 51–56, 75, 83, 89, 96, 100, 103, 115, 121
Communications Workers of America (CWA), 212
Communism and Communists: and AFL, 72, 107, 124, 129–31, 138, 160, 167–69, 181–82, 239n60, 252n1; and CIO, 137–38, 147–49, 166, 170, 173–80, 191, 256n3; and totalitarianism, 127, 160, 167–69
Company unions, 55, 70, 78, 96, 104–5, 120, 124, 130, 145, 162
Congress of Industrial Organizations (CIO): alliance with Franklin Roosevelt; 138–48, 157–63; Communists and, 137–38, 169–70, 173–80; CIO Political Action Committee (PAC), 164–66; industrial organizing campaigns of; 136–41, 144–46, 157–61; merges with AFL to form AFL-CIO, 182; philosophy of, 133, 139, 146–57; scientific management and, 99, 149, 151; splits from AFL, 111, 132–35, 145
Conservatives and conservatism, 38, 75–77, 84–86, 90–91, 99, 114, 132, 140, 143–44, 168, 171, 180, 184, 189, 192, 196–98, 208, 211, 222, 245n13
Conspiracy, 10, 47, 81, 165, 204; conspiracy in restraint of trade, 45, 47, 81–82, 91
Constitutional government, 5–6, 9, 224; in industry, 51–52, 56, 68–69, 98–99, 115, 121, 189; United States Constitution, 16, 84, 93, 114, 140, 143, 168; union constitutions, 28–29, 81–82, 160, 177, 197, 206
Construction industry, 54, 104, 107, 155, 184–85, 206, 209–10, 225–26
Contract, Social, 7–8, 11; union contract, 30, 43, 52, 76–77, 80, 141, 145, 151–52, 157, 160, 171–72, 186–87, 194, 215, 228, 254n32; "yellow-dog" contract, 81, 92, 247n38
Cooke, Morris, 99, 115, 149, 151

Cooperatives, 20–27, 48, 56
Corporations, 32, 50–53, 64, 88–89, 94–97, 125–26, 151, 155–56; "Corporate Campaign," 229
Corruption, 9, 18, 21, 40, 77, 101, 193, 196–97
Cost of Living Adjustment (COLA), 186–87
"Countervailing Power," 211
Craft unions: compared with industrial unions, 73–79, 122–25, 128–35; enable control of labor, 27–34, 43–44, 60–64, 70, 78; formation of, 26–35. *See also* American Federation of Labor (AFL); Voluntarism
Croly, Herbert, 87–89, 94–95, 108
Curtiss-Wright Aircraft, 161

Danbury Hatters, 81, 185
Debs, Eugene Victor, 46–47, 56, 73, 77, 241n35
DeLeon, Daniel, 72–73, 131
Deliberations, democratic, 3–5, 9, 11–13, 16, 57, 116, 135, 152, 163, 168–69, 177, 190, 217–18
Demagogues and demagoguery, 6, 140, 163, 219
Democracy in America. See Tocqueville, Alexis de
Democratic Party, 84, 89–91, 111–12, 115, 199–200, 211–13, 217, 230–31; New Deal Democrats, 116–18, 142–48, 154, 164–66, 170, 174–76; Southern Democrats, 140, 165–66, 176, 208
Democratic theory: American foundations of, 8–16; classical foundations of, 2–8, 190; Frederick Taylor and Ford attack, 57–68; George Meany's interpretation of, 181–83; George Wallace and, 220–22; Industrial Council idea as, 148–56; John Dunlop's "pluralistic industrialism" as, 187–91; Samuel Gompers's voluntarism as, 26–42; Woodrow Wilson and Theodore Roosevelt debate, 84–90
Dirksen, Everett, 207, 261n22
Division of Labor, 14–15, 26–27, 30, 61–62, 65–66, 72, 94–99, 108, 136–37, 187–88, 234n29
Dotson, Donald, 205
"Dual Unionism," 29, 98, 112, 132, 138, 169

ABOUT THE AUTHOR

Clayton Sinyai worked as a hotel dishwasher, machine operator, railroad clerk, and letter carrier before pursuing a Ph.D. in political science at Rutgers University under Wilson Carey McWilliams. Today he is a researcher for the Laborers' International Union of North America (LIUNA).